D1596316

How Choctaws Invented Civilization and
Why Choctaws Will Conquer the World

BOOKS BY D. L. BIRCHFIELD

The Oklahoma Basic Intelligence Test:
New and Collected Elementary, Epistolary,
Autobiographical, and Oratorical Choctologies (1998)
(winner of the Louis Littlecoon Oliver Memorial Prose Award,
from the Native Writers' Circle of the Americas
at the University of Oklahoma)

Field of Honor: A Novel (2004)
(winner of the Spur Award for Best First Novel, from the
Western Writers of America, and the Writer of the Year Award,
from the Wordcraft Circle of Native Writers & Storytellers)

Black Silk Handkerchief: A Hom-Astubby Mystery (2006)
(Volume One in the Hom-Astubby Mystery Series)

(finalist for the 2007 Oklahoma Book Award,
from the Oklahoma Center for the Book
of the Oklahoma Department of Libraries)

The completion of this book was assisted by a
research grant from the University of Lethbridge.

HOW CHOCTAWS
Invented Civilization and
WHY CHOCTAWS
Will Conquer the World

D. L. BIRCHFIELD

UNIVERSITY OF NEW MEXICO PRESS
Albuquerque

© 2007 by the University of New Mexico Press
All rights reserved. Published 2007
Printed in the United States of America

13 12 11 10 09 08 07   1 2 3 4 5 6 7

Library of Congress Cataloging-in-Publication Data

Birchfield, D. L., 1948–
How Choctaws invented civilization and why Choctaws will
conquer the world / D.L. Birchfield.
p. cm.
Includes bibliographical references and index.
ISBN 978-0-8263-3231-8 (cloth : alk. paper)
1. Choctaw Indians—Government relations. 2. Choctaw Indians—Social
conditions. 3. Choctaw Indians—Ethnic identity. 4. United States—Ethnic
relations. 5. United States—Race relations. I. Title.
E99.C8B44 2007
305.897'387—dc22

2007026218

Jacket cartoon illustration by John Goodrich,
Goodrich Cartoonistry, LLC

Book composition by Damien Shay
Body type is Minion 9.5/14
Display type is Trump Mediaeval Bold and Tiger Rag

Contents

Preface

This work is a hybrid between academic scholarship and creative nonfiction, and it also employs fiction writing techniques regarding tone, pace, voice, and other things, rather like a heavily plotted novel that's somewhat character driven. One of the central, recurring themes of this book is that the author of it is a wacko, so when the author sounds wacko to you, congratulations, you got the point.

America might have good reason to be fearful of what it might regard as "wacko Indians," especially in the future, though most Americans remain nearly completely ignorant about that.

Perhaps if Americans were to hear some semblance of what a lot of contemporary Indians might sound like if they were to drop their Tonto-talking pose, Americans might get some hint of how completely America has failed to solve its "Indian problem," and what that might mean for the future, in a rapidly technologically accelerating age, where population superiority no longer counts for anything, and where population density has become a crippling liability.

Welcome to the twenty-first century.

There is little about this book, in a general, overall sense, that isn't already well known to Indian intellectuals, academic or otherwise, throughout North America.

Only Americans are ignorant about those things.

Therefore, this book hasn't been written for Indians, except for a few portions of it that are intended largely for their amusement, particularly for the amusement of Choctaws.

This book has been written primarily for Americans.

America is potentially fatally ignorant about nearly anything regarding the sovereignty of Indian nations, and Americans know virtually nothing about America's oldest and most loyal sovereign Indian ally—the Choctaws.

This book teaches some sophisticated principles of law.

It does that both by means of pedagogy and example—the example being how large portions of this book have been written.

The central and rather sophisticated legal lesson this book teaches is that law is not legislation or court decisions or constitutions.

Law, in its most fundamental sense, is custom, it is culture, it is a habit of thinking.

"Laws" have only been legislated, or handed down in court decisions, or embodied in constitutions, for a very brief portion of the immense sweep of human history.

Yet, humans have ruled themselves by "laws" for much of that immense period of their past.

Humans have done that by their customs, by their cultures, by their habits of thinking.

Nothing about that has changed just because we now have legislatures and courts and constitutions.

Those things merely reflect our habits of thinking.

In the kind of republic that the United States has become, American public opinion regarding Indians (i.e., the habits of thinking of the American people) now controls every aspect of law regarding Indians to a severe degree.

That is partly because both legislative and executive branch officials are elected by the populace (which is a direct reflection of public opinion) but more importantly because American courts of law are no longer allowed to intervene in any way that is not subservient to the will of Congress regarding Indians.

That is because the justices of the U.S. Supreme Court abdicated their constitutional responsibilities in 1903, in a chilling declaration in the case of *Lone Wolf v. Hitchcock*, when those broke dicks on the U.S. Supreme Court chose to make the U.S. Supreme Court totally subservient, forever, to the U.S. Congress with respect to all things regarding Indians.

That action by the U.S. Supreme Court in 1903 destroyed the U.S. Constitution, removing its checks and balances.

For more than a century, it has left the sovereign Indian nations, in that portion of North America that is currently still claimed by the United States, at the complete mercy of the elected officials in the U.S. Congress.

That 1903 Supreme Court decision declares that the U.S. Congress has full (plenary) power over Indians and that American courts of law cannot intervene in any way that is not subservient to the will of Congress regarding Indians.

Therefore, for about the last century, Indians have been at the complete mercy of public opinion in the United States.

American law regarding Indians is controlled by what the "average" American voter thinks about Indians, because those voters elect the Congress.

That means that laws cannot be changed regarding Indians until American public opinion (American habits of thinking) about Indians has changed.

If you might have wondered why Indian treaties haven't meant much lately, for about a century, and how it could be that Indian treaties didn't mean much during that time, that's the reason.

The U.S. Supreme Court put the sovereign Indian nations of North America at the mercy of American public opinion by declaring that the U.S. Congress can unilaterally abrogate any clause of any Indian treaty, whenever the Congress might choose to do so and that American courts not only are powerless to intervene but *must assume* that the Congress is acting in good faith, without having the power even to inquire into *that* issue.

Once the American courts had been rendered completely powerless to do anything regarding Indians except interpret congressional legislation (legislation that Congress can change, to circumvent any court interpretation it doesn't like) and to interpret and uphold clauses of Indian treaties that the Congress has not yet abrogated (all of which creates an illusion that American courts still play some role regarding Indians), American public opinion (propelled by ill-conceived and now dangerously ignorant propaganda about Indians, propaganda that was invented and popularized by selfish, powerful vested interests) compelled the Congress to ignore most of the Indian treaties.

The sovereign Indian nations of North America, overwhelmed, ignored, and buried beneath that self-serving American propaganda, have not exactly been jumping for joy at that turn of events.

They haven't submitted to that turn of events, either.

They never will.

They will find a way to reassert their sovereignty, and to regain control of their own lives and their own land, no matter how long that might take.

Frighteningly, some of them will almost surely attempt to do that—no matter what it takes.

If American habits of thinking about Indian sovereignty don't change, then the only alternative that Americans will have, in the long run, will be to destroy themselves, and all that they have ever hoped to be, by turning America into a police state.

It will have to be a police state where everyone is forbidden to read Indian treaties, where it will be a crime to educate any Indian, where it will be against the law for any Indian to learn how to read, or for anyone to study history, or for any American to know that at one time their constitution had a Bill of Rights appended to it.

Indians will make sure of that.

Indians will force Americans to destroy their own nation, if Americans continue destroying Indian nations.

The problem with Indian education is, once you get Indians educated, they read treaties.

That's not going to change. But the world is changing, with dangerous, lightning speed.

For a long time, it did not appear that there would ever be anything that sovereign Indian nations would be able to do about their plight.

But those days are over, and that's a potentially frightening future to contemplate, for everyone, whether or not some Americans might find it inconvenient to contemplate.

That's what this book is about.

It's a message that a handful of selfish, powerful vested interests in America don't want contemporary Americans to hear, because those powerful vested interests fear the decency and sense of justice of their own contemporary American people more than they fear anything else.

But those powerful vested interests don't tell me what to write, or what not to write, or how to write it.

I write what I see.

This book is about the way "American" history and Indian history are taught.

The way those two things are taught is what fuels contemporary American public opinion about Indians.

This book is about the role that propaganda plays in shaping public opinion about Indians, public opinion that has been derived from propaganda, which has masqueraded as "history," which in turn has shaped Indian law.

Portions of this book illustrate that point by being examples of propaganda, albeit of a different slant than most Americans are accustomed to.

To make the point of how "American" history and Indian history have been slanted by American historians and turned into propaganda, and how both "American" history and Indian history can be slanted distinctly differently, portions of this book tell the story of Choctaw history in a way that has been intentionally constructed as a Choctaw imperialistic-propaganda version of Choctaw history, largely for purposes of stark contrast to the way Indian history has most often been dealt with by American historians.

Therefore, some of the ways in which I've dealt with specific topics in Choctaw history are in furtherance of that approach.

That encompasses such things as what's been included in the book, what's been left out, what's been emphasized, etc.

There's a factual basis for treating each of the topics in this book in the manner I treat them, even when it might not necessarily be what I believe, based on my knowledge of lots of other facts.

Reasonable people can interpret facts differently.

I have dealt with things in this book in a way that has seemed to me to best serve the purposes of this book while still giving an overall general survey of Choctaw history that is factually reliable, even though if I were writing a different kind of Choctaw history than this one, and were less concerned with conveying some profound things about law in general, and Indian law in particular, there are probably a number of things I'd treat differently factually, interpret differently, and also treat differently in terms of tone, voice, slant, and any number of other ways.

This book has also been given an obvious and unmistakable author presence.

The author becomes something of a character in the story, to drive home the point that no work of history is written "objectively," that any work of history is nothing more than one person's "opinion," no matter how crafty the standard culture of "historians" might be in giving their books an absence of author presence, which can create an illusion that the pronouncements in those books were handed down by some god who was not "biased" in how those books were crafted, in what was included, in what was left out, and in how it was all slanted, even where those processes might only be subconscious on the part of an "historian."

This book makes the point that the clash of civilizations in North America between the continent's oppressed, ancient, distinguished peoples and the recently arrived, still Medieval-minded, still proselytizing, still cultural genocide waging, European colonizers is still a contemporary event.

That clash of civilizations has not yet passed into "history," has not yet run its course, and, therefore, no so-called "historian" can be anything but some kind of advocacy journalist regarding the brief span of the first five hundred years of that conflict, no matter how "objective" any historian might strive to be.

Everyone alive today has a stake in the outcome, and no one alive today has any idea what that eventual outcome will be.

The clash of civilizations in North America between New World and Old World civilizations might require only another few hundred years to finally play itself out, or it might require thousands of years, or it might be decisively and surprisingly brought to an end tomorrow.

No one alive today has any idea how long it might take, let alone any idea of how that clash might eventually be resolved.

Today, things have never looked brighter for the sovereign Indian nations of North America. Even the possibility that they might eventually reclaim the entire continent entirely for themselves must be considered.

The mushrooming technological advances of the past half-century have changed everything.

That's when everything suddenly started looking very bright for the future of the sovereign Indian nations of North America, more than half a century ago.

Incredibly, Americans are *still* unaware of that.

Incredibly, the sleepy-headed Americans have *still* got their minds locked up tightly in the Medieval mental prison of their Euro-Anglo ethnocentrisms.

That has now become a potentially fatal weakness, and American historians bear the primary responsibility for inflicting upon their own contemporary American people the crippling inability to see themselves the way that the Indian nations have learned to see them.

Americans are now dangerously about two full *generations* behind in even beginning to contemplate how those startling technological advances had already changed everything, more than half a century ago, regarding the nature of future relations between the United States and the sovereign Indian nations of North America.

Americans are a people who invaded a continent, attempted to conquer it, and then, incredibly, left that job half done while *forgetting* about their enemies.

Americans are not much smarter today than they were in Medieval times.

That is partly due to their enormous capacity for self-delusion and partly due to their lack of much capacity for thinking, or planning, in terms of generations.

Whatever continuing technological advances the future might hold will most likely only tip the balance even farther in favor of the Indian nations encountering little difficulty, at the very least, in reasserting their sovereignty.

The only remaining role that Americans will be able to play in that process is in how it will happen.

That is also the only remaining question to be answered, and it's one that the next generation of Americans will most likely provide the answer to.

That answer, whatever it might be, will likely set the course of history in North America, perhaps for the next several generations. It will also determine whether or not that process will take place peacefully, or whether it will elicit demonstrations of raw, brute force from both sides.

Those issues not only preclude any capacity for objectivity by any historian, but most American historians *still* exhibit no awareness that they have been doing a dangerous disservice to their own American people by being little more than advocacy journalists for U.S. imperialism in North America.

That sort of propaganda started becoming dangerous to America six *decades* ago, the instant that the awful mushrooming beauty of those atomic bombs changed everything, the *instant* that despairing oppressed peoples were shown even the possibility of being able to do something about their oppression—oppression that not only is supported by but made *possible* by that American historical propaganda, because the Supreme Court of the United States put the sovereign Indian nations of North America at the mercy of American public opinion.

Instead of writing American history as American propaganda (which just angers poisoned Indians even more), American historians should have been attempting to change American habits of thinking about Indian sovereignty, in an effort to convince poisoned Indians that it will not be necessary to pursue military options in reasserting Indian sovereignty, military options that in the twenty-first century include waging biological warfare (the means by which to do so being easily available), the one thing that even the geniuses in the Department of Homeland Security are well aware that America is helplessly vulnerable to.

Instead of trying to negotiate a settlement with the sovereign Indian nations of this continent, America continues to fritter away its time, blissfully unaware of the odds that, in time, it will be some "wacko Indian" who will be dictating the terms of the American surrender, some Indian, more likely than not, who won't much give a damn what Americans think, about anything.

What has been needed most is for the people who shape American opinion, particularly American historians, to wake up and get themselves into the game.

Not only have American historians proven themselves incapable of even becoming aware that for more than half a century they have been writing for the wrong audience, but they have been nothing less than criminally negligent in stubbornly resisting the efforts of a few enlightened historians among them to remove the artificial methodological blinders that prevent their academic discipline from even getting into the game, which is dealt with at some length in this book and is a recurring topic throughout it.

American historians are capable of making significant contributions in the effort to reason with poisoned Indians.

American historians are highly skilled, highly intelligent people, and even poisoned Indians can be reasoned with, if they can be shown that some progress is being made, or even any effort at all, to change American habits of thinking.

But the academic discipline of "American" history has frittered away more than half a century of precious time by not being able to reorient itself to even find the field of play, let alone get itself into the game, and nobody knows how much time there might be remaining for the critically needed help of American historians to come to the assistance of America's friendly, unpoisoned Indians, like me, who are aware that America has produced many dangerous poisoned Indians.

The only way to take the danger out of that game, and avoid the possibility that the game clock might suddenly stop ticking because America ran out of time, is for America to stop producing poisoned Indians, and then America wouldn't need to be producing any friendly, unpoisoned Indians like me, either.

But, as long as the U.S. Supreme Court continues being inhabited by broke dicks, nobody but the Americans who shape public opinion can do anything to stop America from producing poisoned Indians.

If someone doesn't like my point of view on those things, then they can write their own book and argue differently.

I'll be content to have the historians of future centuries be the judge of who had a clearer comprehension of late twentieth-century and early twenty-first-century America, and what American historians should have been doing to try to identify the issues of that era, and what those American historians might have been doing differently to help avoid, in the remainder of the twenty-first century, the kind of nightmare that I am fearful might be in store for everyone.

This book is a work of synthesis of Choctaw history, based largely on the many scholarly monographs, books, and journal articles that constitute the literature in this field.

Those things are discussed in a bibliographic essay, enough to give an idea of some of the many things that students of Choctaw history should do in approaching the topic.

Archival materials are not discussed much, because I think the bulk of what I have to say in this book can be traced to things that are available in print, and those that can't, well, those old farts have not been with us for a long time.

There are not many sources cited in this book, as most syntheses don't include many citations.

When I do make citations, I do so parenthetically in the text, or merely mention an author's name, usually as a source for some specific concrete detail, such as the amount of money generated from the sale of Choctaw land in Mississippi in the early nineteenth century, or things like statistics relating to the outbreak of smallpox in colonial Boston in the early eighteenth century.

The canon of Choctaw history is now immense, having attracted many scholars over several generations, but the broad outline of Choctaw history, as well as most of the basic facts of Choctaw history, have long since been common knowledge and therefore require no citation. They can be found in many different places. "American" historians have simply failed to integrate them into the "mainstream" telling of American history.

Certainly no student of Choctaw history needs to be told where to find something like the undisputed details of the *Great Medal Minko of Okla Hannali's* military role in the War of 1812, or how he acted decisively to shatter Tecumseh's vision on the eve of that war, or even how he rose to military leadership of the Choctaw Confederation due to his phenomenal military exploits in the West.

Something like his clash with Tecumseh will have been encountered by students of Choctaw history from many different perspectives, from biographers of Tecumseh, such as Alan C. Eckert, from biographers of the *Great Medal Minko of Okla Hannali* himself, such as Anna Lewis, from the reporting of historians such as Angie Debo in her survey of Choctaw history, and from such things as the recollections of John Pitchlynn, the U.S. interpreter to the Choctaws, who was an eyewitness to the dramatic climax of that clash at the time it happened in October of 1811, as reported by the long-winded preacher, Horatio Bardwell Cushman, in his history of the Choctaws, to mention only a very few of the many published sources, the most obvious ones, that have made those things common knowledge for a very long time.

But it's a kind of common knowledge that the mass of Americans, and American popular culture, have remained unaware of, largely because the Choctaw story is the story of America's betrayal of its most loyal Indian military ally, a story that American historians have never quite figured out how to give the right kind of spin.

Some ideas in this book represent my own conclusions or suggestions or speculations about some portion of Choctaw history, after decades of pondering various aspects of it. There are also some things that scholars have noted but haven't dwelt on, which I have emphasized in giving the Choctaw story the particular spin that I have given to it in this book, to suit the purposes of this book.

Chapter One

The Disbelieving Dead

*F*or the last ninety-three million, thirty-one thousand, two hundred and twelve minutes, the mythmakers who created and then popularized the American Myth have found it prudent to say very little about the Choctaws.

Those mythmakers have also been calculating, and at times even careless, in what little they have said about Choctaws, particularly for the general public in things ranging from reference books to major motion pictures.

Accordingly, American popular culture has paid less attention to the Choctaws than to any of the Indian nations in North America that have played the most important roles in American history.

As a result, few contemporary Americans know much about Choctaws or Choctaw history, even though the Choctaw population in 2007 of about two hundred thousand makes them the third-largest Indian nation on the North American continent, and even though the Choctaw people played the most decisive and most pivotally important role in American history of any Indian nation.

Some might think that it is because there has not yet been any such thing as a "Choctaw Indian War" that American popular culture has taken less notice of the Choctaws than of the Indian nations with whom the Americans have clashed violently.

The lack of hostilities between Choctaws and Americans undoubtedly explains in part why Americans have had little awareness of Choctaws.

But that's hardly what the Choctaw story has to tell us about the American Myth and about the American Mythmaking process.

The reason why contemporary Americans know very little about the Choctaw story is because that story does great violence to the American Myth.

It is the story of America's betrayal of its most critically important Indian military ally in all of U.S. history—the strategically located Choctaws.

This is the story of that betrayal, of how it has impacted Choctaw history, of how it has impacted the telling of "American" history by American-imperialist propagandists, and how that betrayal of the Choctaws will impact the future of this continent, the history that has not yet been written.

It will be the story of a few other things, too, things that help in understanding those stories. The threads of all of those things will be tied together into a knot that will tell the story of all of them, a twenty-first-century kind of story.

Choctaw military power made a decisive difference in a frail and infant American republic surviving a deadly threatening time in its early history, when the United States was in grave danger of having its life snuffed out by the British in the War of 1812.

That Choctaw military power had been *feared*.

It was feared because it was under the command of the head-busting, breathtaking genius of a rare kind of visionary terrible-great Choctaw military leader, one who had spent much of his life dancing with his dark side, exhibiting a horrifying compulsion toward dark-side, head-smashing greatness.

His spectacular Choctaw military career was a gift of the poison of hatred.

His capacity for forming visions that were continental in scope was a gift of the genes of the ancient Choctaw people.

The coming together of those two things was what made him that rare kind of terrible-great Choctaw military leader, capable of horrifying things in furtherance of a Choctaw continental vision.

Down through the millennia, the repeated emergence of that kind of rare, terrible-great Choctaw is one of the reasons why, for those many thousands of years, the Choctaw people have known that it is their birthright to be a great imperial-empire people.

The continuing emergence of rare, terrible-great Choctaws like him is one of the reasons why the Choctaw people might succeed in reasserting themselves as one of the great imperial-empire peoples of the world in the twenty-first century.

How he became that kind of rare, terrible-great Choctaw, before the War of 1812, can help us understand many things, not only about him but also about Choctaws.

Sometime along about the early 1780s, as a young, loudmouth braggadocio Choctaw, he began drumming up hair-raising parties of young Choctaw hellions to go, at a fast trot, all the way from Mississippi, and do what young Choctaw hellions had done from time immemorial—kill the dangerous trespassing criminal peoples who were always trying to move from somewhere else to the southern Great Plains, where they tried to steal the buffaloes from the huge Choctaw buffalo herds of that region.

Those trespassing criminal peoples were mostly too haughty and too arrogant to acknowledge the wisdom of the blessings of Choctaw law, and, by the eighteenth century, they were even trying to deny that those buffaloes belonged to the Choctaw people.

By the late eighteenth and early nineteenth centuries, many such dangerous criminally trespassing peoples had fairly recently come pouring into that southern Great Plains region, such as Comanches and Kiowas, who acted as though they did not know that those buffaloes were part of a phenomenal, ancient, far-western Choctaw imperial province and who mostly acted as though they did not care, even if they did know.

Choctaws of the late eighteenth and early nineteenth centuries were in grave danger of losing control of that ancient, far-western Choctaw imperial province. Choctaws had fallen on relatively hard times, compared to their ancient imperial glories.

But that was hardly anything new.

There have been many such crises in the thousands of years of Choctaw history. Weird peoples have always come pouring into that southern Great Plains region, silly peoples who do not know the wisdom of the blessings of Choctaw law.

It's one of the reasons why Choctaws have always felt a compulsion to act in ways that sustain the status of the Choctaw people as one of the few great peoples of the world, so that Choctaws will always maintain the capability of providing those silly peoples with some head-busting incentive to stop being weird, for the benefit of everybody on the whole continent.

The Choctaw people will never give up on finding ways to fulfill their responsibility of maintaining *their* rightful authority in that southern Great Plains region.

The sublime loftiness of the Choctaw achievement of sustaining themselves as one of the few great peoples of the world stretches backward for thousands of years, far into the misty distance of North American history, which encompasses the dominance of the most phenomenally wise peoples in the history of the world, who lorded it over not just that spectacular far-western province of tens of millions of buffaloes but the entire, huge, largest and richest portion of North America, from the Atlantic Ocean all the way to the Rocky Mountains, a wise people the silly Americans have dubbed the "Mound Builders."

The arrogant and potentially fatally ignorant Americans have not had sense enough to know that the oldest, most dominant, most distinguished, most strategically located, and by far the most *dangerous* of those phenomenal, ancient, earth-sculpting "Mound Builder" peoples were the ancestors of the modern Choctaws of the last several hundred years.

Maybe the Choctaw people have fallen on even harder times now than when they started losing control of their spectacular far-western buffalo province, but the Choctaw people had not then, in the late eighteenth century, and they have not now, forgotten the splendor of the thousands of years of their glorious Choctaw imperial-empire birthright.

Choctaws just happen to be in the process of making a comeback, that's all.

Choctaws have been in the process of making that somewhat slow and steady comeback for, oh, at l-e-a-s-t about the last half-millennium or so.

Big-time comebacks can take a little while for any people, no matter how great they are. For a people who are so great that they were once the undisputed *Lords of the North American Continent*, that can be a pretty big comeback, and if that kind of big-time comeback should require a pretty big amount of time, somewhat equal to the bigness of the comeback, so what? Choctaws are a patient people, possessing a patience equal to their greatness.

There was little, however, that was very patient about that young Choctaw, who would become greatly feared by the time of the War of 1812.

The very first hell-raising Choctaw strike force that was drummed up and led to the southern Great Plains by that young braggadocio Choctaw (some scholars say it might have been the second or third one that he led), sometime along about the early 1780s, met with disaster.

He led them into an ambush so deadly that he was the only Choctaw survivor.

Virtually every white person who has left some written hearsay account of that disaster identified some different group of trespassing criminal Indian peoples in the Trans-Mississippi West as the culprits. It hardly matters which particular criminal peoples they were.

His pride was greatly wounded from that debacle, and for the rest of his life he hated them all.

After surviving that ambush, after his disastrous failure of command, he spent months, some accounts say years, staying in the southern Great Plains, reconnoitering that region, studying the habits and the seasonal movements of the kind of criminally trespassing, Choctaw-buffalo-stealing peoples whom he would soon begin chastising severely.

When he finally returned home to the Choctaw core homelands in east-central Mississippi, it was only to immediately drum up the first of what would be an almost never-ending succession of hate filled, revenge strike forces, some of them huge, none of which he would ever again lead into any ambush.

He had learned to be super sensitive to the nuances of military tactics. He had learned that the hard way, and it was a thing for which he quickly began displaying awesome, deadly clever abilities.

From that time onward, for about the next two decades, his rage of hatred for the criminally trespassing peoples of that portion of the Trans-Mississippi West known as the southern Great Plains propelled him to become, by the early nineteenth century, the most terrifying Indian military tactical genius of his generation.

He became something of a Choctaw military police cop, something of a Choctaw supercop, fighting perhaps what might have seemed a lost cause battle, a long-odds crime-fighting battle, ruthlessly policing that almost lost, ancient Choctaw empire in the West.

Perhaps he was determined to rid that ancient Choctaw province of those trespassing criminal peoples to such an extent that *his* generation of Choctaws might be the one that reclaimed that ancient province for its rightful lords and for the wisdom of the blessings of Choctaw law.

It is hard to know his motives at any one stage of his phenomenal career. Probably, during the younger years of his crime-fighting, supercop rise to greatly feared fame among all of the Indian nations, he was just being propelled by the poison of hatred.

About the only thing we know is what he did, mostly in an overall general sense. We know so little of that in much of a concrete, specific-detail way, even though some of what he did in the West resulted in voluminous testimony before U.S. congressional committees, which heard the whiney complaints of trespassing white traders whose trade goods he had confiscated while always being careful not to harm any white people.

One of those white traders was Joseph Bogey, who lost his personal fortune at the eastern edge of the southern Great Plains in 1806, at the Three Forks of the Arkansas River—one of the great natural landmarks of the North American continent, near present-day Tulsa, Oklahoma, a natural landmark that was known to every Indian nation from the Rocky Mountains to the Atlantic coast.

In that ancient Choctaw imperial province, Joseph Bogey, under license from the U.S. government, had been so foolish as to try to engage in trade with the arrogant Osages.

After the Choctaws had taught Bogey *his* lesson as to *whom* he *should* have asked permission *from*, Bogey was able to do nothing but crybaby to the Congress of the United States about the immense fortune he had lost, about $10,000 worth of trade goods (a huge fortune, in the money of that day).

Bogey had last seen his fortune in trade goods being paddled down the Arkansas River, in his many boats, which the Choctaw strike force also confiscated.

That was Bogey's penalty for trespassing on that ancient Choctaw imperial province, without so much as a "by your leave" from the ancient glorious people who could hardly be making much of a comeback if they tolerated criminal trespassers doing whatever they wanted to do, wherever they wanted to, whenever they wanted to, no matter what kind of "license" they might *think* they have.

Sometime before 1805, sometime before the fortieth birthday of that Choctaw great one, his crime-fighting fame had elevated him to undisputed military leadership of all of the tribal divisions of the entire, powerful, strategically located Choctaw Confederation, which controlled the military key to the eastern half of the North American continent, the lower reaches of the mighty Mississippi River.

Under his command, propelled by the bitter poison of his awesome dark-side hatreds, Choctaw military police power had been lightningly hurled and *howled* upon the criminally trespassing, Choctaw-law-less, haughty peoples of the southern portions of the Trans-Mississippi West, all the way to the southern Rocky Mountains.

That Choctaw military police power had been hurled upon hundreds of those criminals at a time, whose last moments were ones of disbelieving terror that their larger military forces had fallen fatally into such brilliant tactical traps that even the disbelieving dead did not know why they had died at the hands of the always restless, always frightening compulsion to greatness of that Choctaw general.

He was a Choctaw general who, in his reckless youth, the Choctaws at first called *Ishtilawata* (the braggart), when his utter lack of fear, some might say utter lack of any semblance of common sense, in charging wounded, cornered, enraged bears, with nothing but a spear in his untrembling teenage hands, had been matched only by his unrestrained boasting about it.

But he was not known as *Ishtilawata* for long. He soon earned the name that history would remember him by, the name by which white people would know him.

By that name, by the time he died, he would become the most beloved and most highly honored Indian, by the American people, in all of American history. Yet, today, most Americans have never even heard of him, by any name.

Sometime before the seminally important negotiations for the Choctaw-American treaty of November 16, 1805 (the fifth Choctaw-U.S. treaty, and the first treaty that he is known for sure to have signed), he had risen to the highest title among his division of the Choctaw Confederation, the title of *Great Medal Minko of Okla Hannali*, when his bitter hatreds, his nearly unquenchable thirst for the blood of his enemies, and his genius for military tactics had produced the slaughter of what was surely far more human beings than any other Indian walking the face of the earth at that time.

The frightening realities of his awesome abilities were part of the rare kind of visionary, terrible-great, farsighted military-police leader that his ancient, distinguished people, themselves a rare kind of people in the world, have produced from time to time for many thousands of years.

The truly great Choctaw cops down through that time have had to be much greater at crime fighting than great, head-busting supercops.

For those thousands of years, those truly great Choctaw cops have been men of vision. Their supercop visions have sprung from the loins of the law and order-loving ancient Choctaw people, who might be the most law and order-loving people the world has ever known, whose destiny, from time to time, seems to be have been to have Choctaw supercops of great vision come springing into the world when they are needed most, to fight whatever great crimes might need fighting.

Their visions have been grounded in the harsh truths of the realities of the mostly lawless world that those Choctaw supercops have come springing into, the kind of world that was in the making at the time that each one of those Choctaw terrible-great ones was walking the earth.

Whether or not the Choctaw people today might still be producing any Choctaw supercops is hard to tell, but it does not l-o-o-k like it.

Some Choctaws say that they do not think that producing that rare kind of visionary Choctaw supercop is even in the genes of the ancient Choctaw people.

They say no, that they think it is mostly the gift of the poison of hatred. But this is my book, so I will tell it the way I want to. If they want to tell it differently, they can write their own damn book.

The United States Army would call that frightening *Great Medal Minko of Okla Hannali* "the Indian general," and would make him a commissioned brigadier general in the United States Army.

General Andrew Jackson would be compelled to say that he was "the greatest Indian I ever knew."

That great Choctaw Indian general was a witty, charming master of repartee, to the delight and amusement of all of the many white people who left some written account of him.

He was a world-class drunkard, to the amazement of every white person who knew him, to the day he died, white people who did not know that he was something of a Choctaw supercop.

They did not know the burdens he carried on his police beat. They had no idea how *many* nations of criminally trespassing Indian peoples had come flooding into the Trans-Mississippi West, acting as though they did not care that those buffalo herds belonged to the Choctaw people, acting as though they did not care that it was *his* head-busting police beat that they were trespassing on. It was enough to make a drunkard out of any conscientious cop.

He had world-class problems. Every so often he went to a few podunk towns on the American frontier, like Memphis and Mobile, and he painted them world-class red. So what? He blew off a little steam and nobody got hurt. He wasn't the first good cop to do that, you know.

He was impoverished all his life, because he gambled away or gave away the immense fortunes that came his way.

His nervous, tension-filled style of oratory, combined with his frightful military reputation, a thing that always hovered at the forefront of the awareness of his listeners, along with their lack of any doubt whatsoever that he meant every word he said, made that particular *Great Medal Minko of Okla Hannali* one of the most spellbinding, most mesmerizing orators of all time, to the shattering of the vision of another great Indian general, a Shawnee Indian general, from way up north in the Ohio country, whom "American" history would regard as *the* most visionary Indian, for other Indians, of all time, and *the* most frightening Indian, to Americans, who ever lived, even though that particular Choctaw *Great Medal Minko of Okla Hannali* possessed a clearer vision for *his* own Choctaw people and even though that particular Choctaw great medal *minko* was *many* times more frightening to other Indian nations than any other Indian.

Few Indians *feared* being against that great Shawnee Indian general, but even the leaves on those great big buckeye-nut-producing horse chestnut trees, way up there in that great Shawnee general's Ohio country, still *tremble* because, when all of the leaf-bearing trees were being born, one big tree looked around at the kind of world that the trees were being born into, and that one big tree saw the terrible deeds that were being done by the very first one of those rare kind of Choctaw great medal *minkos*, and that one big tree thought about what it would be like for all of the trees if one like him were to think that the trees were his enemies.

That is an "oral tradition." "History" cannot properly be written without including such things. Says who? Read Herodotus, to see how he did it. That ancient Greek invented the thing called "history," and he showed how to do it properly.

Still, if you might need a modern translation for that oral tradition, it means that even the very first rare kind of Choctaw great medal *minko*, a very long time ago, was one unforgettable *bad* bastard, even though Choctaws don't remember his name, because, for a long time, Choctaws had a taboo against speaking the names of the dead, and that very first rare kind of terrible-great Choctaw died back during that time.

But the leaves on the trees still remember.

That's because the leaves on the trees were being born at about the same time that the ancient Choctaws started getting alarmed about the weirdness of the poor peoples who did not know the wisdom of the blessings of Choctaw law.

That's approximately when the Choctaws started doing something about that. It propelled them to start becoming the great imperial-empire people who would eventually evolve into what the silly Americans would dub the "Mound Builders."

We know the sequence in which all of that happened, thanks to science, which tells us that about twelve thousand years ago the most recent ice age started coming to an end when the climate started warming up. The big glaciers started melting and going back up north.

During that ice age, which had lasted for many thousands of years, there hadn't been any trees in North America, just cold grasslands south of those huge, three-mile-thick glaciers. Those big glaciers extended down to about the present Canadian border, and even down a little farther in some places.

The cold grasslands south of those huge glaciers were filled with big species of animals. They included big North American elephants called mammoths and mastodons, and a big species of buffalo. It made for good hunting for the saber-toothed tigers, and the dire wolves, and the Choctaws.

For a long time back then the Choctaws were the only humans in North America, and they just wandered around all over the place, lording it over the whole North American continent, when they weren't getting eaten by those big tigers and wolves.

Those ice age Choctaws were broken up into groups of a few dozen people, because that was about what it took to have a good ball team. Whenever two of those groups ran into each other, they would camp together for a while, mostly to have a good ball game.

Eventually, however, some of the smartest groups figured out that they could get their prettiest girls to marry the most promising young athletes from some of those other groups, and make them leave their group and move in with her, and they started putting together ball teams that had one heck of a salty bunch of ballplayers.

Some of those slow-witted other groups started getting beat so bad in those ball games that they decided they didn't want to be Choctaws anymore. They stopped showing up for any ball games and, in time, even forgot how to be Choctaws.

So, even before those big glaciers stared melting, the earliest known repercussions stemming from the recruiting of ball players had resulted in there being silly peoples in North America wandering around who were no longer Choctaws, and some of them started getting really weird.

By about the time those big glaciers started melting, the Choctaws were probably either the people who made the Clovis spear points, or the ones who made the Folsom spear points. I think the Folsom spear points are prettier, so those Folsom people were probably the ones who were the Choctaws back then.

Scientists tell us that it took a long time for those big glaciers to melt, as the climate was warming up. They call that the watershed age, and they say it lasted from about twelve thousand years ago until about seven thousand years ago.

By that time, about seven thousand years ago, the North American continent settled into the climate it has been exhibiting since then. That's also when North America ended up with the plants and animals that survived that enormous climate change. Lots of new plants were also born as a result of that climate change.

By about ten thousand years ago the climate had already become warm enough that coniferous trees decided it was time for them to be born. But they don't have leaves, just needles.

By about eight thousand years ago the deciduous trees, the ones with leaves, decided it was warm enough for them to be born.

That's what books say, anyway, some books. Some books give somewhat different dates for some of those things, but I don't like those books as well because it makes it harder for things to come out just right for what some Choctaws think they know about Choctaw history.

Knowing when the trees-with-leaves were born is how some Choctaws know approximately when the Choctaws got to thinking about how much better everything had been when they had lorded over the whole continent, before so many of those groups had started losing those ball games so bad they'd just dropped out of civilized society and started getting weird.

By then there were a lot of those silly peoples in North America, and they no longer even looked like they had once been Choctaws. They had gotten outrecruited so bad for so long that their gene pool hardly included much athletic ability anymore, and then their puny athletes could mostly only attract ugly girls to marry them, while the Choctaw gene pool, by retaining its prettiest girls and adding great athletes, just kept producing prettier and prettier girls and greater and greater athletes.

By that time, a lot of even sillier peoples had arrived in North America, who were so weird they had gotten themselves run all the way out of Asia, all the way up through Siberia into Alaska, and then down into the rest of North America.

As the climate got warmer, all of those many different and by now very diverse, mostly ugly and puny, peoples started settling down at different places all over North America, and then they mostly just sat around coveting the choicest, richest, most strategic place on that continent, where the Choctaws had settled down—the lower reaches of the greatest river valley of the continent, the mighty Mississippi River.

Those silly peoples did not know that the Choctaws *wanted* them to covet that rich Choctaw land. They didn't know that the Choctaws settled down where they did specifically so that those silly peoples *would* covet Choctaw land.

No people get to be a great imperial-empire people just by being pretty and athletic. That might require little more than their prettiest girls being good sports about certain kinds of things. Figuring out *how* to outrecruit everybody else is an indication of the sort of wisdom that is required.

The ancient Choctaw people were wise in ways that extend far beyond how to fashion themselves into athletic, attractive people. They were wise enough to figure out how to fashion themselves into whatever they wanted to be.

They were wise enough to know that if they settled on land that *was* coveted by other peoples, then the Choctaws would be *burdened* by the knowledge that they *must* continually propel themselves to sustain their greatness, from the simple necessity of being forced to figure out *how* to defend their great land from the covetous eyes of those other peoples.

At that time, about eight thousand years ago, and at that place, along the lower reaches of that great river of the North American continent, is when both the scientists and the Choctaws say that the trees-with-leaves were being born.

The leaves on those newborn trees did not tremble at all until that one big tree looked around and saw what that tree saw, and got to thinking about what that tree thought about, and that is how Choctaws know approximately when they started becoming really alarmed at how weird some of those silly kinds of peoples had gotten, alarmed enough to launch themselves, inspired by the vision and the leadership of that very first rare, terrible-great kind of Choctaw, on the continental quest of taking back all of North America, by becoming a great imperial-empire people, to try to save those other silly kinds of peoples from getting any weirder, for their own good, and for the good of the whole continent.

The Choctaws only say approximately when that started happening, because those scientists are always changing their stories, and you never know what those scientists might come up with next.

It's best to leave a little bit of wiggle room, in case Choctaws might want to change their stories again, to be more in line with anything new those scientists might come up with.

That's the big advantage that the Choctaw people (and, for that matter, the scientists) have over those silly, ancient, Old World Middle Eastern peoples, who didn't have any better luck than to invent writing way too soon for the human species to be able to handle all of its problems, and who then didn't have any better sense than to write down their oldest, silliest stories, which quickly hardened into written-down religions.

Now they are stuck with the embarrassing ignorance of what their ancient ancestors actually believed, and, not being an oral-tradition people like the Choctaws, they've got no way to change those old ignorant stories.

But the imperialist propagandists among the Americans have never had any trouble figuring out how to change "American" history in ways that leave the Choctaws out of the story.

"American" historians have not thought it prudent to tell how it was Choctaw military power, under the leadership of that particular rare kind of visionary Choctaw great medal *minko*, that made a decisive difference in a fledgling American republic surviving the War of 1812.

That is because, in 1830 (only fifteen years after the War of 1812 had ended in 1815), a gang of lawless American imperialists, who had seized control of the U.S. government in 1828, stabbed their Choctaw allies in the back.

The American Mythmakers have never been able to figure out how to put the right kind of spin on that.

As a result, they have suppressed the Choctaw story in their telling of "American" history.

They have suppressed the Choctaw story to such an extent that even the *name* of that particular Choctaw *Great Medal Minko of Okla Hannali* who was walking the earth at the time of the War of 1812 is entirely unknown to an overwhelming majority of contemporary Americans, even though Choctaws long ago gave up on trying not to speak the names of the dead.

If Americans had not betrayed their Choctaw allies, and had not felt compelled to suppress the Choctaw story, that Choctaw great medal *minko* would be *the* Indian hero of unsurpassed stature to Americans.

No other Indian who has ever lived can rival him as the paramount Indian hero of American history.

At the time of his death in 1824 he was easily the most beloved and most highly honored Indian by the American people in all of U.S. history.

What other *Indian* has ever been given a funeral like the one the American people, and the Americans at the highest levels of leadership, gave for him?

That funeral procession was packed with American people in a line that stretched for three long miles through the streets of the recently burned to the ground, freshly rebuilt, magnificent city of Washington, D.C.

That remarkable funeral procession was led, on foot, at the stately pace of sadness, by the greatest American hero of that entire era of U.S. history, the commanding general of the United States Army, General Andrew Jackson.

That commanding general of the United States Army led that funeral procession all the way to the Congressional Cemetery, where that particular *Great Medal Minko of Okla Hannali* was accorded the rare privilege of being laid to rest, in *the* place, at that time, that was reserved for the most revered and most distinguished public servants of the American nation.

He was laid to rest not with the firing of rifles but with the booming of cannons.

The booming of that battery of those United States Army cannons heralded the passing of a Choctaw great one whose rare abilities have been reckoned to be fair-to-middling by the standards that have been set by the greatest Choctaw rare ones like him in the memory of his Choctaw people.

It was nonetheless a Choctaw great one being honored that day, one who had made the most of his middling-great abilities to accomplish great deeds for the American people and for his own Choctaw people.

America had never before seen such a man, and he was laid to rest in what may have been the most impressive United States Army burial ceremony in the history of the United States up to that time, and maybe far beyond that time, a funeral befitting the stature of the rare kind of Choctaw great one whose *vision* had earned the sincere gratitude of the American people.

Americans by the thousands in the nation's capital poured out of their homes, at an inconvenient time, at Christmastime, to honor his memory with much more than merely the full honors of what had been his commissioned rank in the War of 1812, when, as the military leader of a sovereign Indian nation, he was accorded the rank of a brigadier general in the United States Army, when he led a ferocious Choctaw army in howling support of General Jackson's and General Claiborne's U.S. armies in the bloody and decisive battles of the southern theater of the War of 1812, as America was being born in the blood of Choctaws, of Choctaws who died on those battlefields on behalf of America.

But Americans honored that particular *Great Medal Minko of Okla Hannali* for much more than that.

Americans honored him for the role he carved out for himself as one of the few *towering* heroes of American history, one of the few people who had ever been given an opportunity to make a difference in the very survival of the United States, before the War of 1812.

It was a history-changing opportunity he seized, primarily out of fear that to do otherwise might doom his own Choctaw people.

By the sheer force of his personality, and his frightening reputation to other Indian nations, at great risk to himself and to his Choctaw people, he made a profound difference in the very survival of the American nation.

That particular Choctaw *Great Medal Minko of Okla Hannali* made the most profound and the most far-reaching difference in the survival of the United States that any single individual has ever made, Indian or otherwise.

That long-suppressed, long-forgotten moment in *American* history brought the everyday life of the ancient Choctaw people to a standstill, in late October of 1811, when they witnessed a world-changing, breathtaking public confrontation (which, if it were happening today, would be the biggest media event in American history) between that Choctaw *Great Medal Minko of Okla Hannali* and the only other "Indian general" of American history, that Shawnee Indian general from that big horse chestnut tree Ohio country, who would be commissioned a brigadier general in the British army in the ensuing War of 1812, the great Shawnee Indian general that American history would not ever be able to forget, because he was one *bad* bastard who scared the daylight out of the American dream, turning it into a nightmare of darkness.

On that world-history-changing day, that Ohio Indian general, the eloquent and elegant, compellingly persuasive, great visionary Shawnee leader, named Tecumseh, possibly the greatest Indian of that era of North American history, *stumbled*, in what would be the fatal failure to Tecumseh's vision, when he tried to unite the decisively critical, massive military balance of power of the independent, sovereign, southern Indian nations against a vulnerable American people.

The linchpin key to whether Tecumseh succeeded or failed was the strategically located, greatly feared military muscle of the Choctaw Confederation, a military muscle the strength of which Tecumseh and the British generals, and the American generals, had no doubt about, and the military historians have had no doubt about, and the Choctaws and other Indian nations, for a long time, have had no doubt about—a military muscle the strength of which only the mass of the American people and American popular culture have known nothing about.

Tecumseh failed, more than any other reason, because he met his match, in face-to-face debate, with that particular *Great Medal Minko of Okla Hannali*, who was a devoutly committed Choctaw ally of the American people.

He had a *name*, and that name had a Choctaw war honor appended to it that he had earned, which American history has also chosen to forget.

His name was Apushamatahaubi. The *ubi* is a suffix, sometimes spelled *ubbee* or *ubbby*, or *ubih*. It is a war honor that means "killer."

The Americans who do know of him, know of him as Pushmataha. We will call him Pushmataha because that is how he is most commonly known in the literature.

Americans have foolishly thought it prudent to remember him mostly as that charming master of repartee and that amusing world-class drunkard. Americans do not like remembering him as one *bad* bastard of a killer.

In one of the most stirringly dramatic moments in *American* history, as thousands of Choctaws listened, hanging on every word, those two great Indian generals, the two greatest Indians in all of U.S. history, the two biggest, baddest bastards on the face of the continent, went fourteen and one-half rounds for the heavyweight championship of the North American continent, as they pounded each other in the most colossal contest of wills that *American* history would ever see, with the highest stakes hanging in the balance that any debate would ever have—the fate of a frail and infant American republic.

And then, to the horror of that Choctaw champion, as it was time for the fifteenth and final round to begin, with thousands of his own Choctaws judging the bout, he could see that he had lost all of the first fourteen rounds to the power-packed punches of the seductive evil genius of that great dark-side Shawnee heavyweight, spurring that Choctaw champion to say *to hell with debate* and superhumanly come staggering out of his corner for that final round and *deck* that evil genius by landing the most powerful superpunch in all of *American* history, with his desperately delivered, loudly shouted, never disbelieved, head-busting horror of a punch that still makes Choctaws tremble to this day, that convinced them that if *they* sided with Tecumseh, then *he* would start killing all of those thousands of Choctaws right then and right there, taking as many of the bastards down as he could reach before they all got to him, if any of those evilly persuaded, criminally seduced, about-to-die bastards survived his onslaughts and were left alive to try to get to, or to get away from, his head-splattering, blood-red howling tomahawk.

That was a heroic act! That was the courageous act of a *towering* hero of *American* history!

Except.

Well, it didn't happen *exactly* like that.

Okay.

I got a little bit carried away in telling about what happened.

I embellished things a l-i-t-t-l-e bit.

He didn't exactly threaten to start killing everyone right then.

And, he didn't exactly threaten to kill everyone.

I just got a little bit carried away.

The reason he didn't threaten to kill everyone right then was because he could see that he had not lost all of those first fourteen rounds of that fight.

Up to that point, in that fifteenth round, what frightened Pushmataha nearly out of his wits was that he could see that Tecumseh had been successful in swaying about half of the Choctaws to his side, and that raised the horrific specter of a Choctaw civil war.

But it makes little difference that Pushmataha did not threaten to start killing everyone right then, because what he *did* threaten to do was much worse, and it was a threat that was many times more horrifically possible for him to carry out.

In that loudly shouted, horror-knock-out punch, he threatened to ignite that Choctaw civil war himself, a Choctaw civil war that he would start and that he would finish.

He warned his own Choctaw people with the chilling declaration that he would not follow Tecumseh, no matter what they decided to do.

He threatened them that he would lead the roughly one-half of the Choctaws who adhered to his view in a Choctaw civil-war slaughter against the other half of the Choctaws, to make sure that they were not able to do anything to help further Tecumseh's vision.

It all works out the same. He might as well have threatened to start killing all of them right then. What he did threaten to do was much more horrible to contemplate.

And no Choctaw doubted his words.

His loudly shouted horror punch brought that Choctaw conclave to a standstill.

They called time-out.

Venerated *alikchis* were hastily summoned and consulted about what the Choctaw people should do, while the Choctaws engaged in feverish discussions among themselves.

Then the Choctaw people made their decision—that Tecumseh, along with his impressive traveling entourage of about thirty people, were to be expelled from the Choctaw country.

Under Choctaw escort, they were to be taken to the border of the Creek lands to the east, including Tecumseh's gifted interpreter, Seekaboo, who was a Creek, and whose oratorical abilities in either Choctaw or the Muscogee language of most of the Creek towns of the Muscogee Confederation was something to reckon with.

The Choctaw people decided that they would avoid a Choctaw civil war by uniting to follow Pushmataha's leadership in that matter—that the Choctaw people would follow Pushmataha to war on the side of the Americans, against Tecumseh and the British.

The colossal horror punch that Pushmataha threw at his own people, in desperation, to shock his own Choctaw people into contemplating the gravity of what they were deciding, practically forced the Choctaws to side with the Americans, and it made the decisive difference in the infant United States being able to keep from getting crushed by the British and Tecumseh in the War of 1812.

The War of 1812 was that close to being fatally disastrous for the American people.

Chapter Two

The War of Decisive Difference

*I*f the strategically located and powerful Choctaws had sided with Tecumseh and the British in the War of 1812, the other southern Indian nations would have had little choice but to do likewise.

Most of them were itching to join Tecumseh anyway, and they almost did, until they were faced with the horror of becoming the victims of the terrifying tactical genius of that particular Choctaw *Great Medal Minko of Okla Hannali* named Pushmataha, until he, like Tecumseh, met face to face with each one of their national councils, until he, unlike Tecumseh, spent that time telling them exactly what he would do to them.

Those southern Indian nations were faced with the horror of going to war against him, knowing the full extent of the darkest side of what that ruthless, cold-blooded mass murderer had become so horrifyingly famous for.

In the War of 1812, the British would have had little trouble finishing the job of crushing the life out of the pathetically weak United States, if the British could have had nothing more than the additional tipping of the balance of the massive military power of the southern Indian nations behind them, and every military historian has known that.

Only American-imperialist historians have trouble coming to terms with the awful realities of the War of 1812.

They have a hard time finding much of anything to focus on, except the brilliance and the daring of Andrew Jackson.

The British started crushing the life out of the Americans with a bang, by burning Washington, D.C. to the ground, when the awesomely outmatched United States Army turned tail and ran from a battle-hardened British army that had been locked in a death struggle with Napoleon on the European continent for so long that its veterans couldn't keep from laughing at that inept American army, as its terrorized soldiers fled before the terrible power of that British army all the way from Baltimore to what soon became the ashes of the White House and the ashes of the United States Capitol building and the ashes of every other governmental building in the American national capital—every public building but one.

That one American governmental building the British did not burn (at the corner of Eighth Street and I Street) was the headquarters of the United States Marine Corps, which to this day is the oldest public building in the American national capital, because it was the only one that the British general Packenham and Admiral Cockrane left standing, out of respect.

United States Marines had been the only Americans who stood their ground and fought, and died, to the last man, every time the British encountered a pocket of them on their otherwise unimpeded cakewalk through nearly the whole of the massed United States Army from Baltimore to Washington, D.C.

Americans remember those moments not for how the United States Army disintegrated at the moment it was needed most but largely only for the cool-headedness of the president's wife, Dolly Madison, who had the presence of mind to frantically grab precious portraits from the White House, as that British army was approaching the American capital to burn it to the ground.

American historians, for a lot of reasons, all of them terribly embarrassing, don't dwell on the War of 1812.

Canadians love that war, love studying the defensive genius of the towering hero it produced, Major-General Sir Isaac Brock, the British general who defended Canada from the unbelievably inept, bungling attempts of the Americans to invade Canada and conquer the Canadians (who the Americans outnumbered by a ratio of twenty-five to one).

Major-General Sir Isaac Brock is most remembered, by Canadians, for suckering an entire American army into surrendering to him at Detroit, by doing little more than hastily scratching a bluff on a piece of paper, for the

Americans to intercept, in which he pleaded with other British generals to send British reinforcements, for the honor of the Crown, because he had (he claimed) a howling, blood-thirsty horde of Indian auxiliaries with him that he could not control, which scared that American army so badly it surrendered immediately.

Americans don't dwell on those things, nor would any nation. Choctaws haven't dwelled on some things in their history either, particularly when they have not been able to restrain themselves from dancing with their dark side.

Few Americans know much of anything about the War of 1812, except that the southern theater of that war produced a great American hero named General Andrew Jackson, whose many exploits in that war are little known to Americans, except for the Battle of New Orleans, which Americans have come to know about primarily from the popularity of a pretty good popular-culture song.

Popular-culture vehicles, particularly TV and movies, have been an important way many Americans have learned their history.

Occasionally, and increasingly so in recent times, some of those popular-culture vehicles haven't done a bad job of capturing the essence of the spirit of some moments in American history, which can be a lot more fun to absorb than reading some tedious, dull-boring book.

Those tedious, dull-boring books, however, tell us that if that great Shawnee Indian heavyweight named Tecumseh could have delivered those large and powerful southern Indian nations to the British-and-Indian cause, which Tecumseh came so very close to doing, came within one-half round of doing, in that brutal, no-holds-barred bout with Pushmataha, all of the scattered American frontier families in the entire southeastern portion of the continent would have been forced to flee for their lives, or suffer the same fate that befell the hundreds of Americans during the War of 1812 at the massacre of Ft. Mims in 1813, where Tecumseh's fanatical followers among a faction of the Creeks demonstrated how very vulnerable the Americans were, vulnerable even just to that Red Stick faction of the Creeks.

Nobody knows how many more Americans might have died in the Southeast during the War of 1812, but the hundreds of American corpses at Ft. Mims were a chilling barometer of the deadly seriousness of the threat, a threat that sent the Americans into a terrorized panic and spurred General

Andrew Jackson to ferocious activity, a threat that scared the daylights out of that particular Choctaw *Great Medal Minko of Okla Hannali* and spurred him and his Choctaw army to ferocious activity on behalf of the Americans, in concert with the American generals.

That ferocious, howling Choctaw army did its share. It contributed to the slaughter of the powerful Red Stick faction of the Creeks at the Battle of Etowah (Holy Ground) in Alabama, and, to a lesser extent, to the annihilation of General Packenham's entire British army at the Battle of New Orleans in Louisiana.

Nobody got a chance to do very much at the Battle of New Orleans, due to the devastating skills of cannoneers (pirate cannoneers who had been shanghaied by a desperate General Jackson), who blasted that awesome British army into shreds of nearly unidentifiable humans by cannon-turkey-shooting into the massed columns of gallant British soldiers, who just kept marching forward, in phalanx infantry formation, into the mouths of those many cannons, until there weren't very many British soldiers left who were even hardly identifiable, let alone alive.

But if that particular Choctaw *Great Medal Minko of Okla Hannali* had instead been ferociously in league with Tecumseh and the British during the War of 1812, there would never have been any reason for Admiral Cockrane and General Packenham to have been diverted to New Orleans.

The British would have been in control of the vast southeastern portion of the North American continent, and in control of the continent's greatest river, throughout the entire War of 1812.

The war would have been different in critical ways. For the Americans, with their nation already at death's door, with their armies either disintegrating or surrendering all around them, there would never have been any occasion to be writing any songs about Andrew Jackson, if that Choctaw *Great Medal Minko of Okla Hannali* had decided that the American people were his enemies.

The terror of defensive necessity would have compelled the actions of General Jackson and yet the lack of safe passage through those powerful southern Indian nations, which was all that allowed General Jackson's perilously weak, ill-provisioned American army to maneuver throughout that vast expanse, would have prohibited General Jackson from even penetrating the region, and no one knew that better than General Jackson.

Had it not been for that particular Choctaw *Great Medal Minko of Okla Hannali*, and the decision he forced his strategically located, powerful Choctaw people to make, at the most perilous moment in the history of the United States (and at a fair-to-middling perilous moment in Choctaw history, compared to some of the truly perilous moments in the thousands of years of Choctaw history), there would never have been a General Andrew Jackson doing anything that any Americans would want to remember in the War of 1812.

There wouldn't be anyone called Americans to do any remembering.

There wouldn't be any United States of America.

American democratic ideas were a dangerous threat to the global idea of monarchy. That threat would have been exterminated, weeded out of existence.

At the time of the War of 1812, the British monarchy and all of the other terrified monarchies of Europe were ruthlessly attempting to exterminate threats to monarchy on both sides of the Atlantic Ocean—in Napoleon's Europe, in the recently rebelled Atlantic coast British colonies, and in Mexico.

Those monarchies had *seen* what the guillotines of Paris had done to monarchy and aristocracy in France, and they were frightened out of their wits.

The War of 1812 is known as the Second War for American Independence. At that time, the American Revolution had not yet been consolidated, had not yet been consummated, had not yet been made permanent.

All along the Atlantic seaboard, as the British reasserted sovereignty over their rebellious colonies, the remaining leaders of the American colonial rebellion of 1775–83 would have been rounded up and hanged.

The idea of there even being a United States of America would have died on those gallows along with the people who carried around the idea of it in their heads, and nobody knew that better than the American leaders who survived the War of 1812.

After fleeing that awesome British army in a headlong panic, as that army was entering the American national capital to burn it to the ground, it was a reality that had struck terror into every one of them.

The American Revolution survived its near extermination in the War of 1812, but the French Revolution was not allowed any opportunity to resurface after the armies of the European monarchies crushed Napoleon in Europe. The democratic impulses of the French Revolution were smothered under

Prince Metternich's ironhanded orchestration of the reassertion of the power of monarchy throughout Europe.

The same thing would have happened in North America, if Americans had lost the War of 1812.

There would not be any United States of America.

As it happened, it was a close call for the fledgling American Revolution, even with the strong support of the terrifying power of the military reputation of that Choctaw *Great Medal Minko of Okla Hannali*, not just his desperately thrown horror punch that persuaded his Choctaw people to side with the Americans but also his deadly serious threats, which were taken with the deadly seriousness they merited, to kill every southern Indian who sided with Tecumseh and the British, if not during the War of 1812, then to hunt them down and kill them after the war.

Which he did. He killed every one of them that he could find until the day he died, especially the few Choctaws who joined Tecumseh and lived to tell about it, for a little while, until they heard the howling of the one who had told them what he would do to them.

His message was clear, and it was simple: if you side with Tecumseh and the British, you will die. You will die either during the war or you will die after the war. If you do not die some other way, you will die because you will be killed by me.

No one doubted his words, except the Red Stick faction of the Creeks and those very few Choctaws who sneaked away and joined Tecumseh. They joined the disbelieving dead.

That Choctaw *Great Medal Minko of Okla Hannali* worked tirelessly, traveling to, and speaking to, the other southern Indian nations, especially the Creeks, where Tecumseh had relatives and where Tecumseh's personally delivered message was being strongly received.

The decision makers of those Indian nations sat mesmerized by Pushmataha's nervous, tension-filled style of oratory, grimly contemplating the deadly seriousness of his words.

That *Great Medal Minko of Okla Hannali* helped persuade all of the southern Indian nations to provide safe passage and at least some military assistance to General Jackson's army, including most of the Creeks, who helped kill their own powerful Red Stick people in the battles of the War of 1812.

It was not the persuasiveness of Pushmataha that made it possible for him to influence the other southern Indian nations. It was not just the strategic location and the military muscle of the Choctaws.

It was another side of him. It was a dark side.

It was the terror of what he could be, which the disbelieving dead witnessed when they had heard the howling of that particular Choctaw *Great Medal Minko of Okla Hannali.*

The decision makers of those other Indian nations had seen what that howling had done. They knew the awful truth of it.

When he stood before them in council and told them what would happen to them, when he told them what he would do to them, when he told them what would be coming, they did not disbelieve.

They could see it coming.

For that unequalled contribution to *American* history, for that decisive tipping of the balance that made it possible for America to survive its closest brush with death in its entire history, in the War of 1812, Pushmataha should be the most famous Indian in all of American history, an Indian who should be more spectacularly famous than Geronimo, or Crazy Horse, or Sitting Bull, or any other Indian of whom Americans have any knowledge and whose name should be unforgettable to any American.

In 1824, at the time of Pushmataha's death, the leaders of the United States were well aware of how and why their country had survived its near extermination, and those American leaders were incapable of having forgotten the Choctaws or that particular Choctaw *Great Medal Minko of Okla Hannali.*

Pushmataha's death caused the Congress of the United States to pause, not just with a moment of silence to honor his memory but to hear a memorial to his life, on behalf of a sincerely grateful American nation, eloquently spoken by a person of much stature, Senator John Randolph of Virginia.

Name the Indians whom the Congress of the United States has ever honored in that manner.

Name the Indians who lie at rest today in the Congressional Cemetery of the United States. There is another one, another great Choctaw.

Name the Indians who have ever been given a funeral by the American people as spectacular as the funeral the American nation gave for that Choctaw *Great Medal Minko of Okla Hannali*—for *being* a howling Choctaw great medal *minko.*

Name the Indians who have ever acted as decisively on behalf of their own people and the American people, with such far-reaching consequences.

Name the Indians who have ever been as beloved, acknowledged, and honored by the American people.

Name the Indians who have ever contributed as much to the very survival of the United States of America.

That process produces the name of a hero of towering greatness of *American* history, of *mainstream* American history, of unforgettable decisive mainstream American history.

He was a great one, a particular kind of great one, a rare kind of terrible-great one that the Choctaw people produce every now and then.

The Choctaw people have produced many like him, some of them as great, some of them much greater. One like him is born among the Choctaw people every so often.

It is in their ancient genes.

The occasional birthing of Choctaw great medal *minkos* like him is one of the reasons why it is the birthright of Choctaws to be the lords of the most fabulously rich lands on one of the most fabulously rich continents in all the world, the North American continent, a continent which for thousands of years has had a rare kind of special river.

Those ancient Choctaw lands were along the lower reaches of one of the few great rivers of the world that gave the gift of the great riches of its continent to the lower reaches of its great river valley, which made the lower reaches of that great river valley a special kind of place.

Those few special places along the lower reaches of those few great river valleys in all the world are called cradles of civilization.

They are called that for a reason.

Those few great rivers in all the world that gave the riches of their continent to the lower reaches of its special valley can be counted on the fingers of one hand.

The few great peoples of the world that those rare and special places produced, thousands of years ago, can be counted on the fingers of one hand.

One of those few special places in all the world, one of those few cradles of civilization, one of those few places that can be counted on the fingers of one hand, was, for thousands of years, a blessing to the North American continent.

Of those very few great ancient peoples of those very few cradles of civilization in all the world, only one of those peoples has passed through the thousands of years of its history to come into the modern world without having been influenced in any way whatsoever by any of those other peoples of any of the other great cradles of civilization of the world.

There are reasons why the Choctaw people have long been one of the few great peoples of the world.

There are reasons why the Choctaw people have been one of the few great peoples of the world for the kind of time that is counted in years by the thousands.

There are reasons why at the time of the War of 1812 the Choctaw people were still so much closer to being the same ancient, distinguished people of the thousands of years of their history than any of the descendants of any of those other few great cradles of civilization of the world.

And there are reasons why, for all those thousands of years, though many ignorantly arrogant and pompous peoples have joined the disbelieving dead *trying*, no other people in the world have ever been able to wrest that great special land away from the Choctaw people, who for those thousands of years have produced howling great medal *minkos* like him every so often.

It is in their ancient genes.

That particular Choctaw great medal *minko* was at the height of his ancient Choctaw howling powers at the time the infant American Revolution was still struggling to take a deep enough root to gain for itself a nurturing grasp in ground that was in a global garden that was being ruthlessly weeded by powerful global gardeners that considered it a weed.

And the single most important reason why those ruthless global gardeners were not able to reach quite far enough to grasp that American revolutionary plant tightly enough to jerk it out of the ground by its roots was because those ruthless global gardeners were trying to do that at a time when the *Lords of the North American Continent* produced one of their rare, howlingly great Choctaw great medal *minkos* that they produce every so often.

He had a powerful, far-reaching vision for his continent that depended upon the survival of that American Revolution.

He chose those American people to be the one people among the dangerous foreign imperialists that the Lords of the North American Continent will do business with.

He chose the American people so the Choctaw people could employ the power of those people to shield his North American continent from the threats of the dangerous aggressions of the other foreign imperialists, so that his continent might continue receiving the wisdom of the blessings of its rightful lords that it has been receiving for all of those thousands of years.

That particular Choctaw *Great Medal Minko of Okla Hannali* was the Commanding General of the North American Continent.

That Choctaw Commanding General of the North American Continent *willed* that the American Revolution would not be weeded out of existence.

Pushmataha was the Choctaw who willed that those powerful global gardeners would not succeed.

Pushmataha willed that the howling power of one of the few great peoples of the world would come to the aid of that desperately threatened American Revolution.

Pushmataha was the Choctaw who made certain that the American Revolution would not get weeded out of existence.

That particular howling Choctaw *Great Medal Minko of Okla Hannali* was named Pushmataha!

He was the Commanding General of the North American Continent!

Try to remember *at least* his *name.*

He was a Choctaw.

For many thousands of years the Choctaws have been the Lords of the North American Continent. They are one of the few great peoples of the world!

Try to remember *at least* their *name.*

To the many Americans in their nation's capital in 1824 who helped lay the Commanding General of the North American Continent to rest, no one would have believed it could be possible that a day *could* come when *his* name or the name of *his* people would mean nothing to Americans!

Yet, Pushmataha and the Choctaws have been so completely forgotten by the American people it is almost as though they are not now, and have never been, the Lords of the North American Continent!

Except maybe in *their* own minds.

As though Choctaws might be head cases of a peculiar kind.

It is almost as though Choctaws are thought to be so humble and so retiring as to not care to be in the spotlight of any kind of history, American or otherwise.

Okay.

No need to be overstating anything.

I might have overstated something in there a little bit.

Maybe all of that wasn't exactly that way.

Maybe I got a little bit carried away.

Maybe Pushmataha was not the Commanding General of the North American Continent.

Maybe the Choctaws never did have such a rank.

I just got a little bit carried away there.

But it hardly matters.

At that time, in those circumstances, Pushmataha really was the commanding general of the North American continent. It was his vision, as a general, as someone who could see the continental implications due to the American people being here to stay, that made him, at that moment, the commanding general of the North American continent.

He was a general. He was a general for his own Choctaw people *and* for the American people. He was a general of great vision, of continental vision.

He could see that, one way or another, the American people were going to be unstoppable.

He knew that his Choctaw people could not afford to be lined up against the Americans, no matter what.

Plus, he could see a great benefit for his people if they would get themselves lined up with the Americans, a benefit that was continental in scope, an imperial-empire alliance between two imperial peoples that might cut down by several centuries on the comeback time required for his people to complete their comeback, if the Lords of the North American Continent were to piggyback their way to regaining their former ancient imperial glory, a kind of shortcut chance to make that comeback, big-time, from the hard times they had fallen on lately, for the last few hundred years or so.

He knew that his strategically located and militarily muscle-bound Choctaw people held the all-important strategic balance of power in the Southeast. He knew the value of that bargaining chip with the Americans.

He knew that his Choctaw people could be the saviors of the Americans. And he knew that the Americans, in return, would just naturally be properly grateful.

Well, that last part there might have been where he screwed up j-u-s-t a little bit.

But it hardly matters for acknowledging what he did, and for who he was when he did it.

Pushmataha might as well have held the title of Commanding General of the North American Continent at that time. In acting as he did, and in doing what he did, that, in essence, is what he was at that moment in history. He was the commanding general of the North American continent.

It is not too much of a stretch to say that Pushmataha made it possible for there to be a United States of America today. But "American" history has thought it prudent to remember things differently.

Pushmataha did not envision that American-imperialist propagandists would think it prudent to remember anything differently.

Pushmataha did not envision what would happen not long after his death.

It is no accident that American history has thought it prudent to forget both Pushmataha and the Choctaws.

It is no accident that Pushmataha and the Choctaws have been erased, not just from American history but also from American popular culture, to a point that even their name means nothing to contemporary Americans.

The Choctaw problem has been the biggest *propaganda* problem that the imperialists among the Americans have had to face in their telling of "American" history.

It has been the biggest propaganda problem that they have ever faced in all of U.S. history.

The reason why Pushmataha and the Choctaws have been eliminated from "American" history by American-imperialist propagandists has been to cover up the cold-blooded callousness of their betrayal of their Choctaw allies, when, in 1830, a backstabbing gang of imperialists among the Americans, who had seized control of the U.S. government in 1828, suddenly turned upon their Choctaw allies and rewarded their history-changing loyalty by dashing the dreams of the vision that had guided that Choctaw *Great Medal Minko of Okla Hannali*, leaving twentieth-century historians to regard both him and his Choctaw people as primitive, simple-minded fools.

In that year, in 1830, the Choctaw people became the *first* Indian nation to be ruthlessly uprooted from their homes and subjected to the horrors of the infamous Trail of Tears, a backstabbing horror so great it killed Choctaw people by the thousands, possibly as many as one-quarter to one-third of them, under *President* Andrew Jackson's Indian Removal Act of 1830.

Then that backstabbing gang of imperialists among the Americans just went on about their business while making sure that all of the other Americans would forget about the Lords of the North American Continent.

Historians of future centuries will marvel at that.

They will say that the backstabbers thought, since there didn't appear to be anything that the Lords of the North American Continent would ever be able to do about having gotten stabbed in the back, that the backstabbers could get away with doing that.

Those future historians will say, in amazement, that the backstabbers never saw it coming, that they never imagined that the fruits of that betrayal would steadily ripen.

Those future historians, enlightened by hindsight, will be sophisticated enough to know what to look for in the historical record, and they will have pieced together enough of the story by then to be able to tell what happened next.

They will say that the knife-in-the-back of the Choctaw people was tipped with the poison of breach of trust by an *ally*.

They will say that the blade of that knife lodged in a place that could never quite be reached to pull it out, a place where its poison only worked its way deeper.

They will tell how that poison fueled a fiery pain of outrage, deep beneath the surface, at the depth of the poison tip of that blade, the blade of that knife that could never quite be reached to pull it out, no matter how hard the Choctaw people tried.

They will tell how that poison pierced the veins of many Choctaws and was pumped throughout their bodies, how it was pumped through their hearts, poisoning their hearts and turning them cold, how it was pumped through their minds, poisoning their minds and turning them toward the dark side.

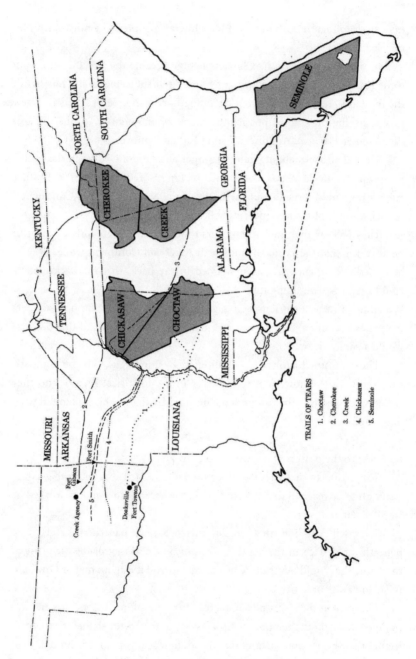

Figure 1: Removal of the Five Tribes
Map courtesy of the University of Oklahoma Press

They will say those things because that poison was injected into the veins of the Lords of the North American Continent from a knife that was embedded in their back five billion, five hundred and eighty one million, eight hundred and seventy three thousand, three hundred and eighty one *ticking* dark-side seconds ago, and poisoned Choctaws have awaited the day that they would be able to do something about that howling pain of poison.

That day has a name. And that day has come.

It is called the twenty-first century.

There is no person on earth, not even any Choctaw, who can say how many Choctaws there might be who have had that poison reach their hearts and turn them cold and who are dancing with their dark side, dancing with a kind of howling twenty-*first*-century nightmare that nobody on earth had ever been able to imagine—until now.

This ticky-tocky talk has been scratched down on paper so that, if nothing else, those future historians will not be able to say that America never saw it coming.

Chapter Three

The Howling Pain
of Poison

The imperialists among the Americans who seized control of the executive and legislative branches of the U.S. government in 1828 betrayed all Americans in 1830 with the passage of the Indian Removal Act, and they betrayed all Americans again in 1832 by delivering a crippling blow to the Supreme Court of the United States.

Those imperialists were a minority faction of the American people, a distinctive, antebellum southern minority that would leave its mark upon America in many other ways that contemporary Americans, including contemporary southerners, are not proud of.

That minority faction seized power during an era of transition in American political life, when all of the political parties were either dying or reshaping themselves, and when a bewildering array of new ones were being born.

The agonizing death throes of the Federalist Party created a chaotic vacuum that new, emerging parties, such as the Whigs, would try to fill, as the Democratic-Republicans were tumultuously reshaping themselves into an emerging Democratic Party. The Republican Party would not be born until the late 1850s. By then the Whig Party, and many others, would be dead.

The political turmoil reached a crescendo in the mid-to-late 1820s. In the election of 1824, so many different presidential candidates from so many different parties won electoral votes that the presidential election had to be decided in the House of Representatives of the U.S. Congress.

The imperialists among the Americans who seized power during that chaotic transition period of the 1820s were people whose values were primarily those of the antebellum South.

They had the decisive advantage of being led by a man of heroic military stature, General Andrew Jackson of Tennessee, who took them all the way to the White House in 1828.

Their attitude regarding the sovereignty of the Indian nations of North America would have a profound influence on later generations of Americans. It was a seminal moment in American history, and in the history of North America.

They changed America from what it might have been to what it would become.

It didn't have to be that way.

And it doesn't have to remain that way.

The Indian Removal Act of 1830 was an act of Congress.

It can be undone by an act of Congress.

The Indian Removal Act of 1830 was approved in the U.S. Senate by the narrowest of margins, revealing a deeply divided American nation that almost succeeded in restraining its greediest and most irresponsible minority faction, that antebellum South, from committing the biggest and most ghastly humanitarian crime in American history.

Amid the political turmoil of that era, it was the temporary political muscle of those like-minded and more united southern states that forced that policy upon all of America, and upon America's future, at a time when national political chaos barely made that possible.

The antebellum southern states would not know any restraint until they were crushed by the military muscle of the rest of America in 1861–65 in the American Civil War, the War Between the States that came a generation too late to preserve the integrity of the American people regarding the sovereign Indian nations of North America.

As that brutal policy of mass uprootings of entire nations of Indian farmers, which Americans had dubbed the "Five Civilized Tribes," was being implemented throughout the South during the 1830s, the injustice of it elicited outraged protests from Americans such as Ralph Waldo Emerson, Daniel Webster, and many others, mostly in the northern states, all to no avail.

America was not yet ready to go to war with its southern states.

Even in that antebellum South, American heroes such as Congressman Davy Crockett of Tennessee voted against the Indian Removal Act of 1830, which brought his immediate defeat in the next election.

There were other statesmen of that antebellum southern region who opposed the Indian Removal Act of 1830, such as Henry Clay of Tennessee, all to no avail.

Men like Davy Crockett and Henry Clay could not overcome the predominant mindset of their fellow antebellum southerners.

That mindset dealt the Supreme Court of the United States a fatal blow, from which the Supreme Court will never be able to recover, when President Andrew Jackson and the state of Georgia simply ignored the decision of the Supreme Court in the case of *Worcester v. Georgia*, in 1832, which would have stopped Indian removal in its tracks. Instead of abiding by the rule of law, the renegade and lawless imperialists among the American people chose to destroy the United States Constitution by refusing to abide by that Supreme Court decision.

Few contemporary Americans seem to have much awareness that America's enduring "Indian problem" is a legacy of the mindset of the antebellum South and a legacy of its blatantly lawless actions against Indians, which will never be submitted to by the sovereign Indian nations of North America.

And few people anywhere seem to have ever had any awareness of the severity of the blow that those unrestrained, mostly southern American-imperialists delivered, in 1830, to the soaring comeback ambitions of their two-peas-in-a-pod, imperial-like-minded Choctaw allies, who themselves had a distinct feeling of having just stepped on a big banana peel, a banana peel on a real steep, real slippery slope (a kind of big-time imperial comeback suddenly gone big-time bad wrong kind of slippery slope).

But those imperialists among the Americans of that era were well aware that they had created two big, backstabbing problems for themselves, an "American" history propaganda problem and a potentially much bigger Choctaw problem. They gave both of their self-made big problems the big attention they merited.

The American-imperialist betrayal of its Choctaw allies quickly became such a threatening Choctaw cancer, so deeply embedded in the vital organs of the emerging American Myth, that the backstabbers began focusing generations of grim determination on the Choctaws, attempting to remove as much of that deeply embedded Choctaw cancer from that emerging American Myth as they could.

The backstabbers viewed the Choctaws as the problem, rather than viewing the traitorous sickness that the backstabbers had inflicted upon their own American nation as the problem.

Ironically, the betrayal of their Choctaw allies denied that emerging American mythos the sublime heights that mythos *might* have soared to, if the American imperialists had honored their alliance with the Lords of the North American Continent, thereby infusing that American mythos with the manifold imperial empowerments it *could* have received from incorporating the validating, homegrown, continental, imperial-empowerment virtues that spring from the thousands of years of the Choctaw people having firmly established *their* birthright to spread the wisdom of the blessings of Choctaw law throughout the continent.

But the American imperialists did not have sense enough to be aware of the many benefits that could have come their way, if they had honored their bargain with the Choctaws and joined together in lording it over all of the silly peoples of that continent, whom the Choctaw people have long known that they have been born to lord it over.

The pansy American imperialists did not tackle their Choctaw problem by attempting to exterminate the Choctaw people, which is undoubtedly the quick and simple solution that the Lords of the North American Continent would have chosen for such a problem.

The American imperialists chose instead to engage in a program of psychological experimentation on the Choctaw people, a program of mental experimentation that they believed to be more humane, trying to find the most effective neutralizing agents (according to their silly Euro-Anglo ethnocentric conceptions) of the things that might make a Choctaw a Choctaw.

They rolled up their sleeves and undertook a determined and bizarre range of experimental tinkerings with unknown parts of the human mind, as though that Choctaw cancer on the vital organs of the American Myth was something that was merely in the minds of the Choctaws, and if their minds might be irradiated just right, then maybe Choctaws would become convinced that they are a people who just shrugged off their betrayal.

The American imperialists have sought that objective by attempting to instill into the Choctaws a mental image of themselves as the happy sidekicks of the white people, by zapping their minds with a wide and weird variety of mental reorientation techniques that might be called Kemo Sabe chemotherapy treatments.

It seems that virtually all of the Choctaws have now been extensively mentally rearranged, if not reoriented, by their minds having been so thoroughly irradiated that way, but the results haven't been exactly what was anticipated.

The white people doing the irradiating haven't exactly been rocket scientists, and the range of the weirdness of the experiments that they have performed on the Choctaws has been so extensive that it has never been fully catalogued.

What has been rather fully catalogued, however, for all the world to see, is that the intensively irradiated, Kemo Sabe-chemotherapied Choctaw people have apparently been entirely mutated into a species of people unlike any other the world has ever known, with a lot of them having gone through life spastically sidekicking out of sync with nearly everything, in an amazing variety of ways.

The American people seem inclined to wonder if the Choctaw people even still know how to be Choctaws.

None of those Americans seem to have ever wondered whether the Choctaws might still think of themselves as the Lords of the North American Continent.

No American has apparently ever had any awareness that the Choctaws for thousands of years have been the Lords of the North American Continent.

No American seems to be wondering if the Choctaws might really still be the Lords of the North American Continent, let alone whether, by the twenty-second century, the Choctaws might have become the Lords of the North American Continent once again.

I wonder if those Americans who don't seem to have ever wondered about any of those things might include those guys at the FBI—FBI as in *Federal Bureau of Investigation*, as in the federal bureau that is supposed to be protecting me from somebody like me.

The range of the experimental things that have been done to the Choctaw people has far surpassed the range of the medical experimentation that the Nazis engaged in during World War II.

But then, those propaganda-spouting and imperial-empire seeking North European Germans only had a few years to conduct their experiments.

The American imperialists have had generations to experiment upon the Choctaws.

Someone must warn the American people that because of what the imperialists among the Americans have done to the most weirdly irradiated, Kemo Sabe-chemotherapied Choctaws that there are Choctaws among the Choctaw people who are in love with the twenty-first century and that there are Choctaws deeply embedded among the American people and scattered throughout the world who are in love with the twenty-first century.

That funny thing that has happened to their fellow Choctaws has fueled a rage in many Choctaws, deep down in many Choctaws, that is another kind of howling pain of poison.

It is coming.

Can you see it coming?

That howling part is coming.

And so is that pain.

Ask not for whom that howling pain is coming.

Ask not what that pain can do for you, ask what you can do for that pain.

That pain will live in history as a day of infamy.

Never in the history of human endeavor have so many felt they owed so little to so few who have known so much pain.

That backstabbing pain has but a little way to fly, and lo, the pain is on the wing.

That pain will not be a crook.

That pain will not have sexual relations with that woman.

That pain will not say tear down that wall.

That pain will not stumble down the stairs.

That pain will not say "no new taxes."

That pain will not sell peanuts.

That pain will not be a haberdasher.

That pain will not fiddle while Rome burns.

That pain will not think therefore it is.

That pain will not seek, nor will it accept, the nomination of its party.

That pain will be the end of all of that, and the end of all that ever was like that.

That howling pain of poison is coming to a theater near you.

That howling pain will not be the pause that refreshes.

That howling pain will most likely be a little bitty dab of African hemorrhagic fever, or anthrax, or bubonic plague, or hantavirus, or smallpox, or, much more likely, some as yet unknown and untreatable cousin of something similar to those sorts of howling painful things, by my carefully calculated odds of 117 to 13, rounded off to whole numbers, after much thought and careful study.

It is coming.

Can you see it coming?

Do you understand why it is coming?

Do you understand why it is unstoppable?

That Kemo Sabe chemotherapy irradiation of the Choctaw people has been coupled with the near elimination from "American" history of hardly any mention of Choctaw removal, a topic that soon joined Pushmataha/Apushamatahaubi among the foremost forbidden things that American-imperialist propagandists would make sure that later generations of Americans would know hardly anything about.

They have succeeded inasmuch as the Trail of Tears has become associated almost exclusively with the Cherokees, whose brutal forced removal, in 1838, occurred years after the Choctaws had become the first nation to suffer that fate, after the Choctaws suffered that fate under far worse conditions, in deadly ill-provisioned forced migrations between 1831–34, in the dead of winter, mostly on foot, rather than in wagons.

The cost to the Choctaw people, among many other things, was the loss of most of their old ones, the great, living repositories of ancient Choctaw knowledge, knowledge that spans many of what Americans call "academic disciplines," and knowledge that spans many things for which Americans have no name, being ignorant, to this day, of almost all of it.

The contemplation of that loss has poisoned the hearts and minds of many Choctaws.

But some of those poisoned Choctaws are aware of an advantage they have gained over their imperialist enemies among the Americans that stems from that Choctaw loss.

Those poisoned Choctaws have known for a long time that sooner or later their imperialist enemies among the Americans might wise up enough to become frightened enough of poisoned Choctaws to prepare a *Big Scouting Report* on what it is that they might be up against in the twenty-first century, ancient Choctaw, games-theoried Big Game that is coming.

And there is one thing that no American seems to know that might sink some real big ship.

America does not seem to have any awareness that the ancient Choctaw knowledge was not told to anyone except very old Choctaws who had become wise enough to receive it, by becoming very old, unless they had been habitual nincompoops, in which case they were told nincompoop versions, mostly just to humor them.

As luck would have it, it was mostly old fart nincompoops who survived removal, and then they got interviewed by missionaries, who did not have any better sense than to publish what they were told.

Someone must warn America that the odds appear to be about 147 to 9 that the *Big Scouting Report* most likely to be put together by the American imperialists who have embedded themselves in the intelligence apparatus of the U.S. government is going to be one big nincompooped thing.

Relying on faulty intelligence has sunk more than one big ship, and somebody in America, somebody who sits in some big chair, needs to figure out that if America does not take some steps to actually learn something about the Choctaw people, particularly more than what the missionaries have thought they have known, then when the imperialists among the Americans are confronted by poisoned Choctaws *everybody* in North America, Indian nations included, is going to be in deep doo-doo (according to my 147 to 9 reckoning, rounded off to whole numbers, after much thought and careful study).

That is why I have taken it upon myself to provide that American big-chair person with some meticulously gathered supplementary intelligence about the Choctaws, to help guide that American big-chair person in this dangerous Big Game that is coming, as any still-loyal, ex-Marine Choctaw would try to do, no matter how weirdly Kemo Sabe chemotherapied any still-loyal, ex-Marine Choctaw like that might be.

So, if I might sidekick somewhat spastically out of sync once in a while, well, that's just the way it is.

Blame the American-imperialist mental experimentations for that.

And so I have scratched this ticky-tocky talk for that *American patriotic* reason. Be sure all you FBI guys out there are clear about that.

In gathering the material for this report, I have had the help, for many years, of many very old Choctaws.

Only one thing worries me about that. Once somebody has become so old that about all they ever do anymore is sit in a chair all the time, how is anybody supposed to be able to tell if they are a nincompoop or not?

So, if my ticky-tocky talk just ends up nincompooping those *Big Scouting Report* odds even worse...oh, well.

No old Choctaws know whether they were told the nincompoop versions or the real versions.

That loss from the horrors of removal, that loss to all the world, not just to the Choctaw people, included among its staggering numbers the most distinguished emeritus *alikchis*, including the greatest one of all of that day, and maybe of any day—the legendary Aihokatubbee.

In the 1820s, Dr. Gideon Lincecum, the American country doctor (a kind of American *alikchi*) who was in the Choctaw country at that time, who learned Choctaw well enough to write a grammar of the Choctaw language, took note of whom the Choctaws paid the most attention to at the time of the removal crisis and reported that Aihokatubbee, as the *tichou minko* (spokesman) for young Moshulatubbee, the *Great Medal Minko of Okla Tannap*, could hold the Choctaws spellbound for hours.

That great man of legend, Aihokatubbee, is a man of legend because he was holding forth not so much on the backstabbing removal crisis but primarily on the topic of what it is that makes a Choctaw a Choctaw, which greatly aided the Choctaw people in determining not to resist their forced removal by force of arms and helped calm the bitter feuding Choctaw factions during the civil-war-threatening crisis among them over whether or not to submit to their removal, discouraging them from employing violence against each other.

And, there was an additionally persuasive thing. By 1830, the imperialists among the Americans had grown strong enough that they would have kicked the peewaddee out of the Choctaws, which had something to do with the Choctaws submitting to their removal. But not much. Choctaws are not afraid to die.

Alikchis of the skill and stature of Aihokatubbee are not born very often. They are not easily made, and they are not easily replaced.

They are not made quietly either.

Sometimes a people must wait many generations for an *alikchi* like that to be made, and it is hardly a secret when that happens.

They say that Aihokatubbee was born of two Choctaws who were so deeply in love that daylight did not come for many hours after their honeymoon night, because they were not anywhere near being done yet when it came time for daylight.

They say that daylight did not dare risk distracting those two lovers for fear that some great Choctaw might not be born if daylight intervened, just from what darkness told daylight about what darkness, and everybody else in that whole damn village, had been hearing all night long, though it seems a pretty sure bet that enough seed had been planted by then to not be worrying about whether or not there might be a crop.

That's the story I heard, anyway, from a very old Choctaw. I don't know if he might have been a nincompoop or not.

Aihokatubbee was but one of the many extraordinary walking, talking libraries of ancient Choctaw knowledge who did not survive the blizzards of removal, having been forced, at his age, to try to walk more than five hundred miles and to try to keep ahead of the bayonets of the United States Army, an army that provided him with nothing but a blanket, so he could try to sleep huddled barefoot around an open fire in the snow.

That was the same United States Army, acting on behalf of the same United States of America, that had so publicly and so gloriously buried Pushmataha/Apushamatahaubi only a few years earlier.

It was the government of the same American people that had committed itself to removing the Choctaws in wagons: "In wagons...the U.S. agree to move the Indians to their new homes...." (Article XVI, "Treaty With The Choctaw, 1830").

But the U.S. government decided, on its own, that the first Choctaw removals in wagons, by private contractors, had been "too expensive."

So the U.S. government put the U.S. Army in charge of all the rest of the Choctaw removals, to save money, even though it was not the U.S. government that was bearing the expense of the Choctaw removals, except temporarily.

The Choctaw people were being accorded the honor of paying all of the expenses of their removals, every penny of it, from the proceeds of the sale of the millions of acres of their remaining Mississippi land.

That land consisted of some of the richest agricultural land in the world, which America would virtually throw away by making it the backbone of the Cotton Kingdom of the South, the accumulated wealth of which America would destroy, a few decades later, in its Civil War of 1861–65.

Under the backstabbing control of the American imperialists who had seized control of the U.S. government, those millions of acres of Choctaw land were being sold to white people, so that those American imperialists would not be inconvenienced with having to part with any of their wealth to pay for those ruthless, expensive, traitorous, multiyear mass uprootings of the Choctaw people.

The American imperialists not only cold-bloodedly forced the removal of the Choctaw people, at a great loss of Choctaw lives, but also charged the Choctaw people $5,097,367.50 for the full cost of it (see H. Glenn Jordan, "Choctaw Colonization in Oklahoma," in *America's Exiles: Indian Colonization in Oklahoma*, ed. Arrell Morgan Gibson [Oklahoma Historical Society, 1976], 31).

That left a balance due to the Choctaws, from the proceeds of the sale of their Mississippi land, of $8,095,614.89 (Jordan 31), which the American government refused to pay to the Choctaws for decades, until it was forced to do so by the U.S. Supreme Court, late in the nineteenth century, by which time virtually every penny of it had to go to pay the decades of accumulated attorney's fees it had cost to "collect" it.

Americans have never displayed any remorse for any of those things.

American imperialists have also never displayed any remorse for the depth of the loss of Choctaw knowledge that they caused, not just to the Choctaw people, but to the whole world, the ancient Choctaw knowledge that had been possessed by the Choctaw old ones, like Aihokatubbee.

The imperialists among the Americans did not care then, and they do not care now.

They have never found it convenient to be burdened by that, and, being unburdened by it, they do not intend to ever do anything about it.

To the contrary, they perceive that they might reap a benefit from what they did. They mock the Choctaws in saying that the depth of the loss that

America's Choctaw ally sustained as a result of that callous betrayal is a rationale for denying the Choctaw people sovereignty.

They say that the depth of the losses that the Choctaws sustained is another thing that is helping Choctaws become properly Kemo Sabe chemotherapy irradiated, which those American imperialists call "assimilated."

Those mocking voices have been claiming that the Choctaws no longer know how to be Choctaws.

Choctaws have been taking note of who those mocking voices are. If you are one of those imperialists among the Americans, did you ever think real hard and real sophisticated thoughts about that? Or do you just mock the Choctaws and then go on about your business, hardly ever thinking about the Lords of the North American Continent after having done your mocking?

Those mocking voices that claim that Choctaws no longer know how to be Choctaws also say that Choctaws should content themselves with concentrating on learning how to absorb the Kemo Sabe chemotherapy irradiations, so they can learn how to be good Tonto-talking Choctaws, on American land, under American law, and that Choctaws should be properly grateful to America that its Choctaw allies were not rewarded with some fate even worse than the horrors of their removal and the mental experimentations that the American imperialists continue performing upon the Choctaw people.

Meanwhile, more recent generations of Choctaws have been bearing the full weight of the *burden* of knowing (throughout the twentieth century, ever since the creation of the illegal state of Oklahoma in 1907 drove home a point to the Choctaws in a way that Choctaws could not avoid becoming aware of) that because of what Choctaws did in the War of 1812 on behalf of the United States of America, Choctaws bear the *primary responsibility* for what the imperialists among the Americans were able to do to all of the other Indian nations during the rest of that nineteenth century.

American-imperialist historians might differ with that assessment of Choctaw responsibility. They can differ with it all they want to. They might be dismissive of it, say it really wasn't that way, say whatever they want to say. They don't count in the Big Game.

They cannot speak to poisoned Choctaws. They don't know *how*.

Only Choctaws can speak to poisoned Choctaws and try to let them know that we know what they know and that we are able to feel what they feel, that we can even express it much the way that they might express it, without sugarcoating of any kind.

But we also know that there is another way besides the dark side, that it doesn't have to be way of the dark side, that we just need more ticky-tocky time.

Just more time, that's all.

Choctaws know what Choctaws did in the War of 1812, and Choctaws know that the other Indian nations know what Choctaws did.

Those other Indian nations know the responsibilities that Choctaws were made aware of (and which Choctaws have been bearing the full weight of the burden of) for the last fifty-two outraged million minutes, ever since the creation of the illegal state of Oklahoma in 1907 drove home that point to Choctaws.

Even heavily rearranged, Kemo Sabe-chemotherapied Choctaws know it. All Choctaws know it. Well, except nincompoops, who know nothing.

Those other Indian nations wait and wonder, wondering when the Choctaw people will do something about the awful weight of the responsibilities the Choctaw people have been burdened with, and they wonder what the Choctaw people have been waiting for.

They wonder if the Choctaw people are still the Lords of the North American Continent. Some of those other Indian people mock the Choctaws about that, which hardly goes unnoticed by the Choctaw people.

Only the American people, with their heads complacently buried in their Euro-Anglo ethnocentrisms, who have been done a dangerous disservice by the American-imperialist propagandists, are ignorant of what will be the most far-reaching, twenty-first-century Big Game that will ever impact their country.

A big part of what will make that such a Big Game owes to what the imperialists among the Americans have done to all of the other Indian nations, which was only made possible by what the Lords of the North American Continent did in the War of 1812 on behalf of America.

The American people have never been able to hear the sound of the poisoned Choctaw ticky-tocky Big Game that awaits them in their twenty-first century, not with their heads buried in their self-made mental prisons. They have never had any comprehension of the enormity of that Big Game, or for how long they have not been seeing or hearing it coming.

But now that the Big Game has all been put into place, Americans can be told what that Big Game sounds like, and they can be told that there is an extraordinary ancient people on this planet who anciently and contemporarily are a people possessed of greatness that few Americans know anything about, and that many Americans have never even heard of, a people called Choctaws, who have been despairing at there appearing to be no way to get rid of the poison that has caused the sound of that Big Game to be filling their ears for the last ninety-three outraged million minutes, which got a twentieth-century boost in volume fifty-two outraged million minutes ago, that howling pain of poison that sounds like "tick-tock, tick-tock, tick-tock."

Many of the things I know, such as knowing that all of the Big Game has already been put into place, are things that I know not just because I have heard a lot of ticky-tocky talk for a long time, and not just because I have looked into the eyes of many poisoned Lords of the North American Continent and have seen it coming for a long time but because I can guess.

It's an ancient power of guessing know-how that was known-how by ancient Choctaws.

What I do not know, I can guess. And if I only know a little, I can guess the rest. I can guess right into the middle of it and know not a lot but enough to guess the rest.

A long-dead, very old Choctaw taught me how to do it.

I found his words deep in the bowels of an archive, recorded in a letter that a missionary had written long ago.

I was able to perceive, from many other things that very old, long-dead Choctaw said, that he was a nincompoop, who only knew nincompoop versions of things.

But from what that nincompoop said about the ancient Choctaw power of guessing, and how he said it, and from what he said, and how he said it, about what I knew were the nincompoop things he said about the rest, I was able to guess the nincompoop parts of what he said about the power of guessing, and that opened up that ancient Choctaw power to guess the rest.

I had little choice but somehow to acquire that ancient Choctaw power of guessing as a research tool, because I didn't quite get this ticky-tocky talk all scratched down in the twentieth century, and now, in expanding it to include a history of the twenty-first century, that's something that hasn't even finished happening yet, so how is anybody who cannot guess the rest going to research the rest of that?

Anyway, that's my story for how I know some of the things I know, and I'm sticking to it.

Be sure all you FBI guys out there are clear about that. I don't *know* nothing about nothing. I'm just *guessing*.

But like G-a-l-i-l-e-o, I do k-n-o-w what I k-n-o-w, no matter what the modern Inquisition might make me say I do not know. And what I was able to know-by-guessing about the second half of the twentieth century, and about the rest of the twenty-first century, scared the daylights out of me.

It spurred me to ferocious activity, if somewhat occasionally spastically sidekickingly, due to those damned Kemo Sabe chemotherapy irradiations.

Only one thing bothers me about how I acquired that ancient power to guess the rest. I know it was a nincompoop who taught me.

Maybe there might be a l-i-t-t-l-e possibility that what I guessed might have actually been a somewhat nincompooped guessing of the rest.

Hey, *you*, in the twenty-third century. Could I *really* guess the rest? How good was I? Fair to middling, out where I learned?

Do you still remember me? Did I make such a nincompooped mess of things that you cannot forget me? Oh, well, I guess there's more than one way to achieve immortality, huh?

Who won the 2197 Super Bowl? How about that World Series? Please don't tell me that they didn't still do those things by then. I can't guess that sort of thing. If I could, I'd be in Las Vegas and would be scratching this in style.

After the War of 1812, Indian military power never again mattered. Americans no longer needed it, and they no longer feared it. The War of 1812 was *the decisive war* for Indians on the North American continent, for all Indians anywhere and everywhere on the continent.

The War of 1812 sealed their fate, every one of them, no matter where they were.

After the War of 1812, no military engagements with any Indians were anything other than utterly predictable in their eventual outcome.

Those subsequent military engagements with Indians were virtually meaningless then, and they have now become nothing more than Hollywood hocus-pocus, something portrayed as stirringly dramatic, in a mindless effort to make those things appear important, to keep world attention deflected from the only Indian war that mattered, the War of 1812.

Tecumseh and the British in the War of 1812 constituted the last hope for Indians.

Every Indian in North America can point to the confrontation between Tecumseh and Apushamatahaubi as the single most decisive event, the one that sealed the fate of all Indians. Choctaws know it, and other Indians know it.

Only Americans are ignorant of it, and there is a reason for that: American-imperialist propaganda.

In the teaching of "American" history in the American public schools by successive generations of American imperialists, the extent of the success of the erasing of the Choctaws from American history, particularly regarding Choctaw contributions to the survival of the United States during the War of 1812, can be gauged by the great silence on the part of millions of Americans in movie theaters throughout the United States in 1959–60.

That's when the premiere American-imperialist icon, John Wayne, was portraying Davy Crockett on the silver screen in *The Alamo*.

That's when John Wayne *howled* these immortal mocking American-imperialist words to the American-imperialist-poisoned Lords of the North American Continent, and to those millions of Americans: "Just speak right up and call me Crockett. Don't bother using my title. Old drunken General Flatford gave it to me in the Choctaw Indian War."

"*The Choctaw Indian War.*"

American audiences did not gasp at hearing those words, at hearing the memory of their Choctaw allies mocked in *that* manner.

American audiences did not even notice. They didn't have any comprehension that America had reached a milestone in its history, and in the history of the Big Game.

By then, the propaganda of the American-imperialist mythmakers had placed nearly all Choctaw things beyond the awareness of nearly all Americans, things that are always so much at the forefront of the awareness of Choctaws.

As that major motion picture demonstrates, it took the American-imperialist mythmakers less than a century and a half to succeed in turning American history completely upside down and standing Choctaw history on its head, to a point that the Choctaws could be publicly mocked, on the grandest stage the Americans have ever invented, by the biggest icon of their imperialism, without any Americans even noticing, without any Americans getting up out of their seats and walking out of those theaters and demanding to be refunded their ticket money and to be ready and willing, itchingly willing, barely containably willing, to punch out, John Wayne style, right then and there, anybody and everybody on this big planet who might refuse to refund that ticket money.

See, I know how many of you Choctaws felt, whether you might have been a poisoned one or not. I also know that many Choctaws were able to just shrug it off.

Some nincompooped ones were even happy just to hear Choctaws being mentioned. They nudged one another with their elbows and said, "Hey, John Wayne mentioned us."

Personally, I am able to overlook that big Duke faux pas, and still happen to think that John Wayne was the second greatest movie actor who ever lived, second only to our Mississippi boy, Elvis, who racked up twenty consecutive million-dollar money-making major motion pictures, the all-time Hollywood record, for a reason.

He was *The King*, that's why.

Just to hear that boy jailhouse rock, or hear whatever else he might want to belt out, sheesh, I'd take some antigag medicine and watch any movie that Mississippi boy ever made.

Some antigag medicine would have been of some help for a lot of Choctaws at that John Wayne *Alamo* movie.

Nobody needs something like an ancient Choctaw power of guessing to know how hearing those words made Choctaws feel.

But I have that power of guessing. You want me to guess the exact amount of money that some of you really outraged Choctaws got back for your ticket refund?

I don't waste my guesses guessing things like that, and if you think I'm going to waste my time researching something like that, you're even crazier than me.

That ancient power of guessing is like charm. When you get it, you only get so much of it, and when you use it all up, it's all gone.

That's why the young guys get all of the good-looking girls. They haven't used up all of their charm yet. Take a good look around and see what us old farts get. If you've still got some charm, keep that in mind and use it sparingly. I wish like hell I'd kept some in reserve.

But I know how Choctaws felt, poisoned or not, and I can guess the rest.

Americans did not do what some of those Choctaws did. They did not demand their money back, not even in ones or twos, let alone en masse. They did not know what had transpired in that quintessential American-imperialist mocking moment.

They did not know that it woke up a lot of sleepy-headed, despairing, poisoned Lords of the North American Continent.

Probably even the people doing the mocking were too sleepy-headed to even be aware of the dangerous thing that they had done.

The screenwriter for *The Alamo*, the late James Edward Grant—*may he rest in peace*—and the late John Wayne—*may he rest in peace*—who directed as well as starred in that Technicolor, howling public mocking of all the Choctaws who died on the battlefields defending America, and all the Choctaws who died in their ruthless forced removal, probably *thought* they could just pick any Indian nation and make up a war, and it wouldn't make any difference whether or not there might ever have been such a war.

Indeed, they could. And they did.

And it did not make any difference, except to poisoned Choctaws sitting in those movie theaters, who did not just shrug it off and go back to concentrating on learning how to be good Americans, on American land, under American law, though many of them had become very skilled at appearing to be good Tonto-talking Choctaws, and many of them by then did not even look like what the sleepy-headed American imperialists think that Choctaws are supposed to look like.

It wasn't that mocking by Hollywood so much as the complete absence of any protest anywhere by any of those millions of Americans who heard those words howled at the Choctaw people that told the Choctaw people how thoroughly that both their loyalty and their multiple betrayals had been erased from the collective memory of the Americans.

It also told the poisoned ones among the Lords of the North American Continent how easily they could move through any part of the fabric of the

American nation that had betrayed their ancient, distinguished people, an American nation that foolishly makes knowledge about anything available to anyone, even extremely dangerous, nightmarish knowledge.

~

Hey, FBI guys, there's a little something that worries me. America has mislaid many really dangerous things over the last half-century or so, no? Didn't I see something mentioned about that on TV?

I wonder why nobody can find those many things, things that are not just nightmarish knowledge but concrete, specific nightmarish things, and things to make nightmarish things.

Has anybody ever done a cataloguing of just how much of that stuff is known to have gone missing?

Whew, it sure seems like a lot, to have just gotten mislaid.

Are there any nuclear devices among those mislaid things that nobody can find? Maybe even some "nucular" devices?

If so, I guess if you make that many thousands of them, a few are bound to get mislaid s-o-m-ewhere.

Oh, well, it'll probably all turn up s-o-m-e day, don't you suppose? You guys have probably been right on top of that problem for a long time anyway, huh?

So what do we have to worry about? We've had the rocket-science FBI guys protecting us.

For a long time.

That Choctaw FBI file decades ago probably had already exceeded the million pages it merited even back then. Huh, FBI guys?

Surely all of you guys weren't running around catching kidnappers and bank robbers for all of those decades, in between chanting that funny litany, "Are you now, or have you ever been, a member of the Communist Party," etc., etc., after backstabbing the Lords of the North American Continent, huh?

You didn't just go on about *your* business and forget about *them*, did you?

You got how many Choctaw code talkers on staff?

Boy, that J. Edgar Hoover was some kind of rocket scientist, huh?

Any of you FBI guys even remember him? Any of you guys even remember those days?

Say, those 1950s, wasn't that when the U.S. Congress was explaining to all of the Indian nations why it had decided to go ahead and "terminate" all of the Indian nations? That House Concurrent Resolution 108 that it actually started implementing?

Seems like I recall something about that in relation to Carl Albert. Any of you FBI guys remember him?

You know, back in the fifties when he was on his way to becoming Speaker of the House, on his way to becoming second in line to succeed to the presidency, where, as Speaker of the House, for a time, he became first in line to succeed to the presidency, in the 1970s, when that silly shifty-eyed Spiro Agnew had to resign the vice presidency of the United States; the Carl Albert who was known as the "Little Giant from Little Dixie," or alternatively as the "Little Drunk from Little Dixie."

That Carl Albert.

You FBI guys were right on top of things back then, right? You guys knew exactly where his "Little Dixie" congressional district in Oklahoma was located, right?

You guys knew how things worked back then, right?

Like things regarding access *from* the highest level of the U.S. government, to things *at* the highest level of the U.S. government, to things that can only be gotten at by being *inside* that highest level of the U.S. government, right?

Like *anything* in the whole goddamn world you want to know about, or want to know how and where and when you could get your hands on it?

And you got the juice to do it?

Like it was one big candy store, and there's nobody guarding the candy but a funny little Bugtussle, Oklahoma, *drunk*, who never had a clue that you've got a great big insatiable sweet tooth?

And wars, both hot and c-o-l-d, going on all over the damn place, and so much candy for nobody to miss a little bit of it. Not right away, anyhow. Those decades, right?

You FBI guys were right on top of that, right?

For decades, right? While that sweetness just kept getting oh so disbelievably sweeter?

Hey, no need to even look into it, right? Most of the ones who knew would be pushing daisies by now anyway. And that wouldn't be finally making the time nice and ripe, would it? And, anyway, they probably wouldn't have left any messages for a good Choctaw code talker to find, right?

A real good Choctaw code talker.

Like one good enough to be holding in his not-too-badly trembling hands the most perilous moments in the history of how many big, crowded places?

You FBI guys got plenty of good code talkers, right?

And, if not, what's to worry about?

It's just some wacko-weird-Choctaw-guessing-the-rest-scout, who thinks he might have guessed something.

"Lieutenant Colonel C-u-s-t-e-r, a scout has returned and says there is s-o-m-ething you might want to t-h-i-n-k about. We might have a l-i-t-t-l-e backstabbing p-r-o-b-l-e-m in this twenty-first c-e-n-t-u-r-y."

Those potentially fatally ignorant, potentially fatally Euro-Anglo ethnocentric American people in the late 1950s included the Hollywood people of the Academy of Motion Pictures, who honored *The Alamo* with Academy Award nominations in 1960 for Best Picture, Best Film Editing, and nominations in quite a number of other categories.

It won only one Academy Award, for Best Sound.

That Academy Award was not for the ticky-tocky sound of that quintessential mocking moment in the history of American popular culture.

It was not for the amplified boost of the sound that was howled into the ears of poisoned Lords of the North American Continent twenty-five outraged million minutes ago.

But s-o-m-e day that amplified boost of that sound might enter the *Oxford Dictionary of the English Language*, in England, as a newly discovered mid-twentieth-century American connotation for the word "motivation."

If the editors of those august tomes that have chronicled the history of the English language for a long time, editors who have included my distant Uncle Bob, might desire some nepotistic ancient Choctaw guessing-the-rest assistance for that new connotation of "motivation," that connotation might be expressed as "something howlingly sufficient to cause the Lords of the North American Continent to dance with their dark side."

The American propagandists who created and then popularized the American Myth (and who had, by then, incidentally erased the Choctaws from the collective American memory as just one by-product of that propaganda) were in no sense American patriots.

They were American *imperialists*, which is something distinctly different from an American *patriot*.

To be an American patriot requires both courage *and* integrity.

You want to know what American patriotism sounds like? It sounds like me.

It sounds like a Choctaw who does not believe that Apushamatahaubi was wrong, or at least does not believe that Tecumseh's way was right, or at least is bothered by the potential problem that if Tecumseh was right then maybe Choctaws were wrong, and Choctaws hate being wrong about *anything*.

Nothing will spur a Choctaw to ferocious activity quite like the desire to prove that Choctaws were not wrong about something, no matter how many dangerous things some Choctaw might have to try to juggle to try to make things come out just right so that Choctaws don't end up being wrong about something.

An American patriot has the courage to unblinkingly face bad things, with untrembling hands, and then has the integrity not to bullshit them up too much when telling about them, not more than a little bit one way or another, unless you've got some good point to make later on in your talk, for which some big bullshitting is just foreshadowing to set things up just right, so everything can come out just right.

Hey, how are you liking the roller-coaster ride so far? Not you FBI guys, you don't count. You illiterate cowards can go back to trying to find a good Choctaw code talker.

The distinction between an American imperialist and an American patriot is somewhat akin to irresponsible and responsible American parenting.

American parents who do nothing when their child becomes a bully do that child no favor, not in the short run, and not in the long run, either.

There is nothing easy for Americans about being a parent, and there is nothing that is easy for them about being a responsible citizen in their republic.

Maybe Americans had to do s-o-m-e of the things that Americans did in order to make America. But there are some things that American imperialists did that they did not have to do, and which there is no reason for them to continue doing.

The renegade, lawless imperialists among the Americans who created that ticking Choctaw propaganda time bomb, and then were so foolish as to plant their fat bottoms so deeply right on top of that ticky-tocky thing, have failed the United States in ways that are far more serious than their irresponsible parenting of the American republic.

The imperialists among the Americans have been extremely dangerous people on the North American continent in ways that go far beyond even their lack of respect for the rule of law.

It has been the mythmaking of their propaganda that has been the most dangerous thing for Indians.

That mythmaking process has dehumanized Indian people and has denied them their fundamental right as nations of people to sustain their remarkable civilizations, free of the tyranny of American cultural genocide.

Not only have contemporary Americans been done the dangerous disservice of not being allowed to know anything about the cancerous American-imperialist betrayal of their Choctaw allies, but they have also not been allowed to know anything about other deadly cancers that have ravished the vital organs of the American National Character as a result of that betrayal.

The long, lingering American-imperialist policy of attempting to execute a death sentence upon the civilization of their Choctaw allies, by inflicting the slow, debilitating cancer of cultural genocide upon Choctaw civilization, is euphemistically called "assimilation."

The attempt to execute that death sentence has been prosecuted by inflicting upon the Choctaw people, and upon the American National Character, an even more deadly kind of cancer, a long, debilitating erosion of Choctaw sovereignty.

Choctaws, who had been highly skilled, town-dwelling *farmers* for thousands of years before the arrival of Europeans, are a people who long ago fashioned a remarkable civilization for themselves that is far superior to that of the American people but who have had to figure out how they can withstand the strenuous efforts of American imperialists to inflict the cancers of many inferior elements of American civilization upon them.

Choctaws are different.

They are not merely different from other Native peoples of North America, but they are markedly distinctive from any other people on earth, and they have a fundamental right to remain different.

Choctaws are decidedly distinctive from Americans.

Consider, for example, the institution of the Choctaw duel. Dueling is well known to Americans from American history.

It's how the great American political genius, Alexander Hamilton, died, on July 11, 1804, in a duel with the shifty-eyed vice president of the United States, Aaron Burr.

Old dueling wounds left the hot-tempered General Andrew Jackson a partial invalid for life, unable even to get out of bed at crucial moments during the War of 1812.

But Vice President Burr and General Jackson survived their duels. As Americans practiced the institution, dueling was designed to settle personal differences between individuals by employing violence to produce a winner and a loser. And it was illegal, participated in on the sly, outside the law, as a matter of "honor," a thing often ignored by prosecutors.

The difference between a Choctaw duel and an American duel was like the difference between a sad dream and a howling nightmare.

Choctaw duels were sad events that were sanctioned by Choctaw law, and the winner was a saddened but much healthier Choctaw community, not either one of the participants.

In a Choctaw duel, both participants died. In early times, they stood facing one another, while each one's assistant, ordinarily their best friend, on signal, at the same time, chopped his friend in the back of the head with an axe.

Later, they might take rifles and go off into the woods and shoot at one another until one was dead, and then the other one would be killed.

The whole thing was over and done with, and Choctaw communities spared themselves the prolonged grief of trying to live with two people who hated each other.

It was a sophisticated mechanism for preserving community harmony, one that demonstrates, without much subtlety, a Choctaw awareness that everyone in a community is affected when two people hate each other and a Choctaw awareness that the kind of prolonged misery springing from that kind of hatred does not have to be tolerated by Choctaw communities.

Choctaw duels were rare events, but the very existence of the institution worked wonders in maintaining a certain decorum of manners, restraint, and tolerance within Choctaw communities, something called civilized behavior.

It was ancient North American civilized behavior, practiced by the Lords of the North American Continent.

It was a far more sophisticated civilized practice than the one devised by Europeans and Americans in attempting to deal with the same problem.

And it was not something that the Lords of the North American Continent had just stumbled into in any recent millennium.

Choctaws have long been far more advanced in the art of civilization than Europeans and Americans.

Choctaws are the product of the North American cradle of civilization. They are an ancient people of the earth, who take a backseat to no one in the art of civilization.

Chapter Four

The Great Imperial
Piggybacked Comeback

*T*he *Great Medal Minko of Okla Hannali* taught the American secretary of
war, General Henry Knox, a lesson in civilized behavior, one that every
other American general took note of, when he challenged General Knox to a
Choctaw duel.

Having been insulted by Knox, Pushmataha bought a barrel of gunpow-
der and fitted it with a fuse. He then sat on that barrel, lit a cigar, and invited
General Knox to sit beside him while he touched his cigar to the fuse.

General Knox declined, which was the only reason that he and
Pushmataha did not die on that day.

Choctaws are not afraid to die.

General Knox never insulted the *Great Medal Minko of Okla Hannali*
again, nor did any other American general, including General Andrew
Jackson, who held both his famous temper and his tongue, in 1820, when
Pushmataha confronted General Jackson with a fraud he appeared to be
attempting to foist upon the Choctaw people, perhaps unintentionally,
General Jackson apparently being the victim of his own pitifully inaccurate
U.S. Army maps.

That dispute occurred at the treaty negotiations in 1820, at Doak's Stand
in the Mississippi Choctaw country. It concerned a point of precise geographical knowledge regarding the *exact* location of the source of the South
Canadian River in the southern Rocky Mountains of present-day northeastern

New Mexico and whether or not any portion of the Red River was to be found "due South" of that source of the South Canadian River.

In that 1820 treaty-negotiation confrontation between Pushmataha and General Jackson, Pushmataha displayed his encyclopedic knowledge of the geography of *his* Trans-Mississippi West, encyclopedic geographical knowledge that had been handed down to him from the thousands of years that the Lords of the North American Continent had been shepherding their continent.

It was encyclopedic geographical knowledge that the particular Choctaw great medal *minko* named Pushmataha had confirmed firsthand, as hundreds of Choctaw generations had done before him.

It was a continent that had hardly been a "wilderness" for the thousands of years that the Lords of the North American Continent, and the other Native nations of that continent, had been intimately acquainted with every part of it, with every watershed, with every watercourse, with every peculiarity, and with every particularity of every part of it.

There was not any part of ancient North America, anywhere, that was unknown. To even be capable of thinking otherwise is nothing less than to take the measure of the foolish (potentially fatally foolish) Euro-Anglo ethnocentrisms.

To this day, Americans *still* believe that they "discovered" a "wilderness." They are not much smarter today than they were in Medieval times.

They are not smart enough to be the lords of this continent, and every Indian nation knows it, and has known it, for a very long time.

When poisoned Choctaws take back the continent, that will likely be hardly any more challenging than taking candy from a baby, not much more challenging than taking candy from a drunk.

The only advantage Americans ever had was their overwhelming numbers and their technology. That is the awful truth that they are facing in their twenty-first century.

American numerical superiority has now become meaningless, and their population density has become a liability, because their technology has been available to anyone, for any purpose.

Whether Americans are smart enough even to ever become aware of that, before it is too late, is the question.

They have not been smart enough to have any awareness that, in the twenty-first century, it is virtually a statistical impossibility that poisoned Indians will not use American technology against Americans, if America continues producing poisoned Indians.

Americans are the only ones who can do anything about that.

But Americans have not even been smart enough to figure out that they have entered their last century, because they allowed themselves to still have an "Indian problem," and Americans have no awareness that they have no option but to fix that problem without delay, if Americans want America to survive as a nation.

Americans have created such potentially insurmountable problems for themselves in making sure that their propaganda has been so pervasive, and so successful, that it remains an open question whether any friendly, still loyal Indian will ever be able to figure out any way even just to get their attention, even just to make them aware that they still have an "Indian problem."

That's how deeply their heads have been buried in the mental prison of their conception of the world, and of their place in it.

Americans appear to care about hardly anything but making money in the here and now, no matter what the consequences might be for other people or for other American generations.

They are not accustomed to having much concern for other people, and they are not accustomed to thinking in terms of generations, for any purpose.

It was partly the many generations of accumulated geographical knowledge that Pushmataha had seen being employed as a powerful military tool in the greatly feared Choctaw military police expeditions that he had participated in during his utterly fearless, bragging, teenage years, before he began drumming up expeditions himself, that eventually helped him become a military leader of tactical genius.

He received that training from Choctaws for whom the examples of tactical military genius, and encyclopedic geographical knowledge, echoed down through the thousands of years that his Choctaw people had been an imperial people.

That millennia of accumulated knowledge helped him earn his ascendancy to the highest rank of military leadership of his people. It was knowledge that helped him achieve the prerequisite terrifying military reputation to ascend to that rank.

But it also helped him achieve much more than that.

It helped him achieve something in 1820 that American-imperialist historians have tried to keep the world from finding out about.

It helped him achieve a thing so great that it would have been unobtainable at that time but for the profound wisdom of his vision.

But because it was a great thing obtained in 1820 *only due* to his vision, only due to the *same* vision that he had acted on in 1811, in fearlessly confronting and defeating Tecumseh's ambitions, the American-imperialist propagandists have made sure that hardly anyone in the world has ever been allowed to know about the great thing that Pushmataha did for his people in 1820, because *no one* can be allowed to know about his vision, and the great thing that he did in 1820 was inextricably tied to that vision.

The great thing that he did in 1820 was the crowning glory of his career.

It was the fulfilling of his vision.

He, virtually single-handedly, in that treaty of 1820 *restored* that ancient southern Great Plains Choctaw imperial province to the Choctaws.

It was a thing that virtually everyone would have thought impossible to do at that time, under the circumstances that prevailed at that time.

But he did it.

He did it against overwhelming odds.

He did it against the kind of overwhelming odds that have the capacity to engage the Choctaw sense of challenge.

He did it in 1820.

And he did it legal and proper, like the cop he was, like the law and order-loving Choctaw that he was, like the worthy shepherd of the North American continent that he was.

It was a great thing for which the American-imperialist historians have denied him his just due, to the endless frustration of the Choctaw people, who lie awake at night trying to figure out how they can make their great imperial comeback, and then, when a Choctaw manages, against overwhelming super-human odds, to bring them back to the glory of those ancient times, nobody is allowed to *know* about it! `

The American imperialists have paid hardly any attention at all to what Pushmataha was doing in the Trans-Mississippi West, or anywhere else, because it has been taboo in "American" history for him to hardly even be mentioned, all because the American imperialists do not want anybody to know that they have betrayed their Choctaw allies.

It is not for a lack of documentation that the world doesn't know about the great thing he did in 1820.

Much of what Pushmataha did in his entire crime-busting military police career in his Trans-Mississippi West is heavily documented in what American historians regard as "historical documentation."

A good big bunch of that evidence, after a ten-year search tracking down as much of the information as she could find, was published in 1959 by a University of Texas-trained historian, Ruth Tennison West, of Commerce, Texas, who offered a voice of sanity from the Lone Star state.

At that time, the Texas culture of historical scholarship was an empire lorded over by the Texas Ranger-whitewashing king of the Texas history professors, Walter Prescott Webb, of the University of Texas, augmented by the awesome anecdotal talents of J. Frank Dobie, occasionally relieved by the blissful breath of Roy Bedichek, that great chronicler of thrilling feats of Texas high school football (see "Southwestern Literature?" in Larry McMurtry's *In A Narrow Grave: Essays On Texas* [University of New Mexico Press, 1987]; originally published in 1968).

Ruth Tennison West published her findings twenty-five million minutes ago, as *The Alamo* was being released, in her concise, even pithy article, "Pushmataha's Travels," in the Summer 1959 issue of the *Chronicles of Oklahoma*, the scholarly historical quarterly of the Oklahoma Historical Society, though she was hardly aware of *what* she was documenting.

It should be especially noted that Pushmataha's hair-raising, crime-busting, howling police capers in the West included ones that engaged, but did not q-u-i-t-e bust, the criminally trespassing, buffalo-stealing crimes of the frightful power of the Great Basin-originating, former great rabbit-hunting nations of Shoshone-speaking peoples who became known as the Comanche nations.

Those trespassing Comanche criminals, only a few generations earlier, had acquired horses and had come thundering out of the Wyoming basin to try to steal the whole damn great southern Choctaw buffalo herds of the southern Great Plains, buffalo herds which the Choctaw people allowed to run loose like buffaloes ought to do, not trying to fence them in, like silly white people do who raise buffaloes today.

Besides, fences would hardly have kept those former rabbit-hunting Comanche nations in their horse-mounted howling thousands from sweeping down out of Wyoming and giving that Choctaw supercop a *Choctaw-southern-buffalo-herd-size-headache* bad enough to drive any great medal *minko* to become a world-class drunkard.

Encyclopedic geographical knowledge can only do so much for you.

But the *Great Medal Minko of Okla Hannali* knew that there was more than one way to skin a bunch of howling, trespassing rabbit hunters.

At those treaty negotiations with his United States allies at Doak's Stand in 1820, that Choctaw supercop was able to cement the capstone achievement of his career *only* because he *had* put his distinguished Choctaw people on the fast track for their big-time, piggybacked, imperial comeback by making it possible for them to become the glorious victorious allies of the United States in the War of 1812.

And it paid off, spectacularly, in 1820.

It was a capstone achievement that also *fixed* that howling rabbit-hunter Comanche headache, but good.

Pushmataha did that by getting his American allies to acknowledge the ancient Choctaw title to a huge and significant portion of the ancient Choctaw empire in the Trans-Mississippi West.

It is a great expanse of the southern Great Plains, and other vast portions of that Trans-Mississippi West, that *was* acknowledged by the Americans as belonging to the ancient Choctaw people in that treaty of 1820.

The *restored* Choctaw imperial empire which that Choctaw supercop carved out for his Choctaw people in that 1820 Choctaw treaty with their United States allies includes huge portions of four present-day states: *all* of the southwestern portion of Arkansas (a Choctaw portion of Arkansas); *all* of the southern half of the illegal state of Oklahoma (a Choctaw half of that illegal state); a *big* chuck of the Texas panhandle (all of the land between the South Canadian River and the Red River, all the way across that Choctaw part of that Texas panhandle); and a stunning Choctaw portion of northeastern New Mexico (to the snow-capped summit of a *Choctaw* Rocky Mountain— well, one side of that mountain, anyway).

That side of that mountain peak, the highest peak in the southern Rocky Mountains, is where the "source" of the South Canadian River is located, which is what forms the western treaty boundary of that Choctaw part of New Mexico.

The treaty says that the western boundary of that Choctaw land runs "due South," from the source of the South Canadian River, to Red River, which is *way* over to the southeast, where the Red River's headwaters are found near the New Mexico border with the Texas panhandle, which is nowhere even n-e-a-r "due South" of the source of the South Canadian River, which was also the squirrelly part of those U.S. Army maps.

Those army maps showed the Red River extending westward to a point *due south* of the source of the South Canadian River, which caused Pushmataha to take his pipe hatchet handle and trace upon the ground a precise map of that huge region, to show General Jackson how squirrelly his U.S. Army maps were.

That was also when Choctaws began pondering how squirrelly that treaty boundary description is.

But General Jackson said don't worry about it, so Choctaws don't worry about it.

If the treaty says "due South" to the Red River, and there is no Red River due south of there, well, that's not a Choctaw problem.

That is an Andrew Jackson "don't worry about it" problem.

That was hardly the only problem. As Pushmataha pointed out to General Jackson, there was also the small detail that the Americans, at that time, did not even claim to own any part of New Mexico, which even they believed belonged to the Mexicans.

But General Jackson said don't worry about that, either. So Choctaws don't worry about that, either.

If the silly Americans want to sell, to the Choctaws, what the Americans do not own, that's called a "quitclaim deed." Then, later, when the Americans do own it, they don't own it, because they already sold it to the Choctaws. That is how a quitclaim deed works.

That Choctaw-American treaty of 1820 leaves the Lords of the North American Continent in what lawyers call "constructive possession" of an immense portion of their ancient Choctaw empire in the West. It includes the heart of their ancient Choctaw southern Great Plains buffalo herd.

After that, the Lords of the North American Continent were confident that the only thing they had to do was sit back and let the military muscle of their imperial allies in the United States Army fix that rabbit-hunter headache of those howling Comanche nations *for* the Choctaw people and fix that headache *but good*.

Which was exactly what happened during the following decades. It required little more than a couple generations.

When Pushmataha negotiated that Choctaw-American treaty of 1820, that Choctaw supercop once again ascended to the sublime heights of being *the* Commanding General of the North American Continent.

He did *that* one more time!

An encore performance!

He did it in 1811!

He did it again in 1820!

In that 1820 treaty, he *did* lead the Choctaw people to their great imperial comeback!

Big-time!

All the way back!

All the way back to Choctaw imperial-empire greatness!

On paper, anyway.

But, in that 1820 new-world-in-the-making, getting it down on *paper* was what counted.

That was the one thing that the Choctaws had learned by then.

In America, it's *paper* that counts.

It's all that counts.

And the Choctaws got it down on paper.

On American paper. Which they had also learned is what counts.

That Choctaw-American treaty of 1820 is both *the* most phenomenal and *the* most overlooked treaty in all of U.S. history.

That treaty affirms the Choctaw title to their restored southern Great Plains buffalo herd in the West, according to the legal and proper ways of the Constitution of the United States.

Those legal and proper *constitutional* ways require not just getting that Choctaw legal title to those lands in the West written down on the legal papers of the Americans, but it also requires getting that 1820 treaty advised and consented to by the United States Senate, which the United States Senate has done, and which can be found in the permanent record of its proceedings, in 7 Stat. 212.

It also means that the 1820 treaty between the Choctaw people and the American people must be proclaimed to the world by the president of the United States, which the president of the United States has done, on January 8, 1821, which makes that Choctaw empire the most phenomenal, *American constitutional*, legal and proper Indian empire on the North American continent.

But American-imperialist propagandists have not wanted anyone to know anything about Choctaws, because the American imperialists have not wanted anyone to know that they have stabbed their Choctaw allies in the back, so they try to keep everyone from finding out anything about that glorious Choctaw empire, and hardly anything else about Choctaws, glorious or otherwise, especially hardly anything about Pushmataha.

There has seemed to be no way to get the American-imperialist propagandists to put the Choctaw people into the story of American history.

But maybe there is a way.

Maybe there is a better way.

Maybe it is time to give up on the American-imperialist historians *ever* doing that and go *over their heads*, over their heads to some *really* powerful people, huh?

Maybe those FBI guys might be guys who can be big-dictionary-connotation "motivated" to *want* the American people to *know* about Choctaws, huh?

Maybe there is more than one way for s-o-m-e new Choctaw supercop to *fix* a howling American-imperialist propaganda headache, huh?

Maybe to circumvent and overpower those American-imperialist propagandists, maybe to go over their heads, big-time, all the way to the F-B-I, maybe just about the only thing that s-o-m-e *new* Choctaw supercop has to do is figure out how to put *all* of those FBI guys *frantically* working around the clock, *every* day and *every* night, for *him*, huh?

Maybe s-o-m-e new Choctaw supercop can become the de facto director of all of those FBI guys, huh?

Those guys in the FBI might not like working for s-o-m-e new Choctaw supercop de facto director of the FBI, and they might like to try to keep that quiet, but if they think that there is any way in these days that they can keep the big-time media from finding out about a Big Game that compels nearly all of those FBI guys, nearly all the time, at all of those FBI field offices, to be doing s-o-m-ething that someb-o-d-y *directs* them to d-o-o-o, then maybe we'll just *see* who the new Choctaw supercop de facto director of the FBI might be, huh?

If they t-h-i-n-k that this little t-o-y-i-n-g with their heads, in this little s-a-l-v-o of this Big-time propaganda war, is all that is c-o-m-i-n-g, if they think what l-i-t-t-l-e that has been mentioned so far about all that scares someb-o-d-y about what poisoned Choctaws have probably been up to, then maybe those FBI guys do not have a clue that long before s-o-m-e new Choctaw supercop is through, even the newest cub reporter on the city desk of the most podunk paper in the most podunk city in the most podunk country in the most podunk backwater part of the world will know *who* is the de facto director of *every* FBI guy, huh?

After all, it is the responsibility of citizens to convey their fears about potential threats to the security of America, and maybe even threats *just to* the security of American-imperialist propaganda, and those FBI guys have not even begun to be tipped off about what s-o-m-ebody's worst fears might be about the many poisoned-Choctaw schemes that are probably being hatched out there *right now*, huh?

Those FBI guys will have no choice but to warn the whole world about poisoned Choctaws, and to tell the whole world *why* Choctaws became poisoned.

Those FBI guys will have to give those warnings on a *media-event* daily basis, until the awareness about poisoned Choctaws, and *why* Choctaws became poisoned, has reached what the advertising executives call a "global saturation level," huh?

Then that unreturnable ball will be bounding across the court of the desperately galloping, futilely swinging, nothing but air-smashing American-imperialist propagandists, who can then *try* to figure out what in the hell they can do, huh?

I will save them the effort of the headache. There will be nothing that they will be able to do.

The Choctaw people *will* become a prominent part of the *American* telling of "American" history, by my carefully calculated odds of 737 to 3, rounded off to whole numbers, after much thought and careful study.

And you just heard how that will be made to happen, and how it will all come out just right.

That 1820 new-world-in-the-making, gotten-down-on-legal-paper, American constitutional, *Choctaw* empire stretches *halfway across* the North American continent.

It stretches from the present-day Alabama-Mississippi border in the Deep South, to the top of the highest peak in the southern Rocky Mountains, to the top of the 13,161-foot peak of Mt. Wheeler, named, apparently, for the wheeler-dealer Choctaws.

That is the tallest peak in New Mexico, which overlooks the sacred Blue Lake of Taos Pueblo, the sacred Blue Lake that was *restored* to the ownership of the ancient, distinguished people of Taos Pueblo by President Richard M. Nixon, for whose 1960 presidential campaign I had both the foresight and the good sense, in the seventh grade, to serve as the chairman of at my junior high school and to eloquently represent his political positions in debate before the assembled student body, against that evil, tricky ninth grader who was the chairman of the Kennedy campaign at that junior high school, who knew what a Mao was, which I had neglected to find out anything about.

But from what that Kennedy man said about it, I was pretty damn sure that my main man, the vice president of the United States, was against it.

And, so what if I was about the only one who had sense enough to vote for Nixon in that 1960 junior high school mock presidential election?

At least I had foresight enough to sense something about that man that made him nearly perfectly suited to sit in that big chair in that big Oval Office, and, sure enough, when he got there, he became the *first* president of the United States (something that *should* have happened in 1960) to *restore* a sacred place to an Indian people, when he restored their sacred Blue Lake to the Taos Pueblo people.

It wasn't that hard to do. He just signed a piece of paper. And voila! The deed was done. A presidential deed.

Which is the presidential precedent that it can be done again, a presidential precedent that was set by the *greatest* president of the United States who ever walked the face of the earth!

Which means that I was *right* in 1960! No matter what all 1,467 of those *other* students thought.

It is in the mountaintop heights overlooking that restored sacred Blue Lake of Taos Pueblo that the source of the South Canadian River is to be found, and that is where the future western boundary of the restored Choctaw imperial empire in the West *will* be found.

That huge 1820 Choctaw treaty empire has only one little gap in that whole sweeping half-continent expanse, just one little bitty gap in southeastern Arkansas, and who in the hell would want *that* swampy place but Quapaws?

In bringing that big slice of the ancient Choctaw western empire into that new-world-in-the-making, the Choctaws did everything right and proper, legal and proper, in arm's-length negotiation with their American allies.

That phenomenal 1820 big-time Choctaw imperial comeback, against overwhelming odds, is something that few American historians have bothered to make themselves aware of, though that is not hard to do, with the historical record about it being so abundant.

American historians haven't bothered doing that partly because, unlike the historians of future centuries, who will be capable of sophisticated perceptions, American historians have never been capable of conceiving of something as dangerous as the twenty-first century, and partly because American historians have never had any comprehension that the single most threatening thing to America, *and* to American-imperialist propaganda, in *their* twenty-first century, would be the Choctaw mental conception of themselves.

That mental conception has been built up for the thousands of years that the Choctaws have been the Lords of the North American Continent, without successfully being challenged by *anybody*, though many pompous peoples have *tried*.

Those American historians, always looking backward, with a peculiar kind of myopia even when they do that, and with no training in how to look forward, have never known that the Choctaw mental conception of themselves was what American historians *should* have been paying attention to.

Americans have now become aware that there are people in the world who have different mental conceptions of themselves, and of the world, than what Americans have.

That's hardly rocket science but rather something that has been known to the world for a very long time.

But, for a very long time, Americans, *thinking* that both America *and* the American-imperialist propaganda was safely isolated from a dangerous world by two big oceans, did not know that the most dangerous part of that world was s-o-m-ething in what they considered to be their own backyard.

No one was allowed to find out about the frightening thing called poisoned Choctaws.

No one was able to foresee that in America's twenty-first century poisoned Choctaws would become the one thing that all of those FBI guys would become so frightened of that those FBI guys would dearly wish they had not been such illiterate cowards about enforcing Indian treaties before it became necessary for them to get a de facto director who would cause them to pee their pants at the very *thought* of pissing *him* off.

That phenomenal 1820 Choctaw imperial empire is real enough, and it was recognized by the United States long enough for Choctaw minds to fully absorb the magnificence of their big-time imperial comeback.

It has hardly been just a paper empire.

Few contemporary Americans are aware that, *because* that 1820 treaty-restored Choctaw imperial empire *does*, in fact, exist, the United States was compelled, for decades, to pay hundreds of thousands of dollars in rent to the Choctaws, so the United States could lease a vast expanse of the southern Great Plains from the Choctaws (land that is currently all of the southwestern portion of the illegal state of Oklahoma), so the Choctaws and the United States could join together in being bountifully generous in providing a place to live for the 1820 new-world-in-the-making *vassals* of the Choctaws, the Comanche and Kiowa nations.

That "Leased District," as it has been called, for the Comanches and the Kiowas, happened to be where they were trespassing and squatting on Choctaw land. It was a multiple-imperial, wheeler-dealer, Choctaw-American real estate rental property arrangement, the underlying legal technicalities and complexities of which it does not appear that any American ever bothered attempting to explain to either the Comanches or the Kiowas.

It also does not appear that the Choctaws ever quite found the time to try to find a Choctaw volunteer to go break the news to either the Comanches or the Kiowas that they had become the vassals of the Lords of the North

American Continent. Choctaws were too busy with other things to ever quite get around to doing that.

To this day, most Comanches and Kiowas seem to have little awareness that they were once for decades the vassals of the Choctaws, at a time when Choctaws had figured out how to fast-track their big-time imperial comeback so that they could become the kind of wheeler-dealer imperialists in that 1820 new-world-in-the-making that Choctaws have always been.

Choctaws did not lose American recognition of that imperial empire until after the American Civil War. The outbreak of that war caused the Americans to violate their treaty obligation of protection of the Choctaws, by withdrawing all American troops from anywhere near the Choctaw Nation, leaving the Choctaws at the mercy of their powerful Confederate States neighbors.

After that war, instead of the American people apologizing to the Choctaws and compensating them for the damages they sustained in that American Civil War, all because the Americans failed to uphold their treaty obligation to protect the Choctaws, the Americans unlawfully (in the treaty of 1866, the last American treaty with the Choctaws) withdrew American recognition of that "Leased District" portion of the Choctaw imperial empire in the West, as an unjust punishment for the Choctaws having done the *only* thing that they *could* do—enter into diplomatic relations with those overwhelmingly powerful Confederate neighbors.

When the U.S. government later began trying to sell portions of that "Leased District" to white "settlers," the U.S. Supreme Court declared that the U.S. government was committing a fraud against the Choctaw people, in violation of that 1866 treaty, but that court did not have the courage to restore American recognition of title to that land to the Choctaws.

By the ploy of that 1866 treaty, the imperialists among the Americans have been trying to get away with penalizing the Choctaws because *America* violated *its* treaty obligation of protecting the Choctaws.

It seems like every few centuries the Choctaw people suffer the frustration of having to sit down and figure out *all over again*, from scratch, how they can do what they were born to do.

The law and order-loving Choctaws know it is their birthright to lord it over the North American continent. It has now become clear that the only way that birthright *can* be restored is for the de facto director of the FBI to be some big-time, head-busting supercop who will enforce a supreme kind of law and order, the supreme law of treaties.

There is no mystery about *how* to do that.

As anyone knows who has ever worked in retail sales, the only way to defeat shoplifters is to *confront* shoplifters.

If shoplifters find that inconvenient, they have only themselves to blame.

The pansies in the FBI have failed to uphold that supreme kind of law and order.

Upholding that supreme kind of law cannot be entrusted to those illiterate cowards who do nothing but pee their pants and run and hide at the very thought of upholding *the supreme law of the land* ("This Constitution, and the Laws of the United States which shall be made in Pursuance thereof; and all Treaties made, or which shall be made, under the authority of the United States, shall be the supreme Law of the Land; and the Judges in every State shall be bound thereby, any Thing in the Constitution or Laws of any State to the Contrary notwithstanding."—Article VI, United States Constitution).

The Choctaw people must always be the lords of this continent. No other people anywhere on earth possess the wisdom and the vision for the good of the whole continent like the wisdom and the vision that is possessed by the Lords of the North American Continent for their continent, and for all of its peoples—well, all except those arrogant Osages, who are just too stubbornly haughty for their own damn good.

The Comanches and Kiowas can be downright arrogant too. The Lords of the North American Continent wish like hell that the few Comanches and Kiowas who have finally found out about that treaty of 1820 had never found out about that, because they facetiously refer to that treaty as "The Great Southern-and-Western, North American, Choctaw *Air-Castle* Empire of 1820."

Any jury of decent Americans would award the Choctaws kazillions of dollars in compensation just for the mental anguish Choctaws have suffered in having to listen to those Comanches and Kiowas.

To obtain American legal confirmation of that ancient Choctaw title to that mostly arid land in the Trans-Mississippi West, the Choctaws exchanged, in 1820, a huge portion of their rich agricultural land in Mississippi, five million acres of it, another big chunk of Choctaw land that would produce great wealth for the Cotton Kingdom of the South.

That means, if you might have been asleep at the wheel, that the Choctaws already owned the land in the West that the Choctaws were removed to a decade later, in the early 1830s, which means that the Choctaws got *nothing* whatsoever for all of their remaining millions of acres of land in Mississippi upon their removal, nothing except, in Article IV of that removal treaty of 1830, a *guarantee* of their perpetual sovereignty over that land in the West in the present-day illegal state of Oklahoma.

That illegal state is at present forty-seven times larger than Rhode Island, and it is five times larger than all of the states of New England combined, according to the *Historical Atlas of Oklahoma*.

That illegal state can be trimmed back far more than in half, and the pittance of leftover parts, mostly the ones that are already ruined, like Tulsa and Oklahoma City and a few other odds and ends, can still be a state, all cabbaged together in some crazy way, without anybody missing the big trimmed-off chunks, which belong to sovereign Indian nations.

And the maps changed too. So the world can see which Indian peoples own which part of that Indian land.

Maybe make up a new edition of Monopoly, using the choice Indian spots for the real estate, to help the world get used to the changes.

It will be up to *you*, American *patriots*, to do something about that.

In 1820, the Lords of the North American Continent did not demand, nor did they ask, that more of their ancient Choctaw empire in the West go into the 1820 new-world-in-the-making Choctaw empire because Choctaws are a reasonable people who are willing to share, even with Comanches, even if Comanches had been so out of touch with reality for so long, busy rabbit hunting in the deserts of the Great Basin for so many millennia, that they did not even know who were the Lords of the North American Continent, and mostly acted like they did not care who they might be.

That 1820 new-world-in-the-making Choctaw empire in the West was forged during that amazing but short period of enormous Choctaw-American goodwill, following the combined glorious victories in the War of 1812 of the profoundly wise, ancient Choctaws and a fledgling, immature American republic, when Americans were properly grateful to their Choctaw allies, and did not hesitate to display generous manifestations of a sincere and heartfelt gratitude, which had been so richly earned by their Choctaw imperial allies.

Choctaws are different.

Little of that difference has anything to do with "assimilation." The Lords of the North American Continent have been very different from all of the other peoples of the world for a very long time.

There are reasons why Americans, early in American history, dubbed Choctaws one of the so-called Five Civilized Tribes, though Choctaws have got their doubts about the validity of the other four ever being mentioned in the same breath with Choctaws, even if many Choctaw things have rubbed off on all of them.

Those American perceptions about Choctaws being a civilized people had largely been based upon an American awareness that Choctaws possessed agricultural skills and a lifestyle that Americans said was similar to frontier Americans, even though many frontier Americans of that era could more accurately be dubbed "hunters and gatherers," not really being anything even remotely similar to the ancient practitioners of the loftily sublime, urban-agricultural civilization of the Lords of the North American Continent.

Choctaws long ago (for simple, sanitary health reasons) had sense enough to stretch out their huge, ancient, formerly densely packed, unhealth-ily unsanitary, so-called "Mound Builder" cities of civilization into towns that sprawled for miles along the creeks in the defensive bastions of the top of the upper watersheds of the core of their homeland—the Choctaw sacred place that Americans call east-central Mississippi.

Americans, scratching their heads, have wondered why Choctaws, who had so much military power that they did not need to live in those hillbilly defensive bastions, who owned so many millions of some of the richest agri-cultural lands in the whole world, would use those rich lands only for their big bountiful deer-hunting preserve and choose to live and farm way up in those hillbilly heights, on the poorest farmland they owned, but there was a reason.

Those sprawling, stretched-out Choctaw towns of that refashioned city of civilization of the Lords of the North American Continent had not just been refashioned, but they had been relocated, far from the deadly river-bottom trading paths that were spreading the fatal European diseases.

Those sprawling Choctaw towns had many public structures and other community areas, particularly the hallowed grounds that make that land sacred, the hallowed grounds that have been consecrated with many generations of

Choctaw blood, the Fields of Honor, the only places allowed to be the law-free sites for contesting the great games of ball called *ishtaboli*—the only place in the Choctaw world where Choctaws were immune from death sentences, the *only* place in the Choctaw world where a Choctaw could cause the death of another Choctaw without forfeiting his or her own life.

That provides a hint of the degree of unrestrained vigor that the Lords of the North American Continent allowed themselves to display in the most passionate endeavor of their lives—seeking victory on the Field of Honor.

Ishtaboli contests were titanic gaming events of the ancient, sophisticatedly games-theoried Lords of the North American Continent, which Americans have regarded merely as some sort of curious pastime, though any American who witnessed *ishtaboli* never forgot it, however little comprehension they might have had of what they were witnessing.

American observers, such as George Catlin, who captured the drama of one of those great *ishtaboli* contests in a painting, and Horatio Bardwell Cushman, who witnessed many of those games, were awestruck by the spectacular nature of those sacred ceremonies.

The perspicacious Cushman was observant enough to note that the Choctaws eagerly wagered every single item of their movable possessions on the outcomes of those great games of ball, and Cushman keenly discerned that it was the most venerated *alikchis*, the ones who were at the height of their powers, who were guiding those contests with the greatest wisdom, care, and skill at their command, occasionally casting what have been characterized as "magical incantations" to influence the course of the game.

That is something that Americans know a lot about, but instead of calling them what they often are, and what they have sometimes spectacularly been—magical incantations—the Americans unimaginatively call them simply "coaching decisions."

In American ball, those decisions, those attempts at magical incantation, are ordinarily made by what Americans apparently regard as sorts of *alikchis*-in-training, which Americans call "offensive and defensive coordinators."

At critical moments of high drama, when some really serious wisdom in the realm of magical incantation is called for, the decision in American ball is made by a full-fledged *alikchi*, which Americans call the "head coach."

At about the time that the painting Catlin and the perspicacious Cushman were never-forgetting *ishtaboli* as the manifestation of the very essence of Choctaw civilization, an American Board missionary, the Reverend Alfred Wright in 1828, was breathlessly publishing his dull-witted, Euro-Anglo ethnocentric big news, informing the world, which would include a long parade of dull-witted, Euro-Anglo ethnocentric anthropologists, that the American missionaries had discovered an Indian people in North America called Choctaws who were so primitive that they had no discernable religious beliefs of hardly any kind, had virtually no religious ceremonies of hardly any kind—that the people called Choctaws had no apparent religion of any kind whatsoever.

Those Medieval-minded, Eurocentric missionaries and anthropologists wouldn't know a good *ball-playing*-religion people if one of them were to kick their butts all the way to Baltimore, let alone be able to comprehend what the *ishtaboli* of the Choctaws is for in Choctaw civilization.

The Lords of the North American Continent wonder why Old World people, instead of trying to kill other people for carrying around different religious conceptions in their heads, don't spend their time putting together good *ishtaboli* teams and finding out on the Field of Honor who gets to have the bragging and the braying rights for a while.

It's called civilized behavior.

Many Choctaws like to engage in some of those Old World religious things, which they can do without affecting anything that has anything to do with being Choctaw.

Many Choctaws do that because they like to sing in public and they like to sing loud, even though they cannot sing at all, and where in the hell else, besides a karaoke bar, can somebody who cannot sing at all demonstrate that so spectacularly in public?

If you get forty of them together, it can sound like forty pregnant cows all going into labor at the same time.

The Lords of the North American Continent tried very hard to spread the wisdom of the blessings of their ancient *ishtaboli* to all of the peoples of the continent, and succeeded to a great extent in doing that, even in spreading it to the silly Sioux, who still haven't figured out why it's a good idea to use *two* *kapucha* sticks rather than just one.

It's been well known, even only to book-knowledge students of Choctaw history—perhaps from Henry S. Halbert's intense historical inquiries into the Choctaws more than a century ago, or some such scholar, which one, Choctaws would prefer to forget about—that the Choctaws and the Creeks once settled the ownership of a disputed watershed that lay between them on the outcome of a great game of ball.

We'll skip who won that game, which is why Choctaws aren't all that interested in remembering exactly who it was who told the world about that.

Americans, particularly American missionaries and anthropologists— the most dull-witted of all Americans, the ones whose minds are most tightly locked up in the Medieval mental prison of their silly Euro-Anglo ethnocentrisms—have never been very perceptive about hardly anything regarding Choctaw civilization, to the endless amusement of the Choctaw people.

Choctaws have known for many generations that American missionaries and academics must be tolerated with both patience and compassion.

The wisdom of the blessings of the *ishtaboli* of the Choctaws should not be confused with the necessity of military police action by the Lords of the North American Continent, on their continent, from time to time. Some peoples will not listen, and they choose to disbelieve wisdom. They choose to join the disbelieving dead.

The superiority of Choctaw civilization extends far beyond such things as Choctaw religion or the institution of the Choctaw duel or the tactical genius of Choctaw military police actions.

The manner of Choctaw executions is also far superior to anything devised by Americans.

The depth of difference between Choctaws and Americans can be illustrated by the death of the most recent person to be publicly executed by the Choctaw Nation, in 1894, who will hardly be the last person to ever suffer that fate.

He was a Choctaw patriot named Silan Lewis—*may he rest in peace*— who unfortunately lost his senses and could not restrain himself from dancing with his dark side.

He was guilty of the crimes for which he was convicted, the murders of other Choctaws in the Choctaw Nation, in the bitter internal Choctaw feud that became, briefly, at an unfortunate moment in Choctaw history that lacked an *alikchi* of the skill and stature of an Aihokatubbee, a shooting war between Choctaw factions over whether or not to resist by force of arms yet *another* betrayal of the Choctaw people by the imperialists among the Americans.

Those American imperialists of *that* era were determined to implement the ultimate tyranny of extinguishing the Choctaw Nation, which they *thought* they had finally accomplished in 1907, by the creation of the illegal state of Oklahoma, in violation of Article IV of the Choctaw removal treaty of 1830.

The Choctaw people bargained for, and obtained, a *guarantee* of their sovereignty in Article IV of that treaty of 1830.

It is not a promise, it is a commitment.

It is the *only* thing that the Choctaw people received for all of their remaining millions of acres of Mississippi land, *and* for suffering the horrors of their removal.

Article IV is free of condescending metaphors about grass growing or water flowing.

That guarantee of Choctaw sovereignty is expressed in eighty-three words, written in plain English that any American *patriot* will have no difficulty comprehending, and it *commits* the United States of America to a *specific* thing:

> The Government and people of the United States are hereby
> obliged to secure to the said Choctaw Nation of Red People the
> jurisdiction and government of all the persons and property that
> may be within their limits west, so that no Territory or State shall
> ever have a right to pass laws for the government of the Choctaw
> Nation of Red People and their descendants; and that no part of
> the land granted them shall ever be embraced in any Territory or
> State.... (Charles J. Kappler, ed., Article IV, "Treaty With The
> Choctaw, 1830," in *Indian Affairs: Laws and Treaties*, vol. 2, *Treaties*
> [Government Printing Office, 1904], 311)

Silan Lewis lost his head and could not restrain himself from dancing with his dark side in trying to get that guarantee of sovereignty honored.

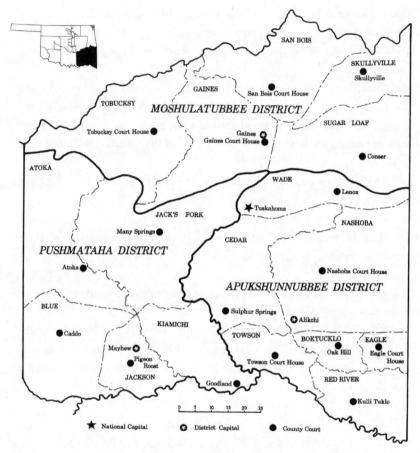

Figure 2: Choctaw Nation: Political Divisions
Map courtesty of the University of Oklahoma Press

Silan Lewis stood trial for his crimes in a Choctaw Nation court of law. He was convicted of those crimes, and he was sentenced to death by that Choctaw Nation court of law. Then he was released.

He was informed of the time and the place that he was to appear for his execution.

He was allowed the dignity of ample time, and personal freedom, to try to accomplish anything really important to him that he had not yet done, and to put his affairs in order, until his day of reckoning for his crimes, as has been the way of Choctaw law from time immemorial.

On that day, and at that place, he came riding in from the hills, as every Choctaw knew he would.

And on that day, and at that place, he was executed by the Choctaw Nation.

Why haven't American courts of law done that, in 1894, or in any other year?

The answer is, simply, that American law and American civilization is *inferior* to Choctaw law and is *inferior* to Choctaw civilization.

Americans have been a people who have had little respect for the rule of law. This would be a matter of little interest to Choctaws, if the imperialists among the Americans did not insist upon continuing to *try* to impose their backward and barbaric civilization upon the Choctaws, as a matter of *tyranny*, mostly as a matter of *state* law.

The renegade, lawless American imperialists have no right to do that.

They had no right to do it in 1830, with Choctaw removal.

They had no right to do it in 1907, with the creation of the illegal state of Oklahoma.

And if they do not voluntarily stop doing it, they will be stopped from doing it in their twenty-first century.

In that twenty-first century, Choctaws, if occasionally somewhat Kemo Sabe-irradiatedly spastically sidekicking, and other Indian nations, will successfully reassert their rightful status as sovereign nations of people, and they will head off whatever howling dance on the dark side might otherwise be in store for the imperialists among the Americans at the hands of the poisoned Lords of the North American Continent.

That the Indian nations have never given up, and will never give up, on reasserting their sovereignty should hardly come as a surprise to contemporary Americans, not if they have been paying attention to their own United States Congress.

In 1975, in explaining to the world why it was passing the Indian Self-Determination and Educational Assistance Act (Public Law 93-638), the U.S. Congress declared: "The Congress... finds ... (2) the Indian people will never surrender their desire to control their relationships both among themselves and with non-Indian governments, organizations, and persons."

"will never surrender."

Twenty-first century Choctaws will prove to other Indian nations, and will prove to the rest of the world, that the American people are capable of being a decent, trustworthy people, no matter how many frustrations Choctaws might have to suffer in proving such a doubtful thing, and no matter how many illiterate cowards in the FBI the Choctaw people might have to trip over in doing that.

Choctaws will do that by patiently spurring American patriots to discover within themselves the motivation to prove that the American people are capable of being a decent, trustworthy people—a present that American patriots can make to the Choctaw people in repayment for the Choctaws having had to bear the expenses of paying for their own forced removal, and a modest present, at that, for American patriots not doing what they should have done a long time ago.

Then things can have been made to work out so that Choctaws will end up having been right in doing what Choctaws did during the War of 1812, and Choctaws *will* end up having been right, even if Choctaws have to rearrange the *whole world* to end up not having been wrong about what Choctaws did in the War of 1812.

Then other Indian nations can shut up and stop pestering Choctaws about the awesome responsibilities that Choctaws have been bearing for having made it possible for there to be a United States of America.

American imperialists might even want to go ahead and surrender right now and save everybody the bother of having had to do much of anything at all, except scratch these few words on these few sheets of paper—not much more than what Major-General Sir Isaac Brock had to do.

Chapter Five

The Contemporarily Distracted Choctaws

By the mid-1970s, the United States government was red-faced with embarrassment at the worldwide media attention being focused on the plight of Indians in North America.

It was a white-hot international media spotlight, a direct result of the spectacular in-your-face, to-hell-with-sugar-coating-it, sometimes armed and violent confrontational tactics of the nothing-left-to-lose, in-and-out-of-jail, bounce-back-and-forth from urban Indian ghettos to desolately impoverished Indian reservations sort of Indian people of the American Indian Movement (AIM), dubbed by the FBI, "Assholes in Moccasins."

Spurred by the international media event sieges of the early 1970s that were brought about by those history-changing, extraordinary, ordinary Indian people, the United States government finally gave up on attempting to maintain the legal fiction that the Choctaw Nation had ceased to exist when the illegal state of Oklahoma had been created in 1907.

Sort of.

The Choctaw people in the illegal state of Oklahoma were "allowed" to write a new, so-called constitution in the mid-1970s, one that had to be approved by the U.S. government, a "constitution" which, by its explicit U.S. government-dictated provisions, attempts to place that newly created "Choctaw Nation *of Oklahoma*" in a subservient role to the illegal state of Oklahoma.

Choctaws, however, were thereby "allowed" to create a severely limited quasi-"government," whose elected officeholders would not be allowed to take office without swearing their allegiance to the constitution of the illegal state of Oklahoma, which reduced that newly created Choctaw entity from a government to an institution of diplomacy that has since that time been serving a transitional diplomatic function as a liaison between the Choctaw people and the American people.

With those foolish and inadequate American-imperialist attempts to put the illegal state of Oklahoma on some sort of life support, while its death knell had begun tolling, the Choctaw people began taking steps toward publicly governing themselves again for the first time in seven decades, after having been forced by the potentially fatally foolish Americans to go underground for the first three-quarters of that century, during which time Choctaws dropped entirely off the American radar screen, becoming virtually invisible, as the Americans, incredibly, seem merely to have assumed that the Lords of the North American Continent simply ceased to exist.

In the mid-1970s, with that newly created Choctaw quasi-governmental/ quasi-diplomatic institution being allowed to function in the light of day, Choctaws began a public process that will eventually lead to the embalming and burial of at least a big portion of that illegal state of Oklahoma, a process that set the Lords of the North American Continent to pondering what sort of public future they might now desire for themselves.

Sort of.

Choctaws haven't gotten very far along with pondering that.

In fact, many Choctaws don't appear to even have begun pondering that, which has given the illegal state of Oklahoma a generation-long reprieve from its embalming and burial, a reprieve that shows no signs of ending any time soon.

Many Choctaws have been distracted.

Many of them got so seriously distracted that no one knows when they might turn their attention to dealing with the illegal state of Oklahoma, or, when they do that, what they might do.

In the late 1960s, a lot of Choctaws were beginning to get riled up, right along with a lot of other Indians. But, in the early 1970s, right at the time that many of those other Indians were beginning to respond to the American

Indian Movement and work themselves into that frenzy that exploded into that phenomenal period of intense and attention-commanding, in-your-face Indian activism, the Choctaw train got uncoupled and sidetracked from all of that.

Indeed, that sidetracking took most Choctaws into such a deep distraction that many, probably most, Choctaws are still nearly completely unaware that there even was a period of intense Indian activism in the 1970s.

Choctaws had virtually nothing to do with that activism, except for a handful of them.

Few Choctaws have any awareness that it was that activism that shamed and frightened the U.S. government into making precipitous capitulations to Indian nations all over the continent, even to those nations, like the Choctaws, that had little awareness of that activism, let alone hardly anything to do with it.

Many Choctaws seem to think that the relatively new "Choctaw Nation of Oklahoma" (whose offices in the mid-1970s Choctaws were suddenly and surprisingly called upon to fill, with a hastily called election for a properly elected diplomatic corps) must have just fallen out of the sky or something.

To this day, few Choctaws know much about the American Indian Movement of the early-to-mid 1970s.

Most Choctaws don't even know who Leonard Peltier might be, or John Trudell, or any Bellecourts, or Dennis Banks, and they think that Russell Means, if they've even heard of him, is a movie star, maybe some Indian who worked his way to Hollywood from Broadway.

It's not that Choctaws suddenly decided to become disinterested in politics during the decade of the 1970s, or suddenly forgot how to recite the litany of the long list of complaints that Choctaws have against those shifty-eyed Okies, or that Choctaws weren't capable of getting riled up to the point of running those Okies right out of here, all the way to Texas, or someplace worse, if there could be anyplace worse.

It was just an accident of history that nobody could do anything about, a thing that caused most Choctaws to be indisposed during nearly the whole decade of the 1970s, to a point that, when Choctaws were finally able to look around, to see what else was going on in the world, all of that intense Indian activism had calmed down to nearly nothing.

Anyone who might try to understand Choctaws, and who might try to understand why Choctaws were so indisposed, must make an effort to comprehend the enduring depth of Choctaws continuing to be, fundamentally and profoundly, an ancient gaming people. Specifically, one important aspect of that continues to be that Choctaws are a particular kind of ancient gaming people—a ball-playing people.

In the early 1970s, a new idea had burst upon the Choctaw world that was so magically mesmerizing, and so embarrassingly frightening, that, for a time, nothing else mattered.

It was called the Wishbone.

From the moment in 1970 that those shifty-eyed Okies suddenly switched to the Wishbone, as a big surprise to their annual, second-Saturday-of-October, *baby-eating-evil*, Wishbone-practicing opponent on that storied Texas-State-Fair Field of Honor in Dallas, when those enemy Okies first handed off, and pretended to hand off, and first pitched, and pretended to pitch, that magically dancing, disappearing, now-you-see-it, now-you-don't Wishbone football, in that shifty-eyed Sooners style, it was a marriage for which heaven truly outdid itself in matching *that* sucker-punch offense with *those* people.

The Choctaws, many of them in the early stages of working themselves into a frenzy, just like a lot of the other Indians, a frenzy that might have quickly spread throughout the nation, possibly exploding into a great howling Choctaw revolt, had to absorb the shock of being confronted with something no Choctaw had anticipated.

With their very own eyes, the Choctaw people, especially their *alikchis*, could see that their enemy had suddenly begun doing something that was very sobering to see—displaying tactical battlefield skills of a level of genius.

That would give any rational people pause, sober or not.

With lightning quickness, nearly every high school and junior high school football team learned how to execute the Wishbone.

Even after years of encountering it, world-class college athletes could not get to where they might need to be to try to defend against all of its shifty-eyed options, let alone the stumble-pup preteen and teenage darling nephews, sons, brothers, cousins, grandnephews, and grandkids during those first few years, who made nearly the whole Choctaw world faint, nearly every time an opponent snapped the ball, on nearly every Field of Honor at nearly every junior high school and high school where any one of those stumble pups might be trying not to disgrace *all* of his relatives.

There might not have been a total of two thousand Choctaw women anywhere on the planet who weren't ready to hitch their skirts and get out there and *show* some darling stumble pup that it didn't take male muscle to make the play, if he might at least be shown *where* he was supposed to be, so he might at least be *trying* to tackle something besides where the ball had just been.

It was the biggest sucker-punch offense the Field of Honor had ever seen.

Every time somebody *thought* they might have figured out how to defend against the Wishbone offense, the two biggest Wishbone magicians on the continent, Coach Barry Switzer of the University of Oklahoma and Coach Bear Bryant of the University of Alabama, sent a Saturday telegram from some world-class Field of Honor that got delivered to thousands of those darling stumble-pup would-be Wishbone defenders in their high school and junior high school football games the next Friday night, keeping nearly the whole of the Choctaw world in a nearly perpetual state of recurring, fainting despair for the better part of the whole decade of the 1970s.

Anybody who doesn't know that wasn't anywhere around very many Choctaws during that decade.

It might not have been so bad if Choctaw emotions and Choctaw indignation hadn't been so heavily weighted toward their darling stumble-pup defenders—if Choctaws hadn't been sophisticated enough to know that you put your best athlete at quarterback, and then you put all of the rest of the best ones on defense, which meant that it was the leftover dregs that were killing their darling stumble-pup defenders.

If a significant portion of a people, including their *alikchis*, is moping around, occasionally exhibiting what the Marine Corps in World War II called the thousand-year stare, then they are just not going to be in any psychological condition to get riled up about much of anything.

It is not too much of a stretch to say that the fundamental reason why history did not record any such thing as what might have been remembered as the Great Howling Choctaw Revolt of the 1970s was because Coach Barry Switzer and Coach Bear Bryant kept inadvertently sucker punching a high percentage of the Lords of the North American Continent, until so many of them were so quickly so punch-drunk, and other kinds of drunk, that in hardly any time at all a point of national incapacitation was reached among the Choctaws.

The only reason that was able to happen is because Choctaws are still Choctaws, still know how to be Choctaws, and cannot do anything to stop being Choctaws.

There is no kind of Kemo Sabe chemotherapy irradiation that will ever be able to do anything about that.

The imperialists among the Americans have failed to keep Choctaws from knowing how to be Choctaws. Those American imperialists are just stuck with Choctaws being Choctaws, whether they like it or not.

All of the other sovereign Indian nations might have gone on the warpath, and Choctaws still might not have known about it.

It might not be too much of a stretch to say that in their hour of need, to keep Choctaws from getting riled up to a point of losing their heads and getting swept up into violence, two extraordinarily unlikely, towering, long-distance *alikchis* arose in the land, with their feet planted firmly on Owen Field and Legion Field, who were possessed of a peculiar but effective way of communicating with Choctaws that ended any possibility of that great howling Choctaw revolt even getting started.

For a long time, nobody had any idea how to slow down the Wishbone, let alone stop it, and that magically disappearing Wishbone football kept bounding right along, all the way past Billy Sims bounding over the Buckeyes in 1977, though that phenomenal bunch of Buckeyes did come awfully close to stopping it, so heartbreakingly, last-second close.

Of course, no Choctaw would pay any attention to that enemy-Okie, University of Oklahoma Sooners football victory over the Ohio State University Buckeyes, except, perhaps, to study it for any tactical lessons it might reveal.

Nevertheless, Choctaws could hardly help noticing how those Buckeyes so gloriously fought their way back from their 20–0 halftime deficit, fought their way back in such a way that it was a downright shame that game could not have lasted just one more quarter, just to see what would have happened.

After those never-say-die Buckeyes had fought back and tied that game, it was nothing short of a crime against nature that those oh-so-close-to-getting-stomped Okie Sooners had to beat those Buckeyes the way they did, on a last second field goal, on that Buckeye home field in Ohio, in front of those fanatical Buckeye home football fans.

That valiant bunch of Buckeyes should have been allowed to try to find their way down south, southwest to be precise, so they could have extended that game for just one more quarter and have had a chance to kick those Okie Sooners on their home field, in front of their home fans.

If s-o-m-e Choctaw had been the de facto director of the FBI at that time, that Choctaw supercop would have declared that Buckeye loss a crime against college football, and that bunch of Buckeyes would have been given the chance to do that very thing.

Maybe it's not too late to invite that bunch of Buckeyes to come on down, and to bring with them the trembling leaves of what is supposed to be the mighty power of their great big horse chestnut tree.

Choctaws mostly only know what those Okie Sooners said about that tree, when those Okie Sooners came back from Ohio after beating those Buckeyes.

Well, that, and what Tecumseh said about that tree.

Those Okie Sooners said that a horse chestnut tree was something to see, that it was ripe with nuts for the picking.

They said that those nuts are called buckeyes, but that they are better for kicking than picking.

Oh Billy-bounded B-u-c-k-e-y-e-s.

One more quarter of foot—ball is c-a-l-l-i-n-g you.

Those Okie Sooners t-a-l-k about you.

They say you are a *F-a-r-q-u-h-a-r-e-d*[*] but far from f-o-r-g-o-t-t-e-n former Okie Sooners f-o-e.

Do you want to p-l-a-y one more q-u-a-r-t-e-r?

They say come on d-o-w-n.

They say take a break from the pounding pace and the eclipsing haze of your Woody-rooted Big Ten second-fiddle place in the annual race with that big bad Ann Arbor tree-climbing thing called a Wolverine that knows how to climb your tree and claw through the bark and bite the tree-hugging heart out of that tree-growing-slow, great big, nut-bearing thing that you call a football team.

Oh untimely time-outing, would-be rout-righting, futilely fighting former foe of a first-half no-show thing that Ohio thought was a football team, they say come on down to Norman town, bring that squirrel-chattering, bird-splattered, great big bird-squawking thing that you call a tree for them to see their ponies horse around.

They'd sooner see their schooner, with horses at a trot, than sing to you your memories of their own Thomas Lott.

They say the only thing you had a chance to win seemed to be the toss of the coin, so take their wind, or take the ball, if you win the toss at all, on their hallowed field of Owen.

Come play rush-rush-rush with them, for just one more quarter, until you play rush-rush and find—a pass to be in order.

They say they don't know what you might do—but when they passed to them *their* OSU, they took two.

They took one from a place called Stillwater, with colors Halloween, and one from sports they can *still* hear holler, from the kick that turned them green.

They say hobble on down to Norman town and they'll refresh your mem-or-y, of how you got that painfully swollen, Big Red Uwe in-jur-y.

They say they play their brand of ball in a great big place that they made out of brand new brick—where they'd love to have, most of all, those same great big buckeye nuts to kick.

For the benefit of the august editors of the *Oxford Dictionary of the English Language*, s-o-m-e Choctaw supercop de facto director of the FBI presents you with a new word:

*FAR'QUHAR'ED, *noun or adj.* [From a double typesetting error in *The Sportsman's Almanac*, by Carley Farquhar (New York: Harper & Row, 1965): "Ohio is a Great Lakes state with Michigan and Lake Erie on the north, Indiana on the west, Pennsylvania on the north-west, and the Ohio River flowing 436 miles as a boundary between West Virginia on the southwest and Kentucky on the south."] *noun.* *geography.* 1. to not know one's northeast from one's northwest, while simultaneously not knowing one's southeast from one's southwest. *noun, sometimes an adj. medical terminology.* 2. a peculiar physiologically induced state of mind, resulting from the optically disorienting act of observing something that is bounding, followed by absorbing a sudden, emotionally wrenching swift kick, said to have been the state of mind of The Ohio State University Buckeye Big Ten football fans, after having been Billy-bounded and Uwe-toe-toasted. Usage example. "What the Buckeyes were was Farquhared."

Double typesetting errors, especially ones like the double typesetting error in *The Sportsman's Almanac*, are rare, but typesetting errors, themselves, are not rare at all.

Most are harmless, but, on occasion, some can have far-reaching consequences.

Those far-reaching consequences can be good or bad, and, on occasion, it can be difficult to determine whether the consequences will turn out to be good or bad.

Encountering certain kinds of typesetting errors can be the first step on a long voyage of discovery that can lead to an awareness that there is nothing sacred about something just because it appears in print.

Many Baby Boomer youngsters in the 1950s boarded that ship for a distinctly indignant kind of voyage of discovery when they discovered the game of chess, as every American generation born to literate, sophisticated households had done before it, as a rite of prepubescent passage.

However, no American generation has ever been so profoundly influenced in that regard by what happened next, because that Baby Boomer generation was the first nearly entire American generation to have saturation access to unsupervised learning, a thing called libraries, and the overwhelming majority of that generation did not come from the literate, sophisticated households that had shepherded the youngsters, the privileged few, of those earlier generations into the world of chess.

What happened next was that a critical core mass of that Baby Boomer generation, born leaders, ones whose attitudes about things would profoundly influence enough of their peers, very early, beginning in prepubescent years, early enough to *drive* that generation, responded to typesetting errors in chess books in a way that molded their entire generation.

That happened because a critical core mass of leaders of that Baby Boomer generation became intrigued with the game of chess enough to do something potentially dangerous, if done on one's own, if done unsupervised in prepubescent years, and that was to learn the sufficiently simple English descriptive chess notation, which opened up the vast library of breath*taking* beauty and heart-wrenching pathos of that captivating and spatially abstract thing called chess, which is a window into the nature of the spatial limitations of the minds of speakers of the Indo-European language family.

That fundamentally flawed language family counts among its foundationally like-minded kinfolks, all in the same tongue-tied breath, the Sanskrit-tongued peoples of ancient India, the Farsi-tongued peoples of ancient Persia, the Attic-tongued peoples of ancient Greece, the Romance-tongued ancient Latins, the Beowulf-spouting breaths of the Germans who invaded the isle of Briton, and many others.

The world of chess that was predominantly being reflected in the recorded games that were being published in the 1950s in chess books for young readers offered a fairly select view of that world. It was a view that looked to the past.

The world of professional chess in the 1950s (and mostly since then) was a dull, boring world, after strategy had overpowered tactics, after an awareness of the full, end-game ramifications of positional play had made it highly unlikely that the interest generated by casual players of the game would be transferable to the modern professional game, as it was being expounded by grandmasters in the 1950s, with the exception of the kind of intrigue that still flickers from the notion of contesting the center of the board, in the opening, with the powers of the pieces rather than with the powers of the pawns.

But hardly any of that mattered for the kinds of recorded games that were most easily and most widely available to prepubescents in the 1950s in chess books aimed at young readers.

Those books featured the dazzling, mid-nineteenth century chess world of the tactical genius of Paul Morphy (1837–84).

That long-dead, tactical-genius chess world was anything but boring, as the prepubescents of that Baby Boomer generation discovered.

If Paul Morphy's tactical genius can't get your blood pumping, then you might not have a pulse.

That led enough of those core Baby Boomers to one of the most saturation-level chess books that was available to them, the *Golden Treasury of Chess*, and to its typesetting errors.

No other generation, since the invention of movable type, ever had to come to grips (entirely on its own, as little kids, first emotionally, and then intellectually, and then spiritually) with the potentially dangerous threat to authority presented by having discovered, while unsupervised, as prepubescents, the soul-shaking, potentially world-changing idea that authority *can* not only be questioned but that it can *be* demonstrably wrong—the authority having been the *print* on the page, and the demonstrably wrong part having been the *typesetting errors* that made that authority demonstrably wrong.

In other words, if authority can screw up, what could there possibly be to believe in?

Many of those Baby Boomers became so disillusioned that they just dropped out and became long-haired hippies.

Many others, however, the core mass of leaders who would drive that generation, rolled up their mental sleeves and threw themselves, and their generation, into the task of making *somebody* pay for their having spent *hours* trying to figure out *how* the *printed* move in *that* chess book not only could *not* be made to make *any* sense whatsoever but was *demonstrably* both illegal *and* impossible.

It was the beginning of the end of the tranquil, carefree America that older Americans knew, and once those Baby Boomers started making somebody pay, it rocked the late 1960s and the early 1970s in a way that no sleepy-headed Dr. Spock had ever imagined was possible.

That silly generation of Baby Boomers has largely been taken at its own assessment of itself.

That self-serving self-assessment, which allowed them, among other things, a rationale for getting real good and high and vibing out on some real good rock and roll, has been most eloquently and most craftily stated, in what is surely the most eloquent and the most crafty way that it could be possible to state it, in the early 1990s, by the Disappointing Duo of William Strauss and Neil Howe, in their curious hybrid blend of sociology, history, and Baby Boomerisms titled *Generations: The History of America's Future, 1584 to 2069.*

That Disappointing Duo of Baby Boomers ought to be made to shovel out all of the stables at Churchill Downs after Derby Day for the great crime of getting everybody's attention, and then following it up with little but some silly obsession with paranormal phenomenon.

Choctaw Baby Boomers, however, had no fear in chomping on something that was nonsense, which was supposed to make sense but remained nonsense, no matter how long it might be pondered on, something like the typesetting errors in the *Golden Treasury of Chess*.

Something like that did not have the capacity to cause Choctaw Baby Boomers to lose respect for authority, or to stop pondering how it might make sense.

Therefore, some Choctaw Baby Boomers were still there, despite type-setting errors, still ooing and aahing and ouching at the beauty and the pathos in the vast library of the recorded essence of the Indo-European mind, when, in 1957, a fourteen-year-old, reincarnated-Paul-Morphy kind of shark, named Robert Fischer, from Brooklyn, New York, came cruising into the treacherous waters of the Lessing J. Rosenwald Tournament in New Jersey, into a room where the biggest sharks between the two biggest oceans in the world had gathered to find out who the biggest shark might be, where that fourteen-year-old, to-hell-with-Botvinik, damn-the-torpedoes, contest-the-center-of-the-board-with-the-powers-of-the-pieces, and-then-you-hide-and-watch-what-happens-next, big sharp-toothed-shark of an utterly fearless and utterly merciless tactician, became the first Baby Boomer to toyingly take a big bite out of history, on a seventeenth move by Black, against a formidable, fully mature, desperately sweating International Master, the toying part being what produced that desperate sweat—*the what-happened-next*, and next, and next, and next, *after* that seventeenth move—which immediately and deafeningly became the first Baby Boomer shot heard round the world, and, to this day, the most resounding sound that any Baby Boomer has thus far made, though that Disappointing Duo of Strauss and Howe did make a pretty loud resounding sound but, thus far, without a what-happened-next, and next, and next.

Instead of getting all upset with authority, and either dropping out and becoming long-haired hippies, or rolling up the sleeves and throwing wild punches for the better part of a decade or two, trying to change the world,

Choctaw Baby Boomers, while keeping an eye on what was going on in the world that might be worth keeping an eye on, tried to understand how big errors could manage to find their way into print.

There were some big ones to ponder.

There was, for example, Columbia University's big, thick, single-volume, paperback *Columbia-Viking Desk Encyclopedia*, which, indeed, might have been edited by Vikings, Vikings who pillaged the Choctaw people with its cryptic, eight-word entry, labeled: "Choctaw Indians":

Were removed to the Indian Territory in 1832.

Those Vikings got the "removed" part right. That's one word out of eight, or 12.5 percent. Not too hot for the Ivy League, huh?

Of course, if you throw into their count the "were," "to," "the," and "in," their percentage goes up dramatically, but that still leaves three out of eight pretty big doozies.

The "Indian Territory" entry in that same encyclopedia was worth noting. It informed the reader that "Indian Territory" did not come into existence until the Indian Intercourse Act of 1834.

Why, oh, why might those Ivy League encyclopedia people have been in such a hurry to get their eight-word "Choctaw Indians" into an "Indian Territory" before that even existed?

Don't they even read their own encyclopedia?

How could the Choctaws have been removed to something that did not even exist at the time the Choctaws were removed?

Isn't historical precision something that we have a right to demand of scholars, or else they get fired or something?

Or might it be that scholars are people who must be kept as scholars, because, if they were to be turned loose on society, they might become pizza makers or something, and then they might inadvertently poison all of us.

So maybe it's thought that the safest thing is to make them professors, so that, at the very least, nobody gets food poisoning.

The thirty-four-word "Choctaw" entry in the *Basic Everyday Encyclopedia* was interesting:

After the Revolution settlers poured into the Gulf area and, in
1831–32, the C moved to a reservation on the Red R in SE
Oklahoma, where they set up a US-style government.

It was the "Gulf area" that those "settlers" were pouring into, huh?

Wasn't it somebody's *country* that they were pouring into? And weren't
the good Choctaw people of their own country already pretty well "settled"
there themselves?

Or do they somehow not count? Not like white people count, huh?
There's a term for that, I think, but I can't recall at the moment what that term
might be. Oh, well, maybe you can think of what that term might be.

Why, oh, why are these *Basic Everyday Encyclopedia* people in such a
hurry to get the Choctaws into an "Oklahoma?"

That is similar to the *Columbia-Viking Desk Encyclopedia* people being in
a hurry to get the Choctaws into an "Indian Territory" that did not yet exist.
Oklahoma did not yet exist, either.

"Oklahoma" is a combination of two Choctaw words, *okla*, people +
houmma, red. It means, literally, "Red People."

One frequently sees and hears the term translated as "Home of the Red
Man" or "Home of the Indians," but "home," or, for that matter, "man," are not
any part of that Choctaw term.

There are lots of Choctaw words that might be translated to mean
"home," in some sense, but none of them are to be found in the term
"Oklahoma."

"Oklahoma" means, simply, "Red People."

That means that the name of the thing that the U.S. government created
in the 1970s, the "Choctaw Nation *of Oklahoma*," to Choctaws, means the
"Choctaw Nation *of Red People*."

That's one of the reasons why the Choctaw people rather liked the name
of their new "entity" that the silly fools in the U.S. government picked out for
them in the 1970s, silly fools who thought that the name they had chosen
would convey to Choctaws their subservience to the illegal state of Oklahoma.

I would say, based upon both what I know and what I can guess, that the
Choctaw people have allowed the silly Americans to hang around as long as
they have simply because they amuse them so much.

The first known geographical usage of the term "Oklahoma" occurred not long after the U.S. Civil War when Choctaw Principal Chief Allen Wright suggested it to the U.S. government as a possible name for the new territory that the U.S. government was contemplating for what is now roughly the western half of the illegal state of Oklahoma, which, indeed, did become a congressionally created entity in 1890, "Oklahoma Territory" (which did not include the sovereign Indian nations of the so-called Five Civilized Tribes in "Indian Territory," in what is now roughly the eastern half of the illegal state of Oklahoma, which continued to be sovereign Indian nations during the so-called Twin Territory era, from 1890 to 1907).

The term "Oklahoma" has no geographical reference connotations whatsoever, for anywhere, until very near the time of the creation of that Oklahoma Territory in 1890. Certainly the Choctaws could not have been removed to any "Oklahoma" in the 1830s—no such place existed at that time, nor for a long time after that.

It's a propaganda technique, one that refers to the past in terms of the present. It's an attempt to pretty up the present by telling a lie about the past.

This *Basic Everyday Encyclopedia* entry could have learned at least *one* thing from those Vikings who pillaged the Choctaws in that other encyclopedia, and that is the one word those Vikings got right—"removed."

The thirty-four words of that *Basic Everyday Encyclopedia* entry make it sound like the brutal removal of the Choctaws was a thing where the Choctaws just decided to pick up and go.

It's propaganda—American-imperialist propaganda. It's a lie, in this case an intentional distortion of history.

Most of what Americans think they know about their own history, in regard to Indians, is that kind of lie—a distortion, sometimes intentionally rendered that way, sometimes just subconsciously or incompetently rendered that way.

Those thirty-four words make it sound like there was already a place called Oklahoma and that the good people of that place made room for the Choctaws by generously letting them have a "reservation" in the southeastern part of it.

A reservation.

Choctaws have trouble finding the word "reservation" anywhere in Article IV of the treaty of 1830 that forced them to remove to the Trans-Mississippi West—to land, which, by the way, for any of you lawyers out there, the Choctaws demanded a "fee simple" title to, which they obtained from the U.S. government.

If you might have been practicing some other kind of law for a long time, which is what most of you have been doing, then dig out your old law school property-law casebooks and brush up a little bit on exactly what "fee simple" means.

It is your country that made that bargain, and it is your country that is going to be held to *exactly* what that means, so take the bother of finding out what it means. You've been zeroed in on your specialties for so long that, like most of the rest of the law you knew at one time, you probably don't remember as much about it as what Choctaws have forgotten.

And if that doesn't make perfect sense to you, then, hey, this is my book.

If you want perfect sense, then go try to make sense of *Polsgraf,* or go visit some of the old law school profs in the loony bin, who got there trying to make sense of such things.

Be advised, however, that some of those old law school profs don't know who they are anymore. So if one of them might be one of the assholes you used to love to hate, don't be looking for any flicker of recognition in their eyes, it ain't there anymore.

Trust me on that, if a trip to the loony bin might not be on your agenda. Lord knows it's getting real close to being on mine.

What Choctaws do find in that Article IV of the removal treaty of 1830 is a rather clear enunciation of a sovereign Choctaw Nation, not any part of any "Territory," not any part of any "State."

That is what the Choctaws were removed to—to their own *sovereign* nation, with *guarantees,* from the American *people,* of that Choctaw sovereignty.

Many Choctaws have been led to wonder where the encyclopedia people find the things that they put in their "Choctaw" entries.

If Choctaws had eight words, or thirty-four words, to play with, they could spend those words better than the encyclopedia people did in the two examples cited above.

Many such examples could be cited.

Something more is obviously at work than typesetting errors. Typesetting errors are one thing. But propaganda is something else.

That encyclopedia propaganda was designed to make sure that nobody but Choctaws knows where the Choctaw people were, in fact, removed to in the 1830s.

Choctaws know that they were not removed to any "Indian Territory" or to any "Oklahoma," but that they were removed to their own sovereign nation.

Only the mass of the American people are ignorant of that. They have been kept ignorant of it by the American-imperialist propagandists, because those imperialists among the Americans fear the decency and sense of justice of their own contemporary American people more than they fear anything else.

Did the twentieth-century encyclopedia people actually think that they could print just any old thing about the Choctaws?

Did they actually think it makes no difference what they print about the Choctaws?

Did they actually think that Choctaws would not sit around, all day long, pondering why such things had found their way into print?

Did they actually think that the Choctaws would not lie awake at night pondering what could be done about such things?

Maybe the imperialists among the Americans had no fear of Choctaw ponderings.

But that was a different century, a century that is no longer with us, a century that didn't have FBI guys being directed by the right sort of person.

Chapter Six

Will the Americans
Ever Get It Right?

*B*ooks are a kind of "stated" authority.

The relationship between those who "state" authority and those who "receive" authority is a curious one.

For that matter, the range of ways that various people have simply responded to things in print, even to things in newspapers, defies belief.

To cite but one weird example, the cowardly Englishman, the great Shakespearean scholar and unofficial chess champion of the world, Howard Staunton (1810–74), after whom the elegantly unobtrusive symbols-for-abstractions called standard "Staunton-design" chess pieces are named, who found it convenient to always be too busy to sit across a chess board from the great New Orleans tactical genius, Paul Morphy, on Morphy's phrenology-impaired reported tour of Europe, nevertheless was such an egomaniac that he actually believed that virtually everything that appeared in print was some-how a veiled reference to him.

That is some kind of egomaniac.

Of course, Staunton *was*, or had been, the strongest chess player in the world, at least, maybe, until Paul Morphy came strolling down the pike.

But the world wasn't quite as aware of Mr. Staunton as he thought it should be, as he, incredibly, in fact, thought that it was.

That was some kind of cuckoo, which would be difficult to imagine having been possible if moveable type had not been invented.

Things were somewhat simpler in a lot of ways before the invention of writing was combined with the invention of movable type to produce weirdos like Howard Staunton, and to produce a peculiar modern problem for peoples such as Choctaws.

In recent generations, Choctaws have found that they must be concerned about what somebody they do not know, and who does not know them, says about Choctaws in a movable-type, stamping-into-mass-distribution-print sort of way, particularly since the gloomy days of the early twentieth century, after the broke dicks on the U.S. Supreme Court flushed the supreme law of the land down the toilet and placed the Choctaws, and all of the other sovereign Indian nations, entirely at the mercy of American public opinion.

Therefore, there are Choctaws who could have been absorbed with how to apply the right magical incantation at the right moment to produce magic on the Field of Honor, or who could be attempting to produce beauty and pathos from the spatial limitations of the abstractions of a distinctly foreign kind of Field of Honor, or, more recently, who could be in some casino, engaged in a good knock-down, drag-out with some slot machine, who, instead, have been compelled to occupy themselves with other things, particularly with the curious sort of "authority" of some things, merely because they have appeared in print.

In the realm of "received" authority, there appear to be some people who assume that anything that has made its way into print must be reliable.

And there have always been some people who assume that anything that has made its way into print must have some nefarious underlying purpose. Some of those people can be really interesting, not just for the way they "receive" things but for the "perceived" purposes they see in them, which, for some of them, no matter how far-fetched that "perception" might be, can nonetheless be amazingly internally consistent.

The ranks of those people running around loose in society *had* been thinned, until, in fairly recent years, a more enlightened tolerance for, or a throwing of the hands into the air and a giving up on them (take your pick), was coupled with the advent of some disassembling, ultramodern medications to allow the release of many of those people back into society from the loony bins.

Somewhere between those extremes are the bulk of the legions of Choctaws who have attempted to "receive" the "authority" of a thing of great evil that burst upon the Choctaw world at about the same time as the Wishbone, in 1970, in the form of Professor Arthur H. DeRosier Jr.'s book, *The Removal of the Choctaw Indians*, from the University of Tennessee Press.

To the hair-pulling frustration of Choctaws, that book by that evil professor, for nearly four decades now, has done more to obscure the 1820 great imperial comeback of the Choctaws than anything else published in the twentieth century.

Most Choctaws, most Choctaws still being loyal allies of the Americans, have been frustrated to tears, fearful that Choctaws are eventually going to be placed in the moral quandary of ending up with *more* land than they are entitled to, all because that evil professor could not even get the *boundary* right for that Choctaw land in the far West.

In his discussion of the Choctaw-U.S. treaty of 1820, which was negotiated at Doak's Stand in the Mississippi Choctaw country, in his chapter 4, "The Treaty of Doak's Stand" (53–69), on page 65, the august Professor DeRosier announced to the world that the western boundary of that Choctaw land in that 1820 treaty is the "headwaters of the *Arkansas River*" (emphasis added).

Ever since that moment, it seems as though the whole world has taken him at his word.

Ever since that moment, nearly every scholar who *has* bothered to take note of that 1820 treaty seems merely to have *assumed* that the august Professor DeRosier *must* have known what he was talking about.

What do Choctaws have to do to get *anyone* to actually *read* their treaties?

The western boundary of that land, as any student of Choctaw history knows, is the "source" of the *South Canadian River*, which could alternatively be said to be the "headwaters" of that river, or, more precisely, the exact spot that can be demonstrated to be the ultimate gravity-influenced place that contributes H_2O to *that* gravity transporter of surface H_2O.

The boundary of the Choctaw land in the far West is found in Article 2 of the treaty of 1820:

> ...bounded as follows:—Beginning on the Arkansas River, where
> the lower boundary line of the Cherokees strikes the same; thence

up the Arkansas to the Canadian Fork, and up the same to its source;
thence due South to the Red River; thence down Red River, three
miles below the mouth of Little River; which empties itself into
Red River on the north side; thence a direct line to the beginning.

We know from unquestioned extrinsic evidence that the "Canadian Fork" is the "South Canadian River," which is by far the longer of the South and North Canadian Rivers.

Both of those Canadian rivers flow downhill across the southern Great Plains, but, in order to make sense of that 1820 treaty boundary description, it is important to know that downhill, in that great big place, is generally from northwest to southeast.

Those two Canadian rivers flow across the present illegal state of Oklahoma, and both now empty into different arms of that great big octopus called Lake Eufaula, which is about halfway between Oklahoma City and the Arkansas border, to the east of Oklahoma City.

Anybody in Oklahoma gets somewhat subconsciously dizzy just being in Oklahoma and trying to walk around in that peculiar cartographically and gravitationally disorienting place, a kind of gravity-induced, land-leaning dizzy, primarily because the state tips way over from the northwest to the southeast, which is what makes the water flow in that direction.

The highest elevation is 4,438 feet, near the farthest western end of the arid high plains of the Oklahoma panhandle, in the far northwest, and from there the land leans steeply down to only 305 feet in the far southeastern tip, which renders most of the rest of the place a 4,133-foot, steeply leaning slippery slope—so people all over the state have to always go around leaning sort of sideways, in trying to keep their balance, and every now and then somebody loses their balance and slips and slides all the way off the thing.

That sideways slippery aspect of that peculiar place, in causing its silly people to try to be facing uphill all the time, as an aid to maintaining their balance, causes them to think, because "up" is always north on their silly round-earth-flattening flat maps, that when they are facing that northwest uphill "up" that they are facing north, and, conversely, they think that their southeast-facing backsides are facing south, because their backsides are pointing toward "down," and that is always south on their silly round-earth-flattening flat maps.

That Farquhared aspect of that place is the very thing that assisted the Choctaws in figuring out why General Andrew Jackson was not worried about there "appearing" to be no Red River "due South" of the "source" of the South Canadian River.

General Jackson's "due South" must have meant the same kind of land-leaning, gravity-induced, water-downhill-flowing kind of "down" kind of south, or down south, or down southeast, that the silly Okies think that their fat behinds are facing, which is in actuality southeast, when their faces are facing uphill, which is northwest, but which their brains think is north, because, on their silly head-flattening flat maps, "up" is north.

Therefore, General Jackson's "due South" = "down south" = "down southeast."

That is the way that gravity brings the water down, and the way that the land leans, which does, indeed, plot a course for that 1820 treaty-boundary description that goes directly from the "source" of the South Canadian River, southeast, directly to a point where such a gravity-and-land-leaning enlightened, earth-knowledged, plotted course does strike the Red River, at the approximate highest point of its headwater heights, near the New Mexico-Texas border, all of which operates to make perfect sense out of the boundary description of that 1820 treaty.

The elusive controlling principle that the example of the Farquhared Okies helped the Choctaws to see was that a gravity-direction interpretation must be the controlling factor for interpreting cardinal directions in the treaty of 1820, because it is watercourses that those boundaries consist of, and that, undoubtedly, was why General Jackson wasn't worried about it.

He knew that it made sense, and, no doubt, he was confident that, in time, the Choctaws would figure out *how* it made sense.

If you go to that Farquhared place called Oklahoma, be warned that the state floral emblem is a poison-berried parasite called the mistletoe—and *that* choice of *those* people for *their* state floral emblem was no accident.

Oklahoma City itself is at about a fifteen-hundred-foot elevation in the approximate center of Oklahoma, at the very place where the famous Cross Timbers meet the Great Plains. The eastern suburbs of Oklahoma City, near

Shawnee, are in the tangle of the Cross Timbers, and the western suburbs of Oklahoma City, near El Reno, are on the Great Plains.

According to the U.S. government, from statistics released along about 1940, Chicago is the "Windy City," beating out Oklahoma City for that honor only by about one-tenth of a mile per hour. That average eleven mile-per-hour wind even makes the little trees on the Great Plains west of Oklahoma City grow up leaning permanently toward the north, even when no wind is blowing, and that wind had a little something to do with putting the dust in the "Dust Bowl."

That Dust Bowl, in the 1930s, is when Oklahoma gave all of its topsoil to Nebraska, which turned it into big-time, disposable, corn-generated wealth that was pumped into football facilities, which is why we are now plagued with Cornhuskers using wind-stolen, Oklahoma topsoil-wealth to display a frightening capacity for learning how to play football.

Those 1940 wind statistics have given Oklahoma City the reputation of being only the second windiest city in the nation, behind Chicago, pending some updating of those statistics to see if the Gulf of Mexico has been getting more upset lately than Chicago's Lake Michigan.

The hot and humid wind that always blows up toward the north from the Gulf of Mexico gets a big hot boost from all the hot air that comes bellowing out of those Texas loudmouths.

All that hot air comes sweeping up the plains across Oklahoma because the Gulf of Mexico is really upset about everything that Texas dumps into the Gulf of Mexico, and the gulf blames Oklahoma, as it should, because it is smart enough to see, on those silly head-flattening flat maps, who is on top with Texas.

When all that hot air comes scorching across the Red River, it collides with cold air sinking down from the north to create the world famous "Tornado Alley" across the middle of Oklahoma, the legendary place where the outraged disgust of that Gulf of Mexico hot air goes on a rip-roaring, tornado-spawning tear each spring, because the Gulf of Mexico is smart enough to know that it should blame Oklahoma for everything that Texas does.

The Okies are very proud of that, because it's *the* big windy indication for *who* is on top with Texas, *any* way you look at it, to such an earth-convincing extent that even the Gulf of Mexico knows it.

So, every time there is a tornado in Oklahoma, sit down and try to figure out what some silly Texan has done now. They have the capacity to screw up so bad that the Gulf of Mexico reserves a special kind of wind for the Texas coast, called hurricanes.

Okies don't seem to care very much that there is a good cracking tornado alley on the subcontinent of India too, maybe an ever better one.

Why doesn't that ever get any press in Oklahoma, huh?

Maybe somebody ought to try figuring out what the Indian Ocean is upset about, and what the Gulf of Mexico is upset about, and why Lake Michigan had gotten really upset at Chicago by 1940.

Oklahoma City is the largest city in the nation, in area, whenever its city council has met after the Los Angeles city council has met. Then, when the Los Angeles city council meets, Oklahoma City is the second largest city in the nation, until the Oklahoma City city council meets again.

That's because in the early 1970s the federal courts started attempting to integrate the Oklahoma City public schools by busing black students out of the northeast Oklahoma City black ghetto into other parts of the Oklahoma City school system, and the Okies responded by opening up what are known as "white flight corridors" into the surrounding central Oklahoma farmland, where the Okies took Oklahoma City (in the form of suburbs, which Oklahoma City then expanded to surround) to damn near the entire center part of the state, to get away from the boundaries of the Oklahoma City school system, without taking the boundaries of the Oklahoma City school system with them (because its boundaries don't include those suburbs), so they could artificially create their good old artificial days of the 1950s again, which, for the most part, they are still living in.

Oklahoma City was created without any Indians, as a result of one of the so-called Oklahoma land runs, which instantly popped up a tent city of ten thousand people overnight.

They say that Rome might not have been built in a day, but Oklahoma City was.

It's quite a place, only now it doesn't have hardly any white people in it anymore. Lots of damn good barbeque and Mexican food places.

The South Canadian River flows along the southern edge of the southern Oklahoma City suburb of Norman, Oklahoma, the home of the University of

Oklahoma, and, coincidentally, also the home of Oklahoma's most famous loony bin.

It is well known in Oklahoma that the mushrooming proliferation of many institutions of higher education all across Oklahoma in the twentieth century was a direct result of twentieth-century Oklahoma children hearing their mothers threatening them that, if they did not behave, then their mothers would "put you in Norman."

That threat, taken with the seriousness with which it was delivered, made the University of Oklahoma, in Norman, a place where the only Oklahoma children who would dare apply for admission were those who were sensible enough to know the difference, or to figure out the difference at some point, between the university in Norman and the loony bin in Norman.

Most of the others ended up at Oklahoma State University, the state's cow college, in the cow town of Stillwater, outside Tulsa in the northeast, which was formerly named Oklahoma Agricultural and Mechanical College, or some such thing, when they were known as the Oklahoma A & M "Aggies," for a lot of good and sufficient reasons, until, out of faculty frustration with those students either not being able to spell "agricultural," or not being able to spell "mechanical," or both, they decided, along about 1960 or 1961 to try being Oklahoma State University for a while, to see if those students might be able to learn how to spell "university," the bulk of them, by then, having mastered how to spell "college." They can't play football worth a damn, either—not way back when, not now, not ever, or else, why haven't they ever won a national championship, huh?

Whereas the University of Oklahoma in Norman has won seven, count 'em, seven *Associated Press* National Championships in football, not some silly collection of forty-eight kazillion billion silly "national championships" like some prissy Southern Cal people claim to have won, who are so prissy that they don't like being called "Southern Cal," and whose football media people spend half their time trying to get the press to call them something besides Southern Cal, whose claimed national championships were awarded by such well-meaning, lofty, but very confused outfits as the "Dogcatchers of the Poor," and other such silly canine-loving entities, who thought that they were trying to help reduce the number of stray dogs in Southern California by helping to promote dog condoms, all stemming from that time that they all saw that big Rose Bowl Trojan Horse-float that was so poorly sculpted that it looked like a big dog.

Those evil, cheating Southern Cal Trojans will someday have it *proven* that they broke the rules, by using, on an embarrassingly big stage, a banned substance called "Whup-Ass," in the most recent University of Oklahoma national championship football game.

It will *further* be proven that the Southern Cal football team got that banned substance after the previous national championship game, from those silly, likewise cheating Louisiana State University Tigers, who should be forced to change their name to the LSU Not-So-Hot-How-*Not*-To-Do-Hurricane-Proof-Plumbing-People.

Those sainted Associated Press National Championship years that tell the tale of the terrible-great dominance of magic, called "Sooners Magic," occurred in 1950, 1955 and 1956 back-to-back, 1974 and 1975 back-to-back, 1985, and 2000.

And, once the no-stone-unturned, NCAA Whup-Ass investigation has been completed, those years will also include 2003, against LSU, and 2004, against Southern Cal, back-to-back.

That Sooners Magic has lost more national championship games than those silly east-west football-field-oriented Okie State Aggies will ever get invited to—for a reason, they cannot play football. That was a "period" there at the end of that.

It's not that I don't like them. I am entirely neutral in the bitter "Bedlam rivalry" between those two Okie schools.

It's just that the Okie State football fans are thoughtlessly irritating when you are trying to watch those two Okie teams play in Norman.

Every time the game is in Norman, the Okie State fans throw firecrackers into the seating sections of the home-team Sooners fans. That doesn't bother the home-team Sooners fans very much. They simply light those firecrackers and throw them back.

But it's damn distracting when you're trying to watch the game, even though it's hardly ever a very good game, because the Okie State people don't know anything more about football than they know about firecrackers.

Which brings us to the question: did the august Professor DeRosier know *anything* about what he was doing?

If that evil professor's misreading of that 1820 treaty boundary description was the only problem with his reporting of the negotiations for the treaty of 1820, he wouldn't have plummeted to the deepest depths of Choctaw infamy, where he has resided for nearly four decades.

But his infamy among Choctaws will always be secure, if for no other reason than putting Choctaws in the moral quandary of being tempted to take more land than what Choctaws know that they are entitled to by the terms of that 1820 treaty.

That has become a nearly unavoidable moral dilemma for Choctaws, because Choctaws can't get *anyone* to read *any* Choctaw treaty.

In the days when the texts of Indian treaties were not instantly available online on the Internet, as they are today, there was no way even for Choctaws to read them except to make a trip to one of the dangerous places called libraries.

Few "American" historians, particularly so-called "mainstream" American historians, have ever bothered to do that.

Few of them have ever read an Indian treaty, any Indian treaty, even today, even with instant Internet access.

The so-called "mainstream" American historians, being, for the most part, little more than propagandists, are dismissive of Indian treaties, as though, somehow, the supreme law of the land does not exist.

Instead of consulting the supreme law of the land to find out for themselves what the supreme law of the land might be, for something like that 1820 Choctaw treaty, they consult DeRosier's book, and they rely on that evil book.

So much of "scholarly" publishing, after DeRosier, places the 1820 western treaty boundary of Choctaw land as the "headwaters of the Arkansas River" that it looks like its going to be impossible to ever convince the Americans otherwise.

It looks like Choctaws are going to be forced to bear the moral burden of swapping the "source" of the South Canadian River for the "headwaters of the Arkansas River" as the western boundary of the Choctaw empire, and then are going to have to try to live with the moral quandary of that having ballooned the size of the Choctaw empire immensely.

Choctaws have gone to the headwaters of the Arkansas River, in the mountainous heights above Leadville, Colorado, to check it out, in anticipation that the million to one near certainty that the Americans will *never* get it right means that the Americans will actually come to believe that the "headwaters of the Arkansas River" *are* that western boundary.

When Choctaws are given no choice but to take that, it will all be the fault of that evil Professor DeRosier.

Chapter Seven

Secret-Scholar Code Talk

*I*n order to understand the enormity of the infamy of the evil Professor DeRosier to Choctaws, a professor who, to Choctaws, is the rough equivalent of what the dastardly evil Professor Moriarty was to Sherlock Holmes, all one need do is consider what DeRosier told the whole wide world about Choctaws, and particularly about Pushmataha, in the fourth chapter of *The Removal of the Choctaw Indians.*

DeRosier first, appropriately enough, in reporting some of the details of the treaty negotiation game, quoted General Andrew Jackson's attempt at pooh-poohing the quality of the Mississippi Choctaw land that the Choctaws would be giving up in the treaty of 1820.

Then DeRosier, on page 65, comments on what General Jackson had said to the Choctaw treaty negotiators:

> For this relatively useless land the United States would give the
> Choctaws all of the magnificent farm and hunting lands from the
> Arkansas River south to the Red River, and west to the headwaters
> of the Arkansas River. As will be seen in a later chapter, none of the
> Indian or white negotiators knew exactly what lands were being
> exchanged, a fact which would cause many headaches for the U.S.
> government in the not too distant future.

DeRosier was unaware that he had unintentionally spouted a twenty-first-century prophecy, in the last portion of his comment.

It should also be noted that DeRosier was doing nothing wrong in speaking facetiously, in capturing the voice of General Jackson regarding how Jackson had characterized the Choctaw land in Mississippi that was being swapped in the treaty of 1820, in capturing the essence of Jackson's pooh-poohing of that land.

It's the part of DeRosier's comment about none of the Indians knowing exactly which lands were being swapped that heralds DeRosier's descent toward the deepest depths of infamy.

Incredibly, this bozo is *typical* of many of the clowns responsible for what has been transmitted to the world about Choctaws, especially in widely disseminated reference works intended for mass consumption by the general public, as illustrated by the encyclopedia examples previously discussed.

How do these Clem Kadiddlehoppers get turned loose on civilized society?

Do they let them out of the loony bins on furloughs?

Just so they can try to outdo one another with what they publish about the Choctaws?

Some of the evil Professor DeRosier's multiplicity of confusions can perhaps be understood, due to his lack of acquaintance with sources that were easily available to him and that he should have made himself familiar with.

If DeRosier had bothered to find out about Pushmataha's career in the far West, he would have known that Pushmataha was intimately acquainted with those arid high plains of present-day western Oklahoma, the Texas panhandle, and eastern New Mexico.

DeRosier has no problem understanding that General Jackson was playing the treaty negotiation game, in pooh-poohing the quality of the land that the U.S. government would be receiving, but DeRosier could not comprehend that there were two sides to that negotiation and that two could play that same game.

Therefore, when DeRosier quoted what an eyewitness, John Hersey, said that Pushmataha said to General Jackson, and then when DeRosier commented on that in his INFAMOUS FOOTNOTE NUMBER 55, DeRosier became the epitome of evil to Choctaws.

According to DeRosier, that eyewitness, John Hersey, reported, in a handwritten letter to Thomas L. McKinney, that Pushmataha told General Jackson the following interestingly secret-scholar-code-talk-doctored things about the land the Choctaws would be receiving in the treaty of 1820:

It is indeed a very extensive land, but a vast amount of it is exceed-
ingly poor and sterile, tractless, sandy deserts, nude of vegetation
of any kind. As to tall trees, there is no timber anywhere except on
the bottom lands, and it is low and boukey [*sic*] even there. The
grass is everywhere very short, and for the game it is not plenty,
except buffalo and deer....The bottoms of the rivers are generally
good soil, but liable to inundation during the spring season, and in
summers the rivers and the creeks dry up and become so salty that
the water is awful to use....[55]

Pushmataha was obviously talking about the arid high plains of the far
West, which constituted a huge portion of the land area described in the
boundaries of that treaty of 1820, land that Pushmataha was intimately
acquainted with, and land he was obviously pooh-poohing, as part of the
treaty negotiation game, just as General Jackson had done.

DeRosier however, knew nothing about Pushmataha's career, and that is
partly what led DeRosier into his INFAMOUS FOOTNOTE NUMBER 55, in
which DeRosier says:

[55]*Ibid.* It is interesting to note that Jackson's assessment of the land
in present-day southeastern Oklahoma was more correct than
Pushmataha's. It is not a sandy, windy, and useless area, but a well-
watered, heavily timbered section of America.

It would be challenging just to catalog the things DeRosier was confused
about. He makes clear, however, in this INFAMOUS FOOTNOTE NUMBER
55 that somehow he had convinced himself that the Choctaws were only gaining American recognition of the Choctaw ownership of "present-day southeastern Oklahoma" in the treaty of 1820, as many other American historians
have done.

How do they do that?

In one breath, this epitome of evil, this dastardly nefarious professor,
can't get the far western boundary of the treaty of 1820 right, but he does seem
to be aware that it is somewhere in the Rocky Mountains, the "headwaters of
the Arkansas River."

In his next breath, somehow, that treaty boundary description miraculously no longer counts for anything, and he reduces the Choctaw land in that treaty of 1820 to "present-day southeastern Oklahoma" while portraying Pushmataha in a way that implies he was some kind of geographically challenged hick who had never been more than five miles from his place of birth.

Maybe there is something about the secret-scholar code talk that might help us figure out more about what scholars like DeRosier are doing, and what they are secretly saying to each other.

The number 55, in superscript at the beginning of the footnote, is secret-scholar code talk. It is a footnote indicator.

If you don't know very much about secret-scholar code talk, then you might not know that the *Ibid.*, which that [55] is nestled up against at the beginning of the footnote, is an abbreviation for *ibidem*, which is a Latin word that is secret-scholar code talk to other scholars that means "in the same place."

That "same place" is referring to the same *thing*, meaning the exact same *source* of the information, a letter or book or interview or whatnot (in this case a handwritten letter) that was cited in the previous footnote, which also cited information from that same letter from John Hersey.

In that previous footnote number 54, DeRosier also imparted a secret-scholar-code-talk message, one that only fellow secret-scholar-code-talk-savvy people are likely to be able to decipher, a secretly coded message about another kind of place, the earthbound physical kind of place, the *building* where those other rare and endangered species of secret-scholar-code-talk-savvy people can find that original, handwritten letter.

In the case of that particular letter, that secret-scholar code talk was telling those rapidly diminishing number of secret-scholar-code-talk-savvy people (trust me on the rapidly diminishing part of that) that John Hersey's handwritten original letter can be found in the National Archives.

Its exact location in the National Archives was all doctored up, by DeRosier, with more secret-scholar code talk, such as MSS, and whatnot, a secret-scholar code talk that history professors *try* to teach to students but which, for the most part, remains a great big secret mystery to most of them, producing the everlasting, hair-pulling, irresistible urgings in those professors to swallow a great big evil pill at the time to compose examinations and fair thee well *fix* their lazy little red wagons *but good*, after those professors have tried to make sense of the pitiful attempts of those students at applying the secret-scholar code talk in their research papers.

That secret-scholar code talk, however, is absolutely essential, so that no Republicans or Democrats, or some other kinds of silly peoples, will know what scholars are secretly saying to each other.

All of those silly peoples, primarily the Republicans and the Democrats, must not be allowed to know how to decipher what the secret-scholar-code-talk messages are saying, because it is deemed essential to society that those silly peoples not know how to find those original documents, so they will not even try to do that, and then they will all be free, all of the time, to be able to focus all of their concentration on keeping everything all screwed up all of the time.

Here's a quiz for you.

Instructions:

First, read what DeRosier said that Pushmataha supposedly said to General Jackson (there are other versions of what Pushmataha said, from other eyewitnesses, but, for this quiz, I am asking you to read what DeRosier told us, which is what DeRosier thought that the chicken-scratching handwriting of John Hersey said).

You should be able to find that without having to be secret-scholar-code-talk savvy and without having to try to figure out where you might need to go, like Washington, D.C., to find and read any original documents, because I just typed the damn thing for you—that quotation in this book just above the quotation of the footnote, the quotation that has the little superscript number [55] at the end of the quotation.

Second, then read DeRosier's [55] footnote that I quoted for you (the one that has the little superscript [55] number at the beginning of it) and find the one word in DeRosier's [55] footnote that DeRosier says that John Hersey said that Pushmataha said to General Jackson, in characterizing that land but which is not in the passage that DeRosier gave us from John Hersey (which is not in the quotation that you were supposed to have read first).

That one word you are looking for is something that DeRosier added on his own, when that evil professor wrote his INFAMOUS FOOTNOTE NUMBER 55.

Go ahead, I'll wait here for you while you go find those two little things that you already just read so you can read them again and identify that one word that DeRosier added.

Now, if you found that one word, why do you suppose that Professor DeRosier would say, in his footnote, that Pushmataha said that one word that isn't in the version that DeRosier gave us of what DeRosier thought that John Hersey had reported that Pushmataha said?

There are thirty-seven immediately apparent possibilities, and some of them can teach us a lot about what scholars do, and don't do.

Possibility #1: That word in DeRosier's footnote that is not in what Pushmataha said in describing that land is DeRosier-turned-linguist, giving us his translation of "*boukey*."

Possibility #2: That word that DeRosier added to Pushmataha's description of that land is DeRosier-turned-linguist, giving us his translation of the secret-scholar-code-talk word "[*sic*]."

Possibility #3: That extra word DeRosier added to what Pushmataha said is DeRosier-turned-linguist, giving us his not-so-hot translation of "inundation."

Possibility #4: That extra word that Arthur DeRosier added in his footnote to what Pushmataha supposedly said is an "Arthurism," which nobody will ever likely figure out.

Possibility #5: That word in DeRosier's footnote that is not in what Pushmataha said in describing that land, was a word that was in the dot-dot-dot, the "...." in the middle of the quotation, or in the dot-dot-dot-dot, the "...." at the end of the quotation.

Okay, we'll skip the other thirty-two immediately apparent possibilities and focus in on that possibility #5.

Those dot-dot-dot-dots are called ellipses, when there are more than one of them. Supposedly only one of them is called an ellipsis. But why anybody but a doo-doo brain wouldn't call only one of them a "period" is beyond me.

Okay, so maybe I am a doo-doo brain, because I do happen to know why only one of them is not called a period, which is primarily because a period is an entirely different thing, even if a period does happen to appear to be identically the same thing. The difference is in what it is and what it does.

What ellipses do is talk. They talk in a secret-scholar code talk. They talk to the secret-scholar-code-talk-savvy people.

Ellipses tell those savvy people that something in the original document has been left out of the quotation, and the ellipses show them exactly where it has been left out, which is exactly where the ellipses have been substituted for whatever was omitted.

We do not know *what* was omitted, because the dots do not tell us that. So, in that regard, they are more "show" than "tell." They only show *where* something was left out, and they only tell us that something *was* left out.

The ellipses are actually pretty darn stingy about telling us hardly anything. They probably don't ever just kick back and have a good time, either. And they probably beat their kids too and all the time go around being sour-mouthed and not much fun.

The dots *could* tell us all about what was omitted, if they weren't such party poopers, if they were to invite some party-animal dashes over to their house and get to spinning some jailhouse rock on the old music box, and fool around and rock-and-roll some real good boogie-woogie dots and dashes at us in Morse code.

But, if they were going to do that, and tell us *that* way all about what was omitted, then we might as well not have had anything omitted at all, at least for Morse-code-savvy people.

However, the secret-scholar code talk does not use Morse code, and even to suggest using Morse code in the secret-scholar code talk, especially in conjunction with boogie-woogie, rock-and-roll dots and dashes, is about the dumbest damn thing that I ever heard.

So, if you suggest that sort of thing again, you will have to go to your room. I mean it. I don't have the patience for that sort of foolishness.

Ellipses are serious business. They are the most critically important part of the secret-scholar code talk.

Ellipses ordinarily come in clusters of three dots or four dots, and there are exactly one million kazillion secret-scholar-code-talk rules for how and when and where to properly use ellipses.

There are also secret-scholar-code-talk rules for anything and everything else that you might be likely to think of for nearly anything regarding the English language.

That is partly because the secret-scholar-code-talk keys, which are called style manuals, or manuals of style, ordinarily incorporate their choice of some particular, *specific* dictionary as the arbiter for anything not covered in the style manual, and that specific dictionary thus becomes *the* reference that is to be used as the authority for how any nuances must be dealt with that might arise from interpretation of any of the secret-scholar-code-talk "rules" in the particular style manual that specified that dictionary.

This aspect of the secret-scholar-code-talk keys (style manuals), this incorporation of a specific dictionary authority, is one of the most critically important means by which those who seek to control the dissemination of knowledge (and who seek to control how people think and what people think about) attempt to achieve that end.

The dictionaries most frequently incorporated into the secret-scholar-code-talk keys are ones descended from the pervasive influence of that always-go-around-sour-mouthed prescriptive grammarian, Noah Webster, and his Bowdlerizing, Puritanical vision of the English language.

The primary reason, however, for why there are now exactly one million kazillion secret-scholar-code-talk rules, for nearly everything, is because there are now that many different editions of style manuals, with each one having different rules.

By far the most famous style manual is the *Chicago Manual of Style*, of the University of Chicago Press, a big thick book that tells publishers how to convert a typewritten manuscript into a book and tells authors how to type the footnotes and about a million other things in their typewritten manuscript.

The *Chicago Manual of Style* is the preferred standard of the discipline of history, primarily because nothing else on earth could possibly be quite so tediously boring to try to read, not even anything that those history professors write themselves, though there are a few of them who can give that old *Chicago Manual of Style* a good run for its money.

The *Chicago Manual of Style* has a condensed version, for students, known as "Turabian," for a Kate Turabian, who invented the thing, the condensed student version.

She did that when she was the dissertations secretary for the graduate school of the University of Chicago, back around the middle of the twentieth century.

She took pity on the poor graduate students at that university, and, because *she* had to know the rules in the big thick *Chicago Manual of Style*, and those graduate students mostly did not have a clue how to make sense of them, or how to determine which rules might be the really important ones, she knocked off a few mimeographed sheets, mimeographed because that was before there were any photocopy machines (now those mimeographed sheets are a rare collector's item), of the most important rules that doctoral students should know for how to type their doctoral dissertations.

Those students found that so useful that they brought her candy, and flowers, and ice cream, and they begged her to add a few more sheets.

So, she did. And it was so popular that she hit upon the idea of turning it into a very slim little paperback book, the first edition of which is still fairly easy enough to find that it isn't much of a collector's item, unless you might not have one yet, in which case you might want to keep it on your list of things to acquire.

Then, each time the University of Chicago Press published a new edition of that big thick *Chicago Manual of Style*, which it does fairly frequently (at a rate of more than a dozen new editions per century, in a frantic attempt to keep up with accelerating technological changes in book publishing), Kate Turabian also published a new edition of her little paperback "Turabian" rule book for students, to incorporate the new rules of the University of Chicago Press, the ones that were the most appropriate for student research papers.

With each new edition of her little "Turabian" rule book, it would get thicker and thicker, until, while it wasn't anywhere nearly as big as the big thick *Chicago Manual of Style*, her little rule book soon got to be about as confusingly complex for most of the students who had to try to make sense of it, which, by the 1960s, included virtually every college student, both undergraduate and graduate students, virtually everywhere.

Those students, most of them, were ordinarily trying to make sense of her rule book hastily, in the wee hours of the night, as they were sleepily and frantically trying to finish typing "according to Turabian" the footnotes, bibliography, and many other secret-scholar-code-talk-doctored things that they were supposed to be doing throughout their research paper.

That research paper had been assigned to them for weeks or months, but they had only begun researching and writing it, rather feverishly, the previous day.

By those wee hours of the night, only hours before that research paper was due, those students were at a point where they didn't much care anymore what Turabian's rules, or anybody's rules, might be.

They were, in fact, just a little bit ticked off, knowing that a portion of their grade for that research paper would be based on how well they were able to demonstrate an understanding of, and an application of, those Turabian–University of Chicago Press rules.

Of course, they might have been ticked off at themselves, if they had thought about it, which few apparently ever did very often, that the other portion of their grade would be based upon the hasty research and writing they'd done to produce the awful, stinking-to-high-heaven thing that they were about to turn in to some history professor, who would not be amused when he reached, like as not, rather deep into the beginning of the alphabet to assign that paper a grade.

Every student everywhere *had* to buy a copy of Kate Turabian's little rule book.

She became richer than God.

She eventually bought the University of Chicago, just to have something to play with, and then she bought all of Chicago, and then all of Illinois, and then she started spreading out from there, and she long ago owned all of the earth, and long ago finished buying all of Mars, and she is now thought to be way out near the edge of our solar system, or somewhere beyond, still buying every damn thing in sight.

So, by the 1960s everybody on every campus all over the country thought that she was God, because that's what happens when you own everything, and so every department of just about every college and university made its students do their research papers "according to Turabian," which was about the only style manual around in those days, about the only one that students were required to use.

And so, everybody tried to learn *her* rules, and everybody thought that her rules, which were actually the rules of the University of Chicago Press, were the *only* way that it could be possible for something to be done right.

And everything was okay, until along came the really pissed off Baby Boomers, the ones who were determined to make *somebody* pay, because of those typos in that *Golden Treasury of Chess*.

Those Baby Boomers took a good look around, and they saw that it was the history professors who were terrorizing their students the most with the "Turabian" rules.

Those Baby Boomers could see that it was those history professors who were the ones who just loved sitting around in the evening actually *reading*, page-by-page, the great big thick *Chicago Manual of Style*, and comparing it with Turabian's little rule book, and doing that with a lip-smacking, eye-darting determination to be the very first one who might catch even just one little tiny thing that Kate Turabian might not have condensed *exactly right*, which they sat around in the evening trying to do every time Kate Turabian put out a new edition of her little rule book.

Those history professors were probably not consciously aware that they were smacking their lips and darting their eyes while they were doing that, but that was the very thing that tipped off those Baby Boomers that there were some professors on campus who might have a few loose screws that somebody should maybe try tightening up just a little bit.

Those Baby Boomers could see that while those history professors were sitting around in the evening doing that, those history professors were concentrating on it so intensely that they wouldn't let any TV be turned on in the house, or allow any boogie-woogie blaring radio to be playing, and if anybody made so much as a peep, like their kids, then they would beat their kids, and then they would mostly just go around being all sour-mouthed all the time.

And their wives, if one of them wanted to communicate with her history-professor husband, then she had to write out her wifely message on paper, being careful to print in block letters so that somebody else could read it, and then she had to go to that history department, and she had to contribute to its secret, annual beer-bash fund, by paying money to hire an amanuensis at that history department, who would take her money, probably money for food for her little kiddies, and that amanuensis would convert her carefully printed wifely message into an *exactly right* presentation that was typed, double-spaced, and properly footnoted, all according to the big thick *Chicago Manual of Style*, so that she could take it back home and give it to her history-professor husband that evening, when he was in a somewhat less than usual sour-mouthed mood, due to the special dinner that she had cooked for him, and, under those circumstances, he would read it, marking any fuzzy verbs and whatnot with an always-sharpened red pencil.

If he marked any typos, then she would get really pissed, because she hadn't been the one who typed it, but she didn't dare say anything, and she just had to be a meek, wifely wife, but his bacon and eggs at breakfast wouldn't be done too hot the next morning.

And those Baby Boomers said, ah ha, *there* is the authority that they had been looking for.

And those Baby Boomers decided to *make them pay.*

Those Baby Boomers could see that it was those mean old history professors who were the silly, prissy authority people.

Those Baby Boomers could see that it was those history professors who were the ones who insisted that everything be done exactly right, that anything that *could* be gotten *exactly* right *must* be gotten *exactly* right, that every little comma, and every little word in every little quoted thing in every research paper and in everything else, like those amanuenced wifely messages, *must* be gotten *exactly* right, because they were things that *could* be gotten exactly right.

Those Baby Boomers had seen how those mean old history professors would even go to the library themselves and spend delicious hours there, darting their eyes while looking at the books and whatnot that the students had quoted from, just for the lip-smacking pleasure of finding one little mis-quoted comma, or any little *anything* else that some student had not quoted *exactly* right, because it *could* be gotten *exactly* right, because it *deserved* and it *demanded* and it *must* receive the exact *precise* attention to *detail* that both *could* and *should* be gotten *exactly* right.

And those Baby Boomers said, ah ha, *here* are the swine who have led us down the primrose path.

Here are the people who have been telling us that we must get things *exactly* right, creating an *expectation* in the innocent, unsuspecting masses of young people that the real world would be a place where the people who would be out there in that real world, who would have paying jobs, who would be get-ting paid to *get* things exactly right, *would* be out there getting everything exactly right, but, when it is two a.m., and you have been spending sleepless, bleary-eyed hours trying to make sense out of that move in that *Golden Treasury of Chess*, where are they, huh?

Home in bed, all snuggled up nice and cozy, without a care in the world, not even knowing that their bacon and eggs at breakfast won't be done so hot, all snuggled up nice and contented, after probably having beaten their kids, all snuggled up not *caring* that they are teaching a big lie, not caring, no matter what they say about how it *should* be done, that the doo-doo brains who are the ones who *actually* do it, *screw* it up.

So those Baby Boomers vented all of that frustration on those mean old history professors, and they didn't let up until they had fixed their little red wagons but good.

Those Baby Boomers crybabied to the English department, and then they crybabied to the psychology department, and then they crybabied to whomever would listen to their complaint, wherever anybody would, that *they* wanted a different style manual.

And, back in those days, what students wanted, students got, otherwise they would just take over the whole damn place.

And so, now there is the Modern Language Association (MLA) style manual, for English professionals; and the APA (American Psychological Association) style manual; and the Merriam-Webster's dictionary-appendix style manual; and the McGraw-Hill publishing company style manual, and exactly enough others to total exactly one kazillion different style manuals.

That one kazillion includes a U.S. Department of Defense style manual, which has fifty-five pages of rules just regarding hyphens. That is to help the military personnel in the U.S. Armed Forces comprehend what they are required to read in order to know how to defend the country. To help them do that, every word containing more than three syllables must be hyphenated, to give the troops a better chance of figuring out what that word might be.

There are, of course, many other military style manuals, with different rules. Now there are different rules out the kazoo, for anything and everything.

Now there are style manuals out the kazoo.

There are now so many different ones for so many different things, and so many different kinds of them, that there are now exactly one kazillion different kinds of style manuals, all with different rules.

That's how pissed off about that *Golden Treasury of Chess* that those Baby Boomers were, and still are, and will go their graves still being pissed off about, after having paused, on the last day of their lives, and on the day before that, and on the day before that, at an idle moment, to glance around the horizon, and narrow their eyes, and knit their brows, and wonder what other kind of style manual they might get somebody to come up with, just so they can stick it to those mean old history professors one more time before they die.

And there used to be only about one style manual. Well, there were a few others way back when, like AP and this and that, but not many, until those Baby Boomers came along.

Those Baby Boomers are evilly cunning.

Not only did they insist that there be exactly one kazillion different kinds of style manuals, but then they insisted that each one of them put out exactly one million successive editions of itself, and that each one change every one of its rules in each new edition.

That's why we now have exactly one million kazillion rules for the only *one* proper way to use ellipses.

One kazillion different kinds of style manuals, multiplied by one million successive editions of each one, gives us exactly one million kazillion *proper* ways to do it, each one of which is the *only* proper way that it can be *allowed* to be done.

Which means that you have got to be pretty damn dumb to do it in *any* way that would not be proper in some edition of some style manual.

But students will figure out how to do that.

Even if there might be only *one* way that it *could* be done wrong, they will find that way, trust me on that.

It also means that in order to make the most surefooted sense out of the secret-scholar code talk that was applied to the evil professor DeRosier's book, you must find out which one of the evilly baby-boomered kazillion different secret-scholar-code-talk style manuals to use and then *try* to find a copy of that, which will be some long out-of-print edition of the style manual, because *The Removal of the Choctaw Indians*, by that Moriartied Kadiddlehopper, was submitted for publication nearly forty years ago.

Most libraries don't keep older editions of the secret-scholar-code-talk keys, partly because most library people cannot imagine why anybody might want one and partly because if they did keep them they would take up all of the bookshelf space, and there wouldn't be any room for any other books.

Bookstores don't sell the old editions because those old editions went out of print when the next edition came out.

And used bookstore people will look at you with that blankness in the eyes that tells you that the hand they just dropped beneath the counter is resting on that .357 Magnum that's been sitting there unused for seventeen years, just for the day, which, apparently, has finally arrived, when someone truly dangerous would walk into *their* used bookstore looking for some squirrelly, useless thing like *that*.

To try to make sense out of how the secret-scholar-code-talk things were done in DeRosier's book, you must know which press published that Kadiddlehoppered thing, so you can try to find out which secret-scholar code talk that press favored at that time.

If a press would say, as part of the details of publication on the copyright page, which edition of which secret-scholar-code-talk version was applied to that particular book, it would make things a lot easier, especially for scholars trying to make sense out of the things in the book many years, or decades, or centuries, or millennia after the book was published.

The press ordinarily controls the choice of which secret-scholar-code-talk version will be used to convert the typewritten manuscript of an author into a published book.

It's the secret-scholar-code-talk whizzes, called copy editors (who might be freelance copy editors who live and do their work elsewhere and who are contracted by a press on a book-by-book basis) who apply the particular press-chosen version of a secret-scholar code talk to what the author wrote.

The copy editor changes what the author wrote.

The copy editor does that wherever necessary to conform to the secret-scholar-code-talk version (and dictionary) that the press favors, which can include nearly everything under the sun, to an extent that, when you see what you wrote, you didn't write it anymore, and it doesn't mean the same thing, which can happen in an amazing million different ways.

When working with a quality press, an author will have a chance to make corrections to the copy-edited manuscript, after the copy-editing stage and, later, will also have a chance to proofread, for typographer's errors, the nearly finished product, after the book has been typeset for publication (called page proofs or galley proofs).

However, depending upon the contractual arrangements between the author and the press, and a lot of other factors (such as the coming and going of different editors during the life of that publishing project, to mention just one common way that things can go wrong), an author might not even see the thing before it is in print, with their name on it, after it has been secret-scholar code talk changed by somebody else, which is a big secret about publishing that hardly anyone but authors seem to have much awareness of, which seems very strange, given the level of interest in other First Amendment issues.

Most people seem to think that the name of the person on a book is the person who wrote that book.

Publishing, except for self-publishing, is a collaborative process, the more quality the press and its product, the more collaborative.

It's a process that, despite contracts, despite nearly everything else, must be based on mutual trust, mutual respect, and give-and-take, where necessary, and on an awareness that reasonable people can differ and the understanding that the ultimate objective is to publish the best book that can be produced, for which, for quality publishing, a few good cooks in the kitchen can be a good thing for everyone.

Quality publishing is both an expensive process and a time-consuming one. These days, university presses, and some education-oriented commercial presses, are about the only ones that even attempt quality publishing anymore.

Most of the old, big commercial publishing houses in America have now been bought by a handful of big corporations, who run them strictly as a bottom-line, money-making operation.

Editors at those presses, who once actually did some editing, handling maybe 15–20 books a year, now handle 80–120 books a year. They've ceased being editors and have become merely cogs in a wheel.

They barely have time to glance through the manuscripts they "edit" and have become entirely dependent on copy editors to prepare a manuscript for publication.

That can be particularly vexing for Indians writing about Indians because some of the secret-scholar-code-talk things, the arbitrary "rules" that copy editors will apply to a manuscript, insist upon silly Euro-Anglo ethnocentrisms, often of anthropological origin, that have a "point of view" about Indians.

Often they are things that non-Indians are oblivious to, which even seasoned editors can have difficulty comprehending when an attempt is made to explain some of those things to them, such as the anthropological usage, sanctioned by Merriam-Webster, of using the singular for the plural when referring to Indian nations, thus reducing Indian nations to the status of animals (the Apache, the horse, the mule).

Copy editors will routinely change "the Apaches" to "the Apache" everywhere in a manuscript, but not my copy editors, not unless they want to spend the rest of their lives cowering indoors, hiding from lightning.

For books published some time ago, there might not be anybody currently at a press who has more than a fuzzy idea of how things were done before they got there, if that press is even still in business.

Often the easiest thing to do, for a lot of books, a lot of the time, will be to study how the secret-scholar code talk was done throughout the book to see if it was done consistently, and, if so, from that you can figure out what the rules must have been at that time at that press, or at least for that book.

And, if it does not readily appear that there were any rules, well, then you are on your own if you want to try to figure out what it might be that you might be holding in your hand.

The ellipses is one of the biggest secret-scholar-code-talk secrets, one that almost always goes unnoticed, because there isn't anything there to notice, except for some dots.

Scholars must leave some things out of what is quoted because a lot of that stuff is of no value for any purpose.

However, much of Indian history is to be found in the ellipses of quotations in books about Indians.

Those little dots can be like a bird dog pointing the way to the game you are hunting.

So don't overlook the ellipses in the quotations of books about Indians if you want to have some fun finding out for yourself what got excised from the quotation.

That extra word in that evil Kadiddlehoppper's INFAMOUS FOOTNOTE NUMBER 55, by the way, is "windy," though "useless" was also a gratuitous offering. But I like "windy" better, and it's my quiz.

And no, "windy" is not what *boukey* means, or *sic*, or inundation, though a case can be made that boukey = useless.

It should also be noted that the evil Professor DeRosier, in common with almost all of the Kadiddlehoppered community of American historians, is helpless to resist engaging in American-imperialist propaganda in his INFAMOUS FOOTNOTE NUMBER 55.

He leaves out a word, as would almost all of his fellow "American" historians.

He refers to the sovereign Choctaw land in the Trans-Mississippi West as being a part of "America," rather than being a part of "North America."

It is not a sandy, windy, and useless area, but a well-watered, heavily timbered section of America.

That evil professor's use of a *political* term of reference (implying that the land is a portion of the United States), rather than a *geographical* term of reference (which would be politically neutral), is a dead giveaway that DeRosier is writing propaganda, that it has an American-imperialist point of view.

American imperialists might *wish* that the portion of North America that DeRosier is discussing were a part of "America," as a matter of U.S. Indian *policy*, but that is nothing but wishful thinking on the part of American imperialists, especially when they are discussing something like the treaty of 1820 and the land in the Trans-Mississippi West that it deals with—a discussion they *should* be engaging in as a matter of *law*, as a matter of Indian treaty law, as a matter of the supreme law of the land of the United States Constitution, rather than as a matter of U.S. Indian *policy*.

The language in the treaty of 1820 is explicit that the Choctaw land in the Trans-Mississippi West is a place where Choctaws can get far away *from* America.

The "Preamble" of that treaty explicitly states that the land in the West is intended:

> ...to perpetuate them as a nation, by exchanging, for a small part
> of their land here, a country beyond the Mississippi River, where
> all, who live by hunting and will not work, may be collected and
> settled together....

Some of DeRosier's multiplicity of confusions can be explained on the basis of a few things that modern-day Moriarty did not know, and that explanation is also the thing that lets the evil professor escape from the deepest depths of infamy.

Sort of.

His bibliography does not list the one key source that might have cleared up a lot of his confusions—Ruth Tennison West's 1959 *Chronicles of Oklahoma* article, "Pushmataha's Travels," where, in the very first paragraph, DeRosier could have alerted himself to the big resounding sound of the public embarrassment that he was about to let go of, by virtue of releasing the big bunch of beans in his book.

However, t-e-c-h-n-i-c-a-l-l-y, a scholar can only be held accountable for the knowledge that is to be found in the books and other things that are listed in the bibliography.

So, read your books backward, and if the bibliography is not worth a second glance, why bother reading that book?

This applies especially if the book purports to be about some particular topic that you know something about. If the things that are critical to comprehending that topic, let alone for trying to explain that topic to others, are nowhere to be found in the bibliography, then a good question to ask might be why that book even got published.

Another lesson that can be learned from DeRosier is that when you write your own books, anything that you might want to say, that would be difficult to say, if your bibliography were to contain reliable knowledge to the contrary, can be gotten around by simply leaving those things out of your bibliography.

That way, you've got your bases covered.

You can "scholar" away as ignorantly as you please, and, like as not, nobody will even notice.

And, if someone might actually notice, then you can't be held accountable for it, because your bibliography says that you did not know better.

Call it "the Doozy Rule of DeRosier."

So, the evil professor gets off on a technicality, and, in the process, he gives us a lesson or two in how to write bad books, and how to cover your bases about that, too.

Say what you will about him, but Arthur DeRosier was no dummy.

This picking on poor old Professor DeRosier has been intentionally delayed for decades, until now when he is undoubtedly either no longer with us, or else, if he might still be with us, is undoubtedly so old that he probably does not know who he is anymore.

The primary reason for that delay has been, as attested by every *Big Scouting Report* on him, that he was such a kindly disposed, well-intentioned person that no Choctaw would want to hurt his feelings.

Another reason is that the last thing Choctaws would want to do is scare off scholars who might contribute something to our knowledge of Choctaw history but who might fear that if they make one little tiny mistake, in one little tiny footnote, then they might get lambasted by Choctaws, but good.

Have no fear.

If you screw it up, be informed that, depending upon *how* bad you screw it up, you will not be lambasted until you are either no longer with us or until you have become so old that you probably won't even know who you are anymore, and, in either case, what would you care then what anybody might say about you?

Choctaws are a patient people.

Choctaws can wait a good long time to deliver a good lambasting, and Choctaws can find other things to be doing in the meantime, just as many Choctaws in the 1970s were not too greatly concerned that a whole lot of irons in the fire weren't too close anymore to any flames to be likely to be doing any branding anytime soon, at a time when something more pressing was suddenly commanding their attention, called the Wishbone.

"Pressing," mind you, being used here in the sense of pressing a branding iron to something, so we don't have any mixed metaphors creeping into anything.

Most of the Lords of the North American Continent got so deeply distracted by the Wishbone during that decade of the 1970s that they missed out on what might have been their opportunity to get riled up and ride that wave of momentum of intense Indian activism to no telling where.

Most of them, at least the unpoisoned ones, now appear more or less distractedly focused on studying the tactical lessons that might be learned from what that world-class football team of those shifty-eyed Sooners has been doing lately and probably wrestling with the colossal headache (with a

Comanche-buffalo-herd-stealing-size-headache) of trying to figure out how the illegal state of Oklahoma might be buried without disrupting that football team, which is an abstract intellectual task so daunting that any rational person would be tempted to indulge in a quantity of refreshing beverage every now and then.

That might even be a more colossal-size headache than the one that made a world-class drunkard out of the Commanding General of the North American Continent.

If a big headache like that can do that to him, it can do that to a-n-ybody.

Perhaps there is enough ticky-tocky time to examine a few aspects of Choctaw history, and American history, in an attempt to understand why Choctaws persist in maintaining a separate sovereign identity from Americans, and how things had gotten to a point, a century ago, that the imperialists among the Americans attempted to extinguish the Choctaw Nation, and how things had gotten to a point, by half a century ago, that Choctaws had been so completely eliminated from the American telling of American history that the Lords of the North American Continent could be howlingly mocked on the grand public stage of *The Alamo* by none other than John Wayne himself—*may he rest in peace*—without any Americans even noticing.

Chapter Eight

The Good and the Bad About the Americans

*I*n order to understand Choctaw history, it's necessary to review some elementary things about American history.

Most Americans have had American history drilled into them throughout their school years, to a point of boredom with the topic.

But not all readers of this book will be Americans.

Americans should simply skip this chapter.

They should just go on to the next one. They should do that now, just skip to the next chapter.

The last thing an author wants to do is risk boring his readers, and a conscientious author can help certain kinds of readers by alerting them to portions of a book that they don't need to read, some chapter, like this one, that they can skip without missing anything.

So, we'll pause for a moment to give the Americans a chance to thumb through the pages and find the beginning of the next chapter.

We'll catch up with them again in a bit, after tending to this somewhat tedious but necessary task, and then all of the readers will have a chance to be on an equal footing with the Americans with respect to all those things that Americans already know about themselves.

Now, for the rest of us, here are the things that Americans have had drilled into their heads throughout their entire lives, to a point that they are bored with hearing it and certainly don't need any review of it.

First and foremost, Americans are Germans.

Americans are quite touchy about this and will become angry if you do not acknowledge that they are Germans.

Americans will point out that no anthropologist has ever had any difficulty in classifying Americans as Germans, for two simple, fundamental, and irrefutable reasons: that English is a German language, and that their race, commonly called "white people," is the German race.

Americans tell their history like this: their ancestors are three German tribes called Angles, Saxons, and Jutes.

It's from the names of two of those German tribes that the term "Anglo-Saxon" comes from, which is frequently shortened to "Anglos" and is universally understood to mean "white people."

The terms "England" ("Angleland") and "English" ("Anglish") come from the Angles.

Until very recently, about fifteen hundred years ago, those three tribes of so-called white people—Angles, Saxons, and Jutes—were just three of the many tribes of white people known as North European Germans (or NEGs, for short).

This race of so-called white people first came to the attention of the rest of the world when all of them still lived in the forests of northern Europe, in the ancestral homeland of their race, "Germania," as the Romans called it, or "Germany," as it's come to be known.

The civilized and thoroughly alarmed Romans had to *invent* a word for that race of people, in desperately trying to warn the whole world about white people, because nobody had a word that adequately described them, until the Romans gave them the name that they are still known by— "barbarians."

Several things can be said about that race of slobbering barbarians that has come pouring out of the forests of Germania to terrorize the civilized world on both sides of the Atlantic Ocean.

They are not the people who invented the wheel.

They are not the people who invented agriculture.

They are not the people who domesticated farm animals.

They are not the people who invented writing.

They are not the people who invented metallurgy.

In short, compared to other people, even in the Old World, they are not the brightest candles ever lit, which is something that contemporary Americans are acutely aware of, and something they anguish about inconsolably.

Those German barbarians from the forests of northern Europe quickly became the most vexing problem faced by the civilized peoples of the Mediterranean region.

Some of the most famous people of all time, such as General Julius Caesar, gained their fame trying to solve what *continues to be* the most vexing problem faced by civilized peoples—how to restrain the German barbarians.

Not even the awesome power of the Roman empire could restrain the slobbering barbarian tribes of Vandals, Goths, and Visigoths who descended upon Rome and plunged the Western world into its Dark Ages.

At about the same time, beginning about 449, three particular tribes of those German barbarians, the Angles, Saxons, and Jutes, also came pouring out of the forests of Germania. But they slobbered their way to the west instead of going south.

They began invading the islands of Briton, where they have become known as the British Island Germans (or BIGs, for short).

As any of the native Celtic peoples of Briton will tell you, those German barbarians didn't stop being Germans, and they didn't stop being barbarians, just because they left "Germany."

Over the course of the next thousand years, the British Island Germans, in going about the business of being Germans, pillaged and conquered many of those native Celtic peoples of Briton.

By then the barbarians were learning how to sail ocean-going vessels, and they took steps toward becoming dangerous on a global scale, as they began founding German colonies far away.

In 1607, a group of British Island Germans sailed all the way across the Atlantic Ocean and became the North American Germans (or NAGs, for short) when they founded Jamestown, the first settlement in a German colony the barbarians call Virginia.

Other groups of BIGs soon followed, establishing other colonies of NAGs, such as Plymouth Rock in 1620, in a German colony the barbarians call Massachusetts.

Before long, the barbarians had thirteen colonies of North American Germans all along the Atlantic seaboard of North America.

If any Indians have ever wondered *why* the Americans have acted like barbarians, the answer is simple.

They *are* barbarians.

They are the people for whom *that* word was invented.

Because the NEGs and the BIGs and the NAGs could then be found inhabiting so much of the Northern Hemisphere on both sides of the Atlantic Ocean, and because they exhibit such similar behavior, all of the German barbarians have now been lumped together into a classification that the anthropologists call the North Atlantic Culture Area.

It only took a few generations before the colonial NAG barbarians got to squabbling with their BIG barbarian bosses back in Briton.

That squabbling among themselves soon ignited a German civil war, from 1775–83, known as the First North Atlantic German Civil War (or FNAGCW), which was shortly followed, from 1812–15, by the Second North Atlantic German Civil War (known as SNAGCW), which again pitted the British Island Germans against the North American Germans.

The weak and puny NAGs, with the decisive help of the Lords of the North American Continent, survived those wrenching clashes with the much more powerful BIGs and then continued going about the business of being Germans on the North American continent.

That barbarian undertaking led to the horrifyingly brutal North American German Civil War (or NAGCW), from 1861–65, which pitted the Northern North American Germans (NNAGs) against the Southern North American Germans (SNAGs).

The horrific carnage in that North American German Civil War was an occasion for a particularly poignant period of NAG contemplation of their barbarian shortcomings, but that hardly ended the German civil wars.

Their most recent barbarian squabbles among themselves have dominated world history, events known to most people as World War I and World War II but which the NAGs refer to as the First World German Civil War

(FWGCW) and the Second World German Civil War (SWGCW), both of which pitted the NEGs against the combined victorious forces of the BIGs and the NAGs in even more horrifically barbaric slaughters that killed tens of millions of people.

Curiously, the NEGS and the BIGs and the NAGs, in a peculiarly German manner, remain very mindful of their barbarian shortcomings and devote a great amount of their time to lamenting some of the more obviously unfortunate things about their race.

They are acutely aware of their difficulty in getting along with one another and the savage brutality with which they wage their endless and terrifying, ever-escalating civil wars, and they anguish greatly about those things, which, unfortunately, they seem not to be able to do much about.

Their painful awareness of that, however, and of what they regard as other critical flaws in the character of their race, leads them to devote the great bulk of their literature, both written and oral, to a kind of endless sorrowful hand-wringing and a pathetic sort of supplication that somehow they might be able to mend their barbarian ways and take steps toward *trying* to become civilized human beings.

To the endless amusement of Indian people, the Germans value their contemplative and heartfelt expressions of anguish so highly that those among them who prove to be the most poignant, skillful, convincing, and entertaining at revealing how wretched they are receive the highest accolades of their race.

If they do that in a book, they are called novelists.

If they do it from a pulpit, they are called preachers.

If they do it in a classroom, they are called professors.

But regardless of the forum they choose, their message is the same—they are wretched creatures.

They are a curious people, consumed with contemplating little else but their shortcomings, which they now call sins, and devoting the bulk of their intellectual effort to convincing one another that their wretchedness is so deeply ingrained in them that they have no hope for anything approaching happiness.

This has led them, for quite some time now, to become thoroughly superstitious and to devote much of their thoughts to the supernatural, in the hope that there might be some other kind of life after this one to which they will be allowed to escape, which is apparently somewhere up in the clouds.

In order to understand that business about the clouds, you have to understand the religious superstitions of the white people.

About a thousand years ago, from some Middle Eastern mystics, the white people adopted a weird imaginary being as their supreme imaginary being. He's supposed to be sort of a superpowerful kind of superasshole, one with a severe personality disorder, angry, jealous, vengeful—a very repugnant sort of creature to any civilized people.

As you might well imagine, a guy like that, imaginary or not, superpowerful or not, would encounter some real obstacles in trying to get any good-looking woman to let him see her naked. If he weren't superpowerful, he might never get laid.

But, so the story goes, being superpowerful, one day this repulsive and arrogantly haughty imaginary being sweeps down out of the clouds, down into the Middle East, and he knocks up this real doozy of a Jewish gal, who— now, be sure and get this part, because it's pretty important—even though she was a married woman, was still a virgin.

In today's parlance, a gal like that would be known as "high maintenance." Real high maintenance.

That imaginary superpowerful superasshole might have chosen her just for spite, on account of how, even though she had gotten married, she was *so* hoitsy-toitsy that she *still* wouldn't put out.

The kid that resulted from that extraordinarily weird and illicit sexual encounter, as you might well imagine, turned out to be seriously screwed up, which would dang near be predictable, given what we're told about both his mama and his imaginary biological daddy.

The kid may have gotten screwed up simply in trying to come to terms with what his mama told him about *how* he had gotten to be a bastard, and *who* she claimed had knocked her up.

What, exactly, the kid's mama might have told her husband about that seems unclear, but she had to tell him *something*. In any event, what she apparently told the kid about it would be enough to screw up anybody. I mean, this was his *mama*.

And, from all available evidence, the kid didn't have the advantage of growing up in a very enlightened home, considering that, if nothing else, his mama's husband couldn't have been very godawful bright.

From what people who supposedly knew the kid wrote about him decades after he died, and from what they told us that the kid supposedly said to them, there seems little doubt that the kid grew up to be a garden-variety paranoiac schizophrenic suffering severe alternating delusions of grandeur and persecution.

If he were alive today, the poor guy would probably be able to get some medication that might allow him to live a normal life.

There have always been such people in the world. There are so many of them today that modern psychiatric practice has become fairly ho-hum in its knowledge of how to deal with them.

But long ago in the Middle East there was little help available of hardly any kind for people like him, and, when he started acting out his delusions of grandeur, he caused his delusions of persecution to become a reality.

The end, for him, came in a real bad scene, nailed to a cross. That was hardly anything unusual in that time and place.

The Romans are known to have executed about ten thousand people that way during that time. Many of those people were religious mystics like that screwed-up kid. It was a time and place that's known to have produced a lot of weirdos.

However, after that weird kid was dead, all the weirdness about his life got fashioned into a weird kind of religion, which might be called the Cult of the Dead Jew.

That's because, so the story goes, that kid's imaginary biological daddy, that asshole of a superpowerful, angry, vengeful, jealous adulterer up in the clouds, decided to make that dead kid a superpowerful imaginary being, like himself, so that dead kid could someday use his superpowers to come sweeping down to earth and swoop up all of his still-slobbering living followers, and all of his no-longer-slobbering dead followers, and take them with him back up into the clouds, where, presumably, they can all sit around forever slobbering to their heart's content while listening to harp music.

That's about it.

The millions of those barbarians who still believe those foreign Middle Eastern superstitions is a testimony to how much slobber still remains in white people.

But white people not only believe those superstitions, they take them *very* seriously.

Remember, they are not the brightest candles ever lit. They're white people.

So, whatever you do, don't make fun of their religious superstitions.

Oddly enough, for about a thousand years, the Germans have associated a lot of their wretchedness with having sex.

That seems to have happened when those Old World Middle Eastern mystics convinced them that their earliest ancestors committed an "original sin" when they first tried to have sex, and, in doing that, damned all of their descendents to a perpetual condition of congenital incurable wretchedness.

The exact technical details of how they think that their earliest ancestors were not able to figure out how to do the sex act correctly is very fuzzy and has provided an endless source of speculation for Indian people, but the Germans don't seem to know anything about those technical details.

They keep themselves in a state of perpetual ignorance and embarrassment about sex, and their greatest fear seems to be that their children might somehow learn something about sex.

From the time they are tiny tots they've had it drilled into their heads that they are wretched, that anything having to do with their sex organs is "dirty," that there is little they can do about it, and that they had better feel bad about it, or else there must be something truly wrong with them.

Given their level of fear and guilt and secrecy about sex, coupled with their ignorance and embarrassment about it, it shouldn't be surprising that their conception of what sort of afterlife they might escape to apparently does consist of sitting around on clouds, endlessly listening to harp music, where, regardless of what else there might be, there will be no sex.

They believe that their congenital incurable condition damns them to a life of endless toil and drudgery and that if they are not feverishly working at a backbreaking pace from daylight to dark they are committing some kind of blasphemy.

To make sure that they must work nearly all the time, and to make sure that they will have as little leisure time as possible, they developed an economic system that discourages them from sharing hardly anything they acquire with anyone else and that rewards them for hoarding wealth from one another, which forces them to compete with each other for everything, even for food.

To compound all of their other problems, they developed a theory of private ownership of land, so they can live in carefully guarded seclusion, in the most wastefully large house they can finance, presumably so that, when they do have sex, no one will know about it.

From that base, they work and worry themselves into nervous exhaustion in their quest to acquire and hoard as much wealth as they can from all the other Germans, apparently so that everyone else will think that they have no time for anything but work and sleep and therefore don't ever have sex.

In short, they are a severely socially flawed race of people who have entered the modern world with deeply imbedded, culturally instilled personality disorders that extend to some of the most basic things about being human, or even simply to being alive, and they have created both economic and social systems that are virtually guaranteed to result in nothing but perpetual misery.

One thing that was almost calculated to drive the Germans straight up the wall was to come to North America and encounter a nearly naked people who were entirely free of Old World Middle Eastern mysticism, who didn't feel bad about being human, or being alive, or about much of anything else, who had lots of leisure time because they shared with one another, and who had lots of sex and didn't feel bad about doing that, either, considering it merely a natural biological function.

The NAGs might have characterized these newly discovered people in any number of ways, such as socially advanced, happy, well adjusted, normal, but none of those things occurred to the NAGs.

Instead of the Germans seeing examples of what they might become, if only they were capable of shedding their personality disorders and giving it a try, the NAGs rolled up their sleeves and set about the task of trying to transplant Germany to North America, much as the BIGs have been trying to transplant Germany to the British Isles.

For the Native peoples of North America, as well as for the native Celtic peoples who are still stuck under the thumb of the BIGs, the Irish and the Welsh and the Scots, the best strategy seems to be to wait them out, for even now the Germans are in the process of leaving—leaving not just North America, or the British Isles, but leaving earth itself.

The Germans, particularly the NEGs and the NAGs, have demonstrated an ability to focus a lot of their resources on rocket science, after the NEGs invented it and then the NAGs set about perfecting it.

They have coupled this with an elementary sort of entry-level interest in theoretical interstellar physics and have convinced themselves that within a few billion years the sun is going to expand and consume the earth and that their only hope for the survival of their peculiar sort of personality disorders is to rocket themselves to some other planet in some other solar system.

Hopefully, we can all look forward to some day soon when a lot of eager volunteers will help the Germans do that very thing. If we all pitch in, we can have the satisfaction of helping the barbarians achieve their most earnest desires, somewhere up there among the clouds. And, as we are waving good-bye to their last rocket leaving earth, we can remember them as the Outer Space Germans.

Then we can all get back to being well-adjusted normal people and try to clean up the mess they have made of this planet.

We can engage in speculations about how befuddled some other people on some other planet are going to be as they go through the process of getting acquainted with those rocket-riding, suddenly arriving Outer Space Germans, who will no doubt be waving a treaty of peace and friendship, written in plain Anglish, eager to get everybody signed up.

For the present, however, the barbarians are still with us, and the matter of how the NAGs have come to be known as Americans should be addressed, as it reveals much about them.

It is apparently a language evolution thing, a kind of code talk they have developed, in which, when they speak, they only voice part of what they say.

That appears to be why, when they tell us who they are, we only hear part of what they are saying: "(North) American (German)."

It has taken Indians a long time to learn how to translate the silent parts, such as: "(Hey, suckers) We want to negotiate a treaty with you."

Some sort of pyschohistoriographical language analyst will have to figure out how this got started, but there seems a good chance it might stem from their resentment of the power that the BIGs held over them for so long: "(You pompous swine) I'm here to pay my taxes (but not for long)."

Much of American history might need to be rewritten in light of what can now be surmised about the silent parts of what the NAGs were really saying, reaching back to some of the earliest, most famous examples of American public declarations.

Patrick Henry: "Give me liberty (to get rich selling Indian land) or give me death!"

The technique might work just as well for fleshing out more recent American public declarations, based upon educated guesses at what the silent parts might have been.

President Kennedy: "(Marilyn) Ask not what your country can do for you, ask what you can do for (the horniest president in the history of) your country."

President Nixon: "I (really) am not a (very smart) crook."

President Bush: "(How to) Read my lips: (If they do not move at all, I'm not lying—now watch closely) No new taxes."

President Clinton: "(God this had better work) I did not have (a lot of) sexual relations with that woman (yet)."

The psychohistoriographical language analysts will probably find the root of this thing somewhere around the most important date in American history, 1763.

That's the date of the laws that Americans spend most of their time studying in their schools, the laws that were announced in the Royal Proclamation of 1763.

The Americans devote so much time to teaching and studying those laws that their details spring readily from the lips of virtually every schoolchild, and for good reason—the Americans are extraordinarily angry at themselves.

Those laws offered the NAGs their best opportunity to learn how to be civilized people.

It became a lost opportunity that recent generations of NAGs have anguished about inconsolably, convinced that it is absolute proof of the depth of their wretchedness.

Those laws were issued by King George III of the BIGs, after the BIGs booted the French out of North America and inherited French claims to the Mississippi River Valley, and the Ohio River Valley, west of the Appalachian Mountains, in the so-called French and Indian War (1755–63), which is known as the Seven Years' War in Europe.

The reason the BIGs called it the French and Indian War in North America was because the BIGs discovered, to their horror, that they not only had to fight the French but most of the Indians, as well.

That was partly due to the Indian policies of the BIGs.

But it was mostly due to a colossal misunderstanding that led to an unbearable level of frustration on the part of the Indian nations of the Ohio River Valley over the lack of adequate mental health facilities among the colonial NAGs, who at that time were still confined largely to the Atlantic seaboard.

The Indian nations of the Ohio River Valley did not understand that the colonial NAGs liked to invent and play parlor games and that they had invented an exciting new parlor game called Land Speculation, which was a lot like playing Monopoly, but instead of using the kind of funny money Monopoly uses, it used a kind of Indian land-title funny money.

If you wanted to be a big player in that parlor game, you had to form your own "land company," and to do that, all any individual subject of the Crown had to do was grab an Indian, any Indian, get him good and liquored up, and buy, say, the Ohio River Valley from him.

With that "deed," the land company printing press then cranked out real estate "land titles" to farms west of the Appalachian Mountains, beyond the frontier of colonial NAG settlement.

Those pieces of paper weren't worth anything, but they were furiously sold among the colonial NAG parlor game players, who were actually willing to pay money for them, partly because, like a lot of fantasy game players, they soon started having difficulty distinguishing their fantasy game from reality.

Those "land titles" were also traded back and forth, kind of like baseball cards.

Whenever a new land company was formed, everybody wanted to make sure they got some of its "land titles," because, in that fantasy world, they were sort of like a baseball card for a rookie baseball player, and nobody knows when some rookie baseball player might turn out to be a Babe Ruth.

All of that buying and selling and that trading back and forth of those "land titles" was done on the fantasy speculation that one day they might be worth something, which is why they called that parlor game Land Speculation.

The problem created by that Land Speculation parlor game stemmed from there not being any laws in those days to protect the mentally handicapped.

It wasn't long before some mentally handicapped NAG hayseeds, and a few mentally handicapped NAG immigrants stumbling off the boats from Europe—none of whom, due to their mental handicaps, understood that Land Speculation was just a parlor game—started buying some of those funny money land-title pieces of paper and then started going west across the Appalachian Mountains to try to find their "farms," where they found themselves surrounded by a horde of Indian nations, who were not amused at being expected to provide a mental asylum for mentally handicapped NAG hayseeds.

Once the colonial NAG parlor game players discovered that they could get more money for those funny money land-title pieces of paper from mentally handicapped people than from anyone else, they started searching for mentally handicapped North American Germans, and they found a whole bunch of them.

It wasn't long before the Indians in the Ohio River Valley began wondering just how many mentally handicapped NAG hayseeds there might be.

Meanwhile, the last thing that King George III of the BIGs wanted to do was have to fight the next North American colonial war with most of the Indians lined up against the BIGs again.

The king understood perfectly well that it was that Land Speculation parlor game that was causing the problems, and so, in that Royal Proclamation of 1763, the king announced a definitive policy of respect for the rights of the Indian nations, taking great care to write those new laws in language that was plain enough and clear enough that even mentally handicapped hayseed colonial NAGs would understand that if they continued playing that Land Speculation game they would become international criminals.

Those laws, in that Royal Proclamation of 1763, set aside the land west of the Appalachian Mountains for the Indians.

Those laws prohibited the colonial NAGs from speculating in Indian land west of those mountains.

Those laws prohibited individual colonial NAGs from attempting to buy any land west of the mountains from any Indian and declared that no one but the BIG king had the right to buy Indian land.

Those laws prohibited colonial NAGs from trespassing on Indian land west of the Appalachian mountains and ordered the BIG army to engage in the removal of all of the mentally handicapped colonial NAGs who had already gone to the western side of the mountains.

Those laws, as every American schoolchild knows, had a lot of other provisions, all prohibiting or regulating colonial NAG activity west of the Appalachian Mountains, such as requiring colonial NAG traders to apply for a license from the BIG king before even those traveling merchants would be allowed to go anywhere west of the mountains.

The BIG king had solemn treaties with those Indian nations, which he intended to honor.

It was a pivotal moment in German history.

Recent generations of North American Germans, outraged at contemplating what they lost in that pivotal moment, have focused great anger on their most severely mentally handicapped colonial NAGs who became international criminals by violating the laws of that Royal Proclamation of 1763, particularly Daniel Boone, who became perhaps the most famous one to exhibit criminal behavior (overt acts) that would become an unsolvable enduring problem—what to do about mentally handicapped North American Germans who refuse to be restrained by the rule of law, whether that law might be embodied in a royal proclamation, or in the Constitution of the United States, or in a treaty, or even in a decision of the U.S. Supreme Court.

It should be noted at this point that it is transparently unfair that Americans should single out Daniel Boone as the one mentally handicapped American to be the special object of their venom.

He was only one among many.

Indian people have at least some respect for the memory of that poor man's mental handicap, but not Americans.

Americans will not let him rest in peace, and they can be unbelievably cruel.

The depth of American revulsion with Daniel Boone hit its lowest point at a time when television captured the attention of nearly everyone and when, each week, in front of millions of viewers, the memory of his life was parodied so viciously, in a horse-opera TV series so pathetic, that no viewer could watch for more than a few minutes without throwing up.

The anger focused on Daniel Boone by American popular culture, however, has been nothing compared to the anger focused on most of the other colonial NAG leaders by American historians.

Those American historians anguish endlessly in explaining that there was apparently an incredibly large percentage of mentally handicapped people in that colonial NAG population, and they refused to abide by the laws embodied in that Royal Proclamation of 1763, which became the direct cause of the First North Atlantic German Civil War, otherwise known as the American Revolution of 1775–83.

In despair, those American historians lament that colonial NAG leaders such as Patrick Henry, Sam Adams, George Washington, and virtually all of the other famous colonial NAGs of that era could not resist the temptation of trying to get rich by continuing to sell those Land Speculation "land titles" to the large number of mentally handicapped NAGs.

Mournfully, the American history books recount how virtually every one of the colonial NAG revolutionary rabble rousers eventually did get rich from Land Speculation and that in order to continue doing that they had to foment a rebellion to break away from the rule of law of civilized people.

Those American historians gnash their teeth as they ponder the unfortunate train of events that unfolded; how the BIG king unwittingly played right into the hands of the criminally minded element among the colonial NAGs; how the BIG king, seeing that the laws were being blatantly violated, responded by ordering that BIG forts be built all along the Appalachian Mountains, garrisoned with BIG soldiers, to try to hold back the bafflingly large number of mentally handicapped hayseeds in that colonial NAG population and uphold the rule of law of civilized people.

Again and again those American historians study the critical juncture in the drama, when the BIG king decided that it should be those colonial NAGs themselves who should bear the cost of paying for all of those forts, and for providing all of that additional, expensive policing to restrain their own international criminals—in the form of new taxes.

In vain, American historians search for some other connection between that taxation and the battle cry of the criminal element among the colonial NAGs: "No taxation without representation!"

Being historians, they cannot avoid seeing that the NAG criminal rabble rousers were presenting to the world what might appear to be a justifiable complaint, so long as no one inquired into the background details.

But, being historians, they do make those inquiries. And they can give their fellow North American Germans no consoling words to relieve their anguish over how their race failed to recognize an opportunity that they had worn out generations of church pews praying might come their way.

Instead of seizing that opportunity to *try* to learn how to become civilized people (perhaps by building enough mental asylums to hold all of their mentally handicapped people, which might have solved the problem), the colonial NAGs fomented a successful rebellion that turned loose a whole new renegade criminal nation to prey upon the Native peoples of the North American continent, whose civilizations were plunged into their Dark Ages, as they became overwhelmed by successive waves of North American German barbarians, with the leading edge of that—people who would become known as "settlers"—consisting largely of mentally handicapped hayseeds who could not be restrained by anyone or anything.

All of that has left contemporary Americans inconsolably confirmed in their opinion of the depth of their wretchedness.

And they look ever more eagerly to escaping that wretchedness in their afterlife.

And they damn Daniel Boone.

If that had been all there was to the First North Atlantic German Civil War, the entire episode would be mostly remembered today for how a bunch of mentally handicapped people caused a renegade criminal nation to be turned loose on the North American continent.

But it is here that those criminally minded NAGs have confounded the entire world and have diverted attention from what they were doing, and why they were doing it, because that's not the entire story of what they did during their rebellion.

For about two and a half decades after 1763, to the astonishment of the world, those NAGs engaged in one of the most elegant bursts of creative political imagination in the history of the human species.

That burst of genius would bring impressive contributions from literally dozens of NAGs, consuming an entire generation with feverish political invention to such an extent that it would have no equal in Western Civilization short of classical Greece, if even then.

The power of guilt is a truly amazing thing.

That creative burst had to spring from the NAGs not wanting to admit, even to themselves, that what they really wanted to do was go steal Indian land.

Undoubtedly, it was the pronounced German tendency to view themselves as wretched creatures incapable of resisting what they call sin, coupled with the soul-searching seriousness with which they wrestle with those concerns, that caused them not to be able to admit to themselves, or to anyone else, what they really wanted to do.

It had to have been a subconscious burden of guilt that spurred them to try to prove to themselves, more so than to anyone else, that they were being motivated by lofty ideals, for the benefit of all mankind.

No other explanation makes any sense.

There does not appear to be anything else that will bring all of the parts of the puzzle together.

Anyone who has studied that era knows that there is little in the way of cynicism or deception or deceit anywhere among them in the feverish and prolonged creation of those ideologies.

The result was a mass act of self-delusion, a generation of colonial NAGs that was utterly successful in convincing itself of the loftiness of its goals.

So great was that guilt, and their passionate need to deny it, that the colonial NAGs eagerly fed off of one another's ideas, attempting to outdo each other, sparking a generational burst of genius that lasted all the way through an intensive intellectual period of frenzied experimentation with political ideas in which they wrote and rewrote state constitutions for those thirteen NAG colonies, both during and after that revolutionary war itself, which finally reached its crescendo, the embodiment of all of that intellectual and practical experimentation, in 1787, in the writing of the Constitution of the United States.

That could have been a good thing for Indians, if the supremacy clause of that constitution, which declares that treaties are among the only three things that are the supreme law of the land in the United States, had turned out to be, like their treaties, something more than just a lot of hot air.

Article VI of the U.S. Constitution stipulates, in plain Anglish:

This Constitution, and the Laws of the United States which shall be made in Pursuance thereof; and all Treaties made, or which shall be

made, under the Authority of the United States, shall be the
supreme law of the land; and the Judges in every State shall be
bound thereby, any Thing in the Constitution or Laws of any State
to the Contrary notwithstanding.

That clause of the United States Constitution has a peculiar ticky-tocky
sound to it, a familiar sound to the Lords of the North American Continent.

It didn't have to be that way.

It didn't start out that way.

Things didn't really start going bad for the integrity of the U.S.
Constitution until Indian military power no longer mattered, after the War
of 1812.

In 1790, when George Washington, as the precedent-setting first U.S.
president to hold office under that new U.S. Constitution (which stripped the
several states of the power to deal with Indian nations and vested that power
exclusively in the national government), had to set the precedents for how
Indian treaties would be dealt with by the United States, he decided that an
Indian treaty should be dealt with in the same manner as any other treaty
with any other country.

With that first constitutionally processed Indian treaty, "Treaty With The
Creek, 1790," and then with every one of the subsequent 370 or so U.S. treaties
with Indian nations that would be ratified by the United States, extending to
the last treaties which were negotiated, in 1868, and ratified shortly thereafter,
the U.S. government followed the exact same process that it followed for any
treaty with any country, the constitutionally mandated process of initiation,
control, and completion of the negotiation of the treaty by the executive
branch, followed by the submission of the treaty to the U.S. Senate for its constitutionally mandated "Advice and Consent," followed by the publishing and
formal proclamation of the treaty by the president of the United States.

That long history was suddenly, and blatantly unconstitutionally,
brought to an end in 1871, when the U.S. Congress, usurping the constitutionally explicit delegation of the treaty making power to the executive branch of
the U.S. government, declared that the United States would no longer enter
into treaties with Indian nations.

That act of Congress in 1871 was couched in these words:

Provided, That hereafter no Indian nation or tribe within the territory of the United States shall be acknowledged or recognized as an
independent nation, tribe or power with whom the United States
may contract by treaty; *Provided further*, That nothing herein contained shall be construed to invalidate or impair the obligation of
any treaty heretofore lawfully made and ratified with any such
Indian nation or tribe. (Title 25, United States Code, Section 71)

The executive branch of the U.S. government, whose powers were being
usurped by that unconstitutional action of the legislative branch, did not contest that unconstitutional usurpation of its powers regarding that fundamental U.S. constitutional separation of powers issue, because the executive
branch of the U.S. government was in cahoots with the legislative branch
regarding that matter, and so was the judicial branch of the U.S. government.

The United States Constitution does not work.

Its last hope for integrity was lost in the early twentieth century, and the
thing that broke its back was the greed to get what little was left, by then, of
Indian land.

The deathblow to the integrity of the U.S. Constitution came in 1903, in
the U.S. Supreme Court decision of *Lone Wolf v. Hitchcock*.

In that *Lone Wolf* case, the Kiowa Nation tried to stop the illegal allotment of its land, in that ancient Choctaw southern Great Plains imperial
province.

The United States government was allotting that Kiowa land so that the
"surplus" Indian land could be sold to white "settlers," under legislation
enacted by the U.S. Congress, in blatant violation of the specific provisions of
the Kiowa treaty with the United States known as the Medicine Lodge Creek
Treaty of October 21, 1867, blatant violations of that treaty that the U.S. government admitted in court that it was committing.

That Kiowa man, Lone Wolf, in whose name that suit was brought, was
also known as "Mamaday." His grandson, N. Scott Momaday, would graduate from the University of New Mexico and would win the Wallace Stegner
Fellowship for graduate studies in creative writing at Stanford University,
the same graduate studies fellowship at Stanford that was won by students
who became such prominent novelists as Ken Kesey, who would write such

works as *One Flew Over the Cuckoo's Nest*, which would become a major motion picture, and Larry McMurtry, who would win the Pulitzer Prize for literature for *Lonesome Dove*, which would become a major motion picture as a TV miniseries.

In the late 1960s, N. Scott Momaday, by then Dr. Momaday, by then teaching at Stanford himself, would win the Pulitzer Prize for literature for his novel *House Made of Dawn*, an event that would finally force Anglish departments in American universities to begin teaching courses in Native American literature, finally wresting it away from anthropology departments, where it had been ignored for generations as "folklore."

In *Lone Wolf v. Hitchcock*, the Supreme Court of the United States declares that the U.S. Congress has full (plenary) power over Indian nations, that the U.S. Congress can unilaterally violate any clause of any Indian treaty whenever it might choose to do so, entirely on its own, that the U.S. Congress can legislate all Indian affairs on its own, without making treaties with Indian nations, without any consultation with Indian nations, without any consent from Indian nations, and that the courts of the United States are powerless to intervene, that the courts of the United States must assume, without having the power to make any inquiry into the matter, that the Congress is acting in good faith, because, according to that 1903 Supreme Court of the United States, dealing with Indian nations is a "political matter."

That has remained the law of the land in the United States to this day.

The reason why those broke dicks on the Supreme Court of the United States turned tail and ran, and ran as fast and as far as they could run, in that 1903 *Lone Wolf* case, was because of what happened to the U.S. Supreme Court in 1832.

In 1832, in the famous case of *Worcester v. Georgia*, the U.S. Supreme Court, then presided over by Chief Justice John Marshall, declares that the state of Georgia (or, by extension, any state) cannot extend its state laws over the Cherokee Nation (or, by extension, any Indian nation).

That 1832 U.S. Supreme Court ruling has the power to reverse the removal of the Indian nations and restore their ancient homelands to them.

In the 1830s, the threat of subjection to state law was the leverage that forced the so-called Five Civilized Tribes to confront the awful specter of submitting to their removal, or resisting by force of arms. Only the Seminoles, in Florida, resisted by force of arms—successfully, it might be noted.

The renegade criminal element that had seized control of the U.S. government in 1828 knew that it was perpetrating a fraud upon the Indian nations, a fraud of pretending to be powerless to stop the states from extending their laws over the Indian nations.

There can be no question that it was that fraud that forced the illegal removal of the Choctaws. In the "Preamble" of the Choctaw removal treaty of 1830, that fraud is couched in plain Anglish:

> Whereas, the General Assembly of the State of Mississippi has extended the laws of said State to persons and property within the chartered limits of the same, and the President of the United States has said that he cannot protect the Choctaw people from the operation of these laws; Now therefore that the Choctaw may live under their own laws in peace with the United States and the State of Mississippi they have determined to sell their land east of the Mississippi and have accordingly agreed to the following articles of treaty.... (Charles J. Kappler, Preamble, "Treaty With The Choctaw, 1830," in *Indian Affairs: Laws and Treaties*, vol. 2, *Treaties* [Government Printing Office, 1904], 310–11)

In its decision in the *Worcester* case, the U.S. Supreme Court has moved decisively to put an end to that fraud, which has the power to restore those ancient Choctaw homelands to the Choctaws.

But, to the shock of the U.S. Supreme Court, the U.S. government simply ignored that U.S. Supreme Court ruling and has been ignoring it ever since, as though it does not exist.

As a result of that *Worcester* case, the U.S. Supreme Court has discovered, to its horror, that it has no way of enforcing its decisions.

It has no army.

It has nothing but the papers it hands down, the papers that its decisions are written on.

The U.S. Supreme Court has no way to deal directly with criminals of any kind, particularly if those criminals have seized control of other branches of the government.

In 1832, the U.S. Supreme Court discovered that it is powerless to do anything, that it is totally dependent upon the federal and state governments to honor its decisions.

That 1832 case, in favor of the Cherokees, broke the back of the United States Supreme Court, and it broke the back of the United States Constitution.

There was nothing left to the U.S. Supreme Court after that but to hope that the passage of time might heal the severe blow it had sustained, and that, in time, it might regain at least some of its authority.

By 1903 that had happened, in large measure, until, for only the second time in its history, the U.S. Supreme Court was offered the opportunity to try to stop the imperialists among the Americans from taking Indian land illegally.

In 1903, the justices of that U.S. Supreme Court peed their pants when they remembered what happened to the Supreme Court in 1832, when the Court had actually tried to enforce the rule of law, when the Court had actually tried to stop the illegal taking of Indian land.

To try to reserve for the Supreme Court at least some role in the U.S. government, in matters not related to Indians, those 1903 Supreme Court justices abdicated their responsibilities under the United States Constitution, and they abdicated their power to the U.S. Congress, forever.

Supreme Court justices have been made aware that the Court cannot survive another staggering blow like the one it has been dealt by the chilling fact that its 1832 decision is still being blatantly and illegally ignored, as though it does not exist.

Those Supreme Court justices in 1903 were also in cahoots with the aims of the Congress regarding Indians.

Those Supreme Court justices did not care what happened to Indians.

They did not value Indian civilization.

Perhaps most important of all, they knew that Indians were helpless to resist, in that century.

Ever since 1903, the Supreme Court of the United States has had nothing whatsoever to do with dispensing any kind of justice for Indians.

The Supreme Court maintains an appearance of ruling on things regarding Indians, an appearance that evaporates when one realizes that the Court rules on nothing except what its masters in the U.S. Congress legislate regarding Indians, or on treaties or clauses of treaties that the Court's masters in the U.S. Congress have not abrogated.

When the U.S. Supreme Court declared, in 1903, that Indian affairs are a "political matter," for which the U.S. Congress has full power, the Supreme Court turned tail and ran, forever, from the central, most critical problem that the United States ever has faced, or ever will face.

And there is virtually no chance of any United States Supreme Court ever mounting the courage to attempt to do anything otherwise.

They are the biggest cowards on the face of the earth.

The United States Constitution no longer has any checks and balances.

Indians, for more than a century, have been at the complete mercy of the U.S. Congress, which is driven by public opinion, which means that public opinion regarding Indians has been translated directly into U.S. law regarding Indians.

The U.S. Constitution had checks and balances, at one time, until America chose to flush them down the toilet. America did that, for more than any other reason, so that it could employ unilateral congressional legislation to bulldoze the "allotment" of Indian land in "Indian Territory" and create the illegal state of Oklahoma, over the vigorous, outraged protests of the Indian people, in violation of their treaties, Indian people who were helpless to resist, in that century.

America did that, just for that little bit of Indian land that was left, just to be able to accommodate the demands of a few more of the wretched masses of Europeans, peoples who could not stand their own culture and history any longer, to a degree that they had been seduced by that torch-bearing Beckoning Bitch that rises up out of the sea in New York harbor, that gift of the French people, that statue that was screaming at the top of her lungs all the way across the ocean, "Come steal Indian land! It's free! There's a little bit of it left, if you hurry!"

Just to get that little bit of Indian land that still belonged to Indian nations, America flushed the integrity of the Constitution of the United States down the toilet.

Perhaps even worse for the mental health of the ancient Choctaw people, the Americans methodically, and with breathtaking suddenness, exterminated virtually every one of the tens of millions of buffaloes in that phenomenal southern Great Plains thousands-of-years-old Choctaw buffalo herd, a thing perhaps about as old as the Choctaw mental conception of themselves, delivering a disorienting blow to those continentally oriented, imperial Choctaw minds, creating a confusion of wondering what there could possibly be anymore that was spectacularly worthy enough for Choctaws to even want to try to make an imperial comeback for.

With the U.S. Constitution in shreds, with the Choctaw Nation in shreds, with the Choctaw buffalo herd in shreds, with no big-time Choctaw imperial comeback in anything but shreds, the late nineteenth century and early twentieth century, coming only about a half-century after that 1820 big-time Choctaw imperial comeback had seemed like such a gloriously good piggy-backed sure thing, and only about a century after the birth of the U.S. Constitution, turned into one of the most gloomy periods in Choctaw history.

Surely no one, at the birth of that U.S. Constitution, could have foreseen what the next century would hold.

That constitution had been born with so much promise.

The people of the world, Indian people in particular, have never known quite what to think about the combination of extraordinary NAG achievement, self-delusion, good intentions, and unfulfilled promise in that extraordinary document.

It's not possible to study that period from 1763 to 1787 without developing a profound respect for its American creative genius, and a profound sadness for its failed promise, to say nothing of the apparent near certainty, in order to account for the large percentage of mentally handicapped people in that colonial NAG population, that a lot of the hayseed sex in those days *had* to be happening on the sly between brothers and sisters.

And surely it's not possible to look at that U.S. Constitution birthing era, at least with the degree of detachment that Indian people can muster, without being able to see that the Royal Proclamation of 1763 was the unglamorous root cause of the phenomenal North American German intellectual achievements that era produced.

That era has left the world both deeply suspicious and decidedly in awe of the North American Germans.

Nobody can afford to be anything but a little unsure of what they might be capable of, both good and bad, and there will undoubtedly be a few melancholy, ambivalent, deep sighs when we wave good-bye to their last rocket leaving earth.

Chapter Nine

Ticky-Tocky Talk

*I*n 1975, it should be noted, when it announced its findings regarding Indian self-determination, the U.S. Congress informed the world that Indian people will never surrender their desire to control their relationships among themselves.

The continuing tyranny of Choctaws and other Indian nations being subjected to the laws of the illegal state of Oklahoma, which deny Indian people their fundamental right to control their relationships among themselves, is one of the primary reasons that will make the burying of the illegal state of Oklahoma necessary.

Few Americans have much comprehension that state governments have been imposing a tyranny upon Indians in that regard.

Many Americans seem to think that it is American wealth that is at risk in Indian demands for Indian sovereignty.

Few Indians have much interest in accumulating or hoarding wealth. The fundamental liberty of Indian people being able to maintain the nature of their relationships among themselves matters much more to them.

The nature of Indian relationships among themselves, and the reasons why Indians have developed some of those relationships, have always been bewildering things for Americans, who have been blind to such things as the superiority of Choctaw family life, compared to American family life, especially in the way Choctaws have protected their women from their husbands and their children from their parents.

Choctaws figured out how to do that, which is by having a husband become a member of the wife's extended family, so that the wife is surrounded by her male relatives, making spousal abuse much less likely to occur, and by having the legal authority for a child rest with the oldest maternal uncle, not because parents don't love their children but because they love them too much, are too emotionally close to them to be able to see what is best for each child.

Americans put their women and children at potentially grave risk, at the mercy of a father-patriarch, without built-in family and community safeguards, and they have insisted, as a matter of state law, as a matter of state tyranny, that all of the Indian people must be forced to become like them.

Americans haven't been able to imagine why everyone wouldn't want to be like them.

Nowhere has the depth of difference between Choctaws and Americans been more profound than regarding the role of women in the two civilizations.

Choctaws are matrilineal, meaning that descent is traced through the female line rather than through the male line, the latter being the Biblical-Hebrew patrilineal system of the colonizers.

There was nothing sacred about the ancient Hebrew way of doing anything, except to the ancient Hebrews.

If some of the Americans want to adopt any of those foreign, Old World Middle Eastern things for themselves, that's their business, but they have no right to impose any of it upon the Choctaws, which they attempt to do as a matter of tyranny, as a matter of state law.

Choctaws are a people as ancient and as distinguished as the ancient, distinguished Hebrews.

American civilization has been a long time approaching anything even remotely similar to the equality of Choctaw women in Choctaw civilization.

The fact that Americans are now finally approaching the Choctaw achievement in that regard is one hopeful indication that the American nation might finally be maturing enough to begin taking responsibility for its actions.

Throughout much of American civilization, an American wife was the legal chattel of her husband.

She could be beaten or raped by her husband without her having any legal recourse.

She suffered severe restrictions on her ability to own property, and she could not vote.

In the 1870s, she became a criminal, subject to felony prosecution by extremely dangerous American men, such as Anthony Comstock, who ruthlessly hunted any American woman down and prosecuted her unmercifully, if she had sought to use any form of contraception or attempted to disseminate any information about birth control to other women, and who boasted for decades about the many American women whose lives he had ruined in this way.

Nineteenth-century American women were not able to imagine why Choctaw women wouldn't want to be like them.

They still cannot imagine why Choctaw women do not want to be like them.

Nineteenth-century Choctaw women are known to have held one specific, extraordinary power over Choctaw men that was deeply profound, a power that was so enlightened and civilized that few women anywhere in the world have ever dreamt of exercising anything like it, on a regular basis, over their men.

Choctaw women had the power of completely disarming Choctaw men when Choctaw women thought it prudent to do so, under appropriate circumstances.

And while the circumstances giving rise to that power were fairly narrowly defined, it was not a power in name only but a power that Choctaw women exercised with some regularity, as the circumstances giving rise to it occurred with some regularity.

What other civilization has ever handed that kind of power to women?

Stripped of weapons, men are virtually helpless to engage in much of any kind of conflict, except, perhaps, wrestling, a thing not likely to result in much harm.

It was a power of such an elevated level of civilization that if women today in all of the nations of the world could have that power there might never again be any such thing as war.

Yet, hardly any so-called scholars ever mention that phenomenal aspect of Choctaw civilization, even though it was a power that Choctaw women exercised on such a regular basis that there are hardly any Choctaw men known to history who avoided being completely disarmed by Choctaw women, not just once, but many times.

The procedure for doing that was perhaps best described, and perhaps best explained, by John Watkins, an eyewitness to it in the early nineteenth century, who left a written account of it. Watkins described it in this manner:

> In the winter of 1824–5, there was a large encampment of Choctaws on the lands of David Hunt, in Jefferson county, near my residence. As usual, the women were engaged in picking cotton; the men had just returned from a successful hunting expedition. They had sold their deer and bear skins, jerked venison and bears' oil, bought blankets, powder, lead and other articles of prime necessity, including an abundant supply of fire water (*ishko homi*), and as a sequence all of them, except one, got beastly drunk. It was a custom among them that one of their number should keep sober, to take care of those who were incapable of taking care of themselves, hence the adage, "one sober Indian," which at that day was in use among white men in like condition. There was another preliminary that was never departed from. The women, before the wassail begun, took from them their guns, knives and tomahawks, so if an affray should happen, they would be in no condition to inflict injury on each other. (John A. Watkins, "The Choctaws in Mississippi," in *A Choctaw Source Book*, ed. John H. Peterson Jr. [Garland, 1985], 72)

Americans have also attempted to take credit for things they have no right to credit themselves for.

Mostly out of ignorance, Americans have deluded themselves into thinking that they have brought the blessings of freedom of speech and freedom of assembly to North America.

The Choctaw achievement regarding freedom of speech and freedom of assembly ranks with the achievement of any people of any time or in any place in the history of the world.

Picture a hot summer day in Mississippi, where a large, round, brush arbor has been constructed, one with a big hole in the center of the roof.

Tiers of benches in the shade along the walls, like stadium seats, are filled with hundreds of Choctaws, all around the interior of the structure. In the center stands the person who is speaking at the moment.

Anyone may address the assembly, as long as they stand beneath that hole in the center of the roof, in the blistering heat of the Mississippi summer sun.

Choctaws in the 1820s told Dr. Gideon Lincecum that they could bear to remain comfortably seated in the shade and listen, for as long as the person speaking cared to stand in the sun and speak.

One might ponder what that has to say, not just regarding freedom of speech and freedom of assembly but also about cultivating the virtues of brevity and conciseness.

Where, among the Americans, is anything even approaching the majesty of the Choctaw achievement regarding freedom of speech?

The New England town meeting seems to be about the closest that the Americans have come to it.

Most Choctaws, both men and women, both historically and contemporarily, have lived their lives without any particular interest in the activities or objectives of institutions of any kind.

This remarkable feature of Choctaw civilization, which is shared to some degree by many other Indian nations, has led some perceptive scholars, in attempting to comprehend Choctaws, to conclude that the Choctaws are a people who don't believe they exist for the benefit of any political, religious, or economic organization, including so-called "Choctaw governments."

Choctaw sovereignty resides, has always resided, and shall always remain in its Choctaw communities.

Choctaws tried the ill-fitting, foreign, American-model "governmental" experience in the last half of the nineteenth century.

Choctaws tried very hard to adjust to it. It was an experiment that Choctaws participated in with great gusto.

That turned out to be somewhat of a process that revealed how eminently susceptible to the temptation of bribery Choctaws can be.

Angie Debo, the seminally important American historian of the 1866–1907 Choctaw American-model governmental era (which was the focus of her original research for her doctoral dissertation in history in 1934 at the University of Oklahoma) had no difficulty calling bribery by its name, though she might have been unaware that it is a tricky topic when dealing with Indians, because Indian leaders are so often redistributors of wealth to their people.

That great historian (and gentle, frail white woman), Angie Debo, author of so many significant works of scholarship regarding Indians, and a severe critic of American imperialists, whom she was wont to call what they are, "imperialists," could never gain admittance to the American-imperialist dominated, male university history faculties, and could obtain no higher station in American academe than the position of "maps librarian" at Oklahoma State University.

There is one critically important area in which Europeans and Americans have *thought* that their achievements were well ahead of the Choctaws, which has, in time, turned out not to be the case.

Americans have taken great pride in their economic system and its related technologies. Americans have been blind to the fact that Choctaws attained the highest level of economic sophistication that is possible to attain on earth, that of being biodegradable, endlessly renewable, and adequate for their needs.

Americans, however, have now learned chilling, planet-threatening lessons that would tell them, if they might be capable of paying attention, how profoundly more sophisticated Choctaws were than the foreign imperialists who arrived on the North American continent five centuries ago.

Eighteenth-century Europeans can perhaps be forgiven for having been blind to the Choctaw achievement in economics. At that time, Europeans were not sophisticated enough to realize where their technology was leading them.

In the mid-to-late twentieth century, however, after that Euro-Anglo technology had been coupled with unchecked mass consumerism, many Americans finally became disillusioned with their "theory of progress," as they began choking on their industrial and chemical filth, and began trying to figure out how they might survive their acid rain, the unchecked proliferation of the deadly poison of their nuclear waste, and all else that their unchecked and little-regulated "progress" had wrought.

Some of them began figuring out that they live their lives in a frantic kind of debt peonage, desperately trying to pay for things that they do not need and which the earth will not be able to afford much longer.

In time, perhaps, Choctaws might be capable of recreating their economic achievement.

In time, perhaps, the demonstration of how the Choctaw people and other Indian nations might be able to do that might become important to the long-range health of the earth.

In time, perhaps, even the imperialists among the Americans might be capable of seeing that it is not in their best interests to meddle with Choctaw economic philosophies, Choctaw land use, Choctaw family structures, Choctaw law, Choctaw land, or anything else that is Choctaw, except Choctaw trade, which is the only right that Americans have acquired, which they acquired by arm's-length treaty negotiation, not by their own unilateral legislation, which has been nothing but the duress of forcing people to do things that they were helpless to resist, and then attempting to give that an appearance of legality.

On January 3, 1786, in the first Choctaw treaty with the Americans, at Hopewell in South Carolina, the sovereign American people and the sovereign Choctaw people freely and voluntarily entered into a treaty relationship that is known in international law as a protectorate.

A protectorate relationship is one of the best-known and least controversial arrangements between nations in the field of international law.

In gaining that protectorate relationship, the Choctaw Nation voluntarily surrendered to the United States the right to regulate Choctaw trade, which is the most common thing that a smaller nation typically surrenders to a larger nation in gaining the obligation of protection by that stronger nation.

Choctaw trade is the only thing that Americans have ever had any right to regulate for the Choctaws, which was acquired in arm's-length treaty negotiations between those two sovereign nations.

No small nation surrenders its sovereignty by entering into a protectorate relationship with a stronger nation.

If that were not true, strong nations would not be able to entice smaller nations into entering into protectorate relationships with them, which large nations earnestly desire to do in their competitions with other large nations.

Much propaganda damage against Indians regarding Indian treaties has been done, perhaps unintentionally, certainly ignorantly, by historians who have not been trained in the law and who have had no awareness of rules of law, called canons of construction, that U.S. courts must follow in interpreting Indian treaties.

The canons of construction for interpreting Indian treaties, which the U.S. Supreme Court began handing down nearly two hundred years ago, are necessary because the written version of an Indian treaty was committed to paper in a foreign language (Anglish), and the written version of a treaty cannot prevail over what the Indians had been told orally that they would be agreeing to by signing the treaty.

Some historians have quoted Article VIII of "Treaty With The Choctaw, 1786" and have asserted, out of ignorance of Indian treaty law, that the Choctaws surrendered their sovereignty to the United States by virtue of that article of that treaty.

Any knowledge at all of Choctaw history and U.S. history at that time should have been enough to tell those historians differently, but some American historians haven't been particularly interested in applying to American history what they know about the realities of Indian history before the War of 1812.

When that lack of interest has been combined with ignorance of Indian treaty law, the result has been enough to satisfy powerful segments of the American nation, who haven't thought it to be in their best interests for the American public to know very much about Indian treaty law.

Article VIII of that 1786 Choctaw-U.S. treaty states:

For the benefit and comfort of the Indians, and for the prevention of injuries or oppressions on the part of the citizens or Indians, the United States in Congress assembled, shall have the sole and exclusive right of regulating the trade with the Indians, and managing all their affairs in such manner as they think proper.

It's the last portion of that article, "and managing all their affairs in such manner as they think proper," that has been propagandized in the attempt to say that the language of that portion of that article applies to anything other than Choctaw trade.

The bulk of the archival records for that negotiation process of that 1786 treaty at Hopewell, records that reveal what the Choctaws were told orally that they were agreeing to, can be found in the Draper Manuscripts, 14 U 56-92, and in the American State Papers.

If some competent, conscientious historians who have been trained in the law and trained in Indian treaty history might want to roll up their sleeves and delve into those archival materials and attempt to make a case that the Choctaws surrendered their sovereignty in that Article VIII of that 1786 treaty, have at it. Lots of luck. It'll be news to the U.S. Supreme Court.

The canons of construction for interpreting Indian treaties have been summarized in many U.S. court decisions. Many different U.S. court decisions could be quoted to convey an idea of what those canons are and how they have been applied to Indian treaties.

In 1983, Judge Pell of the U.S. Court of Appeals for the Seventh Circuit gave a succinct summary of those canons of construction in the case of *Lac Courte Oreilles Band of Lake Superior Chippewa Indians v. Wisconsin*, more commonly now known as the *Voigt* decision, or the Chippewa spearfishing decision, which upheld Chippewa off-reservation fishing rights dating from their treaties of 1837 and 1842 (treaties the U.S. Congress had not abrogated).

In that federal appellate court decision, Judge Pell says, "First, the Supreme Court has held that Indian treaties must be construed as the Indians understood them."

Judge Pell then quotes Chief Justice John Marshall's first enunciation of those canons of construction, in the famous 1832 U.S. Supreme Court case of *Worcester v. Georgia*, in which Chief Justice Marshall declares:

> The language used in treaties with the Indians should never be
> construed to their prejudice. If words can be made use of, which
> are susceptible of a more extended meaning than their plain
> import, as connected with the tenor of the treaty, they should be
> considered as used only in the latter sense.... How the words of the
> treaty were understood by this unlettered people, rather than their
> critical meaning, should form the rule of construction.

In that 1983 federal appellate court *Voigt* decision, Judge Pell then declares:

In *Jones v. Meehan*, 175 U.S. 1, 11 (1899), the Court stated that a "treaty must therefore be construed, not according to the technical meaning of its words to learned lawyers, but in the sense in which they would naturally be understood by the Indians." The Supreme Court has applied this canon of construction because the Indians and the Government were not bargaining from positions of equal strength, *Choctaw Nation v. United States*, 119 U.S. 1, 28 (1886); the Indians' comprehension of treaty terms depended on interpreters employed by the Government, *id.*; and, finally, because the Indians were unfamiliar with the legal manner of expression, *id.* For all these reasons, Indian treaties must be construed as the Indians understood them.

A second—and related—rule of construction is that ambiguous words and phrases in Indian treaties have been resolved in favor of the Indians. *Arizona v. California*, 373 U.S. 546, 599–601 (1963); *Alaska Pacific Fisheries v. United States*, 248 U.S. 78, 89 (1918); *Winters v. United States*, 207 U.S. 564, 576–77 (1908). This rule is particularly applicable if the language of a treaty supports two inferences, one favoring the Indians and one the Government....

A summary listing of the four primary U.S. canons of construction for interpreting Indian treaties that have been enunciated by U.S. courts thus far can be found in Professor Ronald Satz's excellent study of that *Voigt* decision, which is a study of its historical background and the vicious white backlash in northern Wisconsin in the 1980s that had to be dealt with firmly by the federal courts, entitled *Chippewa Treaty Rights: The Reserved Rights of Wisconsin's Chippewa Indians in Historical Perspective* (Madison: Wisconsin Academy of Sciences, Arts and Letters, 1991).

The Supreme Court of Canada has thus far enunciated nine canons of construction for interpreting Canadian treaties with Indian nations, which are enumerated and summarized by Justice McLachlin of the Supreme Court of Canada in *R. v. Marshall* (reconsideration) (1999) 3 S.C.R 533.

The Canadian canons of construction of Indian treaties are very similar to the U.S. canons, upon which they have been based. Canada, founded in 1867 by the British North America Act, did not begin entering into treaties with Indian nations until 1871, the same year the United States stopped making treaties with Indian nations, though Canada inherited the obligations of all of the previous British treaties with Indian nations.

The Canadian government today has been vigorously entering into modern treaties with Indian nations, as a part of its so-called comprehensive land claims settlement activities, all spurred by the famous 1973 landmark Canadian Supreme Court decision in the case of *Calder v. Attorney General of British Columbia*, S.C.R. 313, regarding the sovereign Nishga'a Nation of North American Native peoples, and by the more recent, equally big kick-in-the-butt to the government of Canada, and to the imperialistic interests of Canada, delivered by the famous 1997 case of *Delgamuukw v. British Columbia*, 3 S.C.R. 1010, regarding the Gitksan and the Wet'suwet'en sovereign nations of North American Native peoples.

The full text of all of the 370 or so ratified U.S. Indian treaties, including all of the fourteen ratified Choctaw-U.S. treaties (a facsimile reproduction of the 1904 U.S. government printing office publication of the treaties, edited by Charles J. Kappler) can now easily be found online on the Internet, thanks to a project of Oklahoma State University library, funded by a grant from the Coca-Cola Company of Atlanta, Georgia.

Kappler's compilation of U.S. government documents relating to Indian affairs is in five volumes. All of the Indian treaties are in volume 2. A Google search, with a keyword of "Kappler," will take you there.

The facsimile reproduction of those Indian treaties includes the transcription of the names of all of the individual Indians who signed them and also includes Kappler's helpful margin gloss of supplementary information about each treaty.

The easiest way to use that website for the treaties is via the index to volume 2, where the Choctaw treaties, for example, are found under "C."

Speaking of Google, enjoy your Internet access while it lasts. It won't last long.

Shutting down freedom of access to the "World Wide Web" has already begun. The Chinese have insisted on it being done for them, to limit the kinds of things that people in that part of the world can have Internet access to.

It'll happen in America too. The pretext for doing that seems likely to be the limiting of access to pornography, for the "protection" of children.

By the time those children are adults, control of the dissemination of knowledge will be back in the hands of the "right people," who will have extended their control to Internet access in America. The kind of Internet access we know today will be a thing of the past.

So, read the Indian treaties while you still can.

The only reason the protectorate relationship between the Choctaw people and the American people that was established by that first Choctaw-American treaty in 1786 at Hopewell is not in full force and effect today is because an unrestrained and lawless gang of American imperialists seized control of the American government in 1828, with the election of Andrew Jackson as president, and those American imperialists soon betrayed the Choctaw people, which was also a betrayal of the American people, who, like the Choctaws, must live with the consequences.

The imperialists among the Americans vigorously deny that they are bound by international law for anything having to do with the Indian nations of North America, which American imperialists have always regarded as being within the national boundaries of the United States.

But that American imperial claim is grounded upon the quicksand of the religious tyranny of Medieval European church law.

It is called the Discovery Doctrine.

Americans tell themselves that America is a country founded upon principles of religious liberty. That is a lie so big it staggers the imagination that anyone could tell it, let alone believe it themselves or convince others to believe it.

But the dangerous thing for Indians about Americans has been that Americans do believe it.

The truth, as every Indian nation has learned to its peril, is that America is a country founded upon principles of religious tyranny, a country founded upon the Discovery Doctrine.

American-imperialist propaganda has been particularly adept at helping Americans forget that the Discovery Doctrine is a doctrine of law, and that the Discovery Doctrine is the legal and philosophical foundation for the American claim to sovereignty over Indian land in North America.

The heart of the Discovery Doctrine is its claim that Indians are not capable of full ownership of their land because they are not monotheistic, proselytizing Christian nations.

That is the law of the land today in the United States. It is the reason why Indian nations, to this day, cannot challenge the American claim to sovereignty over their land in American courts of law.

The Discovery Doctrine is an embarrassment to contemporary Americans, and that is why the religious tyranny that is the heart and soul of the doctrine is rarely ever mentioned.

American schoolchildren are lied to by not having the full extent of the Discovery Doctrine explained to them.

The schoolchildren are taught that Columbus "discovered" America in 1492 and that a succession of other Europeans, including the British, then "discovered" and "claimed" other portions of the continent, without explaining what that means as a matter of American law, why American law proclaims that those "discoveries" confer sovereignty over those lands to Americans, as a matter of religious tyranny.

The Discovery Doctrine has its origins in two papal bulls, in 1452 and 1493, in which the pope declared war on all non-Christians in the new lands being discovered by the Portuguese in Africa (Papal Bull of 1452) and in the new lands being discovered by the Spanish in the so-called New World (Papal Bull of 1493).

The pope, who at that time was the supreme legal authority for all of Europe, declared, as a matter of law, that those new people being discovered could be killed or enslaved and that their lands could be confiscated, *because they were not Christians.*

European unity as well as the dominance of the Roman Catholic Church would soon be shattered by the wars of the Reformation, which would lay waste to vast portions of Europe, as both Protestants and Catholics exterminated every man, woman, and child in some European villages, depopulating entire valleys in some areas, until the Treaty of Westphalia finally ended the religious slaughter among those "civilized" people in 1648.

But one thing that all of the European nations, whether Protestant or Catholic, would remain in agreement about was the legal sanctity of the Discovery Doctrine, including the religious tyranny that is the foundation of the doctrine.

Some Americans, particularly Protestant Americans, might feel little connection with what some pope might have declared, or even with what the European nations might have believed during the so-called era of discovery.

One wonders, however, how much connection those Americans might feel with what the Supreme Court of the United States has declared.

The truly embarrassing thing for the American Myth is that the Indian nations of North America have been placed under the religious tyranny of the Discovery Doctrine by a Supreme Court decision in 1823 by Chief Justice John Marshall.

In that decision, in the case of *Johnson and Graham's Lessee v. M'Intosh*, Chief Justice John Marshall declares (note the present tense, "declares"—because of the legal doctrine of *stare decisis*, the rule of binding precedent attaches to Supreme Court decisions) that the Discovery Doctrine is the law of the land in the United States, that Indian nations are not legally capable of full ownership of their land because they are not Christian nations, which makes them "savages."

"Savages" is legal code talk that means "non-Christian." Though there are important cultural bias and racial bias aspects embedded in that legal code talk as well, the non-Christian aspect constitutes the overwhelming basis of the term "savages," as a matter of law, to this day, right now, in the twenty-first century, in the United States (and in Canada as well).

Very little of American (or Canadian) history regarding Indians can be comprehended without an understanding of the depth of the religious tyranny that has pervaded virtually every aspect of American history regarding Indians.

The religious tyranny of the Discovery Doctrine is the reason why American imperialists in the late nineteenth century openly practiced cultural genocide, particularly against Plains Indians, by, for example, forcibly kidnapping many of those children from many different Indian nations and concentrating them in cultural genocide prisons for Indian children, euphemistically called "Indian boarding schools," where those Indian children were systematically stripped of their religion, their culture, and their language, under color of law, under legislation passed by the United States Congress, under the legal authority of the religious tyranny of the Discovery Doctrine.

That has fueled a rage in many descendants of those children, a rage to do something about what those helpless Indian children could do nothing about.

If Americans think that those enraged Indians cannot or will not do something about that, Americans are fools.

It's a rage of hatred, a rage of hatred against the United States. Incredibly, American propaganda regarding Indians has been so successful in brainwashing Americans into believing that the Indian nations have been conquered, or "assimilated," that Americans appear completely unaware that there are people on this continent who hate the United States with a depth of bitterness that, in the twenty-first century, goes far beyond being dangerous.

By contrast with Plains Indians, the Choctaw Nation had been operating its own national public school system long before "Indian boarding schools" came along in the late nineteenth century.

However, it was in that atmosphere, the most virulent, most unchecked period of the imperialists among the Americans waging cultural genocide against Indians, in the late nineteenth and early twentieth centuries, when Choctaw treaties were brushed aside to make possible the creation of the illegal state of Oklahoma.

Understanding the repressive atmosphere of virulent cultural genocide against Indians at that time is critical to understanding how and why American imperialists attempted to extinguish the Choctaw Nation.

Read Oklahoma textbooks of about a century ago and count the number of times the legal code talk of "savages" appears. See what those textbooks were so proudly proclaiming that their new state was "helping" those "savages" become.

Indians know that America is not only a country founded upon principles of religious tyranny, but that much of American history regarding Indians has been a ruthless and brutal exercise in religious tyranny, backed by the police power of the state.

That religious tyranny has been waged against people who have been virtually helpless to resist, until now, until something came along that began opening up frightening possibilities that no one had ever imagined, that no one in the world had ever been able to imagine, something called the twenty-first century, during which the American people will likely need their endlessly patient, long-suffering Choctaw allies much more than any Americans could ever have imagined, if Americans ever wake up enough to accept that help.

Ignoring the religious tyranny aspects of America's deeply embedded, potentially fatal "Indian problem" will not make it go away.

That religious tyranny, in its many varied aspects, is the root cause of the rage in poisoned Indians.

Poisoned Indians are not going to go away until that religious tyranny has gone away. Poisoned Indians are only going to become progressively more dangerous.

Choctaws have no fear in confronting that problem. Choctaws know more about the multiplicity of complexities of that problem than anybody in the world. It is *the* problem of *this* continent in *this* new century.

It seems unlikely to me that Choctaws will allow that problem to go unresolved indefinitely.

In the twenty-first century, it's just too dangerous for everyone, for Choctaws as well as for everyone else, to wait until something happens before trying to do something about it.

Whether or not Americans ever even become aware of that might become irrelevant.

If Choctaws act, unilaterally, to resolve that problem, let the future historians say that somebody saw it coming.

Chapter Ten

A Ticky-Tocky Choctaw Chalk Talk

*C*hoctaws have no fear in confronting any problem that might need confronting.

In the Choctaw Scheme Of Things (or CSOTs, for short), righting the wrongs of the religious tyranny that has been imposed upon the other Indian nations is like as two peas in a pod to the daunting task that suddenly arose near the middle of the twentieth century, the task of confronting and defeating the machinations of those evil geniuses, Mortimer J. Adler and Robert Maynard Hutchins, who are known to all Choctaws, except nincompoops, as the "Dangerous Duo," who conspired to let loose the unthinkable idea on an innocent world, on December 23, 1939, that college football programs could be abolished.

It was after, so I heard, a half-century of deepening intrigue with the game of American college football had gotten the *alikchis* way beyond being committed to its health and welfare, to the point where they were seeing it as the worthiest next evolutionary stage in the development of *ishtaboli*.

Perhaps the things that had so intrigued the *alikchis* about college football were the tactical challenges stemming from the limited number who could play, and the restrictive nature of the way that they could be deployed as individuals, both offensively and defensively, and how those deployments had to incorporate such high degrees of teamwork and athletic ability.

It was after Choctaws, returning to the Choctaw Nation from Yale, had engineered the incorporation of the Yale "Boola Boola" football fight song into its Trans-Mississippi West reincarnation as the "Boomer Sooner" fight song of the infant, emerging University of Oklahoma football program.

It was after the courageous but somewhat fumble-footed West Point cadet named Dwight David Eisenhower, playing football for the visiting West Point team, had gotten himself multiply splattered, which all the world got to see, by the multiply talented Jim Thorpe, on the Carlisle Indian School football Field of Honor in Pennsylvania.

It was after the *alikchis* had engineered Jim Thorpe's entrenchment as the very first head honcho to sit in the big chair of professional football, from which chair he ran that organization, an organization called the National Football League, or NFL, for short, as its first president.

It was after the near-fatal Coca-Cola-bottle bombardment of Mr. Cisco, the flag-happy-throwing umpire who had thrown a few too many flags in the Oklahoma-Texas football game, who saved his own life, barely, which all the world got to see, by crawling into a rolled up rain tarp that offered him just enough protection from the rain of pop bottles to live to tell about it, and who single-handedly ended the sale of Coca-Cola in bottles at football games.

It was after the mighty Horned Frogs of Texas Christian University had shown the whole world what could be accomplished if your scouting report on your big opponent for your big game ran to thirty-seven densely packed, single-spaced typewritten pages, which greatly interested the *alikchis*.

It was after the legendary Don Faurot had entrenched himself as the head coach of the mighty Missouri Tigers and had proven himself to be possessed of one of the most restlessly unsatisfied and innovative minds in college football, in the considered opinion of the *alikchis*.

It was after the mighty Minnesota Golden Gopher scholar-athlete of the Big Ten Conference, Charles "Bud" Wilkinson, had quarterbacked the 1937 baby-batch of college-graduate athletes, called "College All-Stars," to their first-ever victory over the pros, skunking the mighty Green Bay Packers 6–0 in the College All-Star Game, which hardly went unnoticed by the *alikchis*.

It was about the time that Bear Wolf, the head coach of the howling North Carolina State University Wolfpack football team, had the good sense to hire the Cornell baseball coach, Jim Tatum, and had the even better sense to put him on the road scouting future Wolfpack football opponents, which, for some reason, became a thing of intense interest to the *alikchis*.

More to the point, it was directly after one of the most mediocre coaches in all of college football, named Clark Daniel Shaughnessy, had managed to lose more than twice as many games as he had won, in stinking up the place, during his career as the head coach at the University of Chicago, which was what *should* have been the thing that cost him his job.

But that was *not* what cost him his job, which was the problem. The problem was the evil idea of that Dangerous Duo, the evil idea that would need *confronting*, the evil idea that was realized, when, on that twenty-third day of December of 1939, Robert Maynard Hutchins, as president of the University of Chicago, along with his confidant-sidekick, Mortimer J. Adler, an associate professor, abolished the football program at that university.

Why *that* Dangerous Duo wanted to abolish college football programs has always been a head-scratcher.

Robert Maynard Hutchins, who was by far the most dangerous, and, unfortunately, the most persistently stubborn of that Duo, who hasn't been with us now for a long time—*may he rest in peace*—was a gifted and perceptive exponent of Thomas Aquinas, who himself had been a gifted and perceptive exponent of Aristotle. And Mortimer J. Adler became the most gifted and the most perceptive exponent of Aristotle who has ever lived.

Nothing defined classical Greek life so much as its love of vigorous athleticism.

The ancient Greeks are the people who gave us gymnasiums.

They are the people who gave us the Olympics.

They are the people who gave us Pindar.

The ancient Greeks are one of the few ancient peoples of the world who can still speak to us, to all of us, to any of us, down through the centuries, down through the millennia, with perfect clarity.

They are the people whose playwrights can still make us chuckle, and still make us think, all at the same time, even when one of their greatest playwrights, Aristophanes, playfully sends someone to Hades, out of frustration with other Greek playwrights, to fetch back some great Greek playwright, hoping that not all of those great Greek playwrights, "content among us, will be content in hell."

And, okay. So what if Aristophanes did happen to say that about one particular Greek playwright and not about all Greek playwrights. I happen to like that one Greek playwright that Aristophanes was poking fun at, and this is my book, and I'm not going to stand for having fun poked at that playwright, so if you want to know which particular playwright he was, then you go read Aristophanes.

Nobody will likely ever be able to figure out what motivated Robert Maynard Hutchins. Lord knows the *alikchis* tried hard enough to figure that out, so I heard.

But, thanks to Bill Moyers, of public TV, Mortimer J. Adler's motivations became a lot less head-scratchingly difficult to comprehend, when Moyers coaxed Adler into admitting that he personally hated physical exertion so much that he had failed to receive his bachelor's degree from Columbia University, because he had refused to take the compulsory swimming test that was a component of the physical education requirement for that degree at that time (see, or rather, hear, "A Conversation with Mortimer J. Adler: The Designer of the Syntopicon Talks with Bill Moyers," 58 minutes, AUDIO-TEXT Cassette #38820, from the Center for Cassette Studies, Inc., 8110 Webb Ave., N. Hollywood, CA 91605).

Legions of Choctaws have tried to comprehend the oddities of that Columbia University in those days before World War II, when Mortimer J. Adler had been a student there, in an effort to try to understand Mortimer J. Adler.

Many Choctaws have gone about that quintessential sort of Choctaw task by enlisting the help of the autobiography of the compulsory day-by-day, concrete specific-detail-recording diarist turned autobiographer named Isaac Asimov while admiring the spellbinding way that Asimov turned the ordinary and mundane of daily life into captivating, knowledge-transferring recollections of what it was like to be a student at that Columbia University in those days, in the first volume of his autobiography, *In Memory Yet Green*.

But no amount of acquired knowledge about Columbia University in those days will do as much to explain Mortimer J. Adler as that one carefully coaxed admission that Bill Moyers extracted from him.

However, it is one of the great ironies of history that what that Dangerous Duo of Hutchins and Adler did on December 23, 1939, turned out to be the beginning of the curious chain of events that led to the discovery of one of the greatest things that has ever impacted the game of football, the sublime Split-T Formation.

How that got started, and *how* that got boosted, threw the *alikchis* for one of the biggest loops that they have ever been known to have been thrown for, a loop even bigger than the Wishbone loop they got thrown for in the 1970s, and from which, so I heard, they have still not completely recovered from and had not been anywhere near recovering from at the time the Wishbone came along to sort of double-whammy loop them.

That chain of events got its head-scratching start from that Dangerous Duo of Hutchins and Adler during that winter of 1939–40, but it got a much more head-scratching, much bigger boost from the dumb-as-a-box-of-rocks president of Stanford University, Ray Lyman Wilbur, that same winter.

To this day, it does not appear that anyone knows how Ray Lyman Wilbur happened to be at the 1939 *professional* football game that saw the Chicago Bears maul the Washington Redskins 73–0, by employing *pro football's* fairly new T-Formation offense, which the pathetic Redskins of that day obviously had no clue how to try to defend against, and which, partly because of that massacre in that game, among a few others, was thought to be far too complex for college ball.

It was considered too difficult for college ball primarily because of what was thought to be the insurmountable problem of trying to teach its Philadelphia-lawyer, mind-bogglingly intricate offensive-line blocking schemes to part-time college football offensive linemen.

As full-time college students, they were supposed to be devoting most of their efforts to such time-taxing, intellectually challenging endeavors as trying to advance from arithmetic to mathematics, and learning in a chemistry laboratory why $C_9H_6O_2$ smells like alfalfa, or why alfalfa smells like coumarin, take your pick, and learning how to read so they could learn how to write, or learning how to write so they could learn how to read, take your pick, and other such 1930s hayseed things.

But never underestimate the power of ignorance in high places, particularly in the offices of university presidents.

Exactly how that dumb-as-a-box-of-rocks Ray Lyman Wilbur, who needed to hire a new Stanford football coach, happened to get it in his head that it was the suddenly unemployed former head football coach of the far from even mediocre, recently abolished, University of Chicago *college* football team who was "Chicago's T-Formation man," nobody knows. Trust me on that one. If you know, then you have got a scoop.

It was news to that unemployed Coach Clark Daniel Shaughnessy as much as it was to the rest of the world.

And, say what you will about him, but Coach Clark Daniel Shaughnessy was not slow on the uptake.

When Coach Shaughnessy suddenly found himself in California, listening to a bubbling Ray Lyman Wilbur introduce Coach Shaughnessy to the world as not only the newly hired head coach of the mighty Stanford Indians football team but also as the great coup of the greatest college president-genius to ever influence the game of college football since he had succeeded in stealing "Chicago's T-Formation man" away from Chicago and bringing him to Stanford, Coach Shaughnessy hesitated not at all in stepping forward and performing the first of what would be multiple stunnings of the college football world, when he announced that the Stanford Indians would switch to the T Formation for the 1940 football season.

If he was nothing else, Coach Shaughnessy was, by then, a seasoned hand at navigating the treacherously ignorant waters of college presidents, and he also knew who would be buttering his bread, and, if it all turned out to be nothing but one big belly flop, well, he'd been talking about buying a farm, anyway.

At that point, the Coach Clark Daniel Shaughnessy who would emerge as the greatest chalk talker in the history of college football, with the possible exception of Gomer Jones, began to emerge, as he undertook the daunting task of chalk-talk teaching some sixty new line blocking schemes, shuttling tackles and ends, shifting guards and pulling guards, sometimes featuring a flanker or a man in motion away from the play, or both at the same time, and sometimes with a lot of everything else going on at the same time.

Those chalk-talk students in his audience, that part-time Stanford student offensive line, were the ones whose pitiful attempts at blocking *anybody* had resulted in the old Stanford Single-Wing Formation not even managing to score ten touchdowns in the entire previous season.

That Stanford offensive line was composed of an immortal beer-guzzling group of guards, centers, tackles, and ends who had *earned* their reputation for being the free spirits of the college football world.

They were, in the immortal words of Edwin Pope, more proficient at clearing out roadside taverns than anything else.

But with the amazing chalk-talk transformation of what became the rompingest, stompingest, most sucker-punching bunch of offensive linemen in all of college football, and with the considerable talents of a Bronko Nagurski clone at fullback named Norm Standlee, and, by Coach Shaughnessy having the eye to see that a mediocre, Single-Wing tailback named Frankie Albert could make quite a contribution with his great faking abilities if he were moved to quarterback, where a whole world began opening up for a team whose quarterback operated parallel to the line of scrimmage, Coach Clark Daniel Shaughnessy's 1940 Stanford Indians went on a romping, stomping, history-making tear, beating San Francisco 27–0, Oregon 13–0, Santa Clara 7–6, Washington State 26–14, Southern Cal 21–7, UCLA 20–14, Washington 20–10, Oregon State 28–14, California 13–7, and then Nebraska 21–13 in the 1941 Rose Bowl.

That came to the attention of Bear Wolf's football-world-surveying scout, Jim Tatum, and Syracuse University's graduate student, part-time backfield coach, Charles Wilkinson, and the University of Missouri's Don Faurot.

Faurot immediately began tinkering with Shaughnessy's innovations and, in that process, stumbled upon the Split-T Formation.

When an *alikchi* in the Pentagon shuffled the papers just right during World War II to bring Don Faurot, Jim Tatum, and Charles Wilkinson together at Iowa Navy Preflight School, so the *alikchis* might hear what they might talk about, guess what they spent nearly all of their time talking about?

After World War II ended, and after the *alikchis* had quietly engineered the hiring of Jim Tatum as the head coach of the University of Oklahoma football team, who brought Charles Wilkinson with him as an assistant coach, and after the *alikchis* got wind that Jim Tatum was rule-breakingly dispensing cash to football players, and after the *alikchis* quietly engineered a carefully chalk-talk rehearsed, casual-appearing, chance encounter on a sidewalk of that campus between a cooperative member of that team and the president of the University of Oklahoma, Dr. George Lynn Cross, so the beans could casually be spilled to Dr. Cross that the school was about to be in deep doo-doo if it didn't get rid of Jim Tatum, Dr. Cross quietly told Tatum to find another job before somebody found out about those beans.

After Jim Tatum had left, to become the head coach of the mighty Maryland Terrapins, Charles "Bud" Wilkinson ascended to the head-coaching throne of Owen Field, where Wilkinson employed that pro-football-T-Formation-transformed-by-that-football-abolishing-Dangerous-Duo-and-that-coach-hiring-dumb-as-a-box-of-rocks-Ray-Lyman-Wilbur-into-the-chalk-talk-teaching-Coach-Clark-Daniel-Shaughnessy-and-Coach-Don-Faurot-and-Coach-Jim-Tatum's Split-T Formation to kick the most serious butt in the history of college football, reeling off, at one stretch in the mid-1950s, the untouchable, all-time college record of forty-seven straight victories.

The barely believable sequence of all of those things, so I heard, looped the *alikchis* into never yet quite having figured out whether confronting and defeating the machinations of the Dangerous Duo of Hutchins and Adler was the right thing to do, or whether, maybe, the college football world might need a good shaking up that way from time to time—but what are the odds of it ever working out like that again, huh?

Exactly how the *alikchis* went about confronting and defeating the frightening vision of that Dangerous Duo is not a story for me to tell, no matter how much of it I might have heard a little bit of, and no matter how much of the rest I might have guessed.

Suffice it to say, now that the threat of the evil vision of Mortimer J. Adler and Robert Maynard Hutchins has given way to a climate conducive to the expansion of college football programs, Choctaws might be able to turn their attention to the task of dealing with the religious tyranny that the other Indian nations have suffered under owing to the Discovery Doctrine.

Thanks to the power of American-imperialist propaganda, few contemporary Americans have any awareness of the religious tyranny of the Discovery Doctrine, or of what America did to Indian people after Indians disappeared from Hollywood's silver screen, where Indians were last seen galloping around some wagon train in a circle, getting shot off their horses one by one, leaving the impression that they must have continued galloping around in a circle, getting shot one by one, until they were all gone.

For the most part, Indians are never mentioned in "American" history after that, or in American popular culture.

Americans need not feel bad because they know little about the Discovery Doctrine and the Supreme Court decision in the 1823 *M'Intosh* case.

American lawyers don't even know about the *M'Intosh* decision.

That Supreme Court decision is so embarrassing to contemporary Americans, and it does such great violence to the American Myth, that American law students in American law schools have not even been allowed to be exposed to it.

When it has appeared in American law school textbooks at all, it has been severely edited, so as to soften its most embarrassing aspects.

Law school students, like every other kind of student, don't read much of anything more than what they are required to read, and the reading they are required to do is staggering.

Few law school students, other than a few Indian law school students, have ever dug out and read the full text of that Supreme Court decision.

In their careers, very few American lawyers ever have occasion to have anything to do with American Indian law. No knowledge of the Discovery Doctrine is required for any bar examination.

Very few American lawyers have had any understanding of the Discovery Doctrine, to a point that the nature of the religious tyranny of the Discovery Doctrine basis for the American claim of sovereignty over Indian land in North America eventually became so little known and so little understood by the American legal profession that in the late twentieth century some law professors began finding it a rich source for study and publishing, which has enhanced our understanding of it.

American lawyers are, as a group, among the most ignorant people in America regarding American Indian law.

Some of them, in fact, such as the attorneys for the state of Wisconsin in the Chippewa spearfishing controversy in the 1980s, had their heads so full of little but American-imperialist propaganda regarding Indians that they had to be disciplined by U.S. federal appellate court judges for wasting the court's time by arguing American Indian *policy*, rather than American Indian law.

Not all of American Indian law is against Indians, not by a long shot, as the state of Wisconsin discovered in the 1980s, when the federal courts upheld those Chippewa rights in their treaties of 1837 and 1842.

But the *M'Intosh* decision is one of the most devastating Supreme Court decisions for Indians.

One doesn't have to be a lawyer or a law school student to read a United States Supreme Court decision.

Every Indian in North America should read that 1823 *M'Intosh* decision.

Every Indian community in North America should have a copy of it and read the choicest parts of it to their children and explain to them what it has meant and what it continues to mean.

The *M'Intosh* decision is not particularly easy reading, having been written by an erudite scholar, John Marshall, who was possessed of one of the most sophisticated vocabularies and most brilliant minds of his day and place, and it's about thirty-five pages long.

But it is the dirty little secret that the imperialists among the Americans do not want the contemporary world to know about.

For a long time, the imperialists among the Americans have not even wanted American lawyers to know about it, primarily because the Discovery Doctrine and all of its related legal baggage is so inextricably embedded in American law and American history that there is no way for Americans to extricate themselves from the quicksand of that Medieval church law doctrine, no matter what sort of mumbo-jumbo hocus-pocus some contemporary Supreme Court might try to say, and no matter what kind of spin doctoring American-imperialist historians might do.

The most dangerous thing that Americans could do, in my opinion, would be to try to shift the legal basis for the American claim to sovereignty over Indian land to one based on legal doctrines of conquest or settlement, in some foolish attempt to enshrine, by legal propaganda, what American imperialists regard as the status quo.

That would be putting everything strictly upon a military footing, on a footing of nothing but raw, brute force.

As we enter this young and dangerous century, do Americans *want* to ground their future relations with the Indian nations upon that kind of twenty-first-century military footing?

Americans might want to contemplate what that might mean, and the nature of the risks they would be assuming.

Once Americans were to set themselves on that course of action, there would be no turning back.

Americans might try doing something that few Americans have ever done. They might actually read the *M'Intosh* decision.

The rationale of their nation for what it did, what it has been doing, and what it is *still* doing to sovereign Indian nations is in the *M'Intosh* decision, laid out for all the world to see.

All anybody need do is look.

Today, there is no way to keep Indians from reading the *M'Intosh* decision. It is now easily available online. A Google search will turn it up, compliments of the twenty-first century.

One might note that Chief Justice John Marshall, to his credit, was not particularly happy about grounding the American claim to sovereignty over Indian land upon the religious tyranny of the Discovery Doctrine.

But he had no choice.

Other well-established legal doctrines, such as the doctrine of conquest, or the doctrine of settlement, did not apply. There had not even been any exploration, let alone any conquest or settlement, when Anglish ships skirted the coast, "discovered" the land and "claimed" it for the Crown.

Chief Justice John Marshall and his Supreme Court had no alternative but to adopt and acknowledge the law under which the foreign imperialists *had* claimed sovereignty over Indian land, and his decision in the *M'Intosh* case is, therefore, one of the most tortured and twisted pieces of nonsense ever committed to paper in the Anglish language.

The first thing one should know about the *M'Intosh* decision before reading it is that it does not make any sense, so don't be reading it expecting it to make any sense.

It doesn't make sense to anyone, including John Marshall, who openly admits in his opinion that it doesn't make any sense, in one of the rarest moments of candor in the history of the Supreme Court of the United States.

One might note at this point that the year 1823 is a landmark year in the legal history of all Indians for reasons other than the *M'Intosh* decision. That is also the year that the first Choctaw lawyer was admitted to the bar, the brilliant James Lawrence McDonald.

James Lawrence McDonald had been sent by the Choctaws to study law under the tutelage of a lawyer and judge in Ohio, a Buckeye judge, more than a century and a half before those Buckeyes would be so remarkably Billy-bounded and Uwe-toe-toasted, a man named Judge John McClain, who not long afterward became a justice of the Supreme Court of the United States.

It is worth noting that in 1823, nearly two centuries ago, at a time when many other Indian nations in North America had not even encountered the Americans, or were attempting to respond to them in a variety of other ways, the Lords of the North American Continent had already gotten themselves a Choctaw lawyer admitted to the bar, who had received perhaps the most calculatedly sophisticated education of any Indian of his day, perhaps of nearly any lawyer of that day, Indian or otherwise.

Before being sent to Judge John McClain in Ohio, James Lawrence McDonald had been sent by the Choctaws to the East, for private tutoring from the Reverend Doctor Callahan, who later became president of Princeton College and from whom the Choctaws learned the value of getting their most promising ones privately tutored, by whomever in the world might be best suited for that.

Maybe somebody who might be sitting on some big ticky-tocky thing should have sense enough to take note that this is a documented, undisputed lesson from the historical record, from a people who have been pretty careful not to leave a very big paper trail, a lesson that the Lords of the North American Continent had learned before the clocks began ticking away the more than ninety-six and one-half million minutes that have ticked away since that day.

If Americans cannot get the image knocked out of their heads that Indians are simpleminded primitives, well, then you be the one who guesses the rest.

It is also worth noting, with James Lawrence McDonald's admission to the bar, that for the past 184 years, since the *day* the *M'Intosh* decision was announced, Choctaws have understood perfectly the legal philosophy of religious tyranny that is the heart of the Discovery Doctrine.

And Choctaws knew exactly what to do.

It explains why, in the 1820s, the Choctaw Nation immediately, deliberately, and publicly adopted the religion of the Americans.

It explains why, for the past 184 years, Choctaws have publicly wor-shipped that old dead Jew.

It explains why Choctaws can win *any* all-night hollering and singing and praying contest against *anybody*.

Choctaws are not a people who just fell off the turnip truck. Incredibly, the sleepy-headed Americans have never demonstrated any awareness of that.

With James Lawrence McDonald's admission to the bar in 1823, the Choctaws began responding to the Americans with the kind of legality that Choctaws relish that has characterized so much of Choctaw-American his-tory, and that has contributed, among many other things, to so many Choctaw victories against the government of the United States in the Supreme Court of the United States.

Formal training in American law is nearly a two-centuries-long tradition among Choctaws, a period of quite a few generations during which many Choctaws became lawyers. Today, many Choctaws are lawyers. Many Choctaws are also professors, in many different academic disciplines.

Long ago, the Choctaws began sending their most promising young peo-ple to the East, and to the North, to be educated, often at Yale, often at educa-tional institutions in the Buckeye state.

Some of Horatio Bardwell Cushman's childhood Choctaw friends were ones who went off to some of the Buckeye state's institutions of higher edu-cation, Choctaw friends from Cushman's 1820s Mississippi childhood, where Cushman had been the child of white missionaries to the Choctaws.

That Buckeye state seems to have a knack for calling itself to the atten-tion of the Choctaws.

That happened in a big way in December 1969, when a resounding sound came thundering out of that Buckeye state, from a Yellow Springs, Ohio, pro-fessor, a Buckeye-transplanted brilliant Okie named Judson Jerome.

After that brilliant Okie had gotten about all that anybody could get out of his student days at the University of Oklahoma, and had become an Anglish professor in Ohio, he became potentially dangerously positioned as the worldwide-audience-commanding, seductive, monthly essayist who mas-queraded as the poetry columnist for one of the most influential publications in the world, due to the people its readers would become, *Writer's Digest* mag-azine, which, at that time, was indeed a digest-sized publication.

Whether or not that seductive essayist might or might not have known beans about what he was supposed to have been writing about each month, poetry, is a head-scratching thing which you'll have to ask somebody else about.

But he would not get to the part of his monthly message to the world that was actually about the mechanics of poetry until a few hundred words deep into his monthly column.

When that monthly message finally did get to the topic of poetry, he would invariably hold forth on the manifold mysteries of what is supposed to be some sort of discernible beat to the cadence of the Anglish language, which he accompanied with elucidations of trochees, iambs, spondees, and other mysterious poetry code talk things, which is where most Choctaws, all but really weird Choctaws, would go, huh?

But, regardless of whether or not that monthly columnist might or might not have known beans about poetry, what he could do, frighteningly without fail, was to grab and hold *anybody's* attention in the first few hundred words of his column, which had given him a huge audience of what would likely be, in future generations, extraordinarily influential people, people who write for publication.

And so, it was that potentially dangerously positioned poetry professor who, in December, 1969, paused in his monthly column routine, in that issue of *that* generationally influential publication, to thunder out a soul-shriveling message, which he imparted to the world in "A Chapter of Autobiography."

The thundering part of that message was embodied in the capstone presentation of that "Chapter of Autobiography," an anti-deer-hunting sonnet of his own creation, and not just any kind of anti-deer-hunting sonnet, either, but a *Ouachita Mountains* anti-deer-hunting sonnet.

That got more than just a few Choctaws good and drunk.

Given all of the things that Choctaws already had on their plate, *now* they were faced with the specter of actually having to find out what all of that trochee and iamb and spondee stuff might be about.

Even worse, they might have to try to figure out *what* beat that was supposed to be in the cadence of the anguished Anglish language that those poetry professors kept claiming was there, somewhere, for anybody to hear.

As near as anybody could figure out, that was just their primary squirrelly reason for why they claimed that they were writing poetry when they wrote poetry that didn't rhyme, like poetry ought to, if it wants to claim that it is poetry.

Everybody suspected, so I heard, that all of those poetry professors might just be too damn lazy to make their poems rhyme, so they would just knock off a few lines of prose, break it up into lines that *looked* like poetry, and then kick back with some refreshing beverage and watch TV, like normal people, while all the while getting paid the big bucks to be big professors.

If that might be the case, then you got to hand it to them, if for nothing else, for not being dummies.

But with something like the fate of deer hunting hanging in the balance, Choctaws had no choice but to roll up their sleeves and try to figure out whatever might need to be figured out, just to try to make sense out of whatever it might be that some ominous, Ohio sonnet-spouter might indeed be spouting, so they would know, not just *think* they knew but *know* that they knew, that proper tabs were being kept on him, to make sure that he didn't get something started that might get out of hand and put an end to deer hunting, all for the want of Choctaws not being able to figure out what in the hell it might be that he was spouting.

It quickly developed that his awesome essay skills were hardly the most fearful thing about him.

The very first *Big Scouting Report* on him, so I heard, was an occasion for great alarm in the Choctaw Nation.

That piece of hastily gathered intelligence emphasized that he might be possessed of the sort of single-minded, stubborn determination that is well known, from the many examples of it in history, to have the capacity to change the world, if he were to have the kind of luck that can couple up with that kind of persistence that enables certain people to accomplish amazing things, even something like putting an end to deer hunting.

Things reached a state of panic when a second, incredibly detailed, thorough, and *long* scouting report revealed that, sure enough, he was exhibiting that very characteristic, that very thing that might make him truly dangerous.

He was doggedly, single-mindedly fixated on a sort of long-odds challenging quest that Choctaws can identify with, the challenge of getting the nonsonnet-publishing summit publication in his field, *Poetry*, to publish a sonnet.

In furtherance of that objective, he was said to be writing sonnets out the kazoo, on every kind of topic under the sun, and bombarding the editors of *Poetry* with them, stubbornly determined to make them change their policy about not publishing sonnets, by publishing one of his sonnets.

That *Poetry* journal is quite likely something that you have seen.

That *Poetry* journal was nice-touchingly picked as the most appropriate publication for the intellectually tireless Dr. Hannibal "the Cannibal" Lecter to be perusing, while sitting in his soon-to-be-sprung-from-great-big bird cage, in the movie *The Silence of the Lambs*. That is the same august *Poetry* journal in which the poetry of the Montana Blackfoot Indian, James Welch, appeared, perhaps the only Native American poetry yet to have appeared in that august place, the last I heard—the James Welsh, former Cornell Anglish department faculty member, who is best known for his novels but who should be best known for his poem, "The Man From Washington," among other poems.

That stubbornly persistent assault upon *Poetry* by that dangerously positioned, Ohio-transplanted Okie, anti-deer-hunting sonnet spouter is hardly the sort of thing that is without precedent, even when it comes to poetry and august publishers of poetry.

The most famous example, perhaps, had as its central figure the not-so-hot-poet-father of the great poet who wrote the American mid-twentieth-century-shaking piece of poetry titled *Howl*.

That father of that great poet is most remembered for the *same* sort of determined, single-minded stubbornness that characterized that dangerously positioned anti-deer-hunting sonnet spouter.

The long, persistent quest of that father-of-the-poet-of-*Howl* was a decidedly long-odds quest to get *any* poem of his published in the upstate New York *Epoch*, a distinguished journal of poetry and short stories, that great literature journal of that great cow college of the Ivy League, Cornell University.

That is the great cow college whose great Anglish department gave us Professor William Strunk Jr., as well as Professor Strunk's student, E. B. White, who gave the kiddies *Charlotte's Web*, and who eventually gave all of us a rescued, updated, nearly lost-to-everybody edition of the "little book," the little book that the little Anglish professor, Will Strunk, had used to terrorize generations of Cornell students into a proper respect for authority, which his E. B. White former student titled *The Elements of Style*.

The daily poetry output of that father-of-the-poet-of-*Howl* arrived daily at Cornell, eventually prompting the august Anglish professors of Goldwin-Smith Hall to be daily curious about how that father-of-the-poet-of-*Howl* was coming along, to which, in time, the august professor who was editing that *Epoch* journal was able, in good conscience, to say, "He's getting b-e-t-t-e-r."

If, by some chance, you might not know who that poet was who wrote *Howl*, shame on you. I would tell you who he was, but I am having one of those things that Baby Boomers have begun calling a "senior moment" and cannot recall offhand who he was. I'd look it up for you, but why in the hell would I want to do something like that, when you can look it up?

That kind of persistence of that father-of-the-poet-of-*Howl* might have had the capacity, in the hands of that dangerously positioned, anti-deer-hunting sonnet spouter in Ohio, to wreck one of the greatest conservation comebacks of the twentieth century, the phenomenal comeback, from near extinction in the early twentieth century, of the deer herd of the illegal state of Oklahoma.

Choctaws don't know what they would do if there was no deer hunting.

It's not just the meat that counts, or even the quest for a trophy deer rack, or even the thrill of the hunt, or the camaraderie of the camping out, or the occasion to spend time with cherished relatives who might be away much of the rest of the time, maybe far away, maybe only getting back every few years.

Those things count, but they are not the only things about deer hunting that count.

Choctaws use the example of the deer hunt to scare the hell out of the Choctaw teenage boys, so they don't fool around and get married too young.

Choctaws don't need a *Kinsey Report*, or a *Hite Report*, or much of anything else, besides the example of the deer hunt, to teach the teenage boys what they most need to know about sex.

Whatever it might be that the Choctaw women teach the Choctaw girls, I don't know. You'll have to ask somebody else.

But the boys have no difficulty being impressed by the fact that the over-whelming number of bucks that are killed each fall are the one-and-a-half year-olds, the ones who were the fawns of the previous spring, who have grown their very first set of antlers, and who are going through their very first rut, when, kaboom, they end up on somebody's dinner table.

It's that kaboom part that the Choctaw boys are informed how to avoid, the kaboom being the heaven help them when they *do* get married, if they don't do it just right.

Those Choctaw boys are informed that those one-and-a-half year-old young bucks are *them*, in deer years.

They are informed that those young deer bucks are the rough equivalent of teenage boys.

They are further informed that the male species of the human species hits its all-time, hormone-driven, sexual peak in those very dangerous, kaboom, teenage years, the very peak being roughly about age seventeen, or so.

They are *shown* what that *looks* like. They are shown the silly one-and-a-half year-old bucks, during the rut.

It's not hard to do.

You just climb a tree near where one of those young bucks has urinated in a great big spot that he has scratched out on the ground, among many such spots in *his* constantly patrolled, approximately nine-tenths of an acre of his terrain, not a square acre, mind you, but a crazy-quilted, nine-tenths of an acre of winding paths here and there all over the place that cross the terrain paths of lots of other bucks, as graduate students in Alabama demonstrated conclusively long ago with tracking devices mounted on Whitetail deer.

That young buck is hoping to find where a doe in heat has come along and urinated in one of his big scrapings on the ground. When he finds such a thing, he goes nose to the ground, as fast as he can walk, following her trail, at which point you could be standing near her path and kick the bejesus out of his butt as he walked by and he would hardly notice.

Seeing for themselves how easy it is to kaboom such a preoccupied young buck is a thing that is hoped will make a big impression on those teenage Choctaw boys.

They are informed that *if* the young buck does survive that first rut, then the next rut, they *remember*.

They remember all those kaboom noises from the last rut, and they remember that after that rut, and after all those kaboom noises, that Charlie, and Hank, and Fred, and Tom, and Edward, and a whole bunch of other young bucks of their cohort-peer fawn age group just weren't around anymore.

That's when deer get smart enough to do arithmetic and put two and two together. They figure out what happened to all of those other young bucks that they used to frolic around with. That's when they have survived the most critical time in their lives, and, thereafter, they stand a pretty decent chance of growing old.

They are also informed of the head-scratching fact that the female species of the human species does not hit her sexual peak until her early thirties.

The teenage boys are told that if they can somehow manage to restrain their young-buck equivalent, teenage boy impulses, and can somehow manage to avoid getting kaboomed until they are in their early thirties, too, then they will have a superhorny wife, at a time when they will be able to relax a little and slow down and really enjoy having such a wife.

Whereas, otherwise, sometime along about not long after the honeymoon is over, all hell will begin breaking loose, and they'd wish like hell that they had waited until the time that it is her idea to be doing all the time what he wants to be doing anyway.

All of which is more or less a big lie, which won't do much good against those raging hormones, but what the hell, you've got to tell them something and then hope for the best. Maybe this way they'll at least hang in there once they do get kaboomed, hoping that those better days are down the road.

Until the early 1930s, that illegal state of Oklahoma had a statewide, no-deer-hunting law that supplied lots of deer-hunting Choctaws with a lot of hair-raising, game-warden-outwitting stories to tell to their grandkids.

Lots of Choctaws got to hear both sides of lots of those stories, because some Choctaws were the law and order-loving game wardens, who were trying to catch their own witty deer-hunting brothers and cousins and whatnot.

Some of those law and order-loving Choctaw game wardens did not know how miserably they had failed on some days until their own mother served them venison steaks for their dinner.

By the 1930s, that deer herd had begun to recover enough to sustain a one-day deer-hunting season in a very few counties, which gradually was expanded to more counties, and more days, until, by the time that 1969 thundering sound came thundering out of Ohio, in the form of that anti-deer-hunting sonnet, the deer-hunting season was a late November, statewide, nine-day rifle and shotgun, one-buck-per-person event, sometimes with a doe day on the last day or two, in some counties, to thin the herds, which were already at that time getting too big for the carrying capacity of the range in some places.

That deer-hunting season encompassed two weekends, sandwiching the week in between, with the Friday of the last weekend being the day that the Oklahoma Sooners always set aside, back in those days, for kicking the great big butts of the Nebraska Cornhuskers on the Field of Honor, except maybe one or two times when that didn't work out so hot.

Today, there are so many deer in nearly every county in the illegal state of Oklahoma, except the arid far West, that they are almost at a nuisance level.

There are so many new additional separate hunting seasons that hardly anyone can keep count of them, a multi-deer bow season that lasts for months, a nine-day black-powder rifle season that is a clone of the November rifle season, except the black-powder season is at the ordinary height of the deer rut in mid-to-late October, and many new, easy-to-get, special-permit seasons all over the place, all of that being an attempt to try to keep the immense herd to some sort of manageable level.

All of that is now for the benefit of the Texans, primarily for the multitude of well-to-do, Dallas- and Ft. Worth-area north Texans and the same sort of Oklahoma City and Tulsa people.

They have now nearly locked up all of the "privately owned" land in the illegal state of Oklahoma in Texas-style exclusive "hunting leases," preventing the Indian people from even being able to deer hunt in that soon-to-be-dismantled state, all so the "land owners" can make a little bit more income from "their property."

If the Choctaws, back in 1969, had known *that* would happen, they likely would have pickup truck-caravanned all the way to Yellow Springs, Ohio, just to get that anti-deer-hunting sonnet spouter good and drunk with them and get him all riled up and all worked up to a point where he would turn his awesome sonnet skills, and his awesome capacity for single-minded purpose, to leading a successful crusade to bring an end to the terrible crime of deer hunting in the illegal state of Oklahoma.

That still might not be a bad idea, except, that august Ohio professor—*may he rest in peace*—has not been with us now for quite some time.

The Choctaws have been left with no option but to do what they always did, sort of in reverse, and that is to take the "Big Hunt" advice of their grandmothers and "go far from home to raise hell."

The Choctaws used to go *from* Mississippi *to* the Ouachita Mountains to hunt (Ouachita = Big Hunt, from the Choctaw words, *owa*, hunt + *chito*, big).

Now the Choctaws have to go *from* the Ouachita Mountains *to* Mississippi, and elsewhere in the Deep South, to hunt, where, by the mid-1970s, Louisiana was offering a long deer season with a bag limit of four deer, and Mississippi was offering a nearly all-fall, buck-a-day deer season, and where Florida even had deer seasons that stretched into February.

Many Choctaws, however, were also interested in getting a chance at a record-size trophy deer rack, and they had to do things a bit differently.

By the mid-1970s, when the Texas-style hunting lease was first showing the Choctaws the clear indications that it would, in time, lead to the Indian-in-Oklahoma deer-hunting problem that all Indians in that illegal state face today, the Choctaws tackled that problem by collecting the annual "Big Game" report from every state. Then every edition of the *Boone & Crockett Club Record Book* was perused, along with other information.

The deer kills per county of every county in every state were plotted on a big map, with the exceptionally high deer-kill counties highlighted.

Overlaid on top of that map was another one highlighting every county that had produced at least four typical Whitetail deer racks, in total, from all of the editions of the *Boone & Crockett Club Record Book*.

Overlaid on top of that map was another one highlighting all of the publicly owned land in the United States.

Overlaid on top of that map was another one highlighting all of the land parcels in the nation that inquires had revealed were private forestry empires that were deer hunter-friendly.

From those multiple compilations, the choicest spots were selected, each one of which offered lots of deer, a chance for a trophy deer, and a chance to hunt without having to outwit some game warden.

Except that, for trophy deer racks, the place that has always been over-whelmingly, nothing even remotely close to as good, remains southeastern Saskatchewan, in Canada.

So, if you might happen to go looking for Choctaws in the fall and there might seem to be a shortage of them, there is a fair-to-middling chance they m-i-g-h-t be in Canada, outwitting the game wardens there.

If, however, you might want to do what Choctaws would be doing in the United States, if southeastern Saskatchewan weren't so much better, the places you might want to go include the Oconee National Forest in Georgia, Beltrami County in Minnesota, and, if it might have recovered from the big burp of that big volcano out there awhile back, Stevens County in the state of Washington, which was dangerously downwind of that big burping thing.

Or, you might head for the South Texas Brush Country, if you have a few thousand dollars to spend for a few days on somebody's hunting lease, in that second-best place on the continent.

There are other good places, of course, but there are still some Choctaws going far from home to raise hell at those places, so if you want to know where they are, do your own homework and go about it with the sort of con-tinental vision that Choctaws apply to problem solving.

In the early nineteenth century, that continental vision assisted the Choctaws in figuring out how to get a Choctaw well educated for the practice of law.

James Lawrence McDonald was merely among the first of a long parade of Choctaws who, seeking to comprehend the foreign imperialists, acquired advanced Western-style educations outside the Choctaw Nation.

By 1842, Jonathan Dwight had returned home to the Choctaw Nation from Yale, steeped in Latin and Greek, to begin teaching in the Choctaw Nation school system.

For more than a century and a half, Choctaws have been pursuing advanced Western-style educations, in recent generations in large numbers, some of them in extraordinarily sophisticated disciplines.

Today, finally, entering the twenty-first century, the Lords of the North American Continent lack nothing whatsoever in the way of any resources in any field of human knowledge and, perhaps more importantly, are still possessed of some kinds of ancient knowledge that are beyond the ken of Americans.

The treaty that first Choctaw lawyer negotiated for the Choctaws in 1825 rivals the Choctaw treaty of 1820 (which the treaty of 1825 modified, reducing

American recognition of the extent of the Choctaw imperial empire in the Trans-Mississippi West to the southern half of the present-day illegal state of Oklahoma) as the most astonishing Indian treaty the United States has ever entered into.

It's another Choctaw treaty that the imperialists among the Americans have not wanted the world to know about.

That is partly because, as part of the negotiation process for that 1825 treaty, that first Choctaw lawyer forced the U.S. government to carry out a ruthless program of white removal from Choctaw land in the Trans-Mississippi West, particularly in what is now the southeastern quarter of the illegal state of Oklahoma, where the Choctaws would be removed to only half a dozen years later.

That white removal is what General Andrew Jackson had vehemently and passionately vowed that the United States Army would be committed to doing, during General Jackson's negotiations with the Choctaw Commanding General of the North American Continent and the other members of the Choctaw diplomatic corps at the negotiations for the treaty of 1820, by which the Choctaws had gotten the United States to confirm the Choctaw title to that land in the Trans-Mississippi West.

In the mid-1820s, the U.S. Army successfully completed that program of forced white removal, thereby setting a legal precedent that might become very important in the future for all Indian nations.

In that regard, Americans would not have a Choctaw problem today if the United States had continued using its military muscle to remove illegal intruders from Choctaw land, which is what the United States obligated itself to do, which was clearly stated, and agreed to by the United States, in Article 7 "Treaty With The Choctaw And Chickasaw, 1855":

> ...all persons, with their property, who are not by birth,
> adoption, or otherwise citizens or members of either the
> Choctaw or Chickasaw tribe, and all persons, not being citizens
> or members of either tribe, found within their limits, shall be
> considered intruders, and be removed from, and kept out of
> the same, by the United States agent, assisted if necessary by
> the military....

There is no mystery about *how* to remove intruders from Indian land. The U.S. Army is equal to the task.

It would have been easier to do a century and a half ago. A lot of things about America's "Indian problem" would be easier, if America had chosen a different path for itself.

The failure of the United States to fulfill that treaty obligation, the failure to enforce its own supreme law of the land, resulted in the Choctaw people becoming outnumbered, by a ratio of three to one, by illegal intruders in their own nation by late in the nineteenth century, illegal intruders who then clambered for, and got, their illegal statehood.

In the twenty-first century, the Indian nations of North America, those that might desire to do so, will reassert their rightful status as sovereign nations, in a protectorate relationship with the United States, which is the only way that Indian nations can protect their civilizations from the cultural genocide that the United States and the several states are incapable of not continuing to practice against them.

The Indian civilizations have turned the corner on surviving the colonization of the continent and now have time on their side.

They will also have the Lords of the North American Continent, American patriots, and the twenty-first century on their side.

Indian nations might also have world public opinion on their side, which, in the future, no nation will be able to ignore, particularly the United States.

Most Choctaws, however, would prefer to keep the rest of the world out of the Choctaw dispute with the United States.

The Lords of the North American Continent do not need any other nation's help in any way.

Choctaws are still loyal allies of the American people, notwithstanding the repeated disappointments they have endured in patiently waiting for the American people to mature as a people.

It's only the imperialists among the Americans who are their avowed enemies.

And the ticking of time does not alarm Choctaws, unless the fourth quarter might be ticking away in some fumble-filled fiasco on the Field of Honor.

Choctaw land isn't going anywhere. Long ago, Choctaws anchored it solidly to the earth, so it can't go anywhere.

Contemporary Indians, however, have had the help, and will continue having the help, of many American patriots.

One by-product of the success of American-imperialist propaganda regarding Indians has been something that American imperialists never anticipated, that, in time, they would have created a nation of Americans who believe the American Myth so devoutly that they have been revolted by the truth. Many of them, anyway, those who have made *that* kind of voyage of discovery.

American patriots would like to see the American Myth become true. So would Choctaws.

The Lords of the North American Continent don't hate Americans. They don't want to, anyway. They want to get rid of that poison of hatred.

Choctaws have always been rather intrigued by Americans, have spent more than two centuries studying them, marrying them, living with them, learning them inside and out, sizing them up, finding out what makes them tick, a thing that the American imperialists foolishly neglected to pay any attention to doing.

American imperialists don't even have a scouting report for the Big Game.

Choctaws are also keenly aware that the world is a dangerous place and that American military strength has shielded Choctaws and other Indians from such things as the horrors of Nazi Germany in World War II.

Things like that are one of the reasons why Choctaws entered into their protectorate relationship with the United States.

There are worse things in the world than Americans, and every Indian nation is keenly aware that its prosperity is inextricably tied to the welfare of the United States.

Choctaws also understand the need for American propaganda in the American schools.

One of the primary purposes of those schools is to produce young American stumble pups who will feel good about their country, so they will willingly do their military service, and, when their sergeant says, "Charge that machine gun nest!" will get up out of their foxholes and go charging into that machine gun fire.

All Indians want those young Americans to continue growing up feeling good about their country, so they will continue doing their military service, for the benefit and protection of everyone in North America, Indians included.

Indians would just like for there to be no need of there being any propaganda regarding Indians in that American school propaganda.

The Choctaw story is hardly entirely a story of victimization, either.

Choctaws have benefited enormously from their long, close association with Americans.

That's another reason why Choctaws entered into their protectorate relationship with the United States.

But there are dark sides to that association that few Americans are aware of, an American dark side and a Choctaw dark side.

The Choctaw people have had to wrestle with their dark side for a very long time, a dark side that few people have been aware of, except a few Indian nations that have good reason not to have forgotten.

The Choctaw story is not a story of some angelic Indian people.

Choctaws have never been any closer to being angelic than any other people on earth.

Many human beings have been slaughtered by howling Lords of the North American Continent.

Choctaws have often danced with their dark side, and that dark side has been pulling many Choctaws toward it for a very long time.

Howling Choctaws, who for thousands of years have burst out of nowhere, howling the terrorizing Choctaw war whoop.

If you want to know what that howling sounds like, if you want to hear that war whoop ringing in *your* ears, if you want to hear it until you can't stand it anymore, if you want to hear it so loud, and so long, that you will beg your brain to make you deaf, all you have to do is go to the University of Arkansas on any football Saturday.

The silly Arkansawyers adopted it as their "hog call" for the mighty Arkansas Razorback football team.

Chapter Eleven

The Invisible Ancestors

The European exploration of North America unleashed the deadliest killer the continent has ever known. Scientists call it Variola major.

Most people call it smallpox.

Indians had no resistance to smallpox or any other European disease.

It was nobody's fault.

The destructiveness of European diseases in North America, of which smallpox was only one among many, was the result of the isolation of the Western Hemisphere from the rest of the world during the hundreds of generations that Old World populations had been building up at least some resistance to them.

The deadliest and most massive devastation of those diseases was spread by early Spanish contact long before any other European nations arrived anywhere on the continent.

In the southeastern portion of North America, we will likely never know exactly when smallpox struck the ancestors of the Choctaws.

Whether it might have been in the aftermath of the large expedition of Hernando de Soto, which wandered throughout the Southeast from 1539–42, or whether it might have been spread by Indian traders along the network of Indian trading paths, perhaps from contact with the Spanish colonial outpost of St. Augustine in Florida, which was established in 1565, or even earlier Spanish attempts to establish outposts along the Atlantic coast, or from contact with the crews of ships stopping along the Gulf and Atlantic coasts, or from some other source, no one knows.

One thing we know is that one of the cruelest aspects of smallpox is its long incubation period of eight to fourteen days in an infected person.

During that incubation period an Indian trader, healthy to all outward appearances, had time to travel a great distance on the Indian trading paths before delivering death to some distant Indian population.

Another thing we know is that in the Choctaw homeland during the so-called "Black Hole" of Indian history in the Southeast (roughly the century and a half from about 1540 to about 1690), when Europeans weren't present to record any observations in the eastern half of the interior of the continent, great changes took place.

When Europeans did return to the region, beginning in the late seventeenth century, the Indians were unrecognizably different from what the chroniclers of the Soto expedition had recorded, and hardly any Indians, comparatively, remained alive.

Gone were the teeming masses of river-bottom Indian farmers the Soto expedition had passed through for days on end in the rich agricultural bottomlands of the great river valleys of the region.

Smallpox is a crowd disease, a crowd killer.

In the virgin-soil Indian populations of North America, it could kill with a thoroughness that literally brought the end of the world.

The more crowded together the population, the more deadly the disease.

We know, for example, that in 1836 there were 1,600 Mandans crowded together in their villages on the Upper Missouri River. They are a people well remembered by Americans for their hospitality to the Lewis and Clark expedition three decades earlier.

Some might wonder whatever happened to those Mandans. After smallpox struck them in 1837, only 131 Mandans were left alive. The world they had known had ended.

In the virgin-soil Indian populations of the heavily settled agricultural river bottoms of the Southeast, and in the heavily settled agricultural bottomlands of the Mississippi River Valley and its tributaries, smallpox killed Indian farmers on a cataclysmic scale more than a century before the French began trying to extend their imperial ambitions over that vast region.

The relatively late-arriving French and British colonizers, in the seventeenth century, had no knowledge of that cataclysmic reduction of the Indian population. The French and British had no knowledge at all of what the interior of the continent had been like in the early sixteenth century. They had no access to Spanish records of the 1540s. By the seventeenth century, the observations of the chroniclers of the expedition of Hernando de Soto had even been forgotten by the Spanish.

It was not until near the mid-twentieth century that scholars began comparing those early Spanish records with later French records and discovered the cataclysmic changes that had occurred between 1540 and 1690 in the Indian populations of the interior of the eastern portion of North America.

Long before the British began establishing colonies in North America, European diseases had wiped out nearly all of the ancestors of the Choctaws, the great ancient mound-building civilizations of the Lords of the North American Continent, which the Americans have dubbed the "Mound Builders."

For at least six thousand years, those ancient mound-building civilizations had been expanding and contracting, and reorganizing and changing and expanding again, through various stages of political, social, religious, and economic complexity, at various times, in various areas of that vast region, in the same way that the same thing happened in the other cradles of civilization of the world.

The oldest mound thus far discovered in North America, in the lower reaches of the Mississippi River Valley, in present-day Louisiana, has been reliably dated to about four thousand years before the birth of Julius Caesar.

The late-arriving Anglish colonists, along the Atlantic seaboard, being completely ignorant that those great, complex, North American Indian agricultural civilizations had ever existed in the interior of the continent, did not begin stumbling upon their ruins, for the most part, until after they had refused to be restrained by the rule of law of the Royal Proclamation of 1763 and had gone streaming across the Appalachian Mountains, after surviving their First North Atlantic German Civil War, otherwise known as the American Revolution, which ended in 1783.

The barbarian befuddlement of those North American Germans, upon encountering those "Mound Builder" ruins, a North American German befuddlement that extends to the present day, would be amusing, if that continuing befuddlement didn't have such serious legal consequences for contemporary Indians.

It reveals much about "American" historians, even after all of the evidence that has been unearthed during the past half-century, that they cannot quite get their Anglish minds wrapped around the concept that the lower reaches of the great river of the North American continent is a cradle of civilization.

That is not depicted, to this day, in American history textbooks, in the telling of "mainstream" American history.

For the most part, within the history profession, it's known only by specialists in Indian history, but those people are not allowed to be "mainstream" American historians.

Only "American" historians, properly trained to be American propagandists, can be entrusted to put the "right kind" of spin on things.

Those "American" historians have little difficulty in comprehending that the lower reaches of a very few of the other great rivers of the world have been cradles of civilization.

They extol the virtues of those cradles of civilization in the lower reaches of the Tigris and Euphrates rivers in Mesopotamia, the Nile River in Egypt, and the Yellow River in China.

But at the lower reaches of the great river of the North American continent, the mighty *Misha Sipokni* (older than time), they balk.

The American authors of "Western Civilization" textbooks have little difficulty finding their starting point in Mesopotamia and Egypt, but the authors of "American history" textbooks encounter problems when they search for their starting point.

They have some strange difficulty in seeing the lower reaches of the Mississippi River as that starting point.

Why is that?

Could it be that those American historians are not telling history at all but are telling some other kind of story?

A Medieval kind of story?

Could it be that they are creating propaganda, a kind of brainwashing for the American masses, by carefully limiting the story they tell to the narrow history of one particular *polity*?

Could that be because it is too dangerous to tell the story in any other manner?

Too dangerous as a matter of law?

Of Medieval church law?

Of *contemporary* American law?

Too dangerous to the cultural-bias aspects of the Discovery Doctrine—that Medieval church law doctrine that is the law of the land in the United States today and that *still* must be protected with propaganda?

Could it be that those historians have been so thoroughly brainwashed themselves, in jumping through the hoops of the American graduate schools to become practitioners of the academic discipline of "American history," that they are merely tools of powerful vested interests that deem it imperative, as a matter of American law, that "civilization" be portrayed as having arrived in North America on its Atlantic shores in the seventeenth century in some squalid Anglish ship?

Perhaps those "historians" feel compelled to write "American history" in the chronological sequence in which things were revealed to their dull-witted forebears, and, therefore, they feel compelled to appear ignorant of anything that those slobbering barbarians did not know.

But they don't write European history that way.

American historians have no reluctance in revealing such things as how the geniuses who were running European civilizations, *not so long ago*, found it *imperative* to believe that the sun revolved around the earth, because the earth *had* to be the center of the universe, and to explain why it was imperative that everyone *had* to believe that (because the Church said so), and what happened to people, such as Galileo, who dared to say that a universal authoritarian Church had things a bit demonstrably wrong.

Perceptions such as that color everything American historians write about "European history."

But when it comes to telling about things that the Medieval-minded Americans, from the very outset, had wrong about Indians, well, that isn't relevant, because the job of American historians is to tell how America got to be the way it is today, and if American historians were to interject what we now know about Indians into what Americans didn't know then, well, it isn't that doing such a thing might not be more like what real historians might do, it's just that it wouldn't be the "right thing" to do for "American" history.

That's because American history has high standards and must be written "objectively," the way their fellow German, back in Germany, Leopold von

Ranke, the god they bow to for all aspects of methodology, showed them how to do it in the nineteenth century.

They say that Ranke's method was based on a sophisticated, critical examination of nothing but *written* documents, and, therefore, that's the only proper way to do it, not incorporating the methodologies of any other academic disciplines, such as archaeology, anthropology, historical linguistics, or anything else, not because that might not be more like bringing all of human knowledge to the writing of history, and not because they are attempting to keep Indians from having any kind of voice in that history but because those multidisciplinary methodological things are a hybrid specialty, called "ethnohistory" or "Indian history," and that isn't really "history," not in the sense of Leopold von Ranke's methodology, which is what "distinguishes" the "academic" discipline of history from the other academic "disciplines."

They say that the "methodology" of "history" is what sets "history" apart from other "departments" in a university and allows "history" to make its unique kind of contribution to knowledge, one based only upon written records.

And so, while those hybrid "ethnohistory" methodological things might be relevant for some other academic disciplines (other university academic departments), they are just not "right" or "proper" for history, not "American history," because the "discipline" in the discipline of history means exercising the discipline, the restraint, the restriction, of using nothing but written records.

And, regardless of all of that, Americans are only interested in knowing how their forebears fulfilled their "manifest destiny" to control the whole North American continent, how America got to be the way it is today, not what the slobbering barbarians who were their Medieval-minded German ancestors might have had right or might have had wrong about Indians.

And, anyway, Indians don't really exist anymore, not "real" Indians, and so, since Indians aren't really here, not anymore, they can't even impact the present very much. Statistically, they aren't even much of a part of how America is today, so how could they be justifiably regarded as anything more than an "ethnohistory" sideshow in how America got to be the way it is today? Nobody ever hears hardly anything about them.

And, if they might still really be here, and if they were to start impacting the present, well, that's something that hasn't happened yet, and so that can't even be considered part of history, because it's something that hasn't even happened yet.

So, until that might happen, it's just not the place of American historians to write American history the way they write European history, and be telling, at the very outset of their history books, about all of the things that Americans had wrong about Indians, or doing anything else that might get in the way of aligning and maintaining the tight focus of American historians on what their forebears were thinking and doing.

One wonders when it might occur to those American historians that it might be that tight focus that is the tail wagging the dog.

The biases of American historians are not individual but are institutionalized within the framework of their academic discipline.

They merely do what they have been trained to do, the way they have been trained to do it, and they think about things only within the narrow conceptual framework of the limitations that define the boundaries of their academic discipline.

If they dared to do otherwise, they would fail to clear one or more of the hoops they must jump through in graduate school, or else they would be shuttled off into the ghetto of ethnohistory, where they would be conveniently ignored, because the practitioners of that hybrid are not regarded as "historians" by the academic discipline of American history.

None of this is any kind of conspiracy, not a conscious one, anyway.

It's a result of an accumulation of many small things over time, of paths taken by powerfully influential people, when American history was becoming an academic discipline, largely in the mid-to-late nineteenth century, when the paths that were taken were ones that offered propaganda assistance to the philosophical foundations of the justification of the colonization of the continent, and even then that was largely done as a sort of intuitive subconscious thing.

The academic discipline of American history remains intuitively, rather than consciously, aware that its essential role as an institution of propaganda is *still* essential.

And there is nothing dull-witted about its historians. They are, as a group, the most gifted propagandists who have ever lived, though hardly any of them are aware that they are propagandists.

If those great ancient centers of Indian civilization of the Lords of the North American Continent, those "Mound Builder" centers, had continued to flourish, the history of the colonization of the continent by Europeans and Americans would have been different, and American historians would have found themselves compelled to write their histories at least somewhat differently.

But European diseases destroyed the "Mound Builder" civilizations and killed almost all of their people, hundreds of thousands of people, and possibly as many as several million of them. The numbers are in dispute and likely will remain so.

It would be possible for the American scientific community to find out what those numbers were. There are ways to do that. But that's not likely to happen.

American scientists will likely never know more than a few scattered archaeological details of the destruction of what they call the "Mound Builders" because hardly any Americans have ever shown much interest in investigating much of anything about them, and Americans will likely never display more than a yawning interest in them.

The more sophisticated American-imperialist propagandists have known that it is not in their best interests to have a very complete picture emerge of what the continent in precontact times was like.

Much of the American Myth, and most of American Indian law, is grounded upon the North American continent being portrayed as a "wilderness" untouched by civilized peoples, and the people who were found living there being regarded as "savages."

When the American Myth is denigrated, American-imperialist propagandists defend it with apoplectic fury. Most of the toilers in that enterprise have been conditioned to having that response triggered at a gut level and are not sophisticated enough to know that most of American Indian law is grounded upon that myth.

"Savagery" is not just legal code talk for "non-Christian." It is also legal code talk for portraying a *race* of people as having been incapable of creating the kind of organized political, social, religious, and economic complexity that Europeans regard as "civilized."

It is imperative, as a pillar of American *law*, that the Indians of North America be portrayed and perceived as an unfortunate, inferior *race* of people, who must be taken by the hand and shown how to be "civilized," by benevolent Euro-Anglos, who are entitled to the Indian land for having brought the "blessing" of "civilization" to Indians.

An entire race of people *must* be portrayed that way.

Though "non-Christian" is the inextricable component of the European and American philosophical and legal conceptions of "savagery," the components of racism and cultural bias also loom large in the foundation of those conceptions.

There has been an historical evolution of emphasis in those two aspects of the Discovery Doctrine. Earlier, the religious tyranny aspect was paramount. In more recent times, especially in American *popular* culture (which is the *only* thing that really counts, as a matter of law) the cultural bias aspect of regarding Indian socioeconomic culture as being inferior has become the dominant aspect of the Discovery Doctrine.

Anything that runs counter to that cultural bias, to that philosophical conception that Indians, as a *race* of people are not capable of creating civilization on their own, is a direct threat to contemporary American law.

Racism is *the* essential pillar of American law, of *contemporary* American law.

Law is not legislative acts or constitutions or treaties or Supreme Court decisions.

Law, in its most fundamental sense, is *custom*, it is *culture*, it is a *habit of thinking*.

When a people undergo a sea change in their view of something, in their habit of thinking, formal changes in law are not far behind.

The absolutely essential thing for the American-imperialist propagandists has been, and remains, that the *American people* not be allowed to change their habit of thinking about Indians.

That is the only reason why American-imperialist propagandists have portrayed Indians the way they have.

They do that partly because some of them are greedy. They have vested economic interests and know that being forced to share the continent with sovereign Indian nations would cost them some of their wealth.

For that reason, they *fear* the *American people*, because they know what the American people have the power to do to their vested economic interests.

But that's not all of it.

The darkness of religion is a factor. They perceive that their religion is under attack, and because it is a monotheistic, proselytizing religion, like all such religions, it is intolerant of restraint, let alone attack.

But that's not all of it, either.

Most American imperialists are motivated by something other than greed or religious fanaticism. They are truly concerned for the welfare of their country.

If they can be brought to see that sovereign Indian nations on the North American continent can greatly strengthen the United States by helping eliminate a crippling part of the American Myth, a crippling part that is transparent to all of the other nations of the world, even many imperialists among the Americans might stop opposing Indian sovereignty and allow Indians to bring Indian friendship to the assistance of Americans, which would bring with it a priceless empowerment, a means of enabling the American people finally to mature as a nation and set themselves on the path of becoming all they can be, in the best sense of that conception, to the enormous relief of all of the other nations of the world.

Then Americans can preach their various religions all they want to, to any Indians who might want to listen, without either the proselytizers or the Indians being burdened by the crippling baggage of tyranny, legal or otherwise.

That is how Christians would prefer it to be, anyway. Christians would rather persuade, not compel, converts. Some Indians are Christians. Some are Muslims. Some practice other religions.

Indians would like for there to be no reason for Indians to have anything against any religion and would like for it to be possible for them to continue practicing their *own* many, varied Indian religions, which have been brutally suppressed for generations.

And, along that line of the brutal suppression of Indian religions, university presidents need to gracefully butt out of trying to run college football, need to somehow be able to see that just because some kid comes *out* of college football still not knowing how to read, it's no loss at all, because, as a matter of pure logic, he *had* to have entered college not knowing how to read, and, therefore, he cannot be *any* worse off when he *leaves* college than when he *entered* it, except that, if he could be allowed to play college ball, he'd be a lot better off just for having done that.

As for Americans having to share part of the land and part of the wealth, most Americans care more about the welfare of their country, and few Americans actually have any vested economic interest in denying Indian nations their sovereignty, especially if that were accomplished gradually, over a period of time, with there being something in it for people who might be adversely affected.

Today, in the twenty-first century, most Americans only want to earn a decent living and live their lives in peace.

The overwhelming majority of Americans have matured into a decent people, which is why a handful of greedy and powerful American-imperialist propagandists fear their own American people more than anything else.

Chapter Twelve

How to Get to Be an Invisible Ancestor

*T*he American nation has been a long time maturing.

Throughout their history, Americans who could contribute something in the way of supporting the philosophical foundations of the American Myth have had their careers advanced and have become powerful, dominant people in their fields.

It has extended far beyond such things as "history," most particularly to what has passed for "science" in America.

From the outset, from about the time of the American Revolution, the American knee-jerk reaction upon discovering that there had been in North America what Americans perceive to be complex civilizations was to laugh at the idea that those people could have been Indians or any ancestors of the *race* of Indians.

They must have been some vanished *race* of advanced humans, which Americans dubbed the "Mound Builders."

Mounds were virtually everywhere Americans looked in the interior of the eastern half of the continent.

Today, the American scientific community knows that there were more than one hundred thousand mounds, most of them of modest size, but some of them massive, some of them built in precise geometric arrangements, constructed in accordance with sophisticated astronomical observations that made them annual predictors of the vernal equinox and the summer solstice.

The implications for the kind of political, social, religious, and economic complexity that would have been required to organize and direct the amount of human labor necessary to construct the largest mounds did not fit the cultural bias that informed Euro-Ango ideas of "savagery."

As with the pyramids of ancient Egypt, nothing but the tyranny of organized, authoritarian religion could have directed the kind of labor that had been required for the largest mounds.

And, to Americans, the notion that "lazy" Indians could have had anything to do with constructing even the smaller mounds was preposterous.

The "Mound Builder" center that was eventually found to contain the largest mound, at present-day Cahokia, Illinois, directly across the Mississippi River from present-day St. Louis, Missouri, consisted of more than one hundred substantial earthen mounds in its core area and an unknown number in its suburbs.

The largest mound at Cahokia, now known as Monks Mound, has a base larger than the Great Pyramid of Egypt and towers one hundred feet above the ground. Monks Mound is a flat-topped rectangle occupying about sixteen acres, encompassing approximately thirty football fields, and contains more than twenty-one million cubic feet of dirt, which had been transported one sixty-pound basketful at a time.

The American scientific community now knows that Monks Mound at Cahokia was constructed in fourteen stages over a period of about six or seven centuries, from about the eighth century of the Common Era to the fourteenth century, and that it had been abandoned for about a century or so before the voyage of Columbus, in one of the long cycles of "Mound Builder" expansion and contraction and change that no one understands and that has been little investigated.

Monks Mound and some other portions of the Cahokia core complex now constitute an Illinois historical preservation area, after barely having escaped destruction a few decades ago in the construction of Interstate Highway 55, when, after indifferent American governmental planners had embarked upon a project to build the highway right through the center of the Cahokia ruins, a monumental struggle barely succeeded in getting the highway routed around the complex.

Even at that, a heavily traveled modern arterial street in an Illinois suburb of St. Louis runs right in front of Monks Mound, right through the heart of the core complex. The buildings of downtown St. Louis can be seen in the distance across the river.

From the late eighteenth century through the nineteenth century, Americans were still discovering "Mound Builder" ruins.

The ruins could be very difficult to see, many being nearly invisible. Even large, elaborate complexes had virtually disappeared, having been overgrown with bushes and trees. Entire mature forests had grown up on top of them.

It was possible to be standing in the middle of a "Mound Builder" city without realizing it.

Many of the ruins have not been identified for what they are even today.

There was no organized effort to study the mounds.

For a whole century, from 1782 to 1882, when the U.S. Congress finally, yawningly, appropriated $5,000 a year for a seven-year study of the mounds, it was mostly amateur antiquarians who conducted field investigations of them, beginning with Thomas Jefferson.

In 1782, Jefferson set a standard that would not be followed, making a careful excavation of a mound in Virginia while gathering information for part of his response to a questionnaire from the French government on what was called at that time the "natural history" of North America, which Jefferson eventually published as his *Notes on the State of Virginia*.

It would be late in the next century before any mounds would be excavated with anything approaching the precision and thoughtfulness of Jefferson's meticulously recorded and carefully paced excavation, not until an infant American scientific community had emerged and matured enough in the late nineteenth century to begin producing professionals such as Frederick W. Putnam, who would help found several North American museums, along with a few departments of a new, emerging science called anthropology (the study of man) at a few universities.

From the very outset, late in the eighteenth century, seminally important and widely influential scientific minds, such as Thomas Jefferson's friend, William Bartram, a pioneer of American science, believed the mounds had been built by some vanished *race*.

Bartram himself believed that biblical peoples had built them.

That would be the most widely held belief throughout the nineteenth century, though virtually every ancient nation known to history would be suggested by someone.

As Americans discovered the mounds, they began looting them, finding that many of them held burials containing ancient artifacts, including finely crafted copper replicas of weapons that were no longer used by anyone.

More than a century of unchecked looting would pass before the mounds received any protection of any kind, not until the passage of the Antiquities Act of 1906 (Public Law 59-209).

Throughout the nineteenth century, debate raged over who had built the mounds.

The idea that ancestors of the Indians might have built them had only a few advocates. In 1817, Dr. James H. McCulloh published *Researches on America*, propounding his view that Indians had built them. He followed that up in 1829 with another volume, *Researches, Philosophical and Antiquarian, concerning the Aboriginal History of America.*

That some vanished race of people had built the mounds was the overwhelming view, even among so-called scientists, until late in the nineteenth century. By then, all of the foundations of American law regarding Indians had been grounded on its twin pillars of ignorance and religious bias.

One of the first extensive studies of the mounds was published by an amateur antiquarian, in 1820s by the postmaster of Circleville, Ohio, Caleb Atwater, who excavated many mounds in the area. Atwater believed that the mounds had been built before the biblical flood and that they had been built by Indians, sort of—Hindus from India.

Many people believed that the mounds had been built by the "lost tribes of Israel."

But the mass of Americans, largely illiterate, had little interest in the mounds and little awareness of them, being occupied with building roads, towns, and farms that destroyed the archaeological usefulness of most of the ancient agricultural settlements before they could be studied by anyone, while looters tunneled into the mounds themselves.

In that Medieval-minded climate, Chief Justice John Marshall issued his Discovery Doctrine decision in 1823 in the *M'Intosh* case, in which he took no notice of the "Mound Builders" in writing a long, detailed, Medieval-minded summary of his perception of Indian history.

It was a landmark moment in grounding the twin pillars of Indian law in that quicksand of ignorance and religious bias.

The U.S. Congress then passed the Indian Removal Act of 1830 and promptly began removing the so-called Five Civilized Tribes from the Southeast, beginning with the Choctaws.

In 1839, a study that passed for science was published, pathetically reporting measurements of the brain capacity of eight skulls found in "Mound Builder" graves (termed "Toltecan") compared to eight skulls of recently deceased Indians (termed "Barbarous"), in an effort to determine if the "Toltecan" "Mound Builders" had bigger brains than the "Barbarous" Indians of the mid-nineteenth century.

The comparison of the skulls of the "Toltecan" and the "Barbarous" peoples didn't reveal any difference in brain capacity, but Samuel Morton's publication of his study, *Crania Americana*, helped launch the process that would see grave robbing become a professional academic discipline by early in the twentieth century, under the euphemism of "physical anthropology," under the leadership of Ales Hrdlicka of the Smithsonian Institution.

If Morton's 1839 experiment included a comparison of the brain capacity of any of the slobbering North American German barbarians from any of their cemeteries, he didn't include the results of what that comparison had revealed.

Not until 1840 were even rudimentary conceptions of geologic stratigraphy articulated. In that year Charles Lyell published *Principles of Geology*, giving geology its modern foundation in showing that relative dating could be based on geologic strata, a discovery which, in time, had a profound influence on other branches of science.

In 1848, the recently founded Smithsonian Institution (a curious gift to the U.S. government, for the advancement of knowledge, from a wealthy Anglishman in Angleland named Smith) issued its first publication, a study of the mounds.

But that study had been conducted by Ephraim George Squirer, a small-town Ohio newspaper editor, and Edwin Hamilton Davis, an Ohio physician, both amateur antiquarians. Nevertheless, the careful measurements and other records of their two-year study constitute the only knowledge Americans have of many important sites that have long since disappeared beneath cities and reservoirs. Both men believed that neither Indians nor their ancestors could have built the mounds.

Thus, the first public utterance of the Smithsonian Institution was that a "great race of Mound Builders" had done it, who weren't Indians and who weren't the ancestors of the Indians.

Charles Darwin didn't publish his *Origin of Species* until 1859, which, as with Lyell's *Principles of Geology*, began having a profound effect on science, and, in time, a devastating effect on Medieval-minded European religion.

Charles Darwin, it might be noted, in London, also sponsored for publication Dr. Gideon Lincecum's study of Texas fire ants. Lincecum, that astute observer of the Choctaws in transition in Mississippi in the 1820s, a friend and biographer of Pushmataha, had moved to Texas in the 1840s, where he became perhaps the best self-trained naturalist in the world.

Lincecum's fascinating life story was fashioned into an autobiography from letters he had written, late in life, in the 1870s, to a grandson, and was published in the first decade of the twentieth century in the *Publications of the Mississippi Historical Society*. It's an autobiography that contains observations about the Choctaws that are available nowhere else and which hardly anyone except that great lady of Choctaw history, Dr. Anna Lewis, seems to have attempted to make much use of. A number of students of Choctaw history have consulted Lincecum's biography of Pushmataha, and his retelling of Choctaw traditional stories, but, inexplicably, few seem to have thought that there might be anything in his own autobiography about Choctaws.

Lincecum might possibly have made the most of his meager four months of formal education, in a one-room, backwoods Georgia schoolhouse, at the illiterate age of fourteen, as anyone of his generation, achieving distinction in many things.

But because Lincecum was a vehement opponent of missionary activity among the Choctaws, and a great admirer of Choctaw civilization, his views have been suppressed.

Few historians have made use of the five thousand unpublished pages of Lincecum manuscripts in the Lincecum collection of the University of Texas library.

Lincecum, even in his medical practice, was far ahead of his time, spending six weeks in the 1820s traveling the Mississippi countryside with a Choctaw *alikchi*, learning the medicinal properties of plants, at a time when most of the slobbering North American German "physicians" were still maintaining a Medieval focus on bloodletting, and the administering of doses of poisons, such as mercury, to the unfortunate mass of the American people, who had to rely on them for their health care.

The Smithsonian Institution did not organize its Bureau of Ethnology until March 3, 1879 (which is better known by its later name, as the Bureau of American Ethnology, or BAE).

Thanks to a history of that entity, *The Bureau of American Ethnology: A Partial History*, by Neil M. Judd, we have a sort of candid insider's view that is rare for the way it provides a window into the inner workings and personalities of that governmental bureaucracy. It affords us a certain perspective on the BAE men, such as John R. Swanton, that is seldom as easily obtained for most other late nineteenth- and early twentieth-century scholars.

One of those BAE men, Cyrus Thomas, was put in charge of the 1882 congressionally funded study of the mounds, which was not published until 1894. Thomas believed that some vanished race had built the mounds but an analysis of the evidence that his study revealed caused him to change his mind.

Until late in the nineteenth century, American amateur antiquarians, pseudoscientists, Bible-thumpers, and looters had the mounds all to themselves.

By that time, the clamber for the allotment of Indian land was already ringing the death knell for the Indian nations in "Indian Territory," under the marvelous American theory, as it applied to Choctaws and other Indians from the Southeast, that people who had been farmers for thousands of years would learn how to be civilized if they were forced to become farmers.

But there was more to it than that. The allotment of Indian land would be the only way to finally obtain the blessings of civilization for the "savages," according to Henry Dawes, U.S. senator from Massachusetts, who explained the urgent necessity of allotment.

Senator Dawes explained that the Indians lacked the essential element of "selfishness" to ever become civilized, and that they would continue lacking that essential element as long as they were allowed to continue owning their land in common and sharing with one another.

Little mention was ever made of the intense pressure that whites were applying to the U.S. Congress to find some way to allow them to get their hands on the "excess" Indian land that allotment would produce.

By that time, even the best educated, most literate Americans had been persuaded, by the "father of anthropology," Lewis Henry Morgan, that Indians were "savages."

Morgan, a lawyer, is an embarrassment to contemporary anthropologists, who vehemently deny that he is the "father" of their academic discipline, primarily because Morgan was the first and last anthropologist who was capable of carrying on any kind of conversation, intelligent or otherwise, with anyone who was not a fellow anthropologist.

Today, all anthropologists are required by law, as a humanitarian measure, to eat in special cafes, where the waiters are all anthropology graduate students who have spent years learning how to translate what anthropologists say, because otherwise all of our anthropologists would starve to death, and then we wouldn't have any anthropologists.

Lewis Henry Morgan's persuasively influential *Ancient Societies*, written in plain Anglish and published in 1877, helped convince America that something drastic had to be done to force the poor Indians to pull themselves out of "savagery," for their own good.

At about that time, in the late nineteenth century, an enduring, quintessentially American pall of darkness settled over the "Mound Builders"—the emerging esoteric gobbledygook jargon of an infant anthropology discipline and its research tool of archaeology, a gobbledygook jargon that is tailor-made and guaranteed to bring information about the "Mound Builders" to the attention of no one.

Thus, by according it little in the way of sophisticated attention for about a century and then by burying it in gobbledygook for more than a century, the independent invention of complex civilizations by Indians in North America remains invisible to an even greater extent today than when the forests hid that history.

That has been accomplished partly by the way Americans have compartmentalized the dissemination of knowledge, ensuring that there is a disconnect among the "academic disciplines" of such a nature and depth that it has become virtually impossible even for there to be much of an intelligent conversation among those "disciplines," let alone for a practitioner of one of them, steeped in the esotericism that has grown up within the methodological limitations and conceptual frameworks of his or her own discipline, to make sense of what is said by some practitioner who has been steeped in the gobbledygook jargon and other esoterica of nearly any other discipline.

There are reasons why the peer-reviewed academic journals in nearly all of the academic disciplines, which are proudly proclaimed to be the beating hearts of the contemporary advancement of knowledge in America, have several thousand university libraries for subscribers, and no readers.

There are reasons why powerful vested interests in America saw to it that the best and brightest minds in the country would be incapable of spouting anything but gobbledygook jargon, and then spend their entire careers publishing that gobbledygook in peer-reviewed academic journals that would never have any readers.

One might think that the academic discipline of Anglish would be the one touchstone that all might partake of, particularly its branch of literary criticism, as many people in many different disciplines share a love of literature.

But no one on earth can make sense of the gobbledygook of that branch of learning, except for the graduate students in that narrow specialty, who are forced to spend years learning how to decipher it, and who, at the outset, no doubt weep with joy when they encounter, buried somewhere among it, a sentence consisting of a noun, a verb, and an object without at least one of those three things having been fashioned out of jargon, thus rendering that sentence comprehensible to any literate person.

As it happens, the discipline of American history remains one of the least gobbledygook- and esoterica-burdened of all the academic disciplines.

That is partly because its essential propaganda purpose makes it imperative that it be accessible to all, and partly because the learning of most of the other disciplines has been safely compartmentalized beyond the ken of historians, and partly because American historians have nothing of any significance to say that cannot be gotten, with less tedium, and with a lot more entertainment, from either a novelist or a preacher.

So it is perfectly safe for American historians to be allowed to express themselves with clarity.

The primary message of those American historians, in common with the cosmology of their German culture, and in common with the endless parade of American preachers and novelists, who also perpetuate the German view of things, is that the North American Germans are wretched creatures, who were even more wretched in the past, which is ho-hum news to all Americans.

That ho-hum news is delivered by their historians with a tedium that just cannot compete with a good preacher or novelist conveying pretty much the same message.

Today, the American scientific community appears to be able to say, largely only to one another, that by about the year 1200 the population of Cahokia had grown to about fifty thousand people, which made Cahokia a metropolitan area larger than London or Paris at that time.

That population was augmented by quite a number of largely uninvestigated satellite suburb communities, in that portion of the eastern side of the Mississippi River that is known as "the American bottoms," which are the richest agricultural lands on the North American continent.

The ability to create the kind of population density of Cahokia's urban core is thought to have resulted from a new hybrid of corn, with a shortened growing season from more than 200 days to 120 days, and, perhaps more importantly, from the spread of the cultivation of beans northward from Mexico, which, since it allowed an essential amount of protein to be acquired through agriculture, made the population less dependent on game.

But that degree of urban population density might have been the reason why Cahokia was completely abandoned by about 1350, after its citizens had become intolerably afflicted with well-known diseases that are homegrown, which spring from open sewers in the streets and the other kinds of filth associated with urban crowding in cities all over the world at that time.

The people apparently did not leave Cahokia all at once. It appears they left gradually in groups, until, over the course of about half a century, the ceremonial center of the urban core had been entirely abandoned, at which time the forest began inexorably reclaiming it.

Another factor contributing to Cahokia's decline may have been that it simply ran out of people from outlying areas that it could compel to move into its urban core. It has been well known for a long time that death rates in urban settings outnumber birth rates, and for that reason, the only way that any city can sustain its population is by constant immigration.

Cahokia was only one of many "Mound Builder" centers that flourished throughout the lush river bottoms of the interior of the eastern half of the North American continent, at various places and in different millennia. Those centers waxed and waned and warred with one another, expanding, contracting, and changing, and conducting trade over networks that extended everywhere, even to the northwest Pacific coast.

Some of the centers may have been organized like states, with multiple levels of bureaucracy and standing armies. Much of that is in dispute. Nearly anything about the "Mound Builders" of any millennium is in dispute.

The calamitous fourteenth century (perhaps an even more calamitous century in Europe, which was being terrorized by the infamous Black Death) saw some other ancient civilization centers being abandoned elsewhere on the North American continent, well before the voyage of Columbus.

In the Four Corners region of the Colorado Plateau, ancestral Pueblo peoples were forced, primarily by a decades-long drought, to abandon the spectacular cliff palaces of what is now Mesa Verde National Park, in present-day southwestern Colorado, and seek a more dependable source of water for their sophisticated agriculture, which they largely found in the nearby Rio Grande River Valley watershed in present-day New Mexico.

At about the same time, they were also abandoning all of their other settlements in the Colorado Plateau region, including the center of their civilization, Chaco Canyon, and its Pueblo Bonito, in present-day northwestern New Mexico.

Pueblo Bonito, four stories tall, with eight hundred rooms, was the largest stone-masonry apartment building in the world. One larger than Pueblo Bonito would not be constructed anywhere in the world for another five hundred years, until, late in the nineteenth century, one in New York City finally eclipsed its size.

In present-day southern Arizona, the so-called Hohokam people abandoned one of the most elaborate and most skillfully engineered networks of irrigation canals anywhere in the world. Five centuries later, Americans occupying what is now the city of Phoenix would discover that they only had to clean out the canals and rebuild the sluice gates to put the ancient Hohokam irrigation network back into operation.

The impressive achievements of the Hohokams and of the Ancestral Puebloans did not fit the model of the American cultural-bias aspects of the legal code talk of "savagery" any better than the achievements of the "Mound Builders." The only thing about the Hohokams and Puebloans that did fit that model was the fact that they were non-Christians (which, in actuality, was enough).

When Americans discovered those ruins in the far West in the late nineteenth century, they replayed their befuddlement regarding some supposed vanished race of people that must have constructed those impressive things. Americans invented a supposed vanished race they dubbed "Anasazi" for the distinction of having built the Colorado Plateau ruins in the Four Corners region.

It would take the American scientific community quite some time to figure out that the "Anasazi" were the ancestors of the contemporary Pueblo people, whose history has now been charted for thousands of years in that region, under the name "Basketmakers." Scientists would also be a long time figuring out that the Hohokam people were the ancestors of some of the contemporary Native peoples of present-day southern Arizona.

Many aspects of history in the Southwest have benefited from a clarity that was obtained after astronomer Andrew Douglass discovered dendrochronology, that is, tree-ring dating, early in the twentieth century, which eventually made it possible to know the approximate year that an individual tree was cut for a roof beam in many of the ancient structures that are still standing in that arid climate. A tree-ring calendar for the Southwest has now been established that goes back thousands of years.

Very little of the "Mound Builder" ruins remain undisturbed to be investigated. Most of the mounds yielded little that was valued by the mostly illiterate, so-called pot hunters who looted them, and much of Indian history lies discarded and scattered throughout the underbrush of a vast portion of the eastern half of the continent, spurned by people who had little comprehension of and less regard for what they were destroying.

Some looters, however, hit the jackpot.

The most spectacular haul, during the Great Depression of the 1930s, the so-called King Tut bonanza of North America, occurred at Spiro Mound.

The Spiro Mound complex was located at a gateway to the buffalo plains, in the Arkansas River Valley, downriver from the famous "Three Forks of the

Arkansas," near the Arkansas border of present-day east-central Oklahoma, on land that, until the illegal statehood of Oklahoma in 1907, had been the Choctaw Nation.

The Oklahoma legislature had passed an anti-pot-hunting law not long before Spiro Mound was looted, and fear of that law spurred the looters to extraordinarily hasty excavation and virtual destruction of the Spiro Mound and an equally hasty looting of the fabulous treasures they found there.

They hauled away many large and small finely crafted artworks of copper, the copper having been acquired in trade from the Great Lakes region of the Upper Midwest and then fashioned into such things as large ceremonial hatchets and impressive gorgets.

The looters found glistening black razor-sharp obsidian knives, the obsidian having been imported from what is now Yellowstone National Park in present-day northwestern Wyoming, finely etched large conch shells, imported from the Atlantic coast and Gulf Coast, large quantities of freshwater pearls, elaborately tailored gowns of feathers, pottery, ceremonial pipes, and many other things.

No one knows the full extent of exactly what the looters found. Much of it is in private, often secret, collections around the world.

The damage to Spiro Mound was of such an extent that scholars have been hard pressed to try to reconstruct the sequence of the ancient burials and of one apparent massive reburial that had consolidated generations of accumulated treasure into one chamber.

The massive reburial was apparently a last-ditch effort of the priesthood to reverse ill fortune that shortly afterward resulted in the complete abandonment of the core of the Spiro complex, which had been an important trading partner of Cahokia and other centers throughout the "Mound Builder" world at that time.

Some of the Spiro looters went immediately to Kansas City to show the out-of-state press part of what they had found, to alert the world to what was for sale. The "discovery" became big news throughout the country.

Visions of buried riches, ripe for the taking, not in some far-off place like Egypt but here, in North America, spurred the rural poor throughout the Depression-ravaged nation of the 1930s into seeking out and destroying the few mounds that had not been previously damaged, rendering them archaeologically useless, and they further damaged many of the ones that had already been excavated numerous times.

Archaeologists hastily excavated what remained of Spiro Mound. They discovered some chambers the looters had missed, which contained an impressive array of Spiro artifacts.

The looting of Spiro Mound was about the last time that Americans took any notice of the "Mound Builders," a little more than seven decades ago.

The "Mound Builders" have now largely passed out of the collective American consciousness, not having been the focus of any kind of media event since the Great Depression.

Most Americans today have never even heard of them and remain as oblivious to the achievements that sprang from the North American cradle of civilization as the Medieval-minded Anglish colonists who began arriving in North America in the early seventeenth century.

Chapter Thirteen

The Birth of the Brilliant Choctaw Confederation

*I*t makes little difference whether or not the American academic community ever learns very much about the North American cradle of civilization.

Regardless of what any professors might know, or what they might learn, about Indians, there is virtually no chance that the rest of America will ever become aware of it, now that American professors have been muzzled.

Professors are people who are imprisoned in a self-contained, self-important vacuum.

There are reasons for that.

Long ago, professors allowed themselves to be forced, by the tenure and merit review processes, to do their publishing in periodicals that were never going to have any readers, not even on university campuses.

Even university students who have been full-time students for years have no idea what a peer-reviewed academic journal might be, or how to find one in their university library, or how to tell the difference between one of those journals and a magazine, and few students have any interest in learning what the difference might be, to the hair-pulling frustration of their professors, trust me on that one.

Curiously, virtually no professors seem to be aware that any one of the leading authors of the so-called Indian romance novels, a subcategory in the huge and lucrative genre of women's romance fiction, exerts far more influ-ence on contemporary public opinion about Indians than all of the publish-ing about Indians that all of the professors do combined.

For many years, women's romance fiction, of which the Indian romance novel is a large subcategory, has accounted for approximately half of all of the mass-market paperback publishing in the world.

Indian romance novels, dashed off at a rate of three or four per year by some of the most ignorant people on the planet about Indians, speak to millions of readers. And while those books may be "just fiction," their readers absorb the stereotypes that are characteristic of most of those books, books that are so widely distributed that they are even at point of purchase racks in grocery stores.

It might only be women who read Indian romance novels, but women have been allowed to vote for quite some time, and nobody in America, male or female, reads anything that the professors write.

Few Americans have ever seen a peer-reviewed academic journal, and virtually no Americans ever read one.

There are reasons for that.

Long ago, professors allowed themselves to be rendered incapable of com-municating with anyone except another academic, and even then only if that academic was a fellow practitioner of the same academic discipline, steeped in the mysteries of the gobbledygook jargon of that same branch of learning.

There is a reason for all of those things.

It's not a conspiracy, not a conscious one, anyway. It's more of an intu-itive thing, a result of paths taken at many different times by many different people, stemming from an intuitive, perhaps even subconscious awareness that it is too dangerous to American Indian law for Americans to ever be allowed to know what is known, and what could be known, about the igno-rance and the religious bias that are the twin pillars of American Indian law.

And so, things like the North American cradle of civilization and the so-called "Mound Builder" civilizations that sprang from that cradle of civiliza-tion must always remain unknown, must always remain a mystery, to the mass of American voters, who might vote their conscience, who might express their sense of justice and decency, if they were allowed to know anything about the things that have the capacity to bring down those twin pillars of ignorance and religious bias.

There is no mystery, however, about the name of the horror that brought a sudden end to the "Mound Builder" cycles of expansion and contraction and change—Variola major.

Smallpox.

People in the Old World had been ravaged by that killer for perhaps as long as thirty-five hundred years, long enough to build up some resistance to the disease, after contracting it from domesticated cattle, apparently originally on the subcontinent of India, from which it quickly spread throughout the rest of the Old World.

In all that time, Old World peoples had not discovered that smallpox was transmitted to humans from cattle, and they never learned how to protect themselves from smallpox, which could have been achieved very easily, by close contact with cattle.

"Pretty as a milkmaid," the Anglish were fond of saying, without ever figuring out that the reason their milkmaids had such pretty complexions was because their daily close contact with cattle exposed them to cowpox, a disease that produced a rather mild rash that caused a bit of discomfort for a few days and then provided immunity to smallpox for life.

Europeans lived in perpetual terror of smallpox.

It was a fact of daily life, and death, accounting for what Francis Jennings estimated to have been about 10 percent of all the deaths throughout European history.

It might help account for why Old World peoples sought, and found, so much solace in religion.

In European history, there wasn't much question of whether or not one would contract smallpox. It was more a matter of when that would happen and which form of the disease that might be.

There were less lethal strains of smallpox, at least less lethal for Europeans, who'd had thousands of years for their immune systems to make adjustments, which was what enabled them to have fairly high survival rates.

But smallpox left its ravages even on its survivors, most notably a telltale pockmarked face.

Many historical European portraits were faked by the painter, to the extent of not showing the ravages of smallpox on the faces of the subjects of those portraits. Those people were often kings or queens, people who would have had the head of the painter if the portrait had realistically reflected the unflattering truth.

One Old World strategy for surviving smallpox was to intentionally expose oneself to one of the less lethal strains. Old World peoples learned early that surviving any form of smallpox provided immunity for life.

By the early eighteenth century, some controversial doctors in the Anglish colony of Massachusetts in America were offering wealthy patients a smallpox "inoculation," which required that a patient be at least wealthy enough to afford to be bedridden, under a doctor's care, for about a month.

In addition to being controversial and expensive, smallpox "inoculation" was risky. It was not a vaccine, not a prevention—far from it.

The doctor intentionally infected the patient with one of the less lethal strains of the disease. The patient became gravely ill.

In the smallpox outbreak in colonial Boston in 1721–22, 6 people out of 247, or 2.4 percent, died from the inoculation treatment, while 844 people out of 5,980 who caught smallpox died, about 14 percent (see R. G. Robertson, *Rotting Face: Smallpox and the American Indian* [Caxton Press, 2001], 53).

The controversy surrounding those 1721–22 "inoculations" in colonial Boston did not arise because they involved a sobering amount of risk or that they were only available to the wealthy but because they saved lives.

Some outraged Christians railed against the "inoculations" and even bombed the home of a minister, Cotton Mather, who was supporting them, after Mather had learned of the inoculation technique from an African slave he had purchased, who had been inoculated by his people in Africa.

The outraged Boston religious protestors accused men like Cotton Mather of interfering with their conception of a divine will by helping to spare the lives of people who, in that divine course of events, would have contracted the disease and died.

Those geniuses of that era were the sort of Medieval-minded European imperialists that North American Indians were beginning to get acquainted with.

European diseases continued ravaging Indian communities in North America throughout the seventeenth, eighteenth, and nineteenth centuries, reducing them, sometimes suddenly, by the late nineteenth century, to what would be their lowest levels in the history of the European invasion of the continent.

At that point, the imperialists among the Americans *thought* that they could do anything with sovereign Indian nations that they pleased.

What they did with the southeastern Indian nations that had been forcibly removed to what became "Indian Territory" was force the allotment of their land, sell the "surplus" to whites, and then attempt to maintain the legal fiction that those sovereign Indian nations had been extinguished and that their citizens were thereafter merely citizens of the illegal state of Oklahoma.

There is little about the devastation of European diseases in North America that could have happened much differently in any significant way, except that those diseases might have been even more deadly if they had been spread intentionally. But there is little evidence of that having happened except for a few isolated instances.

When smallpox vaccines became available, Americans made sometimes strenuous and risky efforts to provide that protection to Indian nations, some of which, wary at this point, were uncooperative.

At the time the two hemispheres came into permanent contact there was virtually nothing that could have been done to prevent the devastation from disease that followed.

An intriguing question to ponder is whether portions of the Western Hemisphere might have been ravished by pandemics of Old World diseases in the thousands of years before Columbus.

It seems, statistically, highly unlikely that Columbus could have been the first Old World person to travel across the Atlantic Ocean from the neighborhood of the African Atlantic coast to the Caribbean islands.

It seems much more likely that Columbus was just the first Old World person to make that trip and then make it back to the Old World to tell about it, by odds that I have calculated to be 313 to 3, rounded off to whole numbers, after much thought and careful study.

No boat is needed.

Even a floating tree trunk, or anything else that floats, that gets caught up in the trade winds, in the neighborhood of the Canary Islands off the African Atlantic coast, is going to get transported by those trade winds to the neighborhood of Barbados in the Caribbean Sea, whether it wants to go there or not.

At sea in the tropical latitudes, people have survived on rainwater and turtles for a lot longer than it takes to get from Africa to the Caribbean Sea on the trade winds.

Rather than wondering whether that might have happened before Columbus, the better question seems to be whether any of what might have been several dozen or more Old World people who probably made that trip, down through the millennia of human folly, might have touched off any pandemics of Old World diseases in the Western Hemisphere.

Even dead Europeans or Africans could have reached the Western Hemisphere. A drifting small boat carrying a smallpox corpse, swept across the Atlantic to some Caribbean or Gulf of Mexico shore, could have touched off a pandemic.

Getting back to the Old World, dead or alive, from North America, especially alive, seems the much bigger problem.

The powerful Gulf Stream, as it shoots northward between Cuba and Florida, will take you to Galway Bay in Ireland, but the odds of arriving there alive in what become cold stormy waters don't seem as though they would be as good, particularly if those adventures were the result of the sorts of accidents that had undoubtedly been bringing Old World people, at irregular intervals, to Caribbean and Gulf of Mexico shores from time immemorial.

But longer odds have never meant impossible odds, not if the odds-vexing variable of luck cannot be calculated with any degree of confidence and not if accidental misfortune cannot be given an overshadowing presence in the equation.

If you might need an Anglish translation for that, it means that Indians might have intentionally made the voyage, and might have done so successfully, though I am happier with the equation if they don't have to be alive when they get there.

In a speech at a conference at the University of Oklahoma in the summer of 1992, the dean of Native American scholars, Dr. Jack D. Forbes, now retired, discussed some evidence he had found in European archives indicating that Native peoples had made the voyage from the Western Hemisphere to Ireland, before Columbus, and evidence that Columbus had become aware of that (in remarks made in a plenary session speech at the Returning the Gift: A Festival of North American Native Writers conference, Norman, OK, July 7–10, 1992 [video tape of twenty plenary session speeches from the conference available from Greenfield Review Press, Greenfield Center, New York]).

Today, the annual trade-wind sailing frolic from the Old World to the Caribbean Sea is so routine that there's virtually a traffic jam of small yachts every December that come flooding out of the Mediterranean Sea and sail for the Caribbean, as the hurricane season is ending in the Caribbean.

Even sailing around the world single-handed in a small yacht has become so routine it attracts no interest, since Captain Joshua Slocum became the first person acknowledged to do it, so spectacularly, little more than a century ago.

Today, so many small yachts sail around the world that they have become unwanted nuisances in many of the isolated places that once welcomed them.

Even something like climbing the highest peak in the world, Mt. Everest, has become so routine since Sir Edmund Hillary was the first person known to have done that in 1953 that the Chinese government recently had to remove tons of trash that climbers had abandoned high on that peak.

Some of the things that seemed so spectacular to do, not so long ago, that have now become so routine and ordinary, were not at all impossible to do centuries and millennia ago.

The ancient Chinese and Japanese, Pacific sailors of unquestioned ability, are now known to have reached the Western Hemisphere, as far south as South America, long before Columbus sailed.

One of the easiest things that has ever been possible to do is to ride the trade winds across the Atlantic Ocean from the Old World to the Caribbean Sea. It seems highly likely that it happened, quite a number of times, before Columbus.

Today, there is no doubt that the sixteenth-century devastation of Indian populations, on a massive scale, from Old World diseases spread by the Spanish after Columbus, was overwhelmingly the single most important factor in the short-term subsequent history of the North American continent, for the brief period of the next few hundred years, and it was nobody's fault.

But the consequences of the devastation of European diseases were not tragic for all of the Indian peoples of North America.

In the eastern half of the continent, some Indians benefited enormously from the cataclysm. It freed them from the tyranny of their "Mound Builder" priests.

Being free of the tyranny of religion empowered them to figure out ways to free themselves from other sorts of tyrannies, such as political and economic ones.

In a burst of creative genius, some of them fashioned new institutions for their civilizations and soared to new heights of human achievement.

In one such instance, in the aftermath of the worst phase of the destruction wrought by smallpox, during the so-called Black Hole of Indian history in the southeastern portion of the continent, several remnant groups of smallpox survivors, which included the oldest, most dominant, most distinguished, and by far the most dangerous of the Lords of the North American Continent, fled their devastated agricultural settlements in the river bottoms of the lower reaches of the mighty *Misha Sipokni*.

They took with them their sophisticated knowledge of agriculture, their sophisticated knowledge of *their* continent, their mental conception of themselves, and little else.

They said good riddance to much of the rest of their former lives.

Those people came together from different directions, from different river valleys, from at least three different "Mound Builder" centers, each speaking a mutually intelligible dialect of the same sublime language (see Patricia Galloway, *Choctaw Genesis, 1500–1700* [University of Nebraska Press, 1995], for the range of some of the speculative factors).

It appears that at least one of those smallpox-fleeing groups contained a substantial core portion of the distinctive, formal, ceremonial-tongued upper crust of the most anciently knowledged Lords of the North American Continent.

This we can surmise because their artificially formal version of the Choctaw language not only survived among the Choctaw Confederation but flourished and was mastered by all of the divisions of the confederation and used exclusively for formal interdivisional occasions.

That substantial core portion of that old upper crust of society, however, apparently did not include any surviving members of the priesthood, for reasons that become apparent when the early eighteenth-century Choctaw people are compared with the early eighteenth-century Natchez people.

Some of those smallpox-fleeing people would come to be known as Okla Falaya (Long People), who, from their oral traditions, apparently came from the west or northwest. In Okla Falaya cosmology, the west would represent death.

Those Okla Falaya people might have been descendants of some of the people who had been within the orb of a large "Mound Builder" center across the Mississippi River in present-day northern Louisiana, one that had sprung from what is thought to have been the earliest center of "Mound Builder" civilization in the far distant past. Or perhaps they had once been people within the orb of Cahokia or Spiro or some other center in the western region of the "Mound Builder" sphere.

It would be the Okla Falaya dialect of the Choctaw-Chickasaw language that the missionaries to the Choctaws would present to the world, purporting that it was the "Choctaw language."

Beginning in the second decade of the nineteenth century, those missionaries-turned-not-so-hot-linguists, primarily the two Cyruses, Cyrus Kingsbury and Cyrus Byington, would work tirelessly to publish missionary materials in Okla Falaya, with the assistance of some playful tongues-in-cheeks among the Okla Falaya people.

That "standardization" process, one of attempting, even if inadvertently, to make the Okla Falaya dialect the dominant dialect of the Choctaw language, worked much the same way that it had when William Caxton "standardized" the Anglish language from one of the Anglish dialects of London, beginning about 1475, by publishing books in that London dialect, such as one of the earliest books he published, *The Game and Playe of the Chesse*, after the Old World had finally stumbled upon the invention of movable type in the 1430s, which finally made the publication of books possible.

Printing, as such, even on a mass-distribution scale, had been known for millennia—stamping a coin with the imprint of the image of some emperor or king was printing.

Today, the Okla Falaya dialect, after nearly two centuries of being the "published" version of the Choctaw-Chickasaw language, has become, to Choctaws, approximately what the Choctaw trade jargon (called "Mobilian" trade jargon by historical linguists) had been to all of the Indian nations throughout the vast region of the southeastern portion of the North American continent, for how many generations, stretching back into the most misty reaches of time immemorial, nobody knows.

It is of profound historical significance to note that the pervasive "Mobilian" trade jargon throughout the entire Southeast was based on the

Choctaw language, not on any Muscogee language of the so-called Creeks, and that there is no dispute about that, whatsoever, among any historical linguists.

So when are those historical linguists going to get around to figuring out the significance of that and change the silly names they came up with, haphazardly, for Indian language families, and replace the nomenclature for the broad umbrella of the "Muskogean" language family with the more appropriate, and more accurate, "Choctawan" language family?

Under that broad Choctawan language family umbrella is where the languages of the Muscogee Confederation should be placed, not vice versa.

Some of those Muscogee languages, such as Alabama, are so obviously so recently Choctaw that Alabamans might properly be said to still be Choctaws, particularly since their Louis Littlecoon Oliver achieved the kind of distinction as a poet that might cause Choctaws to be inclined to claim the Alabamans again, if for no other reason than to be able to claim that poet as a Choctaw.

It is also worth noting that the people who are known to have been the most adept at "Mobilian" trade jargon were also the first people in the Southeast to take the bother of finding out that Anglish trade goods were not only less expensive than French trade goods but were also of superior quality.

Those people, the Okla Falayan-speaking Chickasaws, who are clearly just Choctaws of another kind, and who can still skin you alive in a trade if you are not careful, continued to be the premier Indian intertribal merchants throughout a vast portion of North America throughout the so-called colonial era.

Chickasaw traders show up everywhere in those colonial records. There are reasons why, for example, Chickasaw traders were encountered by Lieutenant Wilkinson of the U.S. Army at the Three Forks of the Arkansas in 1806, and there are reasons why, while those Chickasaws may have been far from home, that was nothing new for Chickasaws.

The Okla Falaya dialect of Choctaw, however, is hardly the only dialect of the Choctaw language, and the Okla Falaya people were not the only ones who were fleeing those European diseases during the so-called Black Hole of history in the Southeast.

Some of those smallpox-fleeing people would come to be known as Okla Tannap (People of the Opposite Side), also known as the Ahe Pat Okla

(Potato-Eating People), who apparently came from the northeast, probably having been some of the people within the orb of the large "Mound Builder" center known as Moundville, in present-day northwestern Alabama.

Some of those smallpox-fleeing people would come to be known as Okla Hannali (Six Towns People), who apparently came from somewhere to the south. In Okla Hannali cosmology, the south would represent death.

Perhaps some of the Okla Hannali came from the rich agricultural river bottoms around Mobile Bay and were the people who had encountered and humbled the expedition of Hernando de Soto in October of 1539, at a great loss of life.

All of the other Choctaws would consider the Okla Hannali people to be the most "hillbilly" of all of the Choctaws. All of the other Choctaws would make fun of the Okla Hannali dialect of the Choctaw language.

The Okla Hannali people would also be the most persistent in continuing the beauty-enhancing practice of the artificial sculpting of the foreheads of infants by means of cradleboards, sometimes called head flattening, a practice that is known to have been, at one time, a Siouan cultural characteristic and which hints at the likelihood of conquest by some Siouan people at some point in the fairly recent Okla Hannali past.

Siouan peoples are known to have repeatedly invaded the southeastern portion of the North American continent, where they occasionally left Siouan-speaking peoples, such as the Biloxi people, who were near neighbors of the Okla Hannali in the early eighteenth century.

Many small nations of peoples, and many small remnants of nations of peoples, are known to have inhabited the Southeast in the early eighteenth century, who, for the most part, had entirely disappeared by the early nineteenth century.

The Okla Falaya, Okla Tannap, and Okla Hannali (and perhaps others, perhaps at that time including the Okla Chickasaw, and perhaps including some elusive, wispy people in Choctaw history, such as the ones known as the Okla Chito) fled their former homes in terror.

They got as far away as they could get, in that part of the world, from the devastated "Mound Builder" river-bottom centers and settlements that were spreading the European diseases, and they got as far away from the rest of the world as they could get.

They did that by ascending the streams of the region, from different directions, in present-day east-central Mississippi, while noting the agricultural suitability of the previously uninhabited "terraces" along those upper watercourses, until they had come together at the low crest of those watersheds, to a place that had apparently had some sacred significance for them for quite some time.

There, near the top of that hillbilly stronghold, where they had all independently, and calculatedly and shrewdly, antigravitated themselves to, they apparently adopted the only mound that would have much significance for them, which came to be known as *Nanih Waiya*.

That fairly large sculpted mound of earth, near the very top of the crest of those watersheds, became their acknowledged mother, as those sublimely tongued, wise, ancient peoples, those "Mound Builder" smallpox survivors, who would come to be known as Choctaws, formed a confederation of people who had grown profoundly, hindsightedly enlightened in the ways of the world.

They spread out their magnificent city of civilization into strings and clusters of towns, primarily near the agricultural terraces along the upper watercourses of that core homeland, from which they lorded it over an immense expanse of their ancient domain, the choicest part, land that ranks among the richest agricultural land in the world, land which for thousands of years had given the great gift of the immense riches of the North American continent to them, in tribute to them, as the rightful lords of that continent, to use as their deer-hunting preserve, as any sensible civilized people would do, who know that you can hoe corn damn near anywhere in the Deep South, but try feeding pine needles to deer and see what you get.

The Okla Falaya made their homes along the watercourses on the western side of *Nanih Waiya*, the Okla Tannap made their homes along the watercourses on the northeastern side, and the Okla Hannali made their homes along the watercourses on the southern side.

Perhaps it was because the Okla Falaya, Okla Tannap, and Okla Hannali were all possessed of the advantage of hindsight that accounts for why they became determined to employ the bond-breaking cataclysm of the European diseases that had befallen them to ensure that they never again would live their lives for the benefit of any political, religious, or economic organization.

Certainly they had the knowledge that they had failed to foresee the dangers of allowing too much in the way of organized social and economic complexity, and, as a result, they had found themselves made to suffer the indignity of being compelled to devote their leisure time to the drudgery of hauling millions of basketsful of dirt, for generations on end, for the benefit of somebody else, when they could have been spending that time playing ball.

In that sanctuary, well removed from the rest of the world, deep in the beating heart of the North American cradle of civilization, along the lower reaches of the mighty *Misha Sipokni*, those enlightened, long-distinguished, ancient peoples of the world seized their opportunity to refashion themselves in the face of the terrifying new threat of the deadly diseases that had burst upon them, and in that process they scaled the dizzying heights of the very pinnacle of what any people have ever attained in the elusive art of civilization.

It wasn't long after that before foolish foreigners from across the Atlantic Ocean encountered a shrewdly calculating, hindsightedly enlightened people, who had transformed themselves into an unpretentiously contented, indolently resplendent, leisure-loving nation of ballplayers, every man, woman, and child, a nation who had the advantage of knowing that they had already trod the same dirt basket-burdened path that those foolish foreigners were pompously unaware that they were endlessly, burdensomely, unnecessarily trudging along.

Chapter Fourteen

Choctaw Diplomacy

*A*s the seventeenth century was closing and the eighteenth century dawning, the French became the first of the foolish foreigners to become well acquainted with the Lords of the North American Continent, when those frog-eating Frenchmen began trying to extend their imperial ambitions over the Lower Mississippi River Valley.

The Choctaws nearly bankrupted the French.

For their part, the French helped themselves along that path by literally boasting themselves into near bankruptcy, when it quickly became apparent to the French, and to the Choctaws, and to everyone else, that the Choctaw Confederation, with its population, at that time of perhaps as many as twenty thousand or more people, held the balance of power in the Lower Mississippi River Valley.

The astute, worldly-wise, hindsightedly enlightened Lords of the North American Continent wasted little time in sizing up the French and in adopting a calculated, unpretentious, pitifully self-deprecating response to French posturing—that if the French were, indeed, the powerful, feared, and magnificently wealthy dirt basket-bearing people they boasted of being, then they could easily afford to shower a humble and destitute people, such as their Choctaw friends, with presents, annually, and in such volume as to deter them from any thoughts of alliance with either the Spanish in Florida or the Anglish in the Carolinas, unless, of course, the French might not be as glorious a nation as the Spanish or the Anglish.

With that pose, the Choctaws hit the jackpot.

The French soon learned that they had traveled all the way across the Atlantic Ocean, with visions of empire, only to encounter a strategically located people who would be pathetically shameless in adroitly exploiting their strategic advantage in a way that the Achilles heel of haughtiness of the foolish foreigners would result in those pretentious Frenchmen bearing their basketsful of dirt for the benefit of the indolently resplendent architects who had fashioned themselves into the capstone achievement of the North American cradle of civilization.

The French had no comprehension that they had encountered a people who were far more civilized than themselves.

The French, in common with other Medieval-minded Europeans, were not sophisticated enough to understand that the highest levels of civilization are beyond the reach of peoples who have not freed themselves from political, religious, and economic tyrannies.

Those lofty heights inhabited by the Choctaws are so difficult to scale, and have been so little inhabited, that they are likely to remain beyond the reach of many peoples.

The rarefied air of that pinnacle of civilization inhabited by the Choctaws is a domain of truly meaningful fundamental personal liberties, free of the mental prison of religion, free of dirt basket-bearing for the benefit of others, resplendent with time for the leisurely nurturing of extended family and community relationships, which are among the most important things that make life worth living and which the overwhelming majority of the sovereign Indian nations of North America would maintain can only be obtained by sharing, not by competing with one another for food and other material things, including land.

It is a place that is free of artificial distinctions based on the accumulation and hoarding of wealth, a place where the content of a person's character and the peculiarity of their personality are the most meaningful things in the emergence of the sort of distinctions that are necessary and desirable, where a people can be so little concerned about wealth that they can habitually and enthusiastically wager all of their movable possessions on the outcome of a game of ball or in a good knock-down, drag-out bout with a slot machine, where the odds are appropriately overwhelming enough to be worthy of engaging the Choctaw sense of challenge.

Just because they scale those lofty heights and inhabit that rarefied air doesn't mean there is anything about the Lords of the North American Continent that makes them any smarter than any other people.

How they happened to fall into their bed of roses is largely a result of accidents of history, after they had been launched, themselves, for millennia, along the same dreary dirt basket-burdened path that the Europeans and Americans are still trudging.

The Choctaws have undoubtedly fallen far short of attaining what might be *possible* to attain. There is nothing about their achievement that in any sense approaches perfection.

But they have not squandered their opportunity to stake their claim for having scaled higher than any other people who have ever been allowed by the accidents of history to make that climb.

They have merely done things in a peculiarly Choctaw way.

Just inhabiting the Olympian heights of that higher level of civilization has empowered them with perceptions that are beyond the capacity of Europeans and Americans.

In that rarefied air, the pretensions of dirt basket-bearing peoples can clearly be seen for what they are, and the eighteenth-century Choctaws were neither too haughty nor too proud to figure out how to exploit those silly pretensions.

In fleecing the French, little of anything was required of the Choctaw people, and little more was required of their shameless diplomats than to be cunningly unwilling to discuss virtually anything with the French other than the manifold miseries that those astute Choctaw diplomats eloquently enumerated and insisted were the result of the parsimony of their regally wealthy patrons not having lavished them recently with presents and then growing ominously sullen if another abundance of presents was not immediately forthcoming.

That frightened the French nearly out of their wits, whose imperial foothold in the Lower Mississippi River Valley and adjacent Gulf Coast region was, at best, precarious.

That tactical, self-deprecating Choctaw pose worked so well on the French that the diplomatic corps of the Lords of the North American Continent was inspired to polish that pose throughout the rest of the eighteenth century.

After long experience with the French in Louisiana, the Anglish in the Carolinas, and the Spanish in Florida, the Choctaw diplomatic corps eventually elevated itself to a status of walking, talking works of art in human form, fashioned by human hands to be holistically convincing to the eye and to the ear, a peculiar kind of North American artistic endeavor, a sort of traveling theater, appropriately costumed for maximum effect in the delicate art of fleecing pretentious, Medieval-minded colonizers out of the very shirts off their backs.

The ultimate perfection of that art by the Choctaw diplomatic corps can be gauged by the extent to which the three SNAGs who had been appointed by the Continental Congress of the United States to be the (North) American (German) treaty commissioners to the sovereign southern Indian nations failed to perceive the splendor of the civilization of the Lords of the North American Continent, after entertaining a delegation of thirty-one Choctaw diplomats for nine days at the first (North) American (German) treaty negotiation with Choctaws, after the Choctaws had received an invitation saying, "(Hey, suckers) We want to negotiate a treaty with you."

That occurred in the winter of 1785–86, at the sprawling SNAG plantation named Hopewell, in South Carolina, which was the home of one of those treaty commissioners, the upright, prayerful, Presbyterian deacon Andrew Pickens.

There, on January 4, 1786, shortly after those negotiations had been completed, the three (North) American (German) treaty commissioners reported:

> ...we received an express...informing us of the approach of the
> Choctaws, and they arrived here on the 26th. They had been on the
> path from the 16th of October...and we were, from motives of
> humanity, at their arrival, under the necessity of clothing the whole
> of them, as the weather was very cold, and they were nearly naked,
> before we commenced our negotiations...we could perceive their
> strong hankering after presents could not be abated...They are the
> greatest beggars, and the most indolent creatures we ever saw, and
> yet honest, simple...Their passion for gambling and drinking is
> very great...that they may return without starving, through indo-
> lence, we were necessitated to pack up some proper goods...the

presents . . . and the goods . . . amount to 1,811 dollars. . . . (Benjamin Hawkins, Andrew Pickens, and Joseph Martin to the Honorable Charles Thompson, Esq., January 4, 1786, from Hopewell, South Carolina, *American State Papers*, vol. 2, *Indian Affairs*, 49–50)

That experience at Hopewell made such a lasting impression on the NAGs that they would wait another fourteen years, until 1801, before attempting another treaty negotiation with the astute people who had so artfully fleeced them out of nearly $2,000 in unanticipated negotiation expenses in 1785–86.

That was a budget-busting, enormous amount of money in those days.

In order to help compensate for that unanticipated loss at Hopewell, the three SNAG treaty commissioners immediately began trying to cut their other expenses by dismissing the troop of U.S. Army soldiers that had been providing protection for them during their rounds of serial treaty negotiations with several other sovereign southern Indian nations, most of whom had departed by then, as the Choctaws had arrived very late, on Choctaw time.

Or, perhaps it would be more accurate to say, on Creek time, because, while en route, the Creeks had stolen all of their horses, forcing that entire Choctaw diplomatic delegation to walk all of the rest of the way to Hopewell.

Before sending away their troop of soldiers, the SNAG treaty commissioners felt compelled to take the U.S. Army coats off their backs so there would be some way to cover the near-nakedness of the Choctaw diplomats, undoubtedly partly out of concern for the sensibilities of the God-fearing, somewhat ostentatiously overdressed, good Christian ladies of that sprawling SNAG plantation.

In trying to downplay the extent of their financial losses to other officials of the near-penniless U.S. government, the SNAG treaty commissioners characterized the loss of the army coats as having been of an "old style," anyway.

They took the soldiers' sleeping blankets, too, and gave them to the Choctaw diplomats, who promptly either sold them to buy rum or gambled them away, to the incredulity of the SNAGs, who were shivering in what they considered to be cold weather in that climate.

Those imperial-minded North American Germans had no idea that it would only be another thirty-three years (in 1820, in their seventh treaty with the Lords of the North American Continent) before the deviously clever and likewise imperial-minded people those North American Germans formally met at Hopewell would get those barbarians from Europe to acknowledge Choctaw title to that immense portion of the ancient Choctaw imperial empire in the Trans-Mississippi West.

That spectacular 1820 Choctaw imperial domain would cost the NAGs millions of dollars and decades of effort in attempting to acquire title, piecemeal, to portions of it, from the Lords of the North American Continent.

One aspect of that frustrating North American German endeavor would not be resolved until late in the nineteenth century, when the U.S. Supreme Court would issue a decision declaring that the U.S. government had only been able to acquire title to a portion of that Choctaw empire by resorting to fraud and ordering an additional payment of more than $2,000,000, on top of the $600,000 the North American Germans had already paid in attempting to buy back that portion of it.

In hindsight, it seems almost to have been fated that the Choctaws and the NAGs, so different, and yet so similar, would emerge, in the brief decade-long period of enormous Choctaw-NAG goodwill after the War of 1812, as the wheeler-dealer partners in that 1820 scheme that would bring the Lords of the North American Continent all the way back to imperial-empire greatness.

The treaty negotiations in South Carolina at Hopewell in the winter of 1785–86 would not be the last time the NAGs would discover how expensive it could be to invite Choctaw diplomats to negotiations far from their homeland.

At Washington, D.C., in the winter of 1824–25, the hotel bar bill for the Choctaw diplomats, by itself, would cost the North American Germans $2,500 (see W. David Baird, *Peter Pitchlynn: Chief of the Choctaws* [University of Oklahoma Press, 1972], 17).

The North American German experience at Hopewell, particularly the expensive nature of how the NAGs made the formal acquaintance of a people whose diplomats had arrived very late to gamble and drink and party and take the measure of an incredulous, disgusted, pretentious, upright, prayerful, Medieval-minded people for nine days, at a cost to those slobbering barbarians of more than $200 a day, turned out merely to be a foretelling of the expensive nature of things to come.

In the first half of the eighteenth century, a succession of French governors in Louisiana had gone through more or less the same process of making the acquaintance of the Choctaws that the NAGs experienced in the winter of 1785–86.

But the French officials earlier in that eighteenth century had been much more perceptive than the SNAGs at Hopewell, who characterized those Choctaw diplomats as "honest, simple."

A new French governor of Louisiana, Governor Kerleric, perhaps best summed up the experience of French officials.

Upon meeting the Choctaws, in 1753, Kerleric declared:

> It seems to me that they are true to their plighted faith. But we
> must be the same in our transactions with them. They are men
> who reflect, and who have more logic and precision in their rea-
> soning than it is commonly thought. (Angie Debo, *The Rise and
> Fall of the Choctaw Republic*, 2nd ed. [University of Oklahoma
> Press, 1961], 29; originally published in 1934)

One year later, Kerleric's education had been completed, and he confided:

> I am sufficiently acquainted with the Choctaws to know that they are
> covetous, lying, and treacherous. So that I keep on my guard without
> showing it. (Debo 29)

Governor Kerleric had ample reason to keep on his guard. The things about Choctaws that frightened Kerleric are things that historical spin doctoring has suppressed into the deep background, and it has primarily been Choctaws who have done that spin doctoring, particularly mid-twentieth-century Choctaws who became academics, and who attempted to make the Choctaws more presentable to the pretensions of mid-twentieth-century North American Germans.

Indeed, the Lords of the North American Continent have gained a reputation among historians mostly as skillful, astute practitioners of the art of diplomacy.

The prolonged Choctaw milking of the French is certainly an indication of how Choctaws had ample occasion to acquire the sort of diplomatic skills that have become an important component of their public image. But that public image is largely a result of the tireless efforts of those mid-twentieth-century Choctaw scholars who took such pains to portray Choctaws that way, which wasn't difficult to do, if it was done just right, given how sleepy-headed most people were and how little interest most people had in Choctaws.

Those mid-twentieth-century Choctaw scholars were mostly dignified, professional, academic Choctaw women, who, on occasion, engaged in cat-fights with one another, and with some white female American historians.

Some of those great, mid-twentieth-century Choctaw ladies, such as Muriel Wright (a granddaughter of Allen Wright, the mid-nineteenth-century Principal Chief of the Choctaw Nation, who was a product of the early nineteenth-century Choctaw marriage of the white missionary Alfred Wright), were avowed assimilationists.

Muriel Wright had no hesitation in lambasting the white historian, Dr. Angie Debo, in print, for daring to write Choctaw history, in Debo's 1934 *Rise and Fall of the Choctaw Republic*, as a story of American imperial misdeeds regarding the Choctaws or for daring to imply that Muriel Wright's grandfather might have become a wee bit too susceptible to the temptations of money, take your pick (see Shirley A. Leckie, *Angie Debo: Pioneering Historian* [University of Oklahoma Press, 2000], 55–56).

Muriel Wright was the editor, for decades in the mid-twentieth century, of the Oklahoma Historical Society's quarterly scholarly journal, the *Chronicles of Oklahoma*, and she was the author of many journal articles and widely influential books, including *A Guide to the Indian Tribes of Oklahoma*, as well as Oklahoma history textbooks. Her assimilationist views of how the Choctaw people, Choctaw history, and the histories of other sovereign Indian nations should be portrayed to the public were something to reckon with.

One of those great Choctaw ladies, Dr. Anna Lewis, was descended from Choctaw patriots and was outraged at the betrayal of the Choctaws by the imperialists among the Americans.

After her education in the Choctaw Nation school system, before that school system was abolished by the creation of the illegal state of Oklahoma in 1907, and after graduating from college and then earning an M.A. in history at the University of California at Berkeley, Anna Lewis became, in 1930, the first female of any race to earn the Ph.D. degree from the University of Oklahoma.

Dr. Lewis spent her entire distinguished career researching her magnum opus, her life's work, her biography of Pushmataha, mining archives in Oklahoma, Washington, D.C., Mississippi, and California, among other places, while teaching history at the Oklahoma College for Women in Chickasha, Oklahoma (now the coed University of Science and Arts of Oklahoma). She retired in the late 1950s as head of the history department.

Dr. Lewis didn't much care what the barbarians who had invaded North America might think about the Choctaw history she had to tell, though she took pains to try to make that as palatable as possible in her biography of Pushmataha—not enough pains, apparently, not for the depth of the slobber of the North American German propaganda that the continent had been buried under by the 1950s, propaganda that had created the kind of intellectually repressive police state that allowed dangerous demigods, such as Senator Joseph McCarthy, to flourish and dangerous self-appointed censors, such as "Aware, Inc.," to ruin the lives and careers of even such harmless free thinkers as humorist John Henry Faulk (of much later *Hee Haw* television fame) and mystery novelist Dashiell Hammett (of *Maltese Falcon* fame).

There has never been a "convenient" time for Choctaws to try to get the attention of the American people, and the repressive atmosphere of the 1950s was one of the more "inconvenient" times, when Americans conceived of themselves as locked in a global death struggle with "godless" Communism while remaining unaware that they had created a potentially much more dangerous and much more enduring problem for themselves on the North American continent.

The well-known slobbering excesses of the hysterically repressive atmosphere of the 1950s have much in common with the potential slobbering excesses of the hysterically repressive atmosphere of the early twenty-first-century "Patriot Act" days. And that elicits the same kind of contempt from Choctaws.

Late in life, in failing health, not long before she died, not long after she had retired, Dr. Lewis discovered (twenty-five million minutes ago, as *The Alamo* was playing in theaters across America) that she could not find a reputable press that would publish her life's work.

Instead of giving up, one of the last things she did before she died was to swallow her pride, borrow money, and pay to have the book published by a vanity press in New York (Exposition Press), where her meticulously researched life's work, *Chief Pushmataha, American Patriot: The Story of the Choctaws' Struggle for Survival*, sank like a rock in a pond, to be read by practically no one but Choctaws, who were not particularly pleased that Dr. Lewis's account of Choctaw history, and of NAG history, was not of interest to America.

To this day, Dr. Lewis's telling of Choctaw history has been read by few people but Choctaws, and it is a very rare book, hard to find anywhere, because so few copies were printed (and fewer still were able to be distributed very widely), though there were circulating copies of it in the Oklahoma County Metropolitan Library system in the early 1960s, which continued to circulate into the 1980s, and perhaps into the 1990s, one copy of which ended up being housed in the rare books collection of the Downtown Library branch, which had restrictive access to its holdings.

No buildings on the campus of the University of Oklahoma are named in honor of that very first woman to earn the Ph.D. degree at that institution, some three-quarters of a century after Anna Lewis became the first woman to do that (see her necrology, Winnie Lewis Gravitt, "Anna Lewis: A Great Woman of Oklahoma," *Chronicles of Oklahoma* 40.4 [Winter 1962–63]: 326–29).

In attempting to make Choctaws more presentable to the sort of pompous, pretentious people the Germans in North America had become by the twentieth century, little mention was hardly ever made of what might be characterized as a few rough edges that the Lords of the North American Continent have displayed, even in the diplomatic arena.

In one such instance, in the early eighteenth century, a diplomatic mission from the Chickasaws to the Choctaws, which had been invited by the Choctaws to settle a dispute, found a big howling surprise waiting for them.

Upon entering the Choctaw building that was to have been the site of the negotiations, the Choctaws settled the dispute by falling upon the Chickasaw diplomats with hatchets and knives and killing every one of them.

There is a famous instance of Texans slaughtering a diplomatic delegation of Comanches in much the same manner. That kind of brutal deceit didn't do much to help endear Comanches to Texans, and it didn't do much to help endear Chickasaws to Choctaws, either.

Governor Kerleric's anxiety regarding the Lords of the North American Continent was not merely unfounded paranoia.

It could be a very deadly thing to fall out of favor with the Choctaws, who could be extraordinarily, sucker-punchingly deceitful and ruthless in displaying a chilling dark side.

That was the very last lesson the Natchez people, the Children of the Sun, lived to learn.

After the French had extended their grandiose ambitions to the Native nations of the Gulf region, with their imperial outposts of Biloxi in 1699 (on the present-day Mississippi Gulf Coast), Mobile in 1702 (on the present-day Alabama Gulf Coast), Natchitoches in 1714, and New Orleans in 1718 (both in present-day Louisiana), and once the French had gained enough strength to be useful to the Lords of the North American Continent, the Choctaws employed the French to destroy the Natchez.

The Natchez Nation was the only Indian nation that constituted a potential threat to Choctaw territory along its western flank.

The Natchez were the only eighteenth-century people still possessing a fully functioning "Mound Builder" civilization priesthood, the only "Mound Builder" center that had survived intact into the French colonial era.

The Choctaw destruction of the Natchez, in 1731, was accomplished with a kind of cold-blooded, calculated self-interest that is by far more characteristic of Choctaw foreign policy, which the Lords of the North American Continent practice whenever they might perceive it to be in their best interests to pursue the complete destruction of a rival nation.

In recent times, at least one other nation besides the Natchez is known to have suffered that fate, three-quarters of a century later.

At that time, in the early nineteenth century, Pushmataha would prosecute that Choctaw foreign policy with a tactical military brilliance that would leave nothing but the silence of death in the rich agricultural lands of the Red River Valley, and the valleys of its northern tributaries, west of the Mississippi River, along the southern portion of the Ouachita Mountains, that old, worn down but still rugged mountain range, the eastern half of which is found in present-day southwestern Arkansas, and the western half in present-day southeastern Oklahoma.

They were lands that the Choctaws coveted, largely because that portion of the Red River Valley is the farthest western extension of the "Gulf Coastal

Plain," the one part of the Trans-Mississippi West where Mississippi Choctaws can feel very much at home.

That land would be ruthlessly depopulated by Pushmataha in the years after 1805, so that the Lords of the North American Continent would have a desirable home to be removed to in the Trans-Mississippi West, if their removal should become a reality.

The catalyst for that Choctaw foreign policy had come when the Commanding General of the North American Continent had listened to President Thomas Jefferson's North American German treaty commissioners at Mount Dexter in 1805, as those barbarians vigorously and forcefully presented President Jefferson's plan of pursuing the removal of the sovereign southern Indian nations from the South and concentrating them in a portion of the Trans-Mississippi West.

The Choctaw response to the announcement of that quintessential German idea of racial segregation and concentration brings a chilling darkness to the topic of Indian removal that North American German historians, in keeping with their avoidance of nearly anything having to do with Pushmataha or the Choctaws, have paid little attention to.

North American German historians seem, naively, to have merely assumed that the Trans-Mississippi West was an uninhabited "wilderness" where NAGs could plop down large populations of Indians wherever and whenever they pleased.

Those particular western lands in the Red River Valley that were coveted by the Choctaws had been continuously inhabited for at least a thousand years by Caddoan peoples.

Those extensive and powerful Caddoan nations had been rather fully described by La Harpe in the early eighteenth century, who had found it remarkable that they had Apache slaves, which they'd acquired in trade from the West, from beyond the formidable barrier of the Cross Timbers.

The Cross Timbers had been one of the great natural barriers of the earth since the end of the last ice age, a tangle of densely spaced blackjack and post oak trees and treacherous quicksand river bottoms, a barrier that had kept the immense herds of buffalo to the west of it, a barrier of such depth and endurance that on either side of it the Indians were distinctly different.

That Cross Timber barrier extended through portions of three present-day states: it began in southeastern Kansas where it entered Oklahoma in a fairly narrow belt north of Tulsa and then spread out to encompass much of east-central Oklahoma (where today much of its lower elevations are buried beneath reservoirs, giving Oklahoma, according to the *Historical Atlas of Oklahoma*, more miles of shoreline than Minnesota, the so-called "Land of 10,000 lakes") and the northern portion of west-central Texas.

Those ancient Caddoan peoples of the Red River Valley had the misfortune of discovering that they had made the fatal mistake of standing in the way of Choctaw foreign policy, as prosecuted by a military genius who knew how to annihilate forces far superior in number to his own.

The cold-blooded details of what Pushmataha meant, as he had applied it to those Caddoan peoples, when he boasted, as he often did, "First I scare my enemy, then I kill him," can be found in Gideon Lincecum's 1860 biography, "Life of Apushmataha," which appeared in print for the first time in the first decade of the twentieth century in the *Publications of the Mississippi Historical Society*.

The details of how Pushmataha applied his boast to those villages of Caddoan peoples, in the years after 1805, as a matter of tactical genius, are too horrible to be repeated here.

Suffice it to say, that in executing that policy, Pushmataha employed the predictable certainty that when presented with the necessity of protecting their women, children, and old people, those superior forces would try to do that, only to find that a tactical trap had been sprung on them that made the last moments of their lives a thing of sheer terror, both for what they were witnessing and were helpless to do anything about and for what was happening to them and were also helpless to do anything about.

North American German historians have been content to assume that smallpox and Osage depredations depopulated that entire land, to leave it standing silent and empty to await the removal of the Choctaws to it.

Smallpox and Osages had something to do with it. But those historians haven't wanted to face the awful truth of the role that the Lords of the North American Continent played in providing themselves with the home of their choice in the Trans-Mississippi West.

Choctaws did that, not just as a matter of foreign policy but also as a matter of continental thinking and generational planning that is quintessentially Choctaw.

It was insurance against the day that President Thomas Jefferson's vision of coaxing sovereign Indian nations into moving across the Mississippi River (by giving them unlimited credit at U.S. government trading posts, getting them head over heels in debt, and demanding the exchange of more and more of their land to satisfy the recurring trading post debts, as Jefferson had outlined clearly and explicitly in letters to his secretary of war and the governor of Indiana Territory during the winter of 1802–3, a policy that had caused the Choctaws to run up about $50,000 in trading post debt by 1805, for which Jefferson's U.S. government demanded, and received, Choctaw land in that Treaty of Mount Dexter of 1805) might become something more than coaxing, which was exactly what happened, only twenty-five years after those Mount Dexter treaty negotiations, with the Indian Removal Act of 1830.

Something had happened in 1803 that changed everything, and which caused president Thomas Jefferson's North American Germans to take a giant stride toward becoming continental thinkers themselves, something called the Louisiana Purchase.

In that year, 1803, for the first time, the North American Germans acquired a claim to land west of the Mississippi River, a French claim to land the French had called "Louisiana."

The purchase of that French claim to that land roughly doubled the amount of land in North America being claimed by those unrestrainable German barbarians.

What those North American Germans intended to do with land they claimed was no mystery.

Their intentions had been clearly announced for all the world to see, in the so-called Northwest Ordinance of 1787, which explicitly laid out the procedures for converting that land first into things called "territories," and then into things called "states."

By the time of those Mount Dexter treaty negotiations of 1805, the handwriting was on the wall.

The continent was about to be gobbled up by barbarians who were so pompous and arrogant that they had no hesitation in telling the whole world exactly how they intended to do it, and, at Mount Dexter, they were putting their plans into action, having foolishly picked the Choctaws as the first Indian nation to try those things out on.

The only thing the Lords of the North American Continent could do was to stake their claim to as much of their continent as they could carve out for themselves before those German barbarians gobbled it all up.

Only fifteen years after those Mount Dexter treaty negotiations of 1805, in the treaty of 1820, the Choctaws consummated that profoundly wise, visionary endeavor by obtaining North American German recognition of Choctaw title to those silent and empty Red River valleys, throughout the entire range of the Ouachita (Big Hunt) Mountains, as well as recognition of Choctaw title to the immense sweep of land to the west of those Big Hunt Mountains, all the way to the summit of the highest peak in the southern Rocky Mountains.

At least, at the time of that treaty of 1820, the Choctaws and the U.S. government had intended that those Big Hunt Mountains would remain silent and empty to await the arrival of Choctaws who might desire to move there.

But, as Pushmataha pointed out to General Jackson at the negotiations for that treaty of 1820, those Big Hunt Mountains were already beginning to fill up with unrestrainable Anglish hunters and gatherers from east of the Mississippi River, who could conceive of no higher ambition in life than to aspire to become Arkansawyers, an idea that had burst upon an innocent world on March 2, 1819, when President James Monroe added his signature to the congressional legislation that changed a big portion of Missouri Territory into an "Arkansaw Territory."

That pitiful ambition on the part of those wretched, lawless hayseeds had prompted General Andrew Jackson to vow in 1820 that he would restrain them with the power of the almighty Untied States Army, which would remove those trespassing slobbering barbarians by force.

James Lawrence McDonald, the first Choctaw lawyer, held the United States to that vow, in the negotiations for the treaty of 1825, at least for the western half of those Big Hunt Mountains (present-day southeastern Oklahoma).

The eastern half of those mountains, by 1825, had already become irretrievably barbarized even for the almightiness of the United States Army of the mid-1820s to even want to try to do much about.

Therefore, in 1825, the United States was desperate to get the Choctaws to sell that irretrievably barbarized half of those mountains (present-day southwestern Arkansas) to the United States, so the U.S. Army wouldn't have to deal militarily with all of the North American German hunters and gatherers who were squatting on that Choctaw land.

But McDonald refused to even discuss any such sale until the United States had first fulfilled all of its outstanding treaty obligations to the Choctaws from prior treaties, of which there were quite a few, dating all the way back to the second treaty in 1801.

McDonald also refused to discuss anything until the United States agreed to send the U.S. Army to forcibly evict those trespassing barbarian hayseeds from the western half of those mountains, which finally made at least that portion of those Big Hunt Mountains suitable for civilized people to inhabit.

In many ways, the Choctaw treaty of 1825 stands out as one of the most remarkable negotiations with Indians that the United States has ever conducted, which was acknowledged, at that time, by American leaders such as John C. Calhoun, who were more than a little vexed at encountering an Indian negotiator who had been trained in American law.

In contrast, however, to the methods employed by the Choctaws in the early nineteenth century in exterminating the ancient Native peoples who occupied the Red River valleys of the Ouachita Mountains, and then consolidating as much of that land as Choctaws could get in treaty negotiations with the United States, the Choctaw annihilation of the Natchez in 1731 was accomplished with little more than a coldly calculated and quintessential Choctaw deceit.

In 1731, the Choctaws agreed to conspire with the Natchez, to join them in a combined revolt against the French, then merely sat back and watched when the Natchez rose up and began slaughtering the French at Fort Rosalie, which the French had foolishly founded in 1729 near the Natchez villages.

The Choctaws then calmly joined the French in annihilating the Natchez.

Thus, with little effort, the Lords of the North American Continent succeeded in getting the French to help the Choctaws secure the western flank of their Mississippi Choctaw land, something the French would not have done if they had been asked by the Choctaws to do that, and something the Choctaws would probably not have tried to do on their own.

In executing that Choctaw foreign policy, the last vestige of the "Mound Builder" priesthood, and its way of doing things, as practiced by the Natchez, passed into oblivion.

The endlessly fascinating Natchez were a powerful nation in the Lower Mississippi River Valley. They became the focus of one of John R. Swanton's more outstanding BAE bulletins, *The Indians of the Lower Mississippi River Valley*.

In the first third of the eighteenth century, the center of Natchez civilization was on the eastern bank of the lower Mississippi River, near the site of a French settlement that became the present-day town of Natchez, Mississippi.

In the early decades of the eighteenth century, the French became fairly well acquainted with the Natchez, fought four wars against them, and left detailed accounts of some aspects of their remarkable civilization.

After the Choctaws and the French annihilated the Natchez in the early 1730s, the French sold that last remaining vestige of the "Mound Builder" priesthood into slavery in the Caribbean. A few other surviving Natchez fled to the protection of the Chickasaws in present-day northern Mississippi.

From there, some of the Natchez made their way to the Muscogee Confederation, which came to be known as the Creek Nation, in present-day Georgia and Alabama, on the eastern side of the Choctaw Confederation.

In the mid-twentieth century, what was thought to be the last two surviving native speakers of the Natchez language, two elderly Natchez people, were found living in the Creek Nation in the present-day east-central portion of the illegal state of Oklahoma.

One facet of Natchez life that fascinated at least one early eighteenth-century French observer was the unabashed and unrestrained sexuality of the unmarried Natchez girls. But that was hardly the most remarkable thing the French observed about the Natchez.

In their political and social structure, the Natchez were perplexedly and fundamentally unlike any other Indians ever encountered anywhere in North America by the French or the Anglish, and they have remained entirely unknown to most North American Germans today, having never entered the awareness of American popular culture.

The details of Natchez civilization reduce to rubbish almost all generalizations about "Indians," particularly the silly generalizations of "New Age" faddists, generalizations that are based on some of the cultural details of the relatively insignificant proportion of North American Native peoples who have been called Plains Indians, with whom few other Indian nations have hardly *anything* in common but whom the silly Americans *still* regard as *the* shittin' ass Indians.

The importance of the haughty and arrogant so-called Plains Indians in the immense sweep of North American history has been minimal, and their even more insignificant, unremarkable, and utterly predictable fate in "American" history has been enormously magnified and dramatized by Hollywood, largely because it provides a propaganda vehicle for implying that all of North America's sovereign Indian nations are "conquered" nations, a tactic that, it is hoped, will dissuade anyone from inquiring into the fate of the many Indian nations, such as the Choctaws, who have taken the gamble that, somehow, the North American German barbarians can become a civilized people.

Once that great day has dawned, then the Choctaws can return their attention to *trying* to bring the blessings of Choctaw law to the so-called Plains Indians.

To what degree the tyrants of the Natchez priesthood were typical of the priesthoods of the other ancient "Mound Builder" centers, we will never know.

But the Natchez provide a glimpse of what other "Mound Builders" might have been like, and a glimpse of the kind of life that Choctaws, and many other eastern Indians, escaped from, when European diseases destroyed most of those ancient "Mound Builder" centers during the so-called Black Hole of history in the Southeast.

The Natchez reveal a complexity of social organization of a nature that no one could have imagined.

The most striking feature was the curious built-in social mobility of its otherwise rigid caste system.

The French discovered that the Natchez were organized into four clearly defined and rigid classes of people, which included three classes of royalty (Suns, Nobles, and Honored People) and one class of commoners (Stinkards). The remarkable feature of that social structure was that every member of the royal classes had to marry a Stinkard.

The extraordinarily complex upward and downward social mobility resulting from the calculations of the birth class of the offspring of those marriages insured that, in time, all of the descendants of all of the royal classes would be Stinkards, and the descendants of many of the Stinkards would be royalty.

Peter Farb reported (in *Man's Rise to Civilization*) that the operational flaw in the Natchez system seemed to be that it was continually running low on Stinkards. Thus more Stinkards had to be acquired by adoption through raids on neighboring peoples.

It must have been a shock to those captured people to find themselves adopted by the Natchez so that, as Natchez Stinkards, they could be made available as marriage partners for Natchez royalty, and thus stand a decent chance of living a life of relative comfort and privilege.

It puts a different light on the consequences of losing a war or a battle, or, for that matter, of just getting captured by the enemy.

The highest class of Natchez royalty was their "Mound Builder" priesthood class of absolute power, the Suns.

The highest priest, the Great Sun, was the most important and most critically indispensable person on earth.

No Catholic pope, even at the height of the Dark Ages of the unquestioned authoritarian power of the papacy, ever dreamt of having the kind of power that the Great Sun of the Natchez exercised, as a matter of solemn duty, every day of his life.

Even the sun in the heavens above was subservient to the power of the Great Sun.

If the Great Sun, standing on top of the most sacred temple mound, did not command the sun to rise each morning, the sun would not rise.

Once the sun had been commanded to appear on the eastern horizon, it would be powerless to do anything but remain there, until the Great Sun pointed with his outstretched hand, from east to west across the heavens, to show the sun the course it was to follow that day.

The Great Sun was so indispensable to all life on earth that his feet were never allowed inadvertently to touch the ground. He was borne everywhere he traveled on a litter carried on the shoulders of his servants.

The French observed a funeral of a Great Sun in the early eighteenth century and noted that some of his servants and two of his wives gladly accompanied him to his afterlife. They swallowed a concoction of tobacco juice, which rendered them unconscious, and then they were strangled with a garrote. Some others threw their infants into the flames of the Great Sun's funeral pyre, so they might accompany him to his afterlife.

We can only speculate about how strangely out of whack the world must have come to seem to the last Natchez Great Sun, who spent his last days in humiliating toil as a French slave on a Caribbean island sugar plantation.

And we can only speculate about how out of whack the world must have come to seem to the religious tyrants of other "Mound Builder" centers as the cataclysm of smallpox was destroying their world during the so-called Black Hole of history in the Southeast.

By the late 1730s, after the destruction of the Natchez, the Choctaws began playing the French, in nearby Louisiana, against the more distant Anglish in the Carolinas, as those two bitter European colonial rivals each sought to consolidate an exclusive Choctaw alliance, until the Choctaws lost control of that dangerous game at mid century and found themselves embroiled in the disastrous Choctaw Civil War of 1747–50.

That Choctaw civil war pitted the French-aligned Okla Tannap towns against the attempted Anglish breakaway of the Okla Falaya towns, with the Okla Hannali towns split about equally between those two factions, creating the horror of Okla Hannali people slaughtering other Okla Hannali people, as the Okla Falaya and the Okla Tannap people butchered one another.

As Angie Debo has pointed out, civil wars are prosecuted with more deadly thoroughness than any other kind of war.

The Choctaws were well on their way to exterminating themselves for the benefit of the French and the Anglish, when the slaughter was finally brought to an end, with the complete victory of the French faction, primarily due to a critical inability of the more distant Anglish in the Carolinas to get munitions to their faction of the Choctaw towns at a time when that probably would have resulted in the Choctaw Anglish faction winning that Choctaw civil war.

The horrors of that Choctaw civil war would still be fresh enough in the memory of the Choctaw people, in 1811, to give the horror punch that Pushmataha threw at his own Choctaw people, in his debate with Tecumseh, a deep and frightening emotional impact.

It was a greatly civil-war weakened and demoralized Choctaw Confederation that more or less sat out the so-called French and Indian War that ended in 1763 with the Anglish temporarily booting the French out of North America.

The Choctaws were too far distant from the battlefields of the First North Atlantic German Civil War of 1775–83 for life in the Choctaw Nation to be disrupted by it.

In that first war that the North American Germans waged in trying to gain their independence from the British Island Germans, Choctaws managed to convince the Anglish king that Choctaws were on his side while doing almost nothing for him, except occasionally providing a few Choctaws to accompany frustrated Anglish patrols along the nearby Mississippi River, as the Anglish tried and largely failed to find infrequent, small, rebel North American German raiding parties that came down the river.

To the Anglish colonial revolutionaries, however, the Choctaws provided substantial assistance, in the form of Choctaw scouts who served in the rebel North American German armies of generals Washington, Morgan, Wayne, and Sullivan—the beginning of a long and distinguished Choctaw military service on behalf of the North American Germans that extends to the present day.

On the whole, however, Choctaws mostly bided their time in the last half of the eighteenth century while they regained their numbers and their strength and while new generations of Choctaws received their military training from Choctaw veterans in annual exploits to the Trans-Mississippi West at the end of each bear-hunting season.

By the late eighteenth century, the Choctaw Confederation was once again the premiere power in the Lower Mississippi River Valley, even more strategically dominant than before, with the oblivion of the Natchez—those now nearly forgotten Children of the Sun who had so fascinated the French, until they, like so many others, joined the disbelieving dead.

Chapter Fifteen

The Standing Down of the Choctaw Standing Army

*B*efore the removal of the Choctaws in the 1830s, the Choctaw Confederation was clearly organized into what is known in the political theory of Western Civilization as a state, which means something altogether different from a state of the United States.

A state is defined, by that Western political theory, as a nation that consists of multiple levels of bureaucracy and which has a standing army.

The multiple levels of Choctaw bureaucracy have been fairly easy for historians, political scientists, anthropologists, and others to see.

Multiple administrative levels abounded in the Choctaw Confederation, from the level of confederation division, to division town, to different roles that different kinds of towns played in divisional life. Levels even extended to elaborate cross-divisional clan systems and other sorts of organizational schemes that provided for reciprocal responsibilities in such things as burials or that helped avoid incest in determining the degree of distance by blood for who might be a suitable marriage partner.

The Choctaw standing army has been more difficult for Anglos to see, and they have largely been people who at the same time were reporting that virtually every able-bodied Choctaw male of military age was a full-time career soldier, with hardly any other duties except occasional hunting.

The problem seems to be a self-serving Anglo-Saxo-Juto-ethnocentro barbarian befuddlement that is embedded in their conception of Indians, which led them to characterize Choctaw soldiers as "warriors" or "braves," and which helped them to characterize Indian nations as "chiefdoms" or "tribes," or in any manner other than as a state, any manner that might assist in the philosophical consolidation of the colonization of the continent by denigrating Indian sovereignty, at least within the limitations of their Anglo-Saxo-Juto-ethnocentro conceptions of such things.

It is clear, however, that the Choctaw Confederation had a standing army and that the ranks of that army were filled by virtually every adult male in each community.

The Choctaw standing army consisted of many different units, roughly corresponding to the towns and communities.

Some towns, however, particularly on the borders, were specifically designated as "war" towns (red towns). They were fortified, and their units of the standing army were under obligation to maintain a higher state of readiness.

The Choctaw standing army was essentially organized as a defensive force, though it could be deployed in offensive operations, such as at the Battle of Etowah (Holy Ground) and at the Battle of New Orleans, in the Second North Atlantic German Civil War, otherwise known as the War of 1812.

On the whole, however, other arrangements existed for offensive operations, which were ordinarily conducted on a relatively small scale, as the early military career of Pushmataha in the Trans-Mississippi West illustrates.

But they could be conducted on a larger scale, as the later military career of Pushmataha in the Trans-Mississippi West illustrates.

The Choctaw standing army was divided into three divisions that paralleled the three confederation divisions, each with its own commanding general.

By the time of the fifth Choctaw treaty with the United States, at Mount Dexter in 1805, Pushmataha had become one of those three commanding generals. Most of the unit leaders of the Choctaw standing army were designated as captains.

The generals and the captains were prohibited from exercising any civil powers. They were strictly military men, even though they had related diplomatic functions that allowed them to participate in the Choctaw diplomatic corps, along with other kinds of officials who had civic responsibilities.

Outside of their narrowly defined military and military-related duties, the Choctaw generals and captains were just Choctaw citizens, like any other Choctaw.

Virtually every adult Choctaw male during the confederation period was a full-time, lifelong career soldier in the Choctaw standing army, including those who also had civil responsibilities. Those who were physically unfit for combat served the standing army in other ways.

How and when the Choctaw standing army was organized, and how it evolved over time, are things we will never know, which can only be speculated about.

We merely have glimpses of some aspects of it, now and then, throughout portions of the eighteenth and nineteenth centuries, and, perhaps, the twentieth century.

Among the things we will never know is the impact of a world-changing European terror on the development of the Choctaw standing army, not the terror of European diseases, but a terror that burst upon the Native peoples of the Southeast in 1539, changing their world forever.

No Choctaw had ever seen a horse of any kind, let alone a huge, armor-clad Spanish war horse that had been bred and trained for the specific purpose of carrying a fanatical steel-sword swinging, armor-protected Spaniard into the midst of equally fanatical Muslim soldiers, in the barbarically brutal and bloody centuries-long quest to free Spain from its conquest by Islamic imperialists, which had only finally ended in 1492, the year Columbus sailed.

What we do know, from the chroniclers of the Hernando de Soto expedition, is that when that huge, elaborately provisioned and equipped Spanish army had wound its way around through portions of the Southeast north of its landing point in Florida and arrived in the region of Mobile Bay on the Gulf Coast in October of 1539, at the town of Moma Bina, demanding women and baggage carriers, the battle lasted all day long.

Before the people of Moma Bina trapped many of the Spaniards in the town, and burned it down around them, destroying the baggage the Spaniards had been demanding baggage carriers for, which caused the Spaniards the loss of virtually all of the plunder they had taken from other Native peoples, and virtually every item of equipment and luxury they had brought with them (including such oddities as the chess set found by the people of Moma Bina among the charred ruins of that baggage, perhaps the same one that had been used in Peru, where Soto had been the cavalry captain for the Pizarro brothers, and they had amused themselves by teaching the game to Altahualpa, the king of the Incas, before they strangled him), the Soto chroniclers recorded killing three thousand Moma Bina defenders outside the town, in the day-long waves of cavalry charges that wore out both their horses and their sword-swinging arms, in trampling and hacking to pieces a people who stood their ground amid the terror and inflicted, by Spanish count, 644 arrow wounds that pierced some portion of nearly any place their armor did not cover.

Once the surviving, now impoverished Spanish army had recovered enough from its disaster to be able to travel, it went north, skirting to the east of the upper watershed region of present-day east-central Mississippi, which would become the future core homeland of the Choctaw Confederation, and which archaeological excavations tell us was an uninhabited region at that time.

The Spaniards then swung to the west, to encounter a people in present-day northern Mississippi thought to be ancestors of the Chickasaws, who trapped the Spaniards in a fire so hot that, afterward, the survivors had to build kilns and retemper the steel in their swords.

The Spaniards continued on to the west, ragged, impoverished, their ranks greatly depleted, to cross the Mississippi River and wind around in the Trans-Mississippi West for a time, perhaps coming very close to making contact with the large Spanish expedition of Francisco de Coronado, perhaps somewhere in present-day Kansas or Oklahoma, after Coronado's equally disappointing quest to find another fabulously wealthy Mexico or Peru in present-day Arizona and New Mexico had led a large component of his expedition to wander around on the southern buffalo plains for a time.

Coronado never discovered that there were fabulous riches of gold in the southern Rocky Mountains, and Soto never discovered that there were fabulous riches of gold in the southern Appalachian Mountains.

But, in time, the discovery of gold by Americans all over North America would bring precipitous changes both for Native peoples and for Americans,

each of whom would become destined to suddenly find themselves confronted, in different centuries, with the consequences of that unrestrained
greed for gold.

The discovery of gold brought precipitous changes most brutally for the
Native peoples of California, in the "49er" gold rush of the mid-nineteenth
century.

Many of those Native peoples of California would simply be hunted
down and exterminated to get them out of the way (see Robert F. Heizer, ed.,
*The Destruction of California Indians: A Collection of Documents from the
Period 1847 to 1865 in Which Are Described the Things That Happened to Some
of the Indians of California* [Gibbs Smith, 1974], and Clifford E. Trafzer and
Joel R. Hyer, eds., *"Exterminate Them": Written Accounts of the Murder, Rape,
and Enslavement of Native Americans during the California Gold Rush,
1848–1868* [Michigan State University Press], 1999).

In the northern Great Plains, the confirmation of rumors of gold in 1874
by Lieutenant Colonel George Armstrong Custer, of the U.S. Seventh Cavalry,
which he was only able to confirm by deliberately violating the Treaty of Ft.
Laramie of 1868 and trespassing where the U.S. government had agreed by
that treaty that it would be forbidden to go (the sacred Paha Sapa, Black Hills,
of the Lakota Sioux and Northern Cheyenne peoples), would see the U.S.
Army encouraging the use of the recently completed transcontinental rail-
road to finish the extermination of what had been for many millennia buffalo
herds that numbered in the tens of millions, so that those Native peoples
might be starved, whom the U.S. Army could not defeat in battle, not anywhere in the Bozeman Trail War of the 1860s that had forced the surrender of
the U.S. government in that treaty of 1868, and not anywhere afterward, not
at the Rosebud, not at the Little Big Horn, not anywhere until those Native
peoples had suffered the starvation that compelled them to the temporary
defeat of having no choice but to patiently wait and watch and bide their time
to reclaim their sacred Paha Sapa, which everyone but the colossal fools in the
U.S. government knows is the only thing that they are doing, and which any
odds maker in Las Vegas with any sense would say is a clock that is now ticking in their favor.

For the southeastern Indians, for every nation of southeastern Indians,
and for some clocks that have been ticking for a lot longer than the Paha Sapa

clock, the eventual stumbling upon the site of the mother lode of Cherokee gold, by Georgians, in the Cherokee lands of the southern Appalachian Mountains, in 1829, broke loose the avalanche that overwhelmed all of those nations of Native peoples of the Southeast, no matter how near or how far from that Cherokee gold they happened to be.

For that reason, the phenomenal Southern Gold Rush of 1829 is virtually unknown to everyone in the world, even though it is every bit as stirring a story as the California Gold Rush of 1849.

The unrestrained frenzy to get that Cherokee gold in 1829 would be *the* thing that would uproot all of those civilized nations of Indian farmers from their ancient homelands in the Southeast for perhaps as long as two hundred years (if it should require as much as the first third of the twenty-first century for those ancestral homelands of the so-called Five Civilized Tribes to be restored to them).

In the 1830s, to make it possible for the SNAGs to get that Cherokee gold, the NAGs would not restrain their SNAGs from forcibly uprooting nearly all of the sovereign Indian nations from the Southeast, despite the U.S. Supreme Court trying to stop the horror of how that was being done.

The Southern Gold Rush of 1829, in conjunction with the temporary national political power of the SNAGs who had seized control of the U.S. government in 1828, changed America in ways that are much more profound and much more far reaching than any other event in United States history.

American-imperialist propagandists know that the Southern Gold Rush of 1829 led directly to the Indian Removal Act of 1830, and for that reason they have wanted as little attention paid to that gold rush as possible.

They have succeeded in that.

Most contemporary Americans have never even heard of that phenomenal gold rush.

Hernando de Soto, in the sixteenth century, was merely the first of the foreigners who tried to find that Cherokee gold, and failed.

He failed in a lot of ways.

After their trip to the buffalo plains, the dwindling number of Spaniards of the Soto expedition, absent a dead Hernando de Soto, finally rafted down the Mississippi River, harassed by huge flotillas of Natchez war canoes, and passed out of the lives of the Native peoples of the Southeast.

Sort of.

Those sixteenth-century Spaniards had introduced a new kind of terror that could hardly be forgotten.

It seems reasonable to say that in fashioning themselves into a Choctaw Confederation, the people who did that could hardly have been anything but mindful of that new terror in the world, which might return at any time.

Indeed, a kind of cousin of that kind of terror, the barbarism of the Anglish from the Carolinas, was, by the late seventeenth and early eighteenth centuries, descending upon the Mississippi Choctaws in the form of slave raids.

The Anglish barbarians in the Carolinas, throughout much of the seventeenth century, and the early eighteenth century, were doing much more than raiding Indian nations throughout the Southeast for slaves.

Those Anglish colonial Carolinians were also embroiled in vicious imperial wars with the Spanish in Florida, which, combined with European diseases, brought nearly the complete extermination of the teeming masses of Native peoples who had inhabited Florida.

That resulted in such an empty, beckoning land that segments of the Creeks would begin migrating to Florida from the north, from the Muscogee Confederation of present-day Alabama and Georgia.

By 1775, those onetime members of the Muscogee Confederation had assumed a new identity in Florida as a separate people called Seminoles.

Because the Seminoles gave shelter to escaped black slaves from Georgia, the Georgians would become, in the first quarter of the nineteenth century, as determined to get rid of the Seminoles on their southern border as they became determined to get rid of the Cherokees along their northern border in 1829, once gold had been discovered in that Cherokee country.

All of the reasons for the Indian Removal Act of 1830 are found in the SNAG state of Georgia.

The biggest complication in that story was that the United States desperately wanted to create new states west of Georgia, between Georgia and the Mississippi River (land that would have the Northwest Ordinance applied to it, and then be carved into the states of Mississippi in 1817 and Alabama in 1819), but to do that the United States had to buy from Georgia its claim that it owned all of the land to the west of present-day Georgia, all the way to the Mississippi River.

In 1802, in buying that Georgia claim, President Thomas Jefferson's U.S. government not only had to pay Georgia a substantial amount of cash but also had to give Georgia, in writing, a promise that the U.S. government would "extinguish" Indian title to land that Georgia claimed was within its boundaries, as soon as that could be done.

That was the hammer that Georgia would use to pound the U.S. government into passing the Indian Removal Act of 1830.

Georgians had been pounding the federal government to fulfill that commitment for a quarter of a century when, suddenly, the 1829 gold strike occurred on Cherokee land that Georgia claimed was within its northern boundary.

There is nothing much more complicated about what caused Indian removal than the leverage the state of Georgia had over the U.S. government due to that 1802 promise made by President Thomas Jefferson to Georgia, coupled with Georgia indignation over the Seminole harboring of escaped Georgia slaves.

Indian removal happened when it did because it got precipitously avalanched by the Southern Gold Rush in 1829, at a time when Andrew Jackson, an ally of the Georgians, had just been elected to the presidency.

The fate of the Choctaws in Mississippi was sealed by events far away in Georgia.

Choctaws were involved in none of those events, except as military allies of General Jackson's U.S. Army in its punitive expedition against the Seminoles in the so-called Peninsular Campaign in Florida in 1815, where, led by Pushmataha, the Choctaws further cemented their military alliance with the United States, in a military campaign that was conducted for the benefit of the Georgians, in an attempt to appease the Georgians.

Yet, Choctaws still became the first victims of the Indian Removal Act of 1830.

At the same time that the millennia-old Native inhabitants of Florida were being exterminated by disease and European colonial warfare, making it possible for Creeks to migrate to Florida and become Seminoles, large populations of once-powerful Native peoples of the Atlantic coastal regions of the Carolinas were also being exterminated, a thing the Choctaws could hardly have been unaware of.

The Choctaws are known to have adopted the remnant survivors of the once-powerful Catawbas, who fled to the Choctaws for protection from that terror in the Carolinas.

It was an extraordinarily dangerous world in the days of the formation of the Choctaw Confederation, and afterward.

There were also many threats to Choctaw security from other Indian nations during the era of European colonial rivalry, largely due to the strategy of the European powers of setting their Indian allies against the Indian allies of their European rivals.

Those threats included the near proximity of the Lower Creek towns to the east of the Choctaws, with the Creeks being periodically goaded to raid the Choctaws as a result of Anglish or Spanish imperial intrigues among the Creeks.

That posed a threat primarily to the Okla Tannap towns in the north-eastern portion of the Choctaw Confederation, which were heavily fortified as a result, and to the Okla Hannali towns in the southern portion of the Choctaw Confederation.

But small Creek war parties might lie in wait in ambush virtually anywhere in the vast Choctaw country, beside the paths that led between the Choctaw towns, or beside the paths that led to their great river-bottom deer preserves.

The proximity of the Chickasaw towns on the north side of the Choctaw Confederation also posed a threat to the Okla Tannap towns but even more so to the Okla Falaya towns, especially the ones that were spread out on a long north-south axis along the western side of the Choctaw Confederation.

The Chickasaws were periodically goaded to raid the Choctaws by the Anglish barbarians in the Carolinas, after the Anglish had cemented a firm alliance with the Chickasaws very early in the eighteenth century, which would last until near the end of the century.

That Chickasaw-Anglish alliance would make the Chickasaws the ene-mies of the French-aligned Choctaws for most of the first half of the eigh-teenth century, and it would place the literate Anglishman, James Adair, among the Chickasaws for all of the decades during the middle portion of that century.

In 1775, after returning home to Angleland, James Adair would publish his *History of the Indians* in London, which is a detailed insider's view of the intrigues of the European colonizers in the interior of the North American continent during the middle of the eighteenth century.

Many scholars have questioned Adair's reliability because he so obviously had such a big axe to grind, due to his claim that he got double-crossed financially by his Anglish superiors back in the Carolinas in a scheme to get rich individually on the Indian trade. Portions of his *History of the Indians* is his telling of his side of that dispute, which was probably also his motivation for writing the book.

However, we have the benefit of Lawrence Henry Gipson's sophisticated assessment of Adair's reliability. Gipson spent his life mining the archives of Angleland and France for his monumental, multivolume telling of the titanic eighteenth-century death struggle between Angleland and France for imperial control of the North American continent, which Gipson published before World War II.

In that study, in the fourth chapter of the fourth volume, Gipson felt compelled to pause, in a footnote, while relating the complexities of the machinations of the Anglish and the French in the Lower Mississippi River Valley that resulted in the Choctaw Civil War of 1747–50, to say, regarding the reliability of James Adair, that the many things Adair had said that could be corroborated in either Anglish or French archives turned out to be corroborated in those archives, and therefore Gipson felt compelled to give Adair the benefit of the doubt for those things that could not be corroborated.

That seems to be the most rational and authoritative assessment of Adair's reliability that anyone has offered, and because Adair was situated where he was for so long, was fluent in the Chickasaw/Choctaw language, was in the very center of Chickasaw-Choctaw relations, and was knowledgeable about much wider things, and wrote about those things in great detail in his *History of the Indians*, the issue of his reliability has been an important one, especially for events leading to the Choctaw Civil War of 1747–50, and for the bitter, uncompromising personal motivations for the extraordinarily complex and shifting policies of Shalushamastubbee (Red Shoes), the Okla Falaya Choctaw who was primarily responsible for precipitating the events that led to that Choctaw civil war, who was assassinated as a result of them.

The ever-present threat of small units of Osage hit-and-run raiders coming from across the Mississippi River from the region of the present-day

Missouri Ozarks also made Okla Falaya people vulnerable to sudden attacks near their homes.

To a somewhat lesser extent, that Ni•Kon'ska threat also extended to the Okla Hannali towns in the south.

Those kinds of threats to the western flank, and to the western portion of the southern flank, of the Choctaw Confederation also included other peoples from the Trans-Mississippi West, particularly from the eastern edge of the southern buffalo plains in what is today north-central Texas, western peoples with whom Choctaws had long-standing enmities.

Various individual nations of those mostly Caddoan peoples of present-day north-central Texas were the ones most often suggested by contemporaries of Pushmataha as the nation that had ambushed his first expedition in the West, causing his rage of hatred for all of the peoples of that region.

But the haughty and arrogant Comanches, farther west, and the even more haughty and even more arrogant Ni•Kon'skas, farther north, were also suggested as the ones who had sprung that ambush, as well as Indian nations with names that are not likely to be identifiable today for who they might have been.

The many ever-present threats to Choctaw security, from many different directions, whether from Europeans or from other Indian nations, necessitated the maintenance of the Choctaw standing army.

Those threats also necessitated, among other things, that the full-time career soldiers in that Choctaw standing army be ever at the ready, at nearly all times.

The threat of attack was greatest when Choctaw families traveled anywhere from town to town, or anywhere else, within their nation.

To help ensure a condition of instant readiness when traveling anywhere within the nation, the Choctaw women insisted upon carrying every single item that might need to be carried, so that the unburdened Choctaw men might have maximum freedom of movement in the event of a surprise attack. Split seconds could save lives.

Some students of Indian history might be inclined to note how heavily burdened those Choctaw women were on the trail, carrying everything that needed to be carried, including the men's rifles, while the men sauntered along, unburdened by anything at all, except a tomahawk, knife, and tobacco pouch, and regard that as evidence that Choctaw women occupied a low status in Choctaw life.

It's true that Choctaw women did just about everything that might need doing, while the Choctaw men, when not playing ball or engaging in occasional hunting, more or less just lounged around, more or less all of the time, while the women were endlessly busy doing something, usually together, yapping nonstop, gossiping nonstop, apparently unconcerned about, or even unaware of, what might seem, superficially, to be their low station in Choctaw life.

But one should view those heavily burdened Choctaw women trudging along on those trails not from a perspective of having been required to carry more than their fair share of the load but as exercising a power so profound that there was no way that they would voluntarily relinquish the carrying of those burdens, which was just one small manifestation of their power.

The power those Choctaw women were exercising was one facet of the one tyranny that Choctaw civilization had not been able to free itself of, out of necessity, a military tyranny.

It was the tyranny of the Choctaw standing army over the lives of the men, which pervaded every aspect of life for males, and it was made possible primarily by the power Choctaw women wielded.

As Donald Sutherland so eloquently stated in the movie *JFK*, "The organizing principle of any society is for war. The power of a nation over its people resides in its war powers."

The military tyranny that Choctaw men were subjected to was a tyranny of Choctaw women that compelled Choctaw males, at every stage of their lives, to be military men.

Choctaw women fashioned and shaped Choctaw men in much the same way that a potter shapes a work of clay.

Choctaw women usurped virtually every role in Choctaw life in exercising that power in a way that channeled male behavior like cattle being herded through a chute, leaving most of the males no role in Choctaw life but to be highly disciplined, highly trained killers who would take their place in the Choctaw standing army, and be good for little else, so compelling was the need to have that standing army standing ever at the ready, and for every member of it to be prepared in every way to forfeit his life in an instant.

Every aspect of Choctaw life during the Choctaw Confederation period can be understood on that basis, and there does not appear to be any other basis that will bring all of the parts of the puzzle together.

Choctaw women commanded the all-important province of agriculture, and they allowed Choctaw men no participation in any facet of it, except when their time-sensitive labor might be desirable at such community-wide functions as gathering a harvest.

Choctaw women not only commanded the home. They owned it.

They determined its location among her relatives, they traced family descent through her female line, they claimed the children of the marriage as members-from-birth of her clan, which, among other things, avoided any possibility of child custody disputes, as the children automatically went with the wife's clan in the event of the breakup of the marriage, and Choctaw women determined whom they would marry and when. They determined which of their suitors they might smile upon.

When the terrible tolls that were taken on that Choctaw standing army reduced the number of sexually mature males to a point that there were far too few males to go around, Choctaw women were hardly willing to go without what Pushmataha characterized as "such a desirable thing as a man."

Choctaw women solved that problem by compelling Choctaw men to acquire multiple mothers-in-law.

In pity for their men, Choctaw women decided that a mother-in-law should not be allowed to cast her eyes upon the husband of her daughter, and that she should not be allowed to speak to him, as though that might keep the women of multiple generations in that home, which he occupied only by their grace, from conspiring together to do anything that might reduce his multiple miseries, or the multiple demands on what had better not be a flagging libido.

In compensation for all of that, on occasion, he was allowed to get beastly drunk, under the supervision of Choctaw women, and he was allowed to spend most of his time commiserating with the other similarly situated, full-time career soldiers of the Choctaw standing army.

The power of males was further undermined by the vesting of legal authority for the children of the marriage in the wife's oldest brother, not her husband's oldest brother.

As a practical matter, any uncle, either from her family or from his family, would have had sufficient emotional distance with the child to stand a chance of obtaining the desired increase in the odds that whatever military potential a male child might possess would be identified and honed, for the benefit of the Choctaw standing army.

But having a maternal uncle exercise that authority was one more reminder to Choctaw males in their formative years that they had been born to do what Choctaw women told them to do, and what Choctaw women didn't just tell them to do but compelled them to do, in the organizational scheme of virtually every aspect of Choctaw life, was to fashion themselves into something that would be useful to the Choctaw standing army.

If the time should happen to come when the United States might find itself in trouble with poisoned Choctaws, somebody in the U.S. government might be well advised to try to figure out who the Choctaw women might be that they should be trying to do business with, unless they want to waste the rest of their foolish Anglo-Saxo-Juto-ethnocentro time thinking that the Choctaw people are anything like whatever it might be that they think they are.

Unless, perhaps, the U.S. government might want to take the gamble that Choctaw women are still far too distracted to be able to concentrate on much of anything else except the enormous and unanticipated problem they created for themselves—the problem of white women snatching up Choctaw men as fast as they can, because Choctaw women did such a profoundly enduring job of training Choctaw men to do whatever a woman tells them to do, a gamble which, for the time being, might not be such a bad gamble for the U.S. government to take, at odds that I have calculated to be 16,758,962 to 1, rounded off to whole numbers, after much thought and careful study.

From birth, Choctaw males were subjected to irresistible community and peer pressures that the vigorous, energetic, profoundly powerful Choctaw women had fashioned for them.

As a consequence, the lives of the young males were focused on little else but acquiring the skills that might enable them to obtain the coveted, essential emblem that was necessary for full entry into that Choctaw standing army, the suffix to be appended to their name, which various whites have spelled -*ubi*, -*ubbee*, -*ubby*, or -*ubih*. However it might be spelled, it signified the same thing, killer.

Under the operation of that military tyranny, virtually every adult Choctaw male had killed a human being by the time he was a young adult, or had tried and failed and was still trying.

There was no question about whether a member of the Choctaw standing army would kill when the necessity arose. He had been compelled to prove it.

Likewise, there was no question about how he would respond to the terror of the battlefield. He had been compelled to demonstrate his lack of fear and his willingness to die.

Usually, he had been provided an opportunity to demonstrate those things when it hadn't otherwise been necessary.

To obtain that coveted suffix to his name, especially in times of relative peace with neighboring nations, so as to avoid disrupting relations with those neighboring nations, Choctaw teenage boys who had not yet killed were under severe community and peer pressure, at the end of fall and winter hunting seasons for deer and bear in the Louisiana and Mississippi bottoms, to join one of the expeditions that were forming up to go to the buffalo plains and other places in the Trans-Mississippi West.

There, fast moving, unburdened, roving bands of Choctaws terrorized the people of various portions of the Trans-Mississippi West for how many generations no one knows.

Those expeditions provided the young hellions among them with their opportunity to win that coveted suffix to their name while allowing the Choctaw Confederation to remain a relatively calm, peaceful, diplomatic people at home, owing to the hard-won reputation the Choctaw standing army had earned of being a fanatically fearless and unconquerable defensive force.

In its offensive operations, its generals had at their disposal, among other things, condemned men, Choctaws under death sentences, who had been allowed a last military fling, and who had no reason whatsoever for returning home alive.

Probably most Choctaws never returned to the Trans-Mississippi West, after having had the adventure of their lives as youths.

But some, such as Pushmataha, would become the seasoned veterans drumming up and leading those expeditions. As the years went by, they would find upward mobility in the Choctaw standing army that way.

No one would relish those western expeditions as much, or be more committed to them among his generation, than Pushmataha, whose fame would spread throughout the entire Choctaw Confederation, and beyond, until he had reached the point where he had become the acknowledged commanding general of that Choctaw standing army, and a greatly feared military tactician.

It was Choctaw women who molded the environment that made it possible for the Choctaw people to produce a military leader like Pushmataha.

Choctaw women haven't changed much since those days, and someday they will solve the problem of how to keep their men from being lured away by those white women, unless, perhaps, the white people were to become at least as wise as the ice-age Choctaws, and keep those Choctaw women confounded and distracted, by convincing their prettiest white girls to be good sports about certain kinds of things, even with old fart Choctaws who have used up all of their charm.

When the U.S. Army built enough forts in the Choctaw Nation in the West and garrisoned them with enough soldiers to try to fulfill the American treaty obligation of protection of the Choctaw people, it appears that the Choctaw standing army might finally have been able to stand down.

If that was indeed what happened, then that standing down of that standing army might be, to this day, the one thing that has brought the biggest change in the lives of the Choctaw people since the destruction of their ancestral "Mound Builder" centers.

But, if that Choctaw standing army never did stand down, if, instead, it might have merely embarked upon the task of reorienting the awesome abilities of the Lords of the North American Continent to the task of learning how to play the new game that the North American Germans had taught it, then that might turn out to be the one thing that will bring the biggest changes in the lives of the German people since their arrival on this Choctaw side of the Atlantic Ocean.

If there might be some reason why our curiosity about that would not be satisfied during this twenty-first century, I have not been able to guess what that reason might be, unless it might be that those prettiest white girls will hitch their skirts and forestall everything, by deciding to do their patriotic duty, for the survival of all life on earth, and for the survival of earth itself.

Chapter Sixteen

A Curious
Hillbilly People

*C*hoctaw foreign policy at home was starkly different in every way from
Choctaw foreign policy as prosecuted against other peoples.

Few nations appear to have had *internal* institutions of foreign policy,
but the existence of one such Choctaw institution has been nearly a defining
characteristic of the mental conception of the Lords of the North American
Continent for how to deal, as gracefully as possible, with neighboring nations
of other peoples.

Avoiding bloodshed with neighboring nations was something that
Choctaws valued highly. What might be their most sophisticated "governmental" institution is one geared to reducing the likelihood of bloodshed
with neighbors.

Long ago, the Choctaw Confederation either developed that internal
diplomatic institution, or they inherited it from their ancestors.

That institution actively assists individual Choctaws in resolving problems with neighboring nations. The institution also actively assists neighboring nations (today, largely the United States and the illegal state of Oklahoma)
in resolving problems with individual Choctaws.

The institution is called *fanni minko*.

In the eighteenth century, a *fanni minko* was a Choctaw diplomat of high
rank who was the acknowledged Choctaw liaison with a specific neighboring foreign nation, whether that nation might be an Indian nation or a European nation.

If that nation was located near enough to the Choctaws to make the services of a *fanni minko* desirable, it got a Choctaw *fanni minko* assigned to represent it among the Choctaw people.

The foreign nation was not consulted in the matter, and the appointment was made by the Choctaws.

The *fanni minko* would be a Choctaw of considerable accomplishment, unless the Choctaws had little but contempt for some nation, in which case their Choctaw *fanni minko* would most likely be some Choctaw nincompoop from some prominent family that needed to be humored.

A *fanni minko* was apparently always a male. He continued living among his own Choctaw people while he served as the Choctaw spokesperson to his people for his assigned foreign nation.

He was at times an apologist for that nation, and at all times he attempted to maintain good relations between the two nations. He was someone to whom Choctaws could turn when they had a complaint against that particular nation.

It was a great honor to be a *fanni minko*, particularly for nincompoops, who could hope to attain no higher station in Choctaw life, and who, being nincompoops, rarely ever figured out that the nation they represented was the rough equivalent of some East Popcorn State on some contemporary big-time college football team's early season home football schedule.

However, the nearer the nation, and particularly the bigger the threat that nation might pose from time to time, the more important and powerful their Choctaw *fanni minko* became in Choctaw life.

The institution of the *fanni minko* has proven to be a critically important institution of some flexibility that has changed with the times, particularly regarding the liaison duties with the United States, which have become of paramount importance in recent generations.

Much of recent Choctaw history, the last three centuries or so, has been a story of European and American attempts to impose their foreign and ill-fitting notions of government upon the Choctaws, a folly filled with funnies that began with the French.

Early in the eighteenth century, in their frustration in trying to find someone among the Choctaws with whom they could do business, the French attempted to anoint a friendly and prominent Okla Tannap as the Choctaw "king" while apparently continuing to be completely unaware that they had merely succeeded in discovering who their nincompoop *fanni minko* was among the Choctaws.

The French, however, eventually were able to perceive that a *fanni minko's* powers were entirely dependent upon circumstance while still being unaware that he was merely a *fanni minko*.

In the mid-eighteenth century, an anonymous, frustrated Frenchman confided his perception of the limited powers of the nincompoop that the French thought was their French-anointed "King of the Choctaws":

> This nation is governed by a grand chief whose power is absolute
> only so far as he knows how to make use of his ability, but as dis-
> obedience is not punished among them, and they do not usually do
> what is recommended to them, except when they want to, it may be
> said that it is an ill-disciplined government. ("An Early Account of
> the Choctaw Indians," trans. John R. Swanton, in *A Choctaw Source
> Book*, ed. John Peterson Jr. [Garland, 1985], 54)

By the early nineteenth century, the threat posed by the growing strength of the North American Germans had become so serious that the institution of the *fanni minko* appears to have evolved to a point that the three military leaders of the three branches of the Choctaw Confederation, the great medal *minkos*, might properly be regarded as having exercised, collectively, the institution of the *fanni minko*, as being the *fanni minkos* among the Choctaws for the NAGs.

They had very little in the way of any other kind of power in Choctaw life, a thing the NAGs had difficulty perceiving, and even more difficulty understanding, though military responsibilities, and related matters of foreign policy, came to be of a sort of perpetual paramount importance, which expanded their powers proportionately.

Many Choctaws have regarded, and still regard, the increasingly elaborate foreign "democratic" institutions that the NAGs have attempted to impose upon the Choctaws as *fanni minkos*. The Choctaw Nation has remained in a perpetual state of threat and crisis ever since removal, and, therefore, the powers of those *fanni minkos* have remained, of necessity, substantial.

Even at that, most Choctaws have been content to allow those *fanni minkos* to do their critically important work while paying little attention to them, unless they might have had need of the liaison services they have provided and continue to provide.

There have been many things that the NAGs have had little awareness of regarding Choctaws.

In the early nineteenth century, the NAGs had no comprehension that Choctaws had been reared under the legal authority of their oldest maternal uncle.

Often, as Patricia Galloway has keenly discerned, NAG delegations to the Choctaws were largely wasting their breath in solemnly informing the Choctaws of what "their father, the President" desired for them.

Choctaws listened politely. A father was a person deserving of respect, someone revered, who was kindly disposed toward them but who need not be obeyed.

By World War I the NAGs had invented "Uncle Sam," and they inadvertently helped themselves solve that problem, with their U.S. Army recruiting posters proclaiming "Uncle Sam Wants You."

They hit the jackpot with Choctaws, who responded in droves, providing the important service of becoming the first Indian "code talkers" for the U.S. military in World War I, a service they performed again in World War II, as did other Indian nations, including the Comanches and Navajos.

Choctaws in the eighteenth and early nineteenth centuries displayed a *global* aspect of their mental conception of themselves, one that illustrates how keenly aware the Lords of the North American Continent have always been of occupying a special place in the world—they understood that they were not *merely* the architects of the most sublime expression of the gift of the mighty *Misha Sipokni* to the rest of the world in the way of civilization but that they were also the inheritors of solemn responsibilities in that regard.

Those responsibilities included a periodic and peculiarly Choctaw feat of saving the entire world from destruction, by preventing the sun from being destroyed.

The Lords of the North American Continent did that many times, without ever asking anything in return from any of the other peoples of the earth, considering it merely an obligation of being Choctaw.

The dreaded culprit in those heroic Choctaw undertakings was a black squirrel of enormous size that mischievously and inexplicably, but nonetheless dangerously, periodically tried to eat the sun.

The alarming announcement that the black squirrel was trying once again to eat the sun was always heralded by the shadow of that enormous squirrel falling over a portion of the sun.

Sometimes the black squirrel nearly succeeded in devouring the sun, made apparent by its shadow completely obliterating the sun, which caused bright daylight to turn into near darkness.

The black squirrel, however, was no match for the Choctaws, who, at the first indication of the squirrel's return, dropped everything they had been doing, every man, woman, and child, and began attempting to frighten the squirrel away from the sun by raising the most uproarious racket they could muster.

Early nineteenth-century NAG observers, such as Horatio Bardwell Cushman, were dumbstruck by the spectacle, and by the cacophonous din of all the screaming Choctaw voices, and the women beating their pots and pans together in a terrified frenzy, and the volleys of gunfire, as the men calmly discharged and quickly reloaded their rifles, taking careful aim with each shot, not knowing which bullet might be the telling one. The event was accompanied by the agitated howling of what Cushman described as "their sympathetic dogs" for as long as the threat continued.

But, once the black squirrel had been chased away, everyone went back to what they had been doing, without any self-congratulatory ceremonials or festivals of any kind, it having been just another day's work in the business of being Choctaw.

That heroic Choctaw feat, however, apparently occurred with too little regularity to do much to put the Lords of the North American Continent on the map.

John R. Swanton, of the Bureau of American Ethnology, who for decades in the twentieth century was regarded as the premiere authority on southeastern Indians, particularly Choctaws, began his *Source Material for the Social and Ceremonial Life of the Choctaw Indians*, in 1931 (BAE Bulletin 103), in trying to account for the paucity of that thin volume, by explaining that "there were few customs observable among them sufficiently striking to attract the attention of European travelers" (1).

Anthropologists have also shown little interest in a people whose primary ceremony seemed hardly to vary from sitting around beneath some shade tree talking while, as the Methodist missionary Henry Benson observed in the mid-nineteenth century, displaying an ability to consume prodigious quantities of coffee.

The missionary Alfred Wright, writing in the *Missionary Herald* in 1828, after having spent ten years among the Choctaws, becoming fluent in the Choctaw language, and having made diligent inquiries among the Choctaws for that entire time, is convincing, apparently without being aware of it, in characterizing such religious conceptions as Choctaws might have had in very similar terms to the deism of Thomas Jefferson and Benjamin Franklin, that if anyone or anything might have created the world, they had then gone away and never returned.

Others have characterized Choctaws as believing that the sun is the most important thing in their life, but they do not deem that it requires their worship.

Overlooked, because of the Euro-Anglo-Saxo-Juto ethnocentro silliness of anthropologists and missionaries, in their befuddlement regarding the freedom of the Choctaws from the mental prison of religion, is the essential role that writing played in that process. It was absent.

Without writing, Choctaws have been free to change their stories. Being an oral tradition people, they have been free to change their stories whenever some generation of elders might think it prudent to do that.

They apparently felt it prudent to do that after smallpox destroyed their ancient, ancestral "Mound Builder" centers. How many other times they might have felt it prudent to change their stories, no one knows.

They have not been burdened by the millstone around their neck called writing.

Scholars who have studied Choctaws have been baffled by the wide variety of Choctaw traditional stories that were recorded at one time or another during the first several generations of the Euro-Anglo-Saxo-Juto contact period.

One of the most confusing aspects of that for those scholars has been that Choctaws have had more than one story for virtually everything.

There's a reason for that, one that goes beyond a people being able to change their stories periodically.

There are, and always have been, quite a variety of different kinds of Choctaws.

Virtually none of the people who recorded Choctaw traditional stories thought to inquire whether their informant was an Okla Falaya, an Okla Tannap, an Okla Hannali, or any one of what were apparently at one time a number of other peoples, or remnants of them, within the Choctaw Confederation, particularly among the Okla Hannali.

About the last thing that anyone should anticipate would be that the traditional stories would be the same. The wide variety of details in the stories that have been recorded that did have some basic similarities is an indication of the wide latitude Choctaws have had in their cosmology, as individuals, and from generation to generation.

The Choctaw world has long been a world inhabited by witches and wizards.

Choctaw communities no longer precipitously take off en masse on foot to chase down some witch and kill her, as William Bartram observed during the colonial era.

Nor do Choctaws hold trials for witches and wizards and then hang them, as the Bible-thumping Puritans in colonial Massachusetts once hanged more than a dozen of them, after a proper trial.

Today, Choctaws just talk about them, and speculate about who among them might be one.

On the whole, instead of religion, Choctaws have relied on magic to try to make sense of the world around them.

In earlier times, incantations of various sorts were sought to help bring success in the hunt, in war, in the ball games, and in virtually anything else.

Today, magic continues to play an important role in various aspects of Choctaw life.

When they hit the play button on a slot machine and it hits the jackpot, the magic is working.

For the tens of thousands of times they hit the play button, and it doesn't hit the jackpot, the magic isn't working.

It's not much more complicated than that.

Academics try to make it more complicated than that.

Legions of Choctaws, upon learning that some academics are devoting their careers to the study of gaming, have flocked to their publishing, pregnant with many questions.

Who could be better than professors to supply the answers?

Should they play max coins, every play, to get the maximum benefit of hitting a good pay line?

Or might there be some strategy they could employ that might safely allow them to short-coin the machine, at least part of the time, to make their gambling money go farther?

Is it true that the random number generator in the slot machines must be as random as can be humanly engineered for every play?

Isn't there such a thing as a hot cycle for the machines? And if so, how does that work if the pay lines must be randomly generated for each play?

Or is there really some computer program that the machine is following that has determined in advance the outcome for every play?

Should they continue feeding a cold machine, to take advantage of the law of averages catching up, to their benefit?

Would they be better off if they got on a two-coin-max-play dollar machine at $2 a pop, or a forty-five-max-coin nickel machine at $2.25 a pop?

Should they really never play any credit they've won on any machine, always cashing them out, or will they really come out the same in the long run if they merely roll in a twenty-dollar bill and hit the play button until all the credits are gone, or until they've hit a good pay line, whichever comes first?

What were they doing right when they hit that sixteen-hundred-dollar pay line, and what have they been doing wrong since then?

The questions are endless, and they can barely contain their anticipation when they discover that much of the publishing the professors do is not just about gaming but about Indian gaming and Indian casinos.

But, to their disappointment, the professors offer no answers.

To their disgust, they discover that the professors spend their time compiling things like statistical studies of gambling addictions, and engaging in a lot of moaning and hand-wringing while spinning all manner of theories about what might be done to make good dirt-basket bearers out of "dysfunctional"

Indian people, families, and entire Indian tribes, Indian people who just don't seem to understand that they are supposed to hoard wealth and invest it, so they can borrow against it and finance a bigger house than they need, for the benefit of nobody but bankers, so that an army of dirt-basket bearers can cut down trees that don't need cutting down, and build new houses that don't need to be built, so that everyone can live in expensive seclusion from one another, and not have to risk getting acquainted with their relatives and neighbors, and not have to risk having to share anything, so they can spend all of their time working and worrying themselves into nervous exhaustion, so they can buy things they don't need and then hoard them from everybody else, and things like that, without any indication anywhere that any of those professors have ever even seen a slot machine, let alone have ever gotten on a good hot one for a few minutes.

And so, it's back to the casino, to see if the magic might be working.

Bibliographic Essay

The Sources of
Choctaw History

*I*t doesn't make much difference where you begin your inquiry into Choctaw history.

If you like to do things chronologically but don't feel like starting with the Pleistocene Epoch, then a good place to start is *Choctaw Genesis: 1500–1700*, by Patricia Galloway (University of Nebraska Press, 1995), which provides detailed information about some things that are discussed in chapter 14, and elsewhere, regarding the so-called Black Hole of history.

The eighteenth-century Choctaw experience with the French is also a good place to begin, primarily because, as mentioned in chapter 12, Neil Judd has given us some helpful information, a perceptive view of the inner workings of the Bureau of American Ethnology (BAE, which merged with the U.S. government's Smithsonian Institution in 1965), in *The Bureau of American Ethnology: A Partial History* (University of Oklahoma Press, 1967), which includes some things worth knowing about John R. Swanton, the most tireless scholar of that BAE.

Swanton relied primarily on eighteenth-century French perceptions for most of the information he provides to us about Choctaws.

Swanton is a critically important scholar to study, both the man and his work. And, because his work was published by the U.S. government, and since any copyright interest in his work that he might have had has expired, his BAE bulletins can be reprinted and made available by publishers who do that sort of thing. His work is easily available, and it has been widely consulted ever since it was first published, which was primarily during the first third of the twentieth century.

Swanton's prolific BAE work, the various titles of his many BAE "bulletins" (books), reflect his intense, lifelong study of primary archival documents, which he capped off in 1932 with what has been widely regarded as his capstone contribution, his big thick volume, *The Indians of the Southeastern United States* (BAE Bulletin 137, which isn't even close to being within the top three or four of his most valuable bulletins).

In that capstone achievement, which is only a lesser work due to the extraordinary quality of some of his other BAE bulletins, Swanton did what scholars are supposed to do. He provided us with a synthesis of what he thought he could say about the Indian peoples of that southeastern region, both generally, and, on occasion, individually, a synthesis of what he perceived to be similar and dissimilar about them.

That some later, and, for the most part, fairly recent perceptive scholars have noticed some things that Swanton might have understood better does not detract from his achievements.

Anyone who might try to do what Swanton attempted would quite likely leave a trail of later scholars who would be able to identify some things that might have been understood better.

And later scholars doing what later scholars are supposed to do (try to advance knowledge by identifying flaws in the work of earlier scholars) would likely make different kinds of mistakes than the ones that Swanton, and his critics, might have made.

Swanton has been the authority that most later scholars have relied on for ethnographic information about Choctaws.

It would scarcely be possible to exaggerate his importance for the study of Choctaw history, particularly for the way later scholars have perceived Choctaws, bearing in mind that Swanton was primarily relaying to us the perceptions of Medieval-minded Frenchmen, which, for their comprehension of Choctaw civilization, was the rough equivalent of what you would get if you were to ask a monkey to examine a hockey puck.

Neil Judd's perceptions about Swanton's work should be augmented by those of John H. Peterson, in his introduction to *A Choctaw Source Book* (Garland Publishing, 1985).

The many valuable and often overlooked things that are gathered together and made readily available in that *Source Book* should also not be overlooked.

The bibliographies in Swanton's BAE bulletins will provide you with a gateway to many useful things.

The bibliographies of all of the scholarly works that touch on some aspect of Choctaw history will do the same thing.

Tracking down much of what has been published about Choctaws has already been done for you. Much of that can be found in Clara Sue Kidwell and Charles Roberts's *The Choctaws: A Critical Bibliography* (Newberry Library, 1980).

That bibliography should be supplemented by the sources listed in more recently published things, such as Mary Ann Wells, *Native Land: Mississippi, 1540–1798* (University Press of Mississippi, 1994), Daniel H. Usner Jr., *American Indians in the Lower Mississippi Valley: Social and Economic Histories* (University of Nebraska Press, 1998), James Taylor Carson, *Searching for the Bright Path: Mississippi Choctaws from Prehistory to Removal* (University of Nebraska Press, 1999), Greg O'Brien, *Choctaws in a Revolutionary Age: 1750–1830* (University of Nebraska Press, 2002), Donna Akers, *Living in the Land of Death: The Choctaw Nation, 1830–1860* (Michigan State University Press, 2004), Michelene E. Pesantubbee, *Choctaw Women in a Chaotic World: The Clash of Cultures in the Colonial Southeast* (University of New Mexico Press, 2005), and quite a number of other recent books, journal articles, and anthologies.

You won't need to do much more at the outset but take advantage of all the legwork that has already been done by several successive generations of scholars whose bibliographies point you to much of what has been published about Choctaws.

No one has ever published a satisfactory synthesis of all of Choctaw history.

Many scholars have enhanced our knowledge about specific Choctaw history topics, but no one has even attempted anything more than a cursory synthesis of the entire history of Choctaws.

Choctaw history must be pieced together from many different sources.

Most scholars have focused on some particular period or topic. It's likely to be quite some time before anyone attempts more than a cursory synthesis of the overall history. There are still too many holes in the story, too many things that have never been investigated by anyone.

To get some idea of the problems facing students of Choctaw history in dealing with the materials that have already been published about Choctaws, see the bibliographic essay in Richard White's *The Roots of Dependency: Subsistence, Environment, and Social Change among the Choctaws, Pawnees, and Navajos* (University of Nebraska Press, 1983).

For factual details about Choctaw history, which are ordinarily reliable, even when a Eurocentric spin is being applied to those facts, don't overlook any of the authors who have published anything about Choctaw history, some of whom were discussed in various chapters of this book.

But don't just read some author.

Find out who that author is.

For learning how to do that, ask a reference librarian in any library.

Authors are, generally, not at all shy about providing information about themselves.

Authors know, by becoming a public figure, that they forfeit their right to have any secrets, that, if they should become influential enough for any-one to care, everything about them that could be known, will, in time, be known.

Think about that in regard to the most famous authors you can think of.

Then have a look at their subject headings in the Library of Congress and see for yourself how unquenchable the thirst can be for information about them, which can continue on forever, in the quest to better understand the people who have written influential books.

Therefore, authors know that they have an obligation, in reference works such as *Contemporary Authors*, for example, to provide information about themselves.

Authors are also aware, in the great scheme of things, that whatever con-tributions they might be able to make won't be the last word on anything, that they have biases, even ones that they are probably not consciously aware of, and that the search for truth makes it necessary that their biases will become matters of debate, if they should be so fortunate as to publish something that might be influential enough for anyone to care.

So find out about the people who write the things that influence you.

You have a right to know things about them, and they are aware of that, and it's information that is not difficult to find.

Be aware that just about every scholar who has published about the Choctaws has made some kind of contribution.

Track down and digest all of the contributions that those scholars have made.

At intervals, go back and read things again.

You'll marvel at how much you had missed before, and, in time, you'll learn the heartbreak of disappointment in favorite authors, as you begin to see things about their work that you might wish you weren't able to see.

If you want to be a student of Choctaw history, read everything that's ever been published about the Choctaws and read a lot of things that have been published by Choctaws.

That should include the enlightening, interesting things such as novels, short stories, poetry, autobiography, and creative nonfiction by Choctaw literary practitioners, such as Rilla Askew, LeAnne Howe, Ron Querry, Jim Barnes, Louis Owens, Roxy Gordon, and many others.

You will also need to know about Indians other than the Choctaws. You will need to know about the Indian-nation neighbors of the Choctaws.

Many things about Choctaw history will make no sense at all (or worse, will make the wrong sense) until you read the histories of some neighboring Indian nation, and go, ah ha, so *that* was why such and such was happening in Choctaw history.

Then you will have wished that some of the authors of works on Choctaw history had done the same thing, and maybe they would not have been so confused, or so misleading, in how they characterized some aspect of Choctaw history, which can be demonstrated not to have been that way at all, because of what was happening among the neighbors of the Choctaws that accounts for that aspect in an entirely different way.

You'll also need to bury your mind somewhere far away from the Choctaws and their neighbors, to avoid becoming too narrowly focused, and to have some way of comparing the Choctaw experience with that of other Native peoples of North America.

Ideally, you should pick two or three other Indian nations in different regions of the continent as "secondary" nations for you to focus on. They can be entirely of your own choice, just so long as they are out of the Southeast region.

If you were to choose, for example, the Iroquois Confederation in the Northeast, the Navajos/Navahos in the Southwest, and the Blackfoot/ Blackfeet Confederation in the Northwest, then you could play a game called "pick a year."

You just pick a year, any year, and contemplate what was happening at that time among the Choctaws, Iroquois, Navahos, and the Blackfeet.

That will help you see things about Choctaw history that otherwise might be difficult to see.

Likewise, follow the historian's principle: "Read all around any war."

That means (because the first casualty of war is truth) read books about the War of 1812 that were published in Canada and Great Britain, that were written by Canadian and British scholars.

You'll have difficulty believing you're reading about the same war, given the things that American historians dwell on and the spin doctoring they do.

If you want to be a student of Choctaw history, don't overlook anything.

Read all of the Choctaw treaties with the Americans.

To better understand the historical context of those treaties, read works by historians that detail the history of treaty making, such as Francis Paul Prucha's *American Indian Treaties: The History of a Political Anomaly* (University of California Press, 1994).

But take note that Prucha has an admitted Euro-Anglo ethnocentric bias, which he reveals in his preface.

There, he provides the reader with a few reasons for why he believes it is "appropriate—and even necessary—to consider American Indian treaties largely from the white perspective. Such a course, I know, slights Indian views of the treaties...." (xiv). Rarely do Eurocentrics admit their bias, and Prucha is to be commended for doing that.

Ordinarily, Eurocentrics merely embed their bias in their text, without ever admitting it. Their (unadmitted) Eurocentric bias colors every aspect of the research and publishing that they have done.

Still, much of their work remains useful for its informational factual value, and for the timesaving help provided by the footnotes and bibliographies of their books and journal articles, which often do a competent job of revealing where important source material is to be found. Unfortunately, most of what has been published about Indians in general, and about Indian treaties in particular, by Eurocentric historians, is not good for much else.

Get a law school casebook in Indian law and find out about Indian treaty law.

A casebook is a law school textbook, consisting primarily of edited versions of Supreme Court decisions but also including valuable, helpful narrative explanatory analysis by the law professors who edited the casebook.

One of the propaganda tricks of the Eurocentrics, especially of American historians, is that, when they purport to be writing about Indian treaties and Indian treaty law, they instead write about U.S. Indian *policy*.

U.S. Indian policy and U.S. Indian law are *not* the same thing.

U.S. Indian policy is wishful thinking.

Often it is an expression of what the imperialists among the Americans would *like* to do with the sovereign Indian nations of North America, and frequently it is an expression of their spin for how they would *like* the world to view what they have done.

Very few American historians have been trained in the law.

Eurocentrics literally do not know what they are talking about when they discuss Indian treaties, which is readily apparent to anyone trained in the law from the way they attempt to frame the discussion to every other aspect of the way they proceed from there.

Rarely has any Eurocentric historian displayed even any *awareness* of *elementary* aspects of American Indian treaty law.

They look at Indian treaties, and they quote clauses of those treaties willy-nilly, as though what they are quoting might actually mean what the writing says.

They have no comprehension of the U.S. Supreme Court canons of construction for Indian treaties, the gist of which is that the written version of an Indian treaty does not prevail over what the Indians were told *orally* that they were agreeing to.

Frequently, that was something greatly different from the written version, particularly regarding how delicate sovereignty issues were couched and presented orally, compared to the written version, which was what the American treaty commissioners wanted the world and, often, especially their own superiors to see.

It was easy for an American treaty commissioner to write something in a treaty.

It was another matter to say it face to face to a few dozen, or a few hundred, or, on occasion, a few thousand Indians, often deep in their territory, more often than not Indians who had earned the right to be facing the treaty commissioners by having displayed a rather frequent and consistent willingness to embrace just about any day as a good day to die and who were pretty damn sure they were standing on their own sovereign land.

The propaganda tricks of the Eurocentrics work well when they are being spun merely for American college students or for the American public in general, but they don't work so well when they are presented to federal judges.

Federal judges have no patience for anything that wastes their time.

In the Chippewa spearfishing controversy in Wisconsin in the 1980s, the attorneys for the state of Wisconsin got into hot water with federal appellate court judges, got *disciplined* by those federal judges, for wasting the court's time by arguing U.S. Indian *policy* rather than U.S. Indian law.

Find out what the difference is between those two things.

The propaganda of the Eurocentrics, however, has been so pervasive with the American public generally that segments of that public formed frantic anti-Indian treaty organizations, virtually attempting to revolt against federal courts that upheld Indian treaty rights, from "old" nineteenth-century Indian treaties, in court cases in the Pacific Northwest in the 1960s and in northern Wisconsin in the 1980s, treaties which are not as old, however, as the "old" U.S. Constitution.

Those anti-Indian treaty organizations even tried to block federal court orders from being implemented by staging angry white-backlash protests.

There is no need for that.

If those American citizens are not happy with the obligations of American citizenship, no one is forcing them to remain in the United States.

They are free to emigrate to some other country in the world.

All they have to do is pack up and go.

The American Civil Liberties Union also publishes an excellent concise guide to Indian law, *The Rights of Indians and Tribes: The Authoritative ACLU Guide to Indian and Tribal Rights*, by Stephen L. Pevar, a practicing attorney with long experience at dealing with controversial Indian legal issues (3rd ed., New York University Press, 2004).

A number of other publishers also publish excellent concise summaries, such as *American Indian Law in a Nutshell*, by William C. Canby Jr., a senior judge of the United States Court of Appeals (4th ed., West Publishing Group, 2004).

American Indian law is not that hard to find out about.

However, Eurocentric historians know virtually nothing about it; that is a primary contributing factor in rendering most of what they have published about Indians as pure hogwash.

American historians, the so-called mainstream American historians, write about virtually nothing but U.S. Indian policy, partly because that's all they know.

Find out why the charlatans who call themselves presidents of American universities pee their pants at the thought of having mainstream American historians trained in U.S. Indian treaty law.

It's also not hard to find out what Native legal scholars have contributed, for anyone who will look.

Start by consulting the excellent contributions made by such Native scholars as Robert A. Williams Jr., *The American Indian in Western Legal Thought: The Discourses of Conquest* (Oxford University Press, 1990), Blue Clark, *Lone Wolf v. Hitchcock: Treaty Rights and Indian Law at the End of the Nineteenth Century* (University of Nebraska Press, 1994), David E. Wilkins, *American Indian Sovereignty and the U.S. Supreme Court: The Masking of Justice* (University of Texas Press, 1997), David E. Wilkins and K. Tsianina Lomawaima, *Uneven Ground: American Indian Sovereignty and Federal Law* (University of Oklahoma Press, 2001), and any of a number of books by the late Sioux legal, religious, and political scholar, Vine Deloria Jr.

There are only fourteen ratified Choctaw-U.S. treaties, all in the Charles J. Kappler-U.S. Government Printing Office (1904) compilation (in volume 2).

They are available now online, on the World Wide Web, at an Oklahoma State University library Web site. As mentioned in chapter 9, a Google search (keyword: "Kappler") will take you there.

Don't neglect the much overlooked, so-called Treaty of Camp Holmes of 1835, which is so often overlooked probably because it involved eight sovereign Indian nations.

Also don't overlook the written account of that treaty negotiation by Leonard McPhail, a U.S. Army doctor who was present at those events, and which was published by one of the Oklahoma historical journals some time ago, which journal, offhand, at the moment, I can't recall. I'd look it up for you, but why in the hell would I want to do something like that, when you can look it up?

In Article 4 of that 1835 Treaty of Camp Holmes, eight sovereign Indian nations (Comanches, Wichitas, Choctaws, Creeks, Cherokees, Osages, Quapaws, and Senecas) agreed to share the hunting and trapping rights to the southern Great Plains.

Those rights may have become reserved to those sovereign Indian nations as a result of that treaty. The United States never subsequently purchased those hunting and trapping rights to that vast expanse of land from all of the Indian nations involved in that treaty, which the United States apparently forgot own those hunting and trapping rights in common.

Indeed, after 1835, the United States never purchased any property interest to the southern Great Plains (neither land, or hunting and trapping rights, or anything else) from the Osages, Quapaws, and Senecas. And subsequent U.S. purchases of property interests to the southern Great Plains from the Choctaws, Creeks, and Cherokees were only for specific portions of the vast amount of land covered by the Treaty of Camp Holmes.

In time, those eight sovereign Indian nations (or some combination of them) might organize something along the lines of the Great Lakes Indian Fish and Wildlife Commission, which was formed after the federal courts in the 1980s upheld the reserved Indian rights in treaties regarding the Great Lakes region, treaties of about the same time (1837 and 1842) as that Camp Holmes treaty of 1835.

It's something that can be done without causing anyone any problems, as the Indians in that Great Lakes region have amply demonstrated with their multistate *Indian* fish and wildlife commission, whose careful management of those resources in cooperation with the state and federal authorities has enabled it to increase the amount of fish and wildlife in that region and even build and operate new fish hatcheries.

It's something that has made life better for all of the people in that Great Lakes region, despite the hysterical doom-and-gloom prognostications of the white-backlash rabble rousers of the 1980s, who, surely, by now, can see that they were wrong.

It was not the end of the world in northern Wisconsin. It has merely given Indian people a chance to participate, with dignity, in regulating something that they love, and who took pains to reserve the right unto themselves in treaties.

For information on that reserved Indian treaty rights controversy in Wisconsin, so you might contemplate how the Camp Holmes treaty signatory nations might do something similar, see Ronald N. Satz, *Chippewa Treaty Rights: The Reserved Rights of Wisconsin's Chippewa Indians in Historical Perspective* (Wisconsin Academy of Sciences, Arts and Letters, 1991), and Rick Whaley and Walter Bressette, *Walleye Warriors* (New Society Publishers, 1993).

For your study of Choctaw history, don't overlook the state historical society journals of all of the states.

The detailed histories of the Southern Gold Rush of 1829 (the thing that precipitated Choctaw removal), as well as the long history of placer mining for gold in the South, leading both geographically and chronologically southward down the eastern edge of the Appalachian Mountains, from Virginia all the way, eventually, to the mother lode in the sovereign Cherokee Nation (in what is now, temporarily, regarded as northern Georgia), are to be found in the academic historical journals of the Atlantic seaboard southern states, augmented by only a few books.

In comparison with the California Gold Rush of 1849, the Southern Gold Rush of 1829 has attracted little attention, for which I propose my best guess in chapter 15 of this book.

You will never know what you might find in the historical journals of some far-distant states that might have some connection with Choctaw history, unless you look.

For example, some scholars have become aware that it was the long placer-mining expertise of those largely illiterate southern gold miners (who seem to have produced few diarists or letter writers) that guided that subsequent California Gold Rush of 1849.

The probing of the connections between those two gold rushes is largely to be found in the historical journals of western states, but the question of how the attitudes of those southern placer miners regarding Indians impacted the horrific treatment of Indians in California needs more exploring.

For published documentary collections regarding the carnage wrought upon California's Indians by those gold miners, see chapter 15.

In order to comprehend Choctaw history in the nineteenth century, it's necessary to understand how American attitudes toward Indians evolved during that century, to a point where, by mid century in California, the American National Character was comfortable with simply exterminating any Indians that might be in the way.

The evolution of those American attitudes toward Indians is an aspect of American intellectual history.

Don't overlook the role that Texas played in the hardening of those attitudes. Start with W. W. Newcomb Jr., *The Indians of Texas: From Prehistoric to Modern Times* (University of Texas Press, 1961).

Texans simply exterminated Indians—men, women, and children, such as any Apaches or Comanches they could find, and the entire nation of Karankawas of the Gulf Coast.

There are ironies in this.

If the Texans and the Americans had not eliminated the barrier of the Karankawas, Comanches, and especially the Apaches from the long border between the United States and Mexico, the Americans today would not have much of an "illegal immigration" problem. It would be a foolish Mexican who would be so bold as to venture into that border region, for any purpose.

But Texans could not conceive of any use for Indians of any kind. The ones the Texans did not exterminate, with only a couple of exceptions, they drove out of Texas, including the peaceful Indian agricultural communities of the Sabine River Valley along the border with Louisiana.

The Texans drove Indians out of Texas even if they were peaceful military allies of Texas against other Indians.

That's what happened to the nations of Caddo, Anadarko, Ioni, Waco, Tonkawa, and Peneteka Comanches. They had adopted a range-cattle economy on their more than seventy thousand acres of Texas Indian reservations, in north central Texas, until they precipitously had to flee for their lives to Indian Territory, barely ahead of mobs of Texans who didn't care to make any kind of distinction about any Indians.

Texans were so angry at the Texas Superintendent of Indian Affairs, Robert S. Neighbors, for hurriedly ushering those peaceful Indians across the Red River that they murdered Neighbors when he made the mistake of returning to Texas.

Texas was populated by people moving west from the Deep South, some of whom were veterans of the Southern Gold Rush of 1829, some of whom, after contributing their attitudes toward Indians to the Texas National Character during the era of the independent Republic of Texas, then moved on to offer their placer-mining expertise to the California Gold Rush of 1849, transplanting at the same time their attitudes toward Indians to California.

All of that is relevant for trying to understand the ever-changing nature of the Americans that Choctaws have had to try to figure out how to do business with.

The better you understand any aspect of American history, or any aspect of U.S. Indian history, the better equipped you will be to study Choctaw history and to understand the things that will be happening, and why, as those things begin unfolding in the twenty-first century.

There are many things that have some connection with Choctaw history to be found in academic scholarly journals in disciplines other than history.

For example, one aspect of Gideon Lincecum's phenomenal life, his work as a self-trained naturalist, has attracted the attention of quite a number of scholars, whose publishing has appeared in academic journals far removed from the disciplinary blinders of the discipline of history.

By becoming a student of Choctaw history you'll also have a chance to actually apply things from all of the liberal arts courses that you might have been required to take in college, the sorts of things that college students are required to take before they begin specializing, or "majoring," in some particular, more narrow field of learning.

For example, do this: consult several good, big, hardcover, "standard college" dictionaries in a university library.

Find the geologic time scale in each one of those dictionaries (if a particular dictionary does not have a geologic time scale in it, then I might suggest a few other quick tests that you could give that dictionary, and if it failed those tests also, you could scratch that particular dictionary off of your list of dictionaries to consult, but that's another topic).

Compare the way that the geologic time scale is presented in each one of them.

From that study, you should be able to see that the term "Pleistocene" is an "epoch." You should also be able to see that an "epoch," in the geologic time scale, is a term of art.

It has a precise, narrowly defined meaning that is universally understood by scientists, and, supposedly, is universally understood by all other liberally educated people.

You should also be able to see that the term "Pleistocene" can never be used in conjunction with any other term of art from the geologic time scale. Pleistocene is an epoch, and that's all there is to it.

It can never be an "era" or a "period," for example, because those terms are also terms of art in the geologic time scale.

Next, get a copy of one of the seminally important works of the late Sioux scholar, Vine Deloria Jr., titled *Red Earth, White Lies: Native Americans and the Myth of Scientific Fact* (Scribner, 1995), and read Deloria's chapter 5, "Mythical Pleistocene Hit Men."

It's brilliant work by Deloria, but.

From what you now know about the geologic time scale (from what you now know specifically about "Pleistocene" and "epoch," or what you will know after you've done that dictionary work), see if you can spot the places (places, plural) in that chapter 5 that explain why people in the scientific community did not take that book by Deloria seriously.

Now, you might be aware that Deloria didn't much give a damn whether *they* took it seriously or not, because Deloria wasn't writing that chapter for them.

Deloria was writing it for the legions of Native graduate students who will be spending the next several generations following up on the ideas Deloria presented in that book (Deloria is another sort of Jack D. Forbes, in that regard).

Whether or not Deloria might have known that he was misusing the terminology of the geologic time scale (that is, whether he might have been doing so intentionally, just to tee off the scientific community) is another matter, but Deloria isn't with us anymore, so, if no one knows, if no one ever asked him, we might have missed our chance to find out about that.

But, if you want your work to communicate with the practitioners of some branch of learning, particularly if you'll be calling them things like "every redneck peckerwood who can man a typewriter," which does not tend to amuse them but which is part of what makes Deloria entertaining to read, you might want to try communicating with them a little differently than how Deloria went about it, and try being more courteous, too.

You should also find out, for yourself, what historical linguistics is all about. That's not difficult to do.

Europeans had only the most parochial notions about that branch of learning until 1787, when William Jones (1746–94), a British jurist serving in India, pointed out some fundamental similarities in the lexicon of several widely dispersed languages, between ancient Sanskrit in India, Persian in the Middle East, and some European languages that he was familiar with, such as Greek and Latin. He stumbled upon what is now regarded as the Indo-European language family.

Most of what Eurocentrics now know about how some race of humans, who spoke the same language, separated and eventually spoke mutually unintelligible versions of their language, stems from what William Jones discovered in India, *not so long ago*.

Historical linguistics is one of the most important tools for the study of Indians. Find out something about it.

It's a very simple field of study. To understand what historical linguists do, start by reviewing what you were force-fed in school about the history of the so-called "English" language.

In the reference room of some adequate university library, one worthy of being called a library, locate the 1963 edition of Funk & Wagnalls *Standard College Dictionary* in its collection of dictionaries and read what is probably the best brief essay on the history of the language, by Princeton University etymologist Albert H. Marckwardt, which is in the front matter.

You might also note that Marckwardt's essay was replaced in the 1974 edition of that dictionary by one that was "dumbed down" to accommodate the increasingly alarming erosion of academic skills of American college students, whose attention span, and unwillingness to read much of anything, should be cause for national alarm but isn't.

While you're at it, you might note the similar dumbing down of virtually all of the American college textbooks, the ones that have been in use for decades and that have gone through several successive editions, such as McCrimmon's *Writing with A Purpose*, for English courses, and one by Wallbank and Taylor et al., *Western Civilization*, for history courses. Compare the editions of those books in the 1960s, dense with text, with the later editions. See for yourself the evolution of those textbooks, how they have become mostly picture books, with relatively small portions of text, and even that is now in large print.

Both the erosion of academic skills and the lack of alarm about it are strong indications that America is on its way out as much of a player in the future of the world, a country that now lags far behind many other nations, and which falls farther behind with each passing year.

About all that any rival nation really needs to do is allow Americans to continue being Americans for another generation or two, and Americans will have eliminated themselves from the world stage.

But those are other silly Americans, ones without much intellectual curiosity about hardly anything. After reading Marckwardt's essay, I recommend that you examine a more detailed history of the language, such as David Crystal, *The Cambridge Encyclopedia of the English Language* (Cambridge University Press, 1995), which is highly readable and very entertaining, rich with text and illustrations and engaging sidebars.

Note that any living language *changes* in the course of time.

Beowulf, from the "Old English period" (450–1050), has all the attributes of a foreign language, including grammar that is fundamentally different from that of modern "English."

Note how the language becomes gradually more comprehensible to contemporary readers during the "Middle English period" (1050–1475), to a point, late in that fascinating period of rapid change, where we can almost read Chaucer's *Canterbury Tales* without too much editorial footnote help.

By the "Early Modern English period" (1475–1700), we can pretty much read Shakespeare on our own, with the help of a comprehensive dictionary, such as the *Oxford Dictionary of the English Language*.

For the "Late Modern English period" (1700–present), we don't need any help at all, except the occasional help of a good standard college dictionary.

All living languages have changed in the course of time. They have changed at different rates, and in different ways in different places and under different circumstances, but no language ever stays the same for any great length of time. Historical linguists try to figure out how and why those changes take place and what the various rates of change might be.

Consider another example that you are probably at least somewhat familiar with. Review how the Classical Latin of Julius Caesar became a dead language (as did its contemporary, Old German) simply because, like Old German, Latin evolved through several stages but as different versions of the Latin language in different parts of Europe, as the Latin language spawned the so-called Romance languages (named for the city of Rome), which themselves kept changing until they had become what we know today as Italian, French, Spanish, Portuguese, and a number of other modern Latin languages.

There's nothing different about what historical linguists do in trying to figure out how Indian languages change. The greatest changes occurred after some population split away from some other population, and those groups became geographically separated. But because there are no written records of those changes, historical linguists must try to piece the puzzles together backward, starting with the kind of evidence that William Jones stumbled upon in India, identifiable similarities in some of the most enduring words, such as ones for family members.

There's nothing difficult or mystical about historical linguistics, but bear in mind that Americans have attempted to frame much of the discussion about historical linguistics as self-serving propaganda, which is why contemporary Americans are not even aware that they are Germans, little different, fundamentally, than when they left the forests of northern Europe, *not so long ago*, first descending upon the peoples of the Mediterranean world and plunging their civilization into its Dark Ages and then descending upon the peoples of North America and plunging their civilizations into their Dark Ages.

Always be alert to what those barbarians would like for everyone to regard as "names," and "rules," and "definitions." Propaganda becomes child's play when the propagandists are the ones who get to make up the "names," and the "rules," and the "definitions," and that's true for many of their so-called branches of learning, not just for historical linguistics and such things as what constitutes a "language," what constitutes a "dialect," what constitutes a "language family," and many other things.

Never forget that much of the so-called "learning" that Americans teach in their schools, about nearly everything, is little more than self-serving propaganda, a means of perpetuating *their* view of the world and *their* view of themselves.

By being adept at propaganda, Old Low German got miraculously hocus-pocused into "Old English" by the British Island German and North American German "scholars," who try to deny that their version of the German language is, always has been, and always will be *Anglish*, because they're ashamed of who they are.

Americans are, and always will be, Germans. The whole world has simply been brainwashed into forgetting that "English" (Anglish) is a German language.

About the closest concession they will make to their deeply fundamental and distinctive kind of human roots is a bit of hocus-pocus semantics, which, incredibly, works its propaganda magic, by saying that "English" is merely a "Germanic" language, which is something they don't dwell on. Few Americans even comprehend what that means, and it's not hard for something like that to work when the audience for it wants it to work.

Those modern-day barbarians just don't want to admit, especially to themselves, that they have never stopped being Anglo-Saxon-Jute *German* barbarians, as if that denial, along with a few sleight-of-hand "name" changes for themselves (to "Englishmen" and "Americans"), every time they've merely sailed across a body of water (first the English Channel, and then the Atlantic Ocean), would fool anybody but themselves.

None of the "Romance language" peoples are ashamed of who they are. They know that they've been Latins (speakers of a Latin language) for *thousands* of years, for far too long for them to be anything but Latins, the same way that Americans have been Germans (speakers of a German language) for too many *thousands* of years for Americans to be anything but Germans.

Americans invested too much in anti-"German" war propaganda, during two world wars in the first half of the twentieth century, vicious "total war" death struggles against their fellow Germans, to ever be able to admit that they are Germans too.

Because of the lingering effect of that propaganda, to American ears, the word "German" conjures up an evil image, the image of dangerous aggressors who make unprovoked invasions of other countries in attempting to conquer the land of other peoples while "feeling good" about themselves by being adept at propaganda—the very things that North American Germans, blinded by their own propaganda, are unable to see about themselves.

Americans are, in so many respects, for so many things, totally helpless victims of their own propaganda, to such an extent that Indians have to *explain* to them, in the most elementary terms, not just what they are but even *who* they are.

Where I come from, a man's not ashamed to say. But Americans are deeply ashamed, both of who they are *and* of where they come from, to a point they even deny, to *themselves*, that they are Germans.

Curiously, Americans don't deny that they are still "Anglos," or "Anglo-Saxons," largely because they've been rendered too brain dead by their own propaganda to even *understand* what that means.

Even what *that* means has to be *explained* to them.

It means they are *still* Germans.

Another branch of their learning, archaeology, also has very recent origins. Except for grave-robbing, archaeology doesn't extend back much earlier than Heinrich Schliemann's (1822–90) mid-nineteenth-century idea of trying to excavate the perhaps-mythical ancient city of Troy, of Homeric Trojan horse fame, from Greek oral tradition, an oral tradition that the Greeks eventually committed to writing. Schliemann discovered that the Greek oral tradition about Troy wasn't so mythical, that it was just buried under several layers of city that had been built on top of it.

That wasn't so long ago that Eurocentrics finally stumbled upon archaeology, little more than a century ago.

Many branches of Eurocentric learning have very recent origins, as time goes, as time goes for the Lords of the North American Continent, who have long been curious about the world around them, and about themselves, and who have long been interested in a kind of learning that the foolish foreigners have never had any awareness of.

Many branches of Eurocentric learning, which Americans now take for granted, were not even founded until long after they had grounded the philosophical foundations of their American Indian law on its indefensible twin pillars of barbarian ignorance and Medieval religious tyranny.

Many branches of Eurocentric learning, particularly recent technologically driven ones, are so new that they are mind boggling for many contemporary North American Germans, so new that their old, familiar, entrenched habits of Medieval-mindedness have been desperately trying to integrate them into those Old World habits of thinking, without much success.

Get excited about all of this. It's a new day for Indian studies. There are things to be learned now that no one had ever imagined before, things that might be possible to learn now that were not possible to learn before.

Anthropology is a new Eurocentric idea in the world.

As mentioned in chapter 12, you'll not likely find many anthropologists who will admit it, but Lewis Henry Morgan (1818–81), an American lawyer who conducted meticulous field studies of Mohawk kinship systems in the 1850s, is the father of that American propaganda academic discipline.

The reason anthropologists are uncomfortable with acknowledging Lewis Henry Morgan as the father of their discipline is because he published a colossal stinker of a book in 1877, titled *Ancient Societies*.

In it, Morgan, to the embarrassment of contemporary anthropologists, maintained that humans evolve through a progression of nine stages of "Savagery," "Barbarism," and "Civilization."

Guess who the "Savages" were in Morgan's paradigm, and guess who represented the epitome of "Civilization"?

Morgan's 1877 book was hugely popular in the United States in the late nineteenth century, at the time that whites were clambering for the allotment of the lands that were still held in common by the "Savage" nations. Morgan's book helped provide a "scholarly" rationale for forcing allotment upon the sovereign Indian nations of North America.

Anthropologists would accord Morgan the "honor" of being the "father of anthropology" (based on his other studies), if he hadn't stunk up the place so badly with that book.

Contemporary anthropologists would much rather accord someone like Franz Boaz (1858–1942) that honor. Find out why.

But find out why anthropology continues to be deeply influenced by Lewis Henry Morgan's Euro-Anglo ethnocentric Medieval mindset. It's an academic discipline that did not even begin considering the adoption of a code of ethical conduct for field studies among Native peoples until the 1970s.

Examine *contemporary* college textbooks in anthropology and archaeology and see for yourself how some of the most famous names in anthropology, such as Frank Hamilton Cushing (1857–1900), are praised for their "contributions," and then find out who those people actually were and what they actually did.

Try to find any mention in those textbooks of what Frank Cushing actually did in his "field studies" at Zuni Pueblo that led to him becoming the first person banned for life from all nineteen Pueblos in New Mexico by the All-Indian Pueblo Council.

Frank Cushing's attitude toward Native peoples was fairly typical of anthropologists until very recently. They considered Native peoples their private domain, a domain in which anthropologists could do whatever they pleased.

While you're examining those contemporary textbooks, note the subtle way that the sovereignty of individual Indian nations continues to be denigrated. They are not discussed in these textbooks as individual sovereign nations but are lumped together into "culture areas" and "language families."

That was the primary reason for the founding of the Eurocentric academic discipline of anthropology, to denigrate Native sovereignty by such vehicles.

It's a propaganda tool of the colonizers, one that had served its purpose very well by the time the allotment of Indian land had been accomplished in the early twentieth century.

But it's a propaganda tool that the colonizers continue to find useful today, and it's one that college students never think to question, not even to ask why the American, Canadian, and European nations aren't dealt with in the same manner.

The origins of the academic discipline of physical anthropology, as mentioned in chapter 12, date from the pathetic skull comparisons done by Samuel Morton (1799–1851), published in 1839 in his *Crania Americana*.

But physical anthropology as an academic discipline got its firm grounding under the authoritarian dictates of Ales Hrdlicka (1869–1943), of the Smithsonian Institution, who dominated American "science" for decades in the early twentieth century.

Try to find any mention in any of those college textbooks of what Ales Hrdlicka is most famous for among Indians, which is all that anybody really needs to know about Hrdlicka to understand who and what he was.

When a delegation of Indians, visiting the Smithsonian, became ill and died, Hrdlicka didn't have them buried or their bodies returned to their loved ones. He sent their bodies to Columbia University to be boiled.

After the flesh had been thus removed from their bones, the bones were returned to Hrdlicka, so he could study and add them to his precious collection of grave-robbed bones at the Smithsonian.

Hrdlicka was a force to reckon with, a brilliant Czech who graduated at the head of his class in medical school. It was partly his forceful personality and partly his position at the Smithsonian that allowed him to dominate the American scientific community throughout the early decades of the twentieth century.

Early in his career, Hrdlicka developed a passion for conducting physical examinations of deceased peoples of what he regarded as inferior races of humans—he was particularly interested in the bodies of deceased black people—when he worked as a medical examiner in New York City, from whose various institutions he had an endless supply of cadavers to work with.

But Hrdlicka's dominance of the American scientific community came to an end in a way that is filled with ironies.

Hrdlicka's power was such that he was able to prevent nearly everyone from digging in North American strata that was more than about thirty-five hundred years old, to look for evidence of human habitation on the continent before that time (or even to get funding for such investigations), because Hrdlicka was adamant that there was no such evidence to be found anywhere in North America in strata older than that.

No one was allowed to question Ales Hrdlicka's authoritarian pronouncement that there could not possibly have been humans in North America before that time.

For the manifold ironies of how a self-educated black cowboy in northeastern New Mexico, with a sophisticated interest in science, George McJunkin, brought about the ruin of Hrdlicka's career by discovering the existence, in 1908, of now-famous "Folsom spear points," embedded in the ribs of an extinct species of giant bison, in strata that could be unquestionably dated to about ten thousand years ago (and McJunkin was fully aware of the significance of his discovery to the point of spending many frustrating years before he died in 1922 unsuccessfully trying to get anyone from the American scientific community even to look at the site, in a flood-washed arroyo on the ranch where he was the foreman), and for how Hrdlicka responded to that evidence when it was confirmed later in the 1920s by Jesse

Figgins, the director of a Denver museum, see Tony Hillerman's essay, "Othello in Union County," in Hillerman's outstanding essay collection, *The Great Taos Bank Robbery and Other Indian Country Affairs* (University of New Mexico Press, 1973).

Reading things such as that will be time well spent. The better you understand nineteenth- and twentieth-century America, as Native peoples experienced those centuries, the better you will understand the ignorance of the people who have crafted U.S. Indian policy and the ignorance of the people those policy makers have regarded as authorities in various branches of Eurocentric learning.

Likewise, reading things that will help you better understand how many of the various "departments" (academic disciplines) of contemporary universities are very recent Eurocentric academic inventions will also help you understand how some of those academic disciplines have contributed to the attempted colonization of the sovereign Native nations of North America.

It's a colonization process that is an ongoing, contemporary event, one that has now been in progress for about five centuries, since 1492, and which, to all appearances, might last another five hundred years or longer before it has finally run its course, with no one, at present (except, perhaps, Choctaws), having any idea what the eventual outcome will be.

It's a situation that requires the historian's principle: "There has been no history since Queen Anne's War."

That principle means that no one can write the history of any event until the world has become so irretrievably different that no one alive today has any identifiable stake in the outcome of that event, especially any "historians" who might be attempting to write about it without being aware that they cannot be anything but some kind of advocacy journalist for one side or another.

Everyone alive today, anywhere in the world, has a stake in the eventual outcome of the struggle for control of the North American continent, whether or not they might be aware of the many ways that struggle will affect everyone on the planet.

The sleepy-headed Americans, for quite some time, have operated under the delusion that the struggle for control of the North American continent is a thing that long ago passed into history, that it is no longer a contemporary event.

That might well have appeared to have been the case, until the mid-twentieth century.

But everything changed in the mid-twentieth century.

Since the mid-twentieth century, what to do about the United States has been among the least of the problems facing the Choctaws.

Since the mid-twentieth century, the problem facing the Choctaws has been what to do about the rest of the world, the whole world.

At the end of World War II, Americans were under an *obligation*, to all mankind, to conquer the whole world.

For a brief window of a few years in the late 1940s, Americans, in exclusive possession of atomic weapons, retained, for the first time in the history of the planet, the exclusive means to conquer the whole world.

But Americans, by that time, had brainwashed themselves into believing their own propaganda about themselves.

Americans simply didn't *do* that sort of thing, to hear them tell it.

They weren't aggressors, they weren't invaders, they didn't attempt to conquer other peoples, to hear them tell it.

They lacked an Indian perspective for who and what Americans are, have always been, and, perhaps, will always be.

And, Americans lacked a Choctaw capacity for generational thought and planning, lacked any capacity for trying to look much farther into the future than the next American election, lacked hardly any capacity for even attempting to try to anticipate what the range of possibilities might be for what could happen next.

And so, Americans frittered away their opportunity to do what easily could have been accomplished in the late 1940s, which becomes increasingly more problematical to accomplish the longer it is delayed.

Americans have been unaware, in typical American fashion, that they were, and are, under an obligation to do anything.

They didn't have to become evil. What was needed most was simply someone to force the demilitarization of the planet, but they were not capable of even being aware of that obligation.

And so, the world was allowed to nearly destroy itself in the last half of the twentieth century, and it has been allowed to drift leaderless into the steadily worsening mess of its dangerous twenty-first century.

But have no fear.

Choctaws have probably been right on top of that problem for more than half a century.

Rest assured that everything will be made to come out just right, by odds that I have calculated to be dead even, after much thought and careful study.

But dead even odds are a breeze for Choctaws.

In anticipation of that, if you might want to position yourself to be at a decided advantage for doing business, anywhere on earth, for the remainder of the Holocene Epoch, get yourself a Choctaw language textbook, and some Choctaw language tapes, and begin learning the Choctaw language.

It will be time well spent.

Meanwhile, another thing that can be said about the near future is that our knowledge of the human past is going to increase greatly within the next generation or two, and one facet of that will be contributions by Native scholars that will greatly increase our knowledge of Indian history in North America.

Historical writing is hardly something new.

The history of the writing of history extends back to Herodotus and Thucydides among the ancient Greeks.

But, you can pretty much skip from Thucydides to Leopold von Ranke (1795–1886), the nineteenth-century German historian, to find out how the discipline of history has evolved, at least to hear the American historians tell it.

But do what few *contemporary* American historians have ever done.

Actually take a look at some of Leopold von Ranke's books.

That poor man became a god to American historians in the mid-to-late nineteenth century, a thing that will befuddle anyone who actually looks at his books, including contemporary American historians, who know of Ranke's work only by its reputation in American historiography.

Befuddlement characterizes every aspect of Leopold von Ranke's career. He himself was befuddled to suddenly find himself appointed a professor at the University of Berlin in 1825.

Leopold von Ranke was a grammar school teacher in Prussia in the early 1820s, at a time when Germans were desperately trying to form a national identity as a country, as a German nation, as a German state.

Bear in mind that the very concept of national sovereignty is a relatively new idea in Eurocentric political thought.

It required the cutthroat religious wars of the Reformation, and a lot of bloody unifying of nationalities, to bring into existence the "nations" of Europe we know today.

Italy before its unification in 1890 (the latest Western European population to emerge as a state) was little more than a geographical expression, and the same was true of "Germany" until after the wars of the Reformation.

But Leopold von Ranke published a work of history in 1824 that hit the jackpot in two ways.

It got the powers that be in Berlin slobbering at how it contributed to the mythos of German nation-making, and they snatched Ranke out of that Prussian grammar school and made him a professor in Berlin so fast it made his head spin.

Ranke had also appended an essay to the back of that book, an essay criticizing the methodology of other historians, and that essay got the Americans slobbering at the way it provided a rationale for writing Indians out of "American history."

That silly Prussian grammar school teacher spent the rest of his long life at the University of Berlin publishing books that are little more than endless direct quotations of long, tedious archival documents, with little attempt at analysis, or synthesis, or much of anything else.

If Ranke had purported to be an editor of documentary collections, that would have been one thing, but he purported to be something else—an historian, one who placed an extreme methodological emphasis on "original" documents.

Americans elevated that Prussian grammar school teacher to the status of a god, to the everlasting perplexity of historians in other countries, and corrupted Ranke's silly views on historical methodology to an even sillier notion that the writing of "history" must be based on nothing but "written" records.

American historiographical propaganda proclaimed this to be an "objective" methodology while conveniently overlooking its subjective effect of leaving Indians no voice in the telling of "American history."

That's pretty much where the Euro-Anglo ethnocentric mindset of the discipline of American history, among "mainstream" American historians, has remained ever since.

It has made it easier for them to write "American history" as propaganda but has been good for little else.

To try to understand what makes historians tick, start with Harry Elmer Barnes's *A History of Historical Writing* (University of Oklahoma Press, 1937), and from there, tackle some of the more recent, more sophisticated critical examinations of the discipline of history.

After that, you can delve into the academic journals of the last few decades and read the dozens of delicious articles in which American historians, anthropologists, and ethnohistorians get into great big, claw-sharp, name-calling contests over the issue of how American history should properly be researched and written, particularly when the issue is writing about Indians.

For the several periods of Choctaw history influenced by the Spanish, the easiest and best thing to do is to become a Spanish Borderlands Frontier historian, partly because we have the benefit of about a century of scholarship deriving from the pioneering work of Herbert Eugene Bolton in that field, and from several successive generations of scholarship from Bolton's graduate students, first at the University of Texas, and then, until the mid-twentieth century, at Berkeley. And now we have several more generations of scholars that Bolton's graduate students have produced.

The Choctaw scholar Devon Mihesuah was the fiftieth and last doctoral student of the legendary Professor Donald Worcester (descended from the missionary to the Cherokees of the same name, the namesake of the 1832 U.S. Supreme Court case, *Worcester v. Georgia*, the missionary who did a few years "at hard labor" in a Georgia prison trying to stop Cherokee removal, even *after* he won his case in the U.S. Supreme Court, when the state of Georgia refused to abide by that decision, and refused to release the Reverend Worcester from prison).

Professor Donald Worcester was, himself, one of Bolton's graduate students.

Professor Worcester lived well into his nineties. Even not long before he died, he was sharp-witted, a delight to chat with. He said he turned to writing fiction late in life when he "couldn't remember well enough to write history any longer."

He spent much of his career at Texas Christian University in Fort Worth, Texas, after having spent much of it at the University of New Mexico, participating in the editing of one of the premiere historical journals in that Spanish Borderlands Frontier field of history.

Devon Mihesuah is a chip off of that old block, continuing that tradition of scholarly editing, research, publishing, and teaching.

The dean of the field of Native American studies, Jack D. Forbes, now retired from directing Native American Studies at the University of California at Davis, was himself a doctoral student in the field of the Spanish Borderlands Frontier, at the University of Southern California.

Jack Forbes was one of the first historians to be doctorally, methodologically cross-trained in both history and anthropology.

That happened because, in the 1950s, Southern Cal became, if not the first university, then one of the very first universities, to say, more or less, "enough of this bickering among historians about methodological purity, we'll just offer a joint Ph.D. degree in history and anthropology, and see what happens."

What happened was Jack D. Forbes.

Forbes's career as a Native scholar will keep generations of future Native scholars busy, busy just attempting to follow up on the ideas suggested in his works.

But it's worth noting that the history training of Jack Forbes was that of a Spanish Borderlands Frontier historian, and his doctoral dissertation, published by the University of Oklahoma Press in 1960, *Apache, Navaho, and Spaniard*, is pure Spanish Borderlands Frontier history, of a nature that made one silly anthropologist look not only silly but as dumb as a box of rocks, for having said the silly thing that Forbes refuted in his dissertation.

The Spanish Borderlands Frontier history students of Herbert Eugene Bolton, and the students of Bolton's students, are everywhere, and there is a reason why they are, generation after generation, premiere historians.

Find out what that reason is (hint: they write mostly about the history of Spain in North America, not about British colonists or "American" history, and their work is therefore much less burdened by the kind of propaganda that most "American" historians are helpless to avoid—and if you are an Indian wanting to get a Ph.D. in history, do that in the field of the Spanish Borderlands Frontier, where you'll stand a much greater chance of being trained to be an historian, rather than a propagandist masquerading as an historian).

A good place to start is the synthesis of all of the work that Bolton's generations of students had produced by the late 1960s, which was written by one of Bolton's students, Father John Francis Bannon, titled *The Spanish Borderlands Frontier: 1513–1821* (University of New Mexico Press, 1970).

It's an invaluable work, a shortcut to gaining a very sophisticated entry into that field, and its bibliographic essays, one for each chapter, are worth many times the price of the book.

The Spanish Borderlands Frontier field of history encompasses what is now regarded as the American Southwest and the northern provinces of Mexico, during all of the centuries that Spain claimed and attempted to rule that domain.

If you can first understand the long history of Spain in the Southwest, then you will be much better equipped to try to understand Spain in the Southeast, the history for which, for the most part, emanated from a different Spanish colonial viceroyalty, from the viceroyalty of Cuba, rather than from the viceroyalty of Mexico City, as was the case for the Southwest.

The main thing that allowed Herbert Eugene Bolton to fire the interest of legions and legions of graduate students is easy to understand—the Spanish were the greatest bureaucrats in the world.

Everything in the Spanish empire had to be done with the permission of the Crown, and, therefore, everything that was done was recorded in triplicate (a local copy of the document, a copy at the viceroyalty, and a copy at the Council of the Indies in Spain, in Seville).

Additionally, the various different orders of Spanish priests were, on the whole, extraordinarily literate people, as priests are often wont to be, and the mountains of materials that they have left behind are invaluable.

Therefore, for practically any question that you might be capable of raising about Spanish colonial history, or Indian history during that time, there is a mountain of archival materials to help shed light on what the answer, or answers, might be.

It is an historian's paradise, if you don't mind learning how to read the god-awful, brown-ink-on-brown-paper, sometimes semi-illiterate, frontier chicken-scratching attempts at handwriting, in some archaic-century variety of Spanish, that's required to be able to go mining in those documents.

But you get to spend time in Mexico and Spain (and, someday soon, in Cuba). A little of that will do anybody some good.

If you want to see for yourself what one of those brown-ink-on-brown-paper things looks like, have a look at the collection edited by Donald C. Cutter, *The California Coast: A Bilingual Edition of Documents from the Sutro Collection* (University of Oklahoma Press, 1969), where you'll find a photograph of a very old handwritten Spanish colonial document.

Don't let that one scare you too much. It's a very old one. Later ones, especially from the eighteenth and nineteenth centuries, aren't too bad.

Some sophistication in dealing with Spanish history will be necessary, not just for learning about the Soto expedition in the Southeast from 1539–42, or for learning about the long Spanish presence in Florida and the Spanish colonial intrigues emanating from Florida that either involved or affected the Choctaws, or for learning about the period when the Spanish were in control of New Orleans rather than the French, but also for understanding the depth of the Choctaw claim to portions of present-day Texas and New Mexico, which the silly contemporary people in those places *think* belongs to them.

That means concentrating on that region of the West for the years that Pushmataha was engaged in military activity there (the several decades after about 1780), as well as the several centuries before that.

It can be fun studying that region from a Choctaw perspective, trying, for example, to find some indications of what Pushmataha was doing, and when he was doing it, for which, especially for silly "American" historians, with their artificial, self-serving emphasis on what they regard as "proper historical documentation," one approach is via the Spanish records from New Mexico, Texas, and Louisiana.

They might save themselves some time in piecing that story together if they were to start where other historians have left off, notably Lawrence and Lucia B. Kinnaird, "Choctaws West of the Mississippi, 1766–1800," *Southwestern Historical Quarterly* 83 (April 1980): 349–70, in conjunction with Ruth Tennison West, "Pushmataha's Travels," *Chronicles of Oklahoma* 38.2 (Summer 1959): 162–74; Anna Lewis, *Pushmataha, American Patriot: The Story of the Choctaws' Struggle for Survival* (Exposition Press, 1959); and *Treaties*, vol. 2 of *Indian Affairs, Laws, and Treaties*, compiled by Charles J. Kappler (Government Printing Office, 1904), all of whom documented indications of various portions of that story.

Never forget that Choctaws, and their ancestors, the so-called Mound Builders, have been the dominant power in the most strategic and most bountiful portion of the North American continent, the lower reaches of the great river of that continent, its cradle of civilization, for about as long as North America has been exhibiting its Holocene Epoch climate and that Choctaws have regarded those southern buffalo plains in the far West as their special domain for nearly as long as Choctaws can remember.

Never forget that virtually all of the so-called "Plains Indians" are relatively recent arrivals in that region or that the more strikingly dramatic features of their way of life, and their utterly insignificant role in North American history, were entirely the result of acquiring horses, a fleeting phenomenon that lasted for only about two centuries, hardly more than the wink of an eye in the immensity of the history of the Native peoples of North America.

Thanks to the Spanish colonials in New Mexico, anyone can find out *exactly* when the Comanches arrived there, when they migrated from the northern Rocky Mountains, in the vicinity of present-day Wyoming, to the southern buffalo plains. Comanches appear, for the first time, on the northeastern frontier of New Mexico, along the Colorado Front Range of the Rocky Mountains, in the records of the suddenly alarmed Spanish officials, in the year 1700.

Comanches didn't last very long, trespassing on that special Choctaw domain, and we can say *exactly* how long that was, the year it began, and the year it ended, as well as *how* it ended, with the trespassers being evicted by the military muscle of the military ally of the Choctaws, the U.S. Army.

With only slightly less exactitude, we know the same kind of things for every other so-called "Plains Indian" nation, whether they might be Kiowas, or Plains Apaches, or whomever, who have ever been so bold as to trespass on that special Choctaw domain.

The same kind of things are known for the Lakota Sioux farther north on the buffalo plains, who got pushed far to the west, out onto the northern buffalo plains, from the region of the Great Lakes, beginning late in the seventeenth century. The same kind of things are known for virtually every other nation of so-called "Plains Indians," all the way up and down the buffalo plains.

Find out for yourself when each one of those "Plains Indian" nations arrived on the buffalo plains, and where they came from, and what their lives were like before they became "Plains Indians." It's not that hard to do. Any decent university library will be filled with such information.

Find out approximately when each one of those nations acquired horses, which is what transformed their lives and made them such striking dramatic figures. It's not that hard to find out about.

The first Indian of any kind that the Spanish in New Mexico observed on horseback was a "Navaho Apache" in 1659, the Spanish, at that time, having not yet learned how to distinguish the closely related Navajos and Apaches of the Na Dene peoples, there being, at that time, little difference between them in their physical cultures that Spaniards were aware of.

By the end of that century, by about 1700, horses had spread northward up the plains, to about the present-day Canadian border.

Once you've become aware that the particular kind of horse-mounted so-called "Plains Indians" that the self-serving American propaganda equates with *all* Indians was a fleeting human phenomenon that existed for only about two centuries, and only on that very narrow strip of arid high plains that produces buffalo herd-sustaining vegetation (read Richard White's essay on the Pawnees in the *Roots of Dependency* to find out what that vegetation is and how narrow that strip of high plains actually is), perhaps you'll take a few steps toward acquiring a Choctaw perspective of the North American continent.

Perhaps you'll become interested in actually learning something about the thousands of years of Indian history on this continent. Perhaps you'll even become angry at the propagandists for lying to you about Indians.

More to the point, perhaps you'll begin to appreciate the frustration and the anger of Choctaws, and other agricultural Indian nations, that virtually all of U.S. Indian policy in the second half of the nineteenth century was aimed specifically at the so-called "Plains Indians" but was applied to *all* Indian nations, and regardless of whether they were friend or foe.

The lingering success of that now dangerously ignorant propaganda, aided, throughout the twentieth century, by Hollywood, has created the self-serving stereotypes that most Americans carry around in their heads that equate all Indians with "Plains Indians," a delusion that attaches great significance to events that have almost no significance at all, such as "Custer's Last Stand."

From the end of the War of 1812 until the middle of the twentieth century, Indian military power no longer mattered. Americans no longer needed it, and Americans no longer feared it. From the end of the War of 1812 until the middle of the twentieth century, all American military engagements with Indian nations were utterly predictable in their eventual outcome.

And, for the twenty-first century, never forget that the fleeting human phenomenon of the silly white people who are currently trespassing on that special Choctaw domain in the far West have got thousands of years of history working against them, in conjunction with the Ogallala Aquifer beneath that vast expanse running out of water, in conjunction with the Lords of the North American Continent lying awake at night pondering the things that they have been pondering for more than ninety-three million minutes.

If I were a betting man, I would bet that, before this new century is over, the southern portion of those buffalo plains will once again be teeming with tens of millions of buffaloes, Choctaw buffaloes, and the descendants of the silly white people who are currently trespassing there will be living somewhere else, evicted, if necessary, by the military muscle of the U.S. Army, and those silly "Plains Indians" will have become horse Indians once again on those Choctaw buffalo plains, as the *vassals* of the Choctaws. Is anybody in Las Vegas giving odds on that?

Here's a fun thing to do.

Go into the bowels of Bizzell Library at the University of Oklahoma, and go out of your way to find the ornate and stately 1923 "main library room," which was the "new" library in the Roaring Twenties.

That big room might still be the ornate, stately, and whisper-quiet "reading room" that it was for decades in the last half of the twentieth century, after the library had been hugely expanded with a new addition in the 1950s, and that old 1923 reading room started becoming an out of the way place.

It became a really out of the way place with more recent library expansion, and a new library entrance, far from that old reading room.

In that beautiful old 1923 reading room, in the shelves all along the walls of it, was where, for decades, you could find all of the masters' theses and doctoral dissertations that had been written by the graduate students of the University of Oklahoma since the university was founded.

They were arranged alphabetically, according to the last name of each author, and they might still be kept on those shelves, except some that were moved, fairly recently, sometime in the last decade or so of the twentieth century, to a special, restricted-access collection, because of their fame.

One of those now-famous doctoral dissertations was by Angie Debo. It was one of the ones that was moved to the protection of that special collection.

Before it was moved, you could sit in that grand palace of a reading room and read the "library copy," carbon-copy typescript (complete with the signatures of the faculty members who served on her doctoral committee) of her 1934 history doctoral dissertation on the Choctaw Nation from 1866–1907, exactly the way she typed it (before it was edited, in converting it to a book).

Her dissertation immediately became one of the very early books published by the then-infant University of Oklahoma Press, under the title, *The Rise and Fall of the Choctaw Republic*, and it has been continually in print since 1934. Debo corrected a few minor errors in that book in a 1961 second edition, a few things that she had later discovered she had been mistaken about.

That book by Angie Debo is the single most widely available and best known book about Choctaw history, and that makes it compulsory reading for any student of Choctaw history, due to its enormous influence.

Be aware that the 1866–1907 period of Choctaw history was almost the only portion of Debo's book that was based on her own meticulous and careful mining of archival materials.

The early chapters were primarily chapters that she had to synthesize secondarily from the available work of other scholars in order to provide the reader with some background information about the Choctaws, so the reader might better understand the Choctaw history that she had to tell.

Angie Debo was researching and writing at a time when John R. Swanton had recently published his major contributions about the Choctaws, so she had his BAE bulletins to draw upon.

But Debo was an incredibly conscientious and knowledgeable student of history, with a voracious intellectual appetite, and she had learned an enormous amount about U.S. history in her undergraduate and graduate school days.

Not much intimidated Angie Debo, and, while her 1934 book contains errors, some very famous ones (and its early chapters should be read with the understanding that she had to rely on the work of others to write those chapters), she remains a cracking good historian and virtually everything she published was first-rate.

Angie Debo's work should be read in conjunction with at least two things.

One is the biography of Angie Debo, by Shirley Leckie, *Angie Debo: Pioneering Historian*, published by the University of Oklahoma Press in 2000.

The other one is a video, "Indians, Outlaws, and Angie Debo," which was a national public TV telecast in the late 1980s. That video was available in the Oklahoma County Metropolitan Library System for many years, and still might be.

Find out, from that video, why Angie Debo's meticulously researched revelation of one of the biggest and most pervasive criminal conspiracies of the twentieth century, *And Still The Waters Run* (Princeton University Press, 1940), which involved nearly the whole of the Oklahoma power structure (lawyers, judges, and politicians) in the commission of felonies involving court fraud in the illegal separation of Indians from their allotments, could not be published by the University of Oklahoma Press in the mid-1930s, which, as the infant publishing arm of the University of Oklahoma, was at the mercy of the state legislature for its continued existence (hint: one of the reader report evaluations of her manuscript warned the press that Debo's chapter 4, "The 'Grafter's' Share" was "dangerous.").

Find out why Angie Debo's essay about Oklahoma history got replaced in the WPA guide to Oklahoma, replaced by an essay that contained egregious errors of fact and that celebrated the wonderful frontier spirit of the "settlers," which was published under Debo's name, without her consent or knowledge (hint: the opening sentence in Debo's essay had been, "Although Oklahoma is young as a State, the region came very early within the scope of the white man's imperial ambitions").

For some other perspectives on Angie Debo (who was a white woman), see chapter 9 of this book, and for contributions to the study of Choctaw history from some great Choctaw women, Muriel Wright and Anna Lewis, who were contemporaries of Debo, see chapter 14.

If you enjoy the quiet beauty of that 1923 reading room in Bizzell Library, there's another one you can visit on campus, just as stately.

It's in the building that's directly behind the student union building, on the top floor of Monnet Hall, which for decades, until the mid-1970s, was the University of Oklahoma law school building.

When the law school moved to a new law center at that time, Monnet Hall was given over to housing the Western History Collections and the Manuscripts Division of the University of Oklahoma libraries, which is where you'll find most of the university's holdings for things concerning Choctaw history.

Monnet Hall, appropriately enough, is the one with a big sculpted owl at the top of the building, which, long ago, the engineering students at the University of Oklahoma, in their legendary rivalry with the law students, thought should be painted green, and so they got up there one night and gave the law students a green owl, to find out, so the story goes, if the law students would be smart enough to figure out how to get up there themselves and get rid of that green paint, which, for all I know, might still be green today. It certainly was for a long, long time.

That stately reading room on the top floor of the Western History Collections in Monnet Hall has restricted hours, and it's a place where you'll not be allowed to bring anything inside except a pencil and paper.

It's a closed-stacks library, where the attendants retrieve (slowly) the things you request, from the catacombs that used to be the law library.

I'm not a librarian, but I worked part-time in those old catacombs of that old law school building, when it was a law library, and I worked part-time in the Manuscripts Division of the University of Oklahoma libraries, when it was housed in the basement of Bizzell Library.

I recommend library work.

There's no better way to find out what a library's resources are than by working there.

It also doesn't hurt to learn such things as how to microfilm frail and fragile documents, how to operate what were big, table-mounted cameras in those days—how to handle those old documents.

If you don't know your way around a library, you'll need to learn, if you're going to be a student of Choctaw history.

A good way to learn, in the late 1960s, was to be a shelver at the Denver public library.

That was mostly a closed-stacks system, with most of the books housed in the basement levels of the building.

Patron requests for individual books would arrive in a cylinder, in an air tube.

That's when the race would begin.

It was a Dewey decimal system library.

The rookie bookshelvers would be told the Dewey decimal system call number for the requested book, and off they'd go, to see which one of them had learned the labyrinthine layout of those stacks the best and so be able to get to that book first.

But that was for the rookies.

The guys in the featured races would only be told the title of the book, and they'd have to know the Dewey decimal system well enough to know where to look for that book, and be damn fast in getting there to win.

There weren't any slouches in the featured races.

You got to be capable of competing in the featured races by paying attention to detail while reshelving the books that the library patrons had returned. It didn't take long to figure out where any particular title would most likely be shelved in the Dewey decimal system, and you got paid for learning it to boot.

You could also have a chance to work at some of the branch libraries in Denver, like the one in the black ghetto, where someone was occasionally needed to work late, to lock up afterward, on the nights the Black Panthers held their meetings there, and get a chance to learn that the media image of the Panthers in the late 1960s was a bunch of baloney, that they were just regular guys, exceptionally well-read and articulate regular guys, not sitting around on their fat behinds while there were problems that needed solving.

If you're going to be a student of Choctaw history, a little time spent working in a library will be time well spent.

You'll learn things about libraries that you aren't likely to learn any other way.

If you never visited the Manuscripts Division of the University of Oklahoma when those valuable old documents were housed in the basement of Bizzell Library, you might still be able to get a fair idea of what its public areas were like by visiting the reading room of the library and looking at the historical documents collection of the Oklahoma Historical Society, at the state capitol complex in northeast Oklahoma City, if that old Oklahoma Historical Society building is still there.

That building was also a museum, where generations of Oklahoma City schoolchildren had been bused for field trips, which, for some of them, was one of the most eye-opening experiences of their young lives.

If you're not library savvy, start by visiting that old elegant 1923 reading room in Bizzell Library.

After drinking in its ambiance, find the stairs outside of that old reading room and take them up, up into the pricelessly designed and laid out, glass-floored "old stacks" of Bizzell Library, the stacks where, until that 1950s addition to the library, all of the books of the University of Oklahoma library were to be found.

That very old portion of Bizzell Library might still be where the few books are housed which, for decades, were not recataloged under the Library of Congress system but remained under the Dewey decimal system.

If so, find the 900s in that part of the library, the 900s where the "travel" books are shelved.

In that section, read the shelves (that is, read the titles of the books that are shelved there, going along each shelf from left to right, or right to left, if you might happen to be Persian and might happen to be thinking in Farsi as you do it) until you come to books about "travel" in Colonial America.

You might also be on the lookout for any titles written by Isaac Asimov, always a fun thing to do when in a Dewey decimal system library.

Asimov, the last I heard, was thought perhaps to have been the only person, or one of the few, to have published at least one book in each of the classification categories of the Dewey decimal system.

You can make the Dewey decimal system a little more fun to learn if you keep an eye out for books by Asimov, trying to find all of the titles that he published in all of those Dewey decimal system categories.

Of course, you could look that up, but what fun would that be?

Asimov was an interesting character. As a very young East European immigrant, not yet old enough to go to school, he taught himself how to read Anglish, primarily by being exposed to the things that were written in Anglish in the shop windows on the streets of Brooklyn.

His autobiography is worth reading, particularly the first volume (his two-hundredth book), *In Memory Yet Green: The Autobiography of Isaac Asimov, 1920–1954* (Avon Books, 1979).

He doesn't have much to do with Choctaw history, but trying to find his books, while shelf reading in a Dewey decimal system library, is a fun way to learn that book classification system.

As you are reading the shelves in that travel section, looking for the portion that deals with travel in Colonial America, you might also note any misshelved books that you spot and set them out so the library staff can shelve them properly.

If you happen to be a speed-reader, you might even read any misshelved books that you find, allowing the serendipity of luck to choose a vicarious travel experience for you.

Or, if you might happen to be one of those people that the Evelyn Wood Reading Dynamics Institute stumbles upon from time to time, people who possess what is known as "gestalt field vision," you might read all of the books on all of those shelves, as you are "shelf reading," if you've got a little time to spare and want to enjoy a lot of vicarious travel experiences.

When you find those books on travel in Colonial America, find the one published early in the twentieth century that contains an Anglish translation of a priceless French archival document, the report of the French official (on the eve of the Choctaw Civil War of the mid-eighteenth century) who was sent to visit most of the Choctaw towns in an effort to try to figure out for the French how much of a brewing Choctaw problem the French might have.

For most of the decades of the twentieth century, you might have had to go to France to read that French colonial document in the original, if you didn't trust either the translation skills of the translator or the chicken-scratching, handwriting-deciphering skills of whomever might have rendered a typescript of the document (often not the same person as the translator).

But southerners can now easily access that French document (on microfilm, with secret-scholar-code-talk doctoring things like A31, and what have you), in the library of Louisiana State University in Baton Rouge, probably because it was brought back from France and placed there by Patricia Dillon Wood, my best guess on that.

The primary reason for going into Bizzell Library, and into those old stacks, and finding that Anglish translation of that French document (if Bizzell Library is still to be found arranged in that manner, and if someone doesn't have that book checked out, which wasn't likely back in the old days) is to see for yourself just one of the amazing and surprising variety of places that you might stumble upon *something* having something to do with Choctaw history in a library.

Such a discovery is called serendipity, luck.

But you can make your own luck, by looking in unlikely places.

If you don't look, you won't see.

There is only so much about Choctaw history to be found in the places that are the most obvious places to look.

Much of the rest of it is to be found in places that, really, I cannot imagine why anyone looking for things about Choctaw history would ever have occasion to look there.

But that's for libraries.

And I've already been there, done that.

What needs to be tackled now is the whole world, the great big world that's not in a library.

That's where you come in.

Somewhere in the world *might* be something having something to do with Choctaw history that I missed.

If I missed something, I want to know.

I want you to find it for me, whatever it might be, wherever it might be.

I want the whole wide world to go on a great big scavenger hunt, a hunt for anything having to do with Choctaw history.

Those things could be *anywhere*.

They could be in your neighbor's garbage cans.

Do be careful about looking there until they are not looking. People can be touchy about things like that.

But *look* in their trash.

That neighbor might be the widow of some old professor, and you wouldn't believe what some old widows of some old professors are willing to part with, nay, willing to *throw away*, perhaps out of resentment, once that professor has died, probably because he was one of those mean old professors who sat around in the evenings reading, page by page, that *Chicago Manual of Style*, and going around all sour-mouthed all the time, and making his wife (now that old widow) hire an amanuensis to convert her wifely messages into something that might get his attention long enough for her to communicate something to him.

A lot of those old widows will give away that professor's old books, maybe to some fundraising outfit like the one that hosts the big-barn, month-long, used-book sale in October in Ithaca, New York, where those old Cornell professors have been dying off with a fair degree of regularity for quite some time.

But that old widow is just as likely to *throw away* that old professor's papers and such.

Dang near any place of any size now has *some* kind of institution of higher education, with old, former faculty dying off periodically, and with nobody having any idea of what their lifetime of restless intellectual energy might have led them to.

Many old faculty have moved to places as far away from academe as they can get.

They might be dying off *anywhere*, even in places that don't even know what an institution of higher education might be—some howling, trackless wilderness like Washington, D.C., maybe.

So *look* in the trash of your neighbors, even if they aren't old widows.

One of your neighbors might be the son or daughter, or nephew or niece, or grandchild of that old widow, and *they* might be throwing away the things that she still had lying around when it came her turn to go to one of those peculiar kind of loony bins that masquerade as "nursing homes."

If there is something out there having *anything* to do with Choctaw history that I might have missed, I want to know.

Somewhere out there might be some old professor who might have found something having to do with Choctaw history *before* I could get to it.

Might have found it, could have found it, did find it.

It's the "Didion Principle," derived from the most famous part of Joan Didion's most famous essay, "On Keeping a Notebook," from the December 1966 issue of *Holiday* magazine:

> My approach to daily life ranges from the grossly negligent to the
> merely absent-minded. . . . Perhaps it never did snow that August in
> Vermont; . . . and perhaps no one else felt the ground hardening and
> summer already dead even as we pretended to bask in it, but that
> was how it felt to me, and it might have snowed, could have snowed,
> did snow.

From that famous part of that famous essay, we derive the principle that if it could have been done, it was done, and, conversely, if it can be done, it will be done.

That works two ways, for our purposes.

First is that, much as I hate to admit it, some old professor *might* have found something before I could get to it.

Might have found it, could have found it = *did* find it.

And, secondly, when this worldwide scavenger hunt is over, what we will be saying is: you might have found it, you could have found it = you *did* find it.

Because, if it is out there, I want to see it.

And you are going to find it.

Something having something to do with Choctaw history could have been hidden out there somewhere by some old professor.

Might have been hidden, could have been hidden = *was* hidden.

That old professor might have been an old duffer.

Might have been, could have been = *was* an old duffer.

That old duffer-professor might have hidden it in some nearly forgotten storage facility of the golf club that you might be a member of.

Maybe he put it in some old leather briefcase, maybe on a shelf behind some cans containing no telling what, maybe a shelf that might be hard to get to, maybe a shelf that cannot even be seen, maybe because, for some reason, no one has yet thrown away the leftover parts of some sprinkler system that was replaced a long time ago, which might make that shelf hard to see and hard to get to.

But *move* that old sprinkler system out of the way and *look* on that shelf.

There *might* be something there about Choctaw history.

Old professors, or, for that matter, old duffers, can be devious. If it has been hidden, it might have been hidden anywhere.

For your participation in this worldwide scavenger hunt, a hunt for everything in the world that might have anything to do with Choctaw history, you are going to have to learn how to pay attention to detail. You are going to have to learn how to look.

If you don't look, you won't see.

And if you don't look, and you don't see, and if you do not pay attention to detail, then you won't be doing me any good.

And doing me some good is what this thing is going to be all about.

Because I want to know.

I want to know if I missed anything, and if so, *how* I could have missed *anything*.

I do not want to go to my grave saying, darn, I sure wish I knew whether or not I might have missed *anything*.

Now, I understand that not everyone will want to cheerfully participate in this worldwide scavenger hunt, so I have figured out what to do about that.

I am going to declare myself king of the world.

Of the whole world.

To my knowledge, no one has ever done that, so I can also be regarded as the first king of the whole world.

People are long accustomed to doing everything under the sun, just because it happened to be the royal pleasure of some king.

So, it is going to be *my royal pleasure* that this worldwide scavenger hunt be conducted.

And the grumblers can just hope that I might not have some big-time backup for declaring myself king, like a secret army, or a secret whatever might be sufficient to worry the grumblers enough to sober them up, at least enough to cause them to say, hmmmm, this king guy has got, if nothing else, some cajones, and maybe some backup too.

So, what the hey, how much trouble could it be to go sneaking over to the neighbor's house in the middle of the night and paw through their garbage to see if, by some chance, there *might* be something there that this king guy missed in *his* search.

Better to do that than to risk the displeasure of s-o-m-ebody who might put the whole dang FBI after you.

And, while everybody is at it, if anything is found, then it should be read and analyzed, so I can be briefed on what it was that I might have missed.

And, when everybody is just pretty dad-gum sure that they have turned the whole world upside down, and that they have found anything that there might have been out there to find, then they can come find me at whatever casino I might happen to be at, and I can sit back and hear THE REST OF THE CHOCTAW STORY that I MIGHT have missed.

Is everybody clear on all of this?

Okay, then get started.

Index

Page numbers in italics indicate illustrations.

Adams, Sam (American revolutionary): criminally minded advocate of violating laws of Royal Proclamation of 1763, 153

Adler, Mortimer J. (member of Dangerous Duo): associate professor, University of Chicago, 1939, 181; carefully coaxed admission extracted by Bill Moyers on public TV, 182; Choctaw attempts to understand his motivations, 182; Choctaws compelled to confront evil vision of Dangerous Duo, 179, 186; his education at Columbia University, 182; evil idea of Dangerous Duo, 181, 186; gifted exponent of Aristotle, 181; helped abolish college football at University of Chicago on Dec 23, 1939, 179, 182–83, 186; member of Dangerous Duo with Robert Maynard Hutchins, president, University of Chicago, 179, 181, 186. See also *alikchis*; Choctaw religion; college football; college presidents; Robert Maynard Hutchins; *ishtaboli*; Clark Daniel Shaughnessy

Agnew, Spiro (U.S. vice president): shifty-eyed, forced to resign, 56

Aihokatubbee (early-nineteenth-century Choctaw *alikchi* during removal crisis): birth and death, 46; lack of an *alikchi* in late nineteenth century with his skill and stature, 83; legendary *alikchi*, 45; orator, 45; possessor of ancient Choctaw knowledge, 46; *tichou minko* (spokesman) for Moshulatubbee, *Great Medal Minko of Okla Tannap*, 45. See also *alikchis*

AIM (American Indian Movement): 1970s AIM activism, 87; dubbed by FBI "Assholes in Moccasins," 87; little awareness of AIM activism by most Choctaws, 89; prominent members (Peltier, Trudell, Bellecourts, Banks, Means), 89; why most Choctaws were distracted during 1970s, 89–92

Akers, Donna (Choctaw scholar): *Living in the Land of Death: The Choctaw Nation, 1830–1860*, 295

Alabama: boundary of Choctaw empire, 73; deer study by graduate students, 196; location of Creek Nation, 261; Mobile founded in 1702, 255; Moundville site, 241; Seminoles migrated from, 273; statehood in 1819, 273; University of Alabama football, 91, 92; War of 1812 battle of Etowah (Holy Ground), 24

Alabama (Muscogee Confederation division): language related to Choctaw, 240; poet Louis Littlecoon Oliver, 240

Alamo, The (movie): Academy Award for Best Sound, 57; and article by Ruth Tennison West, 67; and book by Dr. Anna Lewis, 253; James Edward Grant, screenwriter, 54; John Wayne as second-greatest movie actor, 53; John Wayne portraying Davy Crockett howling

337

immortal mocking American-
imperialist words to American-
imperialist-poisoned Lords of the
North American Continent, 52, 137;
lack of American movie audience
reaction, 52; milestone in American
history and history of Big Game,
52; mocking moment might provide new dictionary connotation
for "motivation," 57; people doing
mocking unaware of dangerous
thing they had done, 54; quintessential American-imperialist
mocking moment woke up a lot of
despairing poisoned Lords of the
North American Continent, 54
Albert, Carl (mid-twentieth-century
Speaker of the House): early 1970s
was first in line to succeed to presidency when Vice President Spiro
Agnew resigned, 56; FBI guys were
right on top of things back then,
right?, 56; House Concurrent
Resolution 108, 56; known as "Little
Giant from Little Dixie" and "Little
Drunk from Little Dixie," 56; location of "Little Dixie" congressional
district in Oklahoma, 56; nobody
guarding candy but a funny little
Bugtussle, Oklahoma, drunk, 56;
some wacko-weird-Choctaw-
guessing-the-rest-scout, who
thinks he might have guessed
something, 57
alikchis: as American *alikchis*-in-
training, 80; and American college
football, 179–86; as American full-
fledged *alikchis*, 80; and Coach
Barry Switzer and Coach Bear
Bryant, 91–92; and Dangerous Duo
of Robert Maynard Hutchins and
Mortimer J. Adler, 179, 186; and Dr.
Gideon Lincecum, 45, 223; loss of
many emeritus ones, 45; "magical
incantations" of, 80; and medicinal
properties of plants, 223; not made
quietly, 46; as orators, 45; in
Pentagon, 185; summoning of,

18; and University of Oklahoma,
185; and Wishbone offense, 90–91.
See also Aihokatubbee
All-Indian Pueblo Council (New
Mexico): banned Frank Cushing
for life from all nineteen Pueblos in
New Mexico, 313; examine contemporary college textbooks in anthropology and archaeology and see for
yourself what some of most famous
names are praised for and then find
out who those people actually were
and what they actually did, 312
American bottoms: richest agricultural
lands in North America, 226
American historians: American history
written as American propaganda
started becoming dangerous to
America six decades ago, xiii; biases
are not individual but institutionalized within their academic discipline, 211, 317–19; Choctaw problem
is biggest propaganda problem in
telling of "American" history, 32;
compared with Spanish Borderlands Frontier historians, 319–22;
feel compelled to write "American
history" in chronological sequence
things were revealed to their dull-
witted forebears, 209; have chosen
to forget both Pushmataha and
Choctaws, 32; have never been able
to figure out how to put right kind
of spin on Americans betraying
their Choctaw allies, xvi; how to get
American imperialist-propagan-
dists to put Choctaw people into
story of American history, 71–73;
Leopold von Ranke became a god
to them, 209–10, 317–18; methodology leaves Indians no voice in
telling of "American history," 318;
methodology used for writing
ethnohistory not regarded as real
history by them, 210–11; review of
elementary things about American
history, 139–56; spent last half century writing for wrong audience,

control of U.S. government in 1828
and stabbed their Choctaw allies in
the back, 14, 174; severely criticized
by Angie Debo, 168; their strenuous
efforts to inflict cancers of many
inferior elements of American civilization upon Choctaws, 59; they
are stuck with Choctaws being
Choctaws whether they like it or
not, 92; traitorous sickness of backstabbers, 40; what they never anticipated, 203; wishful thinking of, 134
American Indian Movement. *See* AIM
American Myth, 1, 2; American
religious tyranny against Indians
an embarrassment to myth, 176;
Choctaws and American patriots
would like to see it become true,
203; Choctaw problem biggest
propaganda problem, 32; emerging
American Myth threatened by a
Choctaw cancer deeply embedded
in it, 39–40; *M'Intosh* decision does
great violence to myth, 187; much
of it founded upon North America
being portrayed as a "wilderness,"
212; mythmaking process has dehumanized Indian peoples, 59; people
who contributed to philosophical
foundations of it became powerful
people in their fields, 217; response
of some Americans who believed it
devoutly, 203; is transparent to all
other nations, 214; when it is denigrated, 212
American Mythmakers, 1, 14, 58; have
never been able to figure out how
to put right kind of spin on betraying Choctaw allies, 14
American patriots: characteristics of
and distinction from American
imperialists, 38; Choctaws will have
help of many of them, 203; duty of,
78, 86, 202; they would like to see
American Myth become true, 203;
what they should have done a long
time ago, 86

American people: American historians
have done a dangerous disservice to
them, xiii; American imperialists
betrayed them as well as betraying
Choctaws, 174; American imperialists fear their own American people
more than they fear anything else,
x, 103, 213, 215; capable of being a
decent, trustworthy people, 86;
Choctaw civilization as far superior
to theirs, 59–61, 79–85, 163–67,
237–47; Choctaws are still loyal
allies of them, and it's only
American imperialists among
them who are avowed enemies, 202;
Choctaws have waited patiently for
them to mature as a people, 202,
214; have given guarantees of
Choctaw sovereignty, 102–3; have
had inflicted on them a crippling
inability to see themselves the way
Indian nations have learned to see
them, xii; as ignorant of most of
far-reaching twenty-first-century
Big Game that will ever impact
their country, 49–50; majority of
Americans have matured into a
decent people, 215; Pushmataha
was most honored Indian by them
in all of U.S. history, 14–16, 27–28;
renegade and lawless imperialists
among them chose to destroy U.S.
Constitution, 39; seem inclined to
wonder if Choctaws still know how
to be Choctaws, 41; someone must
warn them, 42, 64–65; will likely
need their Choctaw allies in
twenty-first century more than
they ever imagined, 177
Anasazi. *See* Ancestral Pueblo people
Ancestral Pueblo people (formerly
Anasazi): achievements of did
not fit cultural bias aspects of
Discovery Doctrine legal code-talk
of "savagery," 228; "Anasazi" a supposed vanished race invented by
Americans to explain ruins, 228;
astronomer Andrew Douglass

Boone and Crockett Club: record book, 199. *See also* deer hunting

Boston: smallpox outbreak of 1721–22, xv, 234; outraged Christians bombed home of minister who was supporting inoculations because they saved lives, 234

Bozeman Trail War: Sioux forced the surrender of U.S. in treaty of 1868, 271

Bressette, Walter (author): coauthor with Rick Whaley, *Walleye Warriors* (1993), chronicling vicious white backlash in northern Wisconsin in 1980s when federal courts upheld Chippewa off-reservation spearfishing rights from their treaties of 1837 and 1842, 303

Brock, Sir Isaac (British general in War of 1812): Canadian national hero, bluffed an American army into surrendering to him at Detroit, 22–23, 86

buffaloes: big species of Ice Age buffalo hunted by Ice Age Choctaws, 10; buffalo herds belonged to Choctaw ancestors, so-called Mound Builders, 4; buffalo herd-sustaining vegetation, 324; frightful power of criminally trespassing, buffalo-stealing Comanches, 67; herds exterminated by Americans, 161; herds will one day be restored, 325; southern Great Plains buffalo herds part of ancient Choctaw imperial province, 3–4; trespassing criminal peoples who tried to move to southern Great Plains and steal Choctaw buffalo herds of that region, 3, 5, 9; was Pushmataha's Choctaw military-police, head-busting, supercop beat, 5–9

Bureau of American Ethnology. *See* BAE

Burr, Aaron (U.S. vice president): in 1804 killed Alexander Hamilton in a duel, 60

Bush (U.S. president): subject for study by psychohistoriographical language analysts, 149

Byington, Cyrus (early-nineteenth-century missionary), 239

Caddoan peoples: described by La Harpe in Ouachita Mountains in early eighteenth century, 256; exterminated in Ouachita Mountains by Choctaws, 256–58; speculation by contemporaries of Pushmataha that Caddoan peoples ambushed his early expedition to West, 277

Caesar, Julius (Roman general): gained fame trying to solve what continues to be most vexing problem faced by civilized peoples—how to restrain German barbarians, 141; how his Classical Latin spawned modern Romance languages, 309; oldest mound in North America dates to about 4,000 years before birth of Julius Caesar, 207

Cahokia (largest "Mound Builder" city): 218–19; 226–27; 229, 239; by year 1200 a North American Indian city bigger than London or Paris at that time, 226

Calhoun, John C.: in treaty of 1825 negotiated for Americans against first Choctaw lawyer James Lawrence McDonald, 260

California Gold Rush (1849): compared with Southern Gold Rush of 1829, 303; extermination of Indians by California gold miners, 271; role of southerners and Texans in transplanting their attitudes toward Indians, 305. *See also* Robert F. Heizer; Clifford E. Trafzer

Camp Holmes, treaty of. *See* treaty of 1835

Canby, William C. Jr. (author): *American Indian Law in a Nutshell* (2004), 301

Sioux reclaiming their sacred Paha Sapa (Black Hills), 271. *See also* odds making

Latin, 96, 309, 310

"Leased District": Choctaw land provided as a home for Comanches and Kiowas, 75–76

Leckie, Shirley A. (author): *Angie Debo: Pioneering Historian*, 252

Lewis, Anna (Choctaw scholar): and *The Alamo* (movie), 253; biographer of *Great Medal Minko of Okla Hannali* (Pushmataha), xvi; her career, 253; her *Chief Pushmataha, American Patriot: The Story of the Choctaws' Struggle for Survival*, 253–54, 322; was descended from Choctaw patriots, 252; education, 252–54; first woman of any race to earn Ph.D. degree at University of Oklahoma, 254; made use of Gideon Lincecum's autobiography, 222; necrology, 254; no buildings at University of Oklahoma are named for her, 254

Lewis, Silan (most recent person publicly executed by Choctaw Nation, in 1894), 82–85; as Choctaw patriot, 82; sentenced to death by Choctaw Nation court of law, 84; released after death sentence, returned for his execution, 84–85

Lincecum, Dr. Gideon (physician, naturalist, author): autobiography and career, 222–23; because he was great admirer of Choctaw civilization in 1820s and vehement opponent of missionary activity, his views have been suppressed, 222; Charles Darwin sponsored publication in London of his study of Texas fire ants, 222; hardly anyone but Dr. Anna Lewis made use of his autobiography, 222; observations of Aihokatubbee, 45; observed Choctaw freedom of assembly and freedom of speech, 167; self-trained naturalist, 305; studied medicinal

properties of plants with Choctaw *alikchi*, 223; wrote biography of Pushmataha, 222, 257; wrote grammar of Choctaw language, 45

Little Big Horn, battle of, 271; propaganda of "Custer's Last Stand," 324–25

Lomawaima, K. Tsianina (author): coauthor with David E. Wilkins, *Uneven Ground: American Indian Sovereignty and Federal Law* (2001), 301

Lone Wolf v. Hitchcock (U.S. Supreme Court decision, 1903): deathblow to integrity of U.S. Constitution, 157; declares Congress has full (plenary) power over Indians, ix, 158; declares Congress can unilaterally abrogate any clause of any Indian treaty, ix, 158; for only second time in its history Supreme Court was offered opportunity to stop illegal taking of Indian land, but justices remembered what happened first time, 160; in 1903 Supreme Court destroyed U.S. Constitution, removing its checks and balances, viii; Court abdicated its constitutional responsibilities in 1903; Court put sovereign Indian nations at mercy of public opinion, ix

looting of the mounds, 220; looting of Spiro mound, 228–30

Lords of the North American Continent (Choctaws), 4, 29–30, 33, 35. *See also* Choctaws

Louisiana, French colony of: and Choctaw Civil War, 264, 276; Choctaw fleecing of French, 243–48; founding of French colonies near Choctaws, 255; French governor Kerleric's assessment of Choctaws, 251

Louisiana Purchase: 1803 purchase of French claim to interior of North America west of Mississippi River, 258

Lyell, Charles (author): had profound
influence on other sciences, 221;
one of first to articulate geologic
strata as means of relative dating,
221; his *Principles of Geology* (1840),
221

maps: maps will need changing, 78;
pitiful 1820 U.S. Army maps, 63, 69;
silly round-earth-flattening-flat
maps, 108–9, 110
Marshall, John (early-nineteenth-
century Chief Justice of U.S.
Supreme Court): 158, 171, 176,
188–89, 220–21
Massachusetts: North American
German colony founded in 1620
at Plymouth Rock, 142
massacre of Ft. Mims (War of 1812),
23–24
McCarthy, Joseph (mid-twentieth-
century U.S. Senator from
Wisconsin), 253
McCulloh, Dr. James H. (author):
believed that Indians build the
mounds, 220; his *Researches on
America* (1817), 220; his *Researches,
Philosophical and Antiquarian,
concerning the Aboriginal History
of America* (1829), 220
McDonald, James Lawrence (first
Choctaw lawyer, 1823), 189–91, 200,
259–60
McJunkin, George: black ranch foreman in New Mexico discovered
Folsom site, 314–15
McMurtry, Larry (author):
"Southwestern Literature?" in his
essay collection, *In A Narrow Grave:
Essays on Texas* (1968), 67
McPhail, Leonard (U.S. Army doctor):
diary regarding treaty of 1835,
known as Treaty of Camp Holmes,
301–2
media events: caused by AIM in 1970s,
87; FBI will have to give media-
event warnings about poisoned
Choctaws on a daily basis, 72; 1811

debate between Pushmataha and
Tecumseh would be biggest media
event in U.S. history if it happened
today, 16
Mihesuah, Devon (Choctaw scholar),
319–20
M'Intosh decision (U.S. Supreme Court
decision, 1823): applied Discovery
Doctrine to U.S., 176, 187–88,
190–91; religious tyranny, 176
Mississippi: Choctaw core homelands,
5, 79, 237–43, 270; 1817 statehood,
273; Georgia's claim to it, 273; hunting, 199, 281; *Publications of the
Mississippi Historical Society*, 222,
257; sale of Choctaw land, 47, 77–78,
83, 117–18; slave raids, 273; state
attempted to extend its laws over
Choctaws, 159
Mississippi River: Cahokia largest
"Mound Builder" city, 218;
Choctaw land beyond it in West to
be a place where Choctaws can get
far away from America, 134; French
arrive there, 243–45; how and why
Choctaws settled there, 12; its lower
reaches a cradle of civilization,
28–29, 61, 207–8, 230–32, 243, 246,
323; its valleys decimated by smallpox long before French or British
arrived, 206; *Misha Sipokni* (older
than time), 208; Natchez people,
260–61; strategically located
Choctaws controlled military key
to North America along its lower
reaches, 7
Mobilian trade jargon: used in vast area
of Southeast, based on Choctaw
language, 239–40
Moma Bina, battle of (Oct, 1539): with
Soto expedition, 269–70
Monks Mound (at Cahokia): largest
mound in North America, 218–19
Monroe, James (U.S. president): gave
the world Arkansawyers by creating
"Arkansaw Territory," 259
Morgan, Lewis Henry (mid-nineteenth-
century anthropologist): his *Ancient*

extension any Indian nation), 158; has power to restore ancient Choctaw homelands to Choctaws but is still being ignored by U.S. government, 159; Supreme Court discovered it has no way to deal directly with criminals of any kind, particularly if those criminals have seized control of other branches of U.S. government, 159; Supreme Court discovered it has no way to enforce its decisions, that it has no army, has nothing but papers it hands down, 159; was first enunciation of canons of construction of Indian treaties, 171; was ignored by state of Georgia, 319; when its ruling was ignored it dealt Supreme Court a fatal blow from which Supreme Court will never recover, 39; would have stopped Indian removal but was ignored by President Jackson, 39

Wright, Alfred (early-nineteenth-century missionary): characterized such Choctaw religious beliefs as he could discern in terms very similar to Deism of Thomas Jefferson and Benjamin Franklin, that if anyone or anything had created the world, they had then gone away and never returned, 288; Medieval-minded missionaries and anthropologists wouldn't know a good ball-playing-religion people if one of them were to kick their butts all the way to Baltimore, 81; progenitor of

mid-nineteenth-century Choctaw Principle Chief Allen Wright, who was grandfather of mid-twentieth-century Choctaw scholar Muriel Wright, 252; published his dull-witted, Euro-Anglo ethnocentric big news that he had discovered an Indian people called Choctaws who were so primitive they had no discernible religious beliefs, 81

Wright, Allen (mid-nineteenth-century Principle Chief of Choctaw Nation): grandfather of mid-twentieth-century Choctaw scholar Muriel Wright, 252; not long after U.S. Civil War suggested Choctaw word "Oklahoma" (*okla*, people + *houmma*, red = "Red People") to U.S. government as possible name for new territory it was considering creating, 101

Wright, Muriel (Choctaw scholar): an assimilationist author and editor, 252; her criticisms of Angie Debo, 252, 327; editor of *Chronicles of Oklahoma* and author of *Guide to the Indian Tribes of Oklahoma*, 252

Yale University: Jonathan Dwight first Choctaw to be educated at Yale, by 1842, 200; nineteenth-century Choctaws often educated at Yale, 191

Zuni Pueblo: Frank Cushing barred for life from all pueblos in New Mexico, 313